IMAGINING THE MODERN

Imagining the Modern

THE CULTURES OF NATIONALISM IN CYPRUS

Rebecca Bryant

I.B. TAURIS

LONDON · NEW YORK

Published in 2004 by I.B. Tauris & Co Ltd
6 Salem Road, London W2 4BU
175 Fifth Avenue, New York NY 10010
www.ibtauris.com

In the United States of America and Canada
distributed by Palgrave Macmillan a division of St Martin's Press
175 Fifth Avenue, New York NY 10010

HB ISBN 1 85043 461 1
PB ISBN 1 85043 462 X

HB EAN 978 1 85043 461 0
PB EAN 978 1 85043 462 7

A full CIP record for this book is available from the British Library
A full CIP record is available from the Library of Congress

Library of Congress Catalog Card Number: available

Typeset in Times by JCS Publishing Services
Printed and bound in Great Britain by MPG Books Ltd, Bodmin

Cover picture: "Ölüm, Ağıt, Bekleyiş, Kin" (Death, Mourning, Expectation, Hatred)
by Güner Pir, courtesy of the Turkish Republic of Northern Cyprus National Struggle Museum.

Chapter 2 was originally published as "Bandits and 'Bad Characters': Law as
Anthropological Practice in Cyprus, c. 1900," *Law and History Review*, 21: 2, pp.
244–69 (2003). Chapter 4 was published as "Pashas and Protests: On Revelation and
Enlightenment in Cyprus," *Cultural Dynamics*, special issue, "Epistemologies of
Islam," 13: 3 (2001). Part of Chapter 6 was originally published as "An Education in
Honor: Patriotism and the Greek Schools of Cyprus," in *Cyprus and Its People:
Nation, Identity, and Experience in an Unimaginable Community, 1955–1997*, ed.
Vangelis Calotychos (Boulder, CO: Westview Press), 1998. Versions of Chapters 7
and 8 were published as "The Purity of Spirit and the Power of Blood: A Compara-
tive Perspective on Nation, Gender and Kinship in Cyprus," *The Journal of the
Royal Anthropological Institute* 8: 3 (2002); and "Justice or Respect? A Compara-
tive Perspective on Politics in Cyprus," *Ethnic and Racial Studies* 24: 6 (2001).

Contents

List of Illustrations

For my parents

Acknowledgments

Any endeavor with a decade-long history entails a multitude of debts that are also entangled with friendships, experiences, and intellectual commitments.

My first and primary thanks go to all the many friends and colleagues in Cyprus who made it possible for me to accomplish what was, when I look back on it now, surely a daunting project. For their friendship, support, and in many cases readiness to argue with me, I would like to express my gratitude to Vassos Argyrou, Deirdre Guthrie, Maria Hadjipavlou, Niyazi Kızılyürek, Marios Michaelidhis, Yiannis Papadakis, Yiouli Taki, Hikmet Uluçam, and Neşe Yaşın. I wish to express a special thanks to Rolandos Katsiaounis, with whom I spent many hours over several months, poring over documents and discussing Cypriot history; and to Ali Nesim, who generously shared his knowledge of Turkish Cypriot history by taking the time to introduce me to persons who were important in my research.

There are also persons in more official capacities who aided my work enormously. Nikos Peristianis of Intercollege literally made my work in the south possible by providing me with an institutional home during my research there. He also made possible fruitful discussions around my work by inviting me back to Cyprus on numerous occasions. Daniel Hadjitoffi of the Fulbright Commission in Cyprus was always very supportive of my research, even at times when that was politically difficult. Maro Theodorou and her assistants in the State Archive, as well as Christodhoulos Theodotou of the Archive of the Archbishopric eased the process of sorting through thousands of pages of documents.

Mustafa Haşim Altan, then director of the Turkish Republic of Northern Cyprus State Archive, was always willing to share their resources with me.

For their generous financial support, I would like to express my gratitude to the following agencies and fellowship programs, which provided me with funds for language training, fieldwork, and writing: the Social Science Research Council International Predissertation Fellowship program, with funding from the Ford Foundation; the United States Institute of Peace Jennings Randolph Fellowship program; the Institute for International Exchange/United States Information Agency Fulbright Fellowship program; the Department of Education Fulbright-Hays Dissertation Fellowship program; the University of Chicago Council for Advanced Studies in Peace and International Cooperation Summer Travel Grant fund; the Sawyer Seminar on Religion, Law, and the Construction of Identities Fellowship at the University of Chicago, funded by the Mellon Foundation; the Institute of Turkish Studies Dissertation Writing Grant program; The John D. and Catherine T. MacArthur Foundation Program on Peace and International Cooperation Research and Writing Grant for Individuals; the American University in Cairo summer travel grant program; the Council for Advanced Overseas Research Centers Multi-Country Grant program; and the National Academy of Education/Spencer Foundation Postdoctoral Fellowship program.

The writing of this work has been influenced by many colleagues around the world, though especially in Chicago. At the University of Chicago, my unbounded thanks go to John Comaroff, who was always challenging, supportive, and a model adviser, especially for someone whose work goes somewhat against the grain of conventional anthropology. Paul Friedrich's comments and conversations were always stimulating, often lingering in my mind and influencing my work in ways of which he was probably unaware. I am grateful to Richard Chambers for his support of someone who was, admittedly, an interloper in Ottoman studies.

Friends in Chicago provided and continue to provide both emotional and intellectual sustenance, and I would like especially to mention Laura Blasingame, Kathy Hall, Johanna Schoss, and Kamala Visweswaran. Cornell Fleischer knows the various ways in which this entire project was influenced by him. And Uday Mehta was not only a friend at some of the most critical junctures, but has also been one of the most important influences on the course of my thinking with regard to liberalism and its possible alternatives.

There are two persons whose influence on my work must be acknowledged in their absence. The sudden death of Kostas Kazazis, my Greek teacher, was a great loss to all who benefited from his knowledge and intellectual enthusiasm, and who developed a love of Greek through his enthusiasm and often ribald humor. I feel great sorrow that Valerio Valeri passed away before he was able to see this work. His letters to me in the field, his wide-ranging knowledge, and his readiness to discuss anything, at any time, made him both a friend and a model for me. Without his determined encouragement at critical points, I might never have completed some of the most difficult stages of research and writing.

The final revisions of the book were completed at the Society for the Humanities at Cornell University, where interdisciplinarity was not only realized but proved truly fruitful. My special thanks go to all the fellows of the Society, where our many discussions, and comments received on sections of this work, stimulated me to rethink portions of it and to refine some of its conclusions. In this regard, I am especially grateful to Dominic Boyer for challenging me on certain points on which I certainly needed to be challenged. Dominick LaCapra, director of the Society, provided perhaps the most congenial and collegial environment that I could have enjoyed for completing this project. My colleagues in the anthropology department at Cornell were always welcoming, and I thank them for their hospitality.

Finally, I wish separately to thank two people who have aided and influenced the transformation of this work from dissertation to book. I have been in conversation with Michael Herzfeld for a number of years, a conversation that has resulted in an ongoing, complementary, and I believe productive disagreement. I am grateful to Michael for his support and for his willingness always to extend our conversation. Very special thanks go to Peter Loizos, who probably knows all the ways in which he has influenced my work. His unerring ethnographic sense, uncompromising pragmatism, and unwavering support all helped me through periods when I thought this book might never see its way into print. I'm sure he's relieved that it now has.

My husband, Haldun Gülalp, has always taken the time to read and to question, and my work has greatly benefitted from that questioning. Certainly, the book would not have taken its current form without his critical eye and his engagement.

And my final thanks go to my parents, to whom this book is dedicated. They have always supported me, sometimes despite their better judgment, and even when that meant that I would be very far from them. This book may not be adequate compensation for my absence, but I hope that it will show them why I found it necessary.

A Linguistic Note

The transliteration of Greek is notoriously difficult, and here I have chosen to employ a simplified phonetic system that attempts to replicate the sound of modern Greek or of its Cypriot variant, where necessary.

Turkish uses an expanded Latin alphabet; some of the represented sounds in that modified alphabet are as follows:

Vowels
a as French *a* in *avoir*
â lengthens vowel as in *far*
e as in *bed*
ı as *a* in *serial*
i as *ee* in *tree*
o as French *o* in *note*
ö as French *eu* in *peu*; German *ö*
u as *u* in *rule*
ü as the French *u* in *tu*; German *ü*

Consonants
ç as *ch* in *change*
ğ lengthens preceding vowel
j as the French *j* in *joie*
ş as *sh* in *ship*

Introduction

There are now high hopes that the period of divisive nationalism in Cyprus is coming to an end. Recently, to the surprise and joy of many, thousands of Greek and Turkish Cypriots flooded through the buffer zone that divides the island, many returning for the first time to homes that they had been forced to abandon almost thirty years earlier. The opening of the buffer zone followed on the heels of large-scale protests by Turkish Cypriots, who have been marginalized by the international community and impoverished as a result. For most Turkish Cypriots, nationalist claims collapsed in the face of the opportunity to join the European Union (E.U.), whose duty it would become not only to strengthen their economy but also to ensure peace and safety in the island. Amidst anxieties, longings, and tears of joy, new stories of communal and political belonging are being constructed.

At this moment of transition to a postnational future that is still vague and uncertain, this book tells the story of another such transitional moment: the moment of the rise and clash of nationalisms in the island. As a study of nationalism and the specific period of its rise and decline, this narrative is necessarily bracketed between the prenational and the postnational—or some would say, the premodern and the postmodern. It is bracketed between a moment when the transition to British rule overturned earlier structures of authority and created demands for a representative politics ultimately expressed as nationalism, and a moment when not only nationalism but even traditional representative politics no longer suffice in an island soon to be incorporated into the supranational E.U. Just as the paternalistic politics of the Ottoman heritage no longer sufficed for Cypriots of the late nineteenth century, so the nationalist political games played by the older political players in the island no longer suffice for Cypriots at the beginning of the twenty-first century. In both instances, the result was a groundswell of protest that built the momentum of a quiet, but forceful, revolution.

This book is premised on the belief that a future for Cyprus should be founded on a fuller understanding of the ideologies that divided the island and sustained that division over decades. In particular, it demonstrates how communal belonging and political belonging came to overlap in the island, leading to conflicting political claims. I argue that while differences were always constructed—between Christian and Muslim, elite and villager, educated and uneducated—representative politics led to a gradual overlap of communal belonging and political belonging. One's "real" identity became singular and ethnic, leading in turn to what I describe here as "ethnic estrangement," or the process by which people that one knows may nevertheless appear to be or to become strangers. There is no real contradiction between defining one's group in opposition to a constitutive Other, and getting along with those others when in contact with them. But in modern representative politics claiming rights entails defining oneself as a certain type of person—a citizen—with claims on a particular state. It is here that the theoretical articulation of experience—namely, ideology—comes into play and divides.

This book argues that two conflicting styles of nationalist imagination led to the violent rending of Cyprus in 1974 and afterwards sustained that division. At the same time, the work demonstrates how the conflict emerged through Greek and Turkish Cypriots' encounters with modernity under British colonialism, and through a consequent reimagining of the body politic in a new world in which Cypriots were defined as part of a European periphery. I describe how Muslims and Christians in Cyprus were transformed into Turks and Greeks, and what it meant— epistemologically, ontologically, and politically—when they were. This book, then, is an analysis of diverse styles of nationalism and of nationalism's emergence in modernity. But the book also makes three further claims.

The first claim is that to understand the Cyprus conflict from a truly comparative perspective is to understand not only the larger Greek–Turkish conflict that has periodically shaken the Mediterranean, but also to understand something about the logic of conflict in modernity. The rupture of the island began in the 1878 transition from Ottoman to British rule, which led to hopes for new freedoms that were then frustrated but which ultimately, many decades later, resulted in an armed rebellion (1955–59) led by the *Ethniki Organosis Kiprion Agoniston* (EOKA), or National Organization of Cypriot Fighters. That fight aimed not at independence but at *enosis*, or union of the island with Greece. In response, the Turkish Cypriot minority called for *taksim*, or separation, of the two communities, citing alleged atrocities against Muslims in Crete and

Thrace. The four-year fight of that exclusively Greek Cypriot guerilla organization was opposed not only by British colonizers, but also by Turkish Cypriots, many of whom joined the British forces or otherwise took up guns against EOKA.

When Cyprus was given its independence in 1960, political space in the island was already framed by the terms of ethnonationalisms. Indeed, nationalism first intervened in Cyprus' independence in the form of a difficult constitution, which provided guarantees for the two "national" groups. Nationalism later impeded good governance during 1963–74, when the government at various moments ceased to function effectively because of intercommunal violence. During those same years, many members of the Turkish Cypriot minority fled to enclaves or to larger Turkish villages, which many say they guarded with shotguns.[1] Nationalism brought a Greek coup d'etat in 1974 and then the Turkish military intervention and division of the island. In 1975, those Greeks and Turks who had not already fled to the areas relegated to their respective ethnicities were exchanged *en masse* in a diplomatic maneuver that severed the very important Cypriot ties to land, and altered social relations within each community. Until very recently, the relative quiet of the island had relegated it to a spot rather low on the agendas of international powers. Even now, even in the midst of a revolutionary groundswell, there are indications that at the level of politics, nationalism continues to hinder the search for a workable compromise—a solution to "The Cyprus Problem"—that will guarantee safety, freedom, and respect for all Cypriots.[2]

Hence, the stalemate in Cyprus since the island's division in 1974 has been not only the result of international politics or of Cyprus' position as a pawn in larger power games. And, in contrast to what many analysts have suggested, I argue here that the Cyprus conflict was not only, or even primarily, a result of a British colonial divide-and-rule strategy. Rather, I claim that the ideologies of freedom that emerged under British rule and that allowed Cypriots to imagine a better future for themselves and their children were necessarily imagined in nationalist terms. This was not, I contend, the simple result of irredentist propaganda on the part of the Greek and Turkish states but was, instead, a result of the demands for freedom, equality, and representative politics that emerged under British rule.

The latter assertion depends, in turn, upon an argument that I develop throughout the book and which may be summarized in a second claim, which is that the emergence of representative politics is inextricably

entangled with nationalism. The first four chapters of the book lay the
groundwork for this argument by examining how Cypriots of the late
nineteenth and early twentieth centuries grappled with the decline of traditional hierarchies and the emergence, in their place, of new ways in
which they would represent themselves and be represented by others. In
that transformation, the ontologies that Muslim and Christian Cypriots
used to explain their worlds were also transformed: those ontologies
were made ideological, becoming the ground for politics that also
defined the limits of community. Certain cultural logics appear to
explain one's situation in the world better than others, and so those logics take prominence, becoming hegemonic. As they become hegemonic,
they become part of our everyday worlds, part of the taken-for-granted
and hidden to consciousness. They become part of our way of seeing the
world, and hence an unspoken, and usually unquestioned, part of the
ways in which we explain it.

Throughout the book, I describe fundamental differences between
Greek and Turkish nationalisms in Cyprus, differences that are predicated on a divergence between the communities in the meaning and
logic of history. Greek Cypriot history assumes the primordial inevitability of blood ties, such that Turkish Cypriots are usually seen as
descendants of converted Greeks. In contrast, Turkish Cypriot history
stresses historical contingency (the Ottoman conquest of 1571), accommodation, and acculturation as social foundation. Furthermore, I trace
how those differing meanings of history took on significance and gained
momentum as traditional "high" cultures of the two communities were
made available to the masses.

I contend, then, that nationalism is thoroughly entangled with modern
politics, and that the comparison possible in Cyprus allows us an unusu-
ally privileged perspective on the differing ways in which both
modernity and nationalism may be realized. Moreover, I believe that
only by understanding such differing encounters with modernity will we
be able to outline a theory of nationalism that places it squarely within
modernity, but without reifying it as a "product" to be packaged, sold, or
imitated (the West's influence on the Rest), and without resorting to the
near-primordialism of protonationalism. Nationalism, I argue, is one
possible way of resolving contradictions that I describe here as inherent
in our modern understandings of how freedom should be realized.

The final claim of the book also takes us beyond the national. The
final claim is a semi-Hegelian one: namely, that just as modernity
retained elements of the religious age that preceded it and which it sup-

posedly rejected, so postmodernity reacts to and thereby retains elements of the modern. The project of modernity was essentially an ethical one, aimed at dispelling the illusions of religion and discovering the "real" truths upon which a better life could be founded. The contradiction at the heart of this ethical vision was that it was founded on a belief in the universally human that was realized in culturally specific terms. In the last four chapters of this book, I show how this contradiction worked itself out in Cyprus, with tragic results.

Postmodernity, on the other hand, is a culturalist project, one that reverses the terms of the modernist equation. Whereas modernity asserted a universal vision in which the cultural was contingent but necessary, postmodernity asserts difference as foundational and the universal (conceived in terms of rights) as contingent but necessary. Nationalist projects emerged in modernity, where the supposedly universal ethical principles of democratic representation and rights were realized in culturally specific, and often contradictory, terms, as I discuss in the final chapter. The political projects of postmodernity call for the protection of humans' basic rights to culture. Hence, the ethical problematic at the heart of the contradictions in modernity is replaced in postmodernity by the problematic of culture. The question is no longer "What should we do?" but "Who are we?"

The postnational, then, does not simply replace the national but supplants it dialectically. In nationalist visions, identity is assured; in postnational visions, it is called into question. Just as modernity took as its project prying open the "truths" and ethical demands of religion and replacing them with a purportedly surer foundation in science, postmodernity pried open modernity's illusions of universality. "Identity" is founded in "culture," but both the meaning and political import of those terms are called into question. Nationalism, then, even in its supposed demise, quickly resurfaces in the form of identity politics and the claims of culture. Hence, the need fully to understand the experience of nationalism does not end with the emergence of postnationalism but in fact becomes all the more critical.

That is why this account of conflicting nationalisms in Cyprus is squarely situated within an account of Cypriots' experiences of modernity. The cultural logics that I describe here and which became hegemonic during the period of Cyprus' "modernization" retain hegemony so long as they appear to provide adequate descriptions of their world. Globalization, represented most potently by the postnational European Union, has clearly changed the capacity of those cultural logics to provide adequate explanations for an expanded world. I suggest, however, that the manner in which those cultural logics arose, became hegemonic, and conflicted in Cyprus may help us to understand possible contradictions in the postnational experience.

A politics of personhood

In the past decade or so, nationalism has become a subject of intense fascination for academics at the same time that it has fallen out of moral favor, a victim of globalization and an eruption of unexpectedly bloody conflicts. This has generated an entire subliterature on "good" and "bad" nationalisms, those that promote virtues and those that promote vices. Such categorizations have also captured the public imagination to the extent that many wish to believe that they themselves have a "good" nationalism, while that of others is "bad." The very obvious problem with such an approach is that one constantly has to recalibrate as, for instance, the United States (formerly a "good," incorporative nationalism) adopts as its political policy a xenophobic, and nationalist, imperialism. Moreover, in most current work the constructed, and imposed, nature of nationalism is taken for granted. "Patriot" has become a rather ugly word for many academics, even for those who attempt to understand devotion to the nation-state.

This work attempts to take nationalism seriously on its own terms. Taking nationalism seriously means, I believe, wrestling with the intransigent divide between essentialism and constructivism, and attempting to bridge the gap between "believers" and critics. Taking nationalism seriously has here entailed rejecting both modernist notions of a singular identity and postmodernist notions of fractured identities and instead outlining a notion of nationalist personhood as a skill governed by aesthetic values. Nationalism, I argue here, is certainly something learned, usually through formal schooling. But mastering the signs of "Greekness" does not mean that that is one's singular identity; neither does it mean that it is part of a fractured, perhaps conflicted, identity. It means, rather, that it becomes a skill upon which one can call, much as a good mechanic would not think about which were appropriate tools, and a good pianist would not wonder where to place her hands.

Hence, I argue here that the high cultures of nationalism are also a form of embodied knowledge, an embodied knowledge deployed at appropriate moments. Moreover, I argue that the value of persons is socially related to their capacity to learn and deploy such skills, and that in the past in Cyprus it has been those persons capable of speaking properly, writing well, and performing "Greekness" or "Turkishness" who have commanded respect. As I argue elsewhere, the hierarchy itself is largely determined by those others against whom one casts one's own notions of "civilization." In a new global order supported by new forms of knowledge, it is not surprising that the hierarchy of values within which those skills are deployed should change.

For more than a decade in Cyprus, there has been a growth of "Cypriotness," defined against the Greeks of Greece and the Turks of Turkey. While that "folk culture" had never been lost in the island, it gained acceptance only as it became possible for Cypriots to imagine a world in which they might live and succeed apart from the "mainlands." During interviews that I conducted with EOKA fighters, it was constantly reiterated to me that an independent Cyprus was something that they never imagined; it was simply beyond the horizon of possibility. As Greek Cyprus has grown economically powerful, Greek Cypriots have begun to imagine the possibility of their own cultural independence. And for Turkish Cypriots, the experience of Turkish colonization of the northern part of the island has meant a new definition of the constitutive Other, who is now defined as the non-Cypriot Turk.

Hence, horizons of possibility, limited by constitutive Others, also define the hierarchy of values within which one enacts personhood. The EU has presented new possibilities, new forms of sameness and otherness, and hence a new hierarchy of values in which it is possible not simply to live Cypriotness but even to value it. It should be noted, however, that other possibilities pushed farther down the hierarchy of value do not necessarily die. The aftermath of the September 11, 2001, attacks in the U.S. should serve as fair warning to anyone tempted to believe that globalization and its concomitant valuing of the local will simply eradicate the political logic of which nationalism is the symbolic expression.

A comparative, and historical, anthropology

Comparison's current place in anthropology is ambiguous, even if its history is not. Once central to the very notion of an effective anthropology, comparison was dethroned in the 1960s, along with the "grand theories" that comparison supposedly buttressed. This dismissal of comparison as effective method followed upon critiques of comparison's almost promiscuous use to buttress projects, especially colonial ones, and of the tendency through comparison to reify the cultures that anthropologists study.[3] As the editors of a recent volume observe, anthropology's current take on comparison is of a method easy to use but impossible to think.[4] And it has become impossible to think because, as one of the volume's contributors notes, "[c]omparison implies establishing relations of both similarity and difference and ... will in the same instance reify those constructs."[5]

In other words, behind comparison lurks the specter of essentialism. In the study of nationalism, for instance, the anthropologist supposedly risks falling willy-nilly into the "trap" of nationalist essentializing, in which some putative "reality" and its distorted mirrors are no longer distinguishable. In particular, the anthropologist supposedly risks replicating the same sorts of homogenization that have resulted in the suppression of other political possibilities and other ways of life. Anthropology's mission has become to uncover counterhegemonic and silenced voices, and to explain the mechanisms of their silencing. However, while this provides one critical way of bringing to the surface the manner in which power is hidden because it is hegemonic, there are other questions about the nature of hegemony, and about why certain ideologies become hegemonic when they do, that cannot always be answered in this way.

One other possible way to understand the hegemonic is through a strategy of "strategic essentialism." "Strategic essentialism," according to Gayatry Spivak, is a form of "deconstruction" that consists of "constantly and persistently looking into how truths are produced."[6] One may, in other words, examine the construction of relations of discursive dominance, and how these relations structure social life. But how is one to do this? How is one to investigate regimes of truth, when "truths," by their very nature, appear natural and real, rather than the arbitrary things that they are? The answer of much of postcolonial and subaltern theory has been to play "the West against the Rest," to bring to light the arbitrariness of Western European grand "truths" by setting them side by side with other ways of being-in-the-world with which those grand "truths," in the period of European colonialism, interacted and came into conflict, and against which they often appeared ridiculous. The answer, in other words, has been comparison.

This book represents a similar move, though one relatively rare in anthropology. The postcolonial move of historically setting colonizer against colonized is familiar enough by now. Here, though, I employ comparison of a different sort, one in which I compare the regimes of truth represented by two nationalist ideologies in conflict with each other. The danger in such an approach is that nationalism's claims to represent a whole and bounded culture may be replicated by the anthropologist. This is the importance, I believe, of the historical approach, which takes nationalisms not as primordial but as constructed under specific historical and political circumstances. In the case of Cyprus, those circumstances also included a constitutive Other against whom one's own group was defined. It is important to understand this moiety-like system in order fully to comprehend the dynamism and strength that nationalisms have experienced in the island. Whatever differences may have previously existed, those differences certainly grew starker as nationalist ideologies triumphed in the two communities.

This, in itself, makes comparison not only worthwhile but, I believe, necessary. What makes truths true is that they also are confirmed in experience and provide a way of making sense of the world. While comparison of the sort that I have undertaken here cannot be mobilized to study every dimension of social life, it certainly allows a privileged perspective on the construction of regimes of truth, and it does so by setting those "truths" into rather stark contrast with each other.

The anthropologist Marshall Sahlins coined the phrase "the structure of the conjuncture" to refer to those moments of cultural meeting when cultures and histories conjoin in a particular, contingent event. This, he proposes, is the proper way to analyze history: as moments of cultural conjuncture, with all the social embeddedness that that entails, and with all the syncretisms that that produces. This is just another way of saying that social change is never unidirectional and is always structured by what went before.

Critics of Sahlins' work have argued that it essentializes, taking cultures as whole and given, and looking at the effects of cultural meeting from within the framework of that wholeness. One might alter Sahlins' words and opt instead for the "structure of the disjuncture" to capture the history of the production of essentialisms and the accompanying strategies. While we may always define ourselves through difference from others, the nature of difference takes varying forms over time. Nationalism, however, posits essential difference, and it is my task here to understand the manner in which a nationalism that simplifies and essentializes the complexities of people's lived worlds may nevertheless acquire an explanatory power over experience that aspires to be taken as true.

Plan of the book

When I began research in Cyprus in 1993, I originally intended to conduct ethnographic research in the schools on both sides of the island. Immediately, I faced barriers, such as the refusal of the Republic of Cyprus to grant me the research permissions that I wanted. But while waiting for those permissions and beginning ethnographic work in the neighborhood of Nicosia where I had chosen to live, I also began to research the history of Cypriot education in the British colonial archives. Faced with the dawning comprehension of my vast ignorance of a Cypriot history known to Cypriots but not found in books, as well as the realization that parts of that folk history conflicted with what I found in the archival record, I found myself slowly recognizing that my task had to be not only understanding difference in the present, but also explaining how those differences came to take the form that they have. This has been the academic motivation for this work.

But more importantly, I also found myself growing more and more committed to the belief that an anthropological and comparative rereading of the course of nationalisms in Cyprus would be necessary to provoke a rethinking of those nationalisms and could be instrumental in thinking about how to go beyond them. For this reason the movement of the book is broadly chronological, although the book primarily takes its shape from the momentum of the argument. Part One describes the ways in which the intervention of British colonial rule overturned traditional hierarchies, and how this brought about new definitions of the body politic. These chapters examine the new forms of representation that transformed Cyprus in the twentieth century and linked the authority of the word to the authority of the state in a new moral and political order. The rise of local print media, the breakdown of traditional structures of authority, competition amongst elite groups, and local attempts to transform colonial power all demonstrate the growth of new forms of power tied to print, literacy, and education.

Part Two then shows how the publics that rose from the ashes of the old structures were constituted as linguistic communities and hence "ethnic" ones. These chapters, furthermore, contrast the ways in which Orthodox and Muslim elites struggled and won power in these new public realms. In each case, the triumph of a new class depended upon that class's capacity to participate in and manipulate novel forms of representation in which claims to truth and claims to legitimacy intersected and overlapped.

Part Three then addresses the manner in which literacy and education were tied to the nationalist ideologies of Greece and Turkey. These chapters argue that education in Cyprus was necessary for nationalism because education already embodied community traditions and represented communal continuity. Both the Greek Orthodox and Muslim communities of Cyprus considered the best, most representative, and indeed most virtuous aspects of their own cultures to be embodied in the texts and traditions learned through formal schooling. Moreover, schools in Cyprus came to take over many of the tasks of the family, including a discipline that was explicitly national. At the same time, education in each community created considerably different sorts of persons, and this difference was ultimately realized in the mobilization of students and their teachers for rebellion and counter-rebellion.

Part Four then outlines why the triumph of logocentric politics in Cyprus should have resulted in conflict and violence. There, I show how the logics that sustain historical interpretation are naturalized, and how they have been naturalized differently for each community. I then demonstrate the everyday consequences of these differences for politics in each community and for interpretation of the other. The final chapter brings my analysis to the present, and to the unfortunate, current perpetuation of the dynamics that I describe.

The movement of the book, then, is from representation to epistemology, epistemology to knowledge, knowledge to discourse, and discourse to politics. At the same time, the narrative moves chronologically so that the reader can see the ways in which Cypriots have been driven further apart by the same "modern" institutions—such as a public sphere, representative politics, and increased education—that one might otherwise be tempted to believe should bring them closer together.

The recent changes in Cyprus were unexpected and revolutionary, and they portend an entirely new and hopeful future for the island. My own hope is that that future will be crafted in discussion and debate about the past, expressed as a will to self-understanding and self-searching. If this book helps to ignite that debate, it will accomplish all I could wish.

PART ONE

Stirrings

1. An old cafe of Larnaca. First published in Ohnefalsch-Richter (1994).

2. A modern cafe of Larnaca (1878). First published in Ohnefalsch-Richter (1994).

Introduction

The photograph has no date. It bears the caption "A modern cafe of Larnaca," and in it men in straw hats and fezzes lounge at tables on a neat, seaside promenade. Many wear pressed white suits and ties—even white shoes. Behind them, lettering in English advertising tobacco and cigarettes adorns a building of cool, cut stone. Above this photo is another, "An old cafe of Larnaca in 1878." In that year—the year of the British arrival—the pier is lined with tumble-down mudbrick buildings that front the water, and the path along the bay winds underneath the arches that buttress the balconies. From those buildings jut dangerous-looking wooden shacks supported by stilts in the surf. One must suppose that the dark, indistinguishable figures in those shacks are sipping coffee in the shade.

These photographs are part of the first ethnographic study of Cyprus, published in 1913 from work begun nineteen years before.[1] The author's husband, a "trader of antiquities" had arrived with the British, and so her work—primarily from interviews conducted in Greek—encompasses and encapsulates the first tumultuous, transformative decades of British rule. What her sensitive study reveals most clearly is something that the photographs described above belie: that, for most Cypriots, the transformations wrought by the British presence were not smooth and neat like the stone face of the wharfside cafe, though they may have been so for the men in crisp suits. At the turn of the century, the "progress" that had penetrated urban life had not yet worked its accelerating homogenization outside the old town walls.

Yet that small group of Christian and Muslim men sipping coffee together would frame the terms of an increasingly violent struggle for authority from which would emerge the well-formulated, unquestionable nationalist aspirations that would guide their grandchildren down the path to their own destruction. Cyprus' rapid incorporation into British administrative structures, and the new opportunities that the colonial administration represented, overturned hierarchies, leveled differences,

and presented a fundamental challenge to the spiritual and political leaders of one of the most neglected provinces of the Ottoman domains. The
next chapters will examine *how* those hierarchies were overturned and
what replaced them, as well as the type of imagination that made possible such fundamental changes. Without doubt, Cyprus encountered
that complex of ideas that has come to be known as modernity, and in
doing so both appropriated and transformed it. Wielding a narrative of
progress, these elites fumbled to create citizens and citizenship anew
from the *bricolage* of ideas and materials ready to hand. Their call for
progress "both moral and material" reflected a deep intuition that history
must be remade both as event and as consciousness.

The results of their struggles will form the subject of the next chapters. Here, we want briefly to dwell on the changes that caused a crisis of
authority and authority's recreation. Within the Ottoman Empire, many
distinctions had been based on confession, and much of the power structure had religion at its base. One's communal affiliation was defined,
firstly, by one's *millet*, or religious community, and only afterwards by a
complex of birthplace, profession, and family. Greek Orthodox, Arme-
nians, and Jews were all tried in their own religious courts and were
accountable to their own religious leaders. This meant, in consequence,
that the clerics of these religious minorities had occupied the primary
space for political representation of their peoples within the Ottoman
domain.[2]

The British arrival in Cyprus undermined the political power of the
Orthodox Church both officially and in the popular imagination, as one
can see in the peasants' immediate refusal to pay their yearly dues. As
early as 1880, Archbishop Sofronios complained to the high commissioner that church properties would fall into ruin and that priests would
be left to starve if they were not allowed to use police to collect tithes, a
privilege granted them in the Ottoman imperial *berat*, or certificate, that
confirmed them in office.[3] The Muslim community, on the other hand,
suddenly found that its direct links to the Ottoman central government
had evaporated, and new forms of representation began to take their
place.

The new institutions of British rule provoked attempts to redefine
structures of authority—processes that would accelerate as the turn of
the century approached.[4] Greek Orthodox clergy, having their relations
with the state effectively severed, grappled to retain their political power
in the face of a rising bourgeoisie. Muslim clergy, on the other hand,
sought to fill the power gap created by the evacuation of Ottoman

administrators, redefining the traditional Ottoman roles for the clerics even as they sought to suppress the growing numbers of modernizers of the "Young Turk" persuasion. Most importantly, however, these changes took place as individuals were being redefined as social actors; it was on the basis of such new definitions that authority and its discipline would be worked.

At the turn of the century, when Richter was conducting much of her ethnographic work, the men sitting together in the cafe were battling amongst themselves over modernization and "national" causes. They were merchants, traders, lawyers, doctors, teachers, and clerics of both religions. The town of Larnaca was the bustling seat of speculative enterprise, the only working port, the place where new gadgets were sold and new styles modeled, and the home for hundreds of years of the consuls of those governments that thought Cyprus worthy of their attention. The only significant road in the island connected the town to the walled city of Nicosia—isolated in the center of the Mesaoria plain—and linked the capital's bureaucrats, bazaar merchants, and artisans to the port's shippers, traders, and would-be cosmopolites. Travelers often contrasted the open plan of Larnaca and its relaxed, Levantine houses swept by sea breezes with the closed conservatism of Nicosia's dwellings, which minimized on openings to protect against the sun and sandstorms of the plain in summer.[5] The men in their coffeehouses claimed to speak for the people, at the same time seeking to describe a consensus that would support their claims to authority.

By the start of the twentieth century, Cyprus fairly seethed with new and competing ideas, usually embodied in the Larnaca or Nicosia newspapers and debated in the reading-rooms that were also intellectual clubs, places to drink and debate, and the sites for mobilization of villagers or those who would sway villagers. In the Turkish quarter of Nicosia, the club for conservative Ottoman gentlemen faced the Young Turks' club across a narrow street, so that the turbaned *ulema* had daily—and antagonistic—intercourse with exiles whose counterparts in Istanbul wished to remove the turban from the sultan's pate.

At issue was the future—and by necessity the past. The men in their coffeehouses wrote newspaper articles redolent of local concerns, canvassed the villages, giving speeches full of memorable, muscular rhetoric, and lobbied for laws that would better control the tendencies of a society that they assured themselves they knew. Both the disagreements themselves and the manner in which these struggles were fought demonstrate that such urban elites who saw themselves as progressive leaders never viewed their role as one of imposition but of clarification of a truth that they believed they recognized in their own culture. Their disagreements would become most explicit in debates over education—examined in Part Three—which reflect the struggle to control processes by which bodies of knowledge and norms for determining truth are created. But those truths were ones that such elites believed were inherent to the society, making their practice an anthropology of local life grounded in an epistemology that was eventually articulated through education.

As we will see, the occupation of Cyprus by representatives of the "empire on which the sun never set" effected a paradoxical transformation: During the latter part of the nineteenth century, Cyprus witnessed the overturning of the entrenched, imperial system with its corresponding ideologies, along with a renegotiation of the relations of power within the Greek Orthodox and Muslim communities, which constituted almost the entirety of the island's population. Long subjects of an essentially Mediterranean empire, where even the natural geographical boundaries of an island flowed into the realm that governed them, Cypriots had to become peculiar, "civilized" subjects of a heterogeneous, world imperium before they began to see the distinctness of their island community. Clifford Geertz has noted that "to rework the pattern of social relationships is to rearrange the coordinates of the experienced world. Society's forms are culture's substance."[6] But conversely, to rearrange the coordinates of the experienced world—not only what one can see, but also what one can imagine seeing—is to rework the pattern of social relationships. Form and substance are only heuristically partible.

In this regard, one cannot overestimate the symbolic and historical importance of the Ottoman Empire in the European narrative of world history, since the Ottoman regime more than any other represented "the Other"—a challenging power at the doorstep of Europe—and its decline was seen by many Europeans to usher in the modern world. The "tyranny of the Turks" was vituperated in the European popular press and literature; the "decline of the Ottomans" as a supposed result of the corruption of their race has remained—in one form or another—an accepted, indubitable part of the European narrative of the rise of "civilization." As they acquired lands and peoples in north Africa and the eastern Mediterranean, British and French colonizers often spoke with awe of the world-historical significance of the change in administration. Even in Cyprus, which legally remained an Ottoman province until

1914, one of the clearly defined goals of the British administration was to show "the Turks" how a province *should* be run.

Despite the significance of the Ottoman Empire as premodern, neighboring predecessor to the modern empires of Europe, the former Ottoman realms still suffer from the curious silence that reigns in the postcolonial literature regarding different *styles* of imperial subjectivity and the epistemic shifts that they necessitate. Indeed, the Ottoman Empire was manifestly *un*modern, even though its elites had struggled for more than a century at "modernizing" it. The difficulty for them, however, seems to have been in grasping the fundamental distinction between modernization and modernity: While the former is a narrative of progress, the latter is the condition of the possibility of a subjectivity that requires such narration. It is the latter that makes "peoples with history" in the sense defined by modern European narratives.

In Cyprus, the British arrival made this distinction clear to some, and it created conditions, such as increased literacy and a vibrant local press, that were the cornerstone of the European transition to the age that has been identified as modern. Indeed, one of the fundamental goals of this work is to demonstrate through the contrast of Greek and Turkish Cypriot nationalist sensibilities that, if we are to define an identity that might be called "modern," it is distinguishable not only by its necessary narration, but also by the second-order nature of that narration, which links formal education and writing with the nationalist projects of modernity.

In one of those rare but deliciously lapidary phrases of which Proust was such a master, he remarked that "the forgetful self does not grieve about his forgetfulness precisely because one has forgotten."[7] This was, of course, within the context of his marvelous dismantling of the notion of the constant self—what William James called an abstraction imported into experience. The next chapters will trace a transformation of a sort that can only be observed in retrospect, for actors are notoriously unaware of the processes by which identities are created and shed. It will trace the emergence of a subject so new that the narrative of her own history makes no room for the identity that she's lost along the way. This is an exploration of horizons of possibility, and it represents a conscious attempt to avoid circumscribing and fixing the sets of relations that constitute the representation of our selves that we call "identity."[8] Instead, we will traverse that most dangerous ground of self-identification: that area between subject and culture, between consciousness and its limitations, where truth is defined, and the imaginable becomes the possible.

CHAPTER 1

Rights and Religions

On the Larnaca promenade where Cypriot gentlemen once sipped coffee together, one can stroll today amidst the hum of motorboats, the occasional airplane roar, and the blare of American pop music from seaside pubs. During the day, the bright, white hotels glare in the Cypriot sun, while at night the signs in English are a colorful, neon cacophony advertising traditional Cypriot food, traditional Cypriot drink. In the summer, the beaches are filled with middle-aged tourists and English-speaking Cypriots returned from abroad. Like so much of Cyprus, there is something at once cosmopolitan and parochial about this town, which caters to the passing multitudes, while behind this seafront facade are the neighborhoods where families struggle to build a dowry house, to send their children to England or America for university. Almost every Cypriot has a close family member abroad, but for many the goal of that exile is a successful return to the island. Unfortunately, in such a small place there are too few jobs and too much education, and so too often there is no hope of a permanent return. And so much of Cyprus is cosmopolitan by necessity and parochial by desire.

In fact, despite the tourists, despite the emigrants, and despite Cypriots' constant travels to visit family abroad, the Cyprus of today is in many ways more parochial than it was in the last century, when British colonists arrived in the island. There is, of course, something incongruous in the old photos that show a British steamer banked alongside the Venetian walls of Famagusta, or the neat, well-ordered encampment of British soldiers alongside the narrow streets and crumbling, mudbrick houses of the towns. Indeed, early British descriptions are of a picturesque and isolated island populated by peoples with quaint customs, charming clothes, and terrible manners.

But to take such portraits at face value is to ignore the sources of power and prosperity that were available to Cypriots as members of a vast and still-powerful empire. Cypriots of the time certainly were not isolated, if they ever had been. Cypriots maintained strong links with co-religionists throughout the eastern Mediterranean: the Cypriot Brotherhood of Alexandria funded many of the Greek Orthodox schools; most Cypriot Muslims who received higher education were educated in Cairo or Istanbul; Cypriot merchants traded throughout the Levant; agricultural laborers could find seasonal work in Anatolia; Greek Cypriot masons and goldsmiths made their way to Egypt, where many amassed large fortunes as moneylenders; and many Cypriots appear to have had family members scattered throughout the Mediterranean shores of the Ottoman domains. In the island, the language of commerce was French; the language of administration was Ottoman; and the languages of the people were Cypriot versions of Greek and Turkish. As late as 1911, there were three times as many native Arabic-speakers as English-speakers in Cyprus. And with the Russian Revolution, the Orthodox Church of Cyprus complained that it had lost significant amounts of property in the Ukraine, which had been confiscated by the new government.

British colonists took Cyprus as an island—in other words, as a well-defined and bounded territory—and saw it as a unity containing populations that spoke different languages and worshipped in different fashion. These people they called Cypriots. For the inhabitants themselves, "Cypriot" (*Kıbrıslı* in Turkish or *Kiprios* in Greek) was a designation of origins, but not a significant designation of identity. The Ottoman Empire itself was fluid, with ever-expanding or contracting boundaries, and at the time of the British occupation of Cyprus it still stretched from Tunis across the shores of Tripoli, throughout Egypt, the Hijaz, Syria, and Iraq, and included Bulgaria, Albania, and Macedonia. Cypriots had been able to traverse this far-flung empire because of the several routes to success open through confessional affiliation. The socially relevant identity employed outside one's homeland was primarily one's religious identification, while one's place of birth became relevant only when it established one as part of a particular set of social relationships. Hence, when a wealthy *âlım*, or cleric, from Larnaca traveled to Istanbul for Ramadan, the Cypriot-born grand vizier appointed his compatriot as his personal imam for the holy month.[1] However, it is clear that these inhabitants lived before a time when origins would necessarily imply a subjective identity, since it would only be in an age of equality that origins would become both a source of identity and a source of authority. The inhabitants of Cyprus were subjects, not citizens.

As they traveled, worked, and lived in far-flung parts of the Ottoman domains, what many of these Cypriots experienced is called in Turkish *gurbet* and in Greek *ksenitia*, or being far from one's homeland. The longing for one's homeland is the subject of much poetry and folksong, in which the delights of childhood and the pretty girls of the village are evoked to give to that longing the tangible association of memory. Notably, this meaning of *gurbet* is only possible when the longing that one feels is for a known and remembered land—a particular village nestled in the mountains, a crisp breeze redolent with sage, the familiar faces of childhood friends. In this sense, one could experience that longing within a large island like Cyprus as well as outside it. One could not, however, experience that longing for an imagined land, an imagined community.[2]

This chapter will examine the crisis of authority that resulted from the entry of the British into the island. I will argue in Chapter 2 that the identity of the citizen was not an easy one to acquire, and that its rights and responsibilities were not transparent but problematic. But such an argument will be prefaced here by questions regarding the constitution of authority and a newly emergent demand for consensus. The struggle to define citizenship was also—if not primarily—a struggle to define that authority to which one owed one's allegiance. Because religion and politics had previously been entwined, the crisis of political authority was also, by definition, a crisis of religious authority, and of the role of religion as a form of representation.

In the past, priests who rose in the hierarchy of the Orthodox Church gained increasing political authority, and the archbishop of the auto-cephalous Orthodox Church of Cyprus was recognized as the political as well as spiritual leader of the island's Orthodox Christians. Anyone aspiring to the rank of bishop or above was elected by a popular vote of the adult male Christians in his district. Similarly, the *kadi*, or judge, and the *mufti*, or interpreter of shari'a law, had traditionally interceded for Cypriots with whatever foreign governor administered the island.[3] The mufti, especially, had this role, for he was invariably of Cypriot origin and was elected by the *ulema* and notables of Nicosia.

The entry of the British into Cyprus and the administration of the island by a Protestant power changed all of this. As we will see in this and the next chapters, the transformation of Cypriot subjects into nation-alist citizens required, first and foremost, a new way of linking word and state—a new way of linking the authority of knowledge and the author-ity of politics. In a land in which religion, politics, and identity had for so long been intertwined, the decline of traditional, especially religious, authority issued in a period of violent, spectacular, and blasphemous protests and disputes over the nature of authority. Orthodox Cypriots uniformly refused to pay their yearly tithes without adequate accountability on the part of the bishops who controlled those funds. Muslim Cypriots, on the other hand, were not only joining other Ottoman Muslims in debating the status of "Muslim" as a political identity, but they were also, within Cyprus itself, challenging the right of the *ulema*—and the wealthy families from which they came—to represent the entirety of the community. Those same decades saw equally violent contests and disputes over the creation of "publics"—public spaces, public speech, public behavior. If politics was to be divorced from the religious sphere, what was it to be a politics *of*? What sort of community would that politics represent? And what did it mean to Cypriots that they were promised entry into the modern world? Did that not mean a new sort of knowledge—a sort of knowledge for which there may have been no prior normative corollaries?

This chapter describes Cypriots' encounters with British "equality" and the consequent breakdown of traditional structures of authority. The chapter then examines how, in the wake of that breakdown, the slow transformation of subjects into citizens began. That was a transition accomplished through the advent of a notion of a "public" that emerged through representative politics and new media. The chapter shows, first, the problems entailed in divorcing religion from politics, and how a new form of politics began to emerge. The following sections then look at the role played by bureaucracy and newspapers in "inscribing" a new form of identity dependent upon one's ability to represent oneself in writing. The new role for the word, and those who commanded its power, would ultimately rewrite the state.

Rights and religions

Every spring, the period immediately before Easter begins a series of celebrations that culminate in Kataklysmos, or the Festival of Aphrodite. During Kataklysmos the archbishop travels to the seashore to bless the waters, throws a cross into the sea, and then waits as boys dive from a pier into the still-frigid waves to retrieve it. The festival lasts for several days, marked by the singing contests of oral poets, or *poiitaridhes*. Kataklysmos was historically an island-wide celebration, and both

Greeks and Turks traveled from the remotest corners of the island to attend events in Larnaca and Limassol. On the second day of Easter and before the start of Kataklysmos, Greek Cypriots used to burn the figure of Judas in all the churches and village chapels of the island. This straw man would be set alight immediately outside the chapel, and Ohnefalsch-Richter notes that the figure of Judas was often used as a caricature, giving a mood of satirical play to the proceedings. In the first years of the British occupation, she notes, Greek Cypriots began to dress Judas as a contemporary Englishman, complete with bowler hat and nightstick. And the English of Larnaca, she says, attended the proceedings and celebrated along with the Orthodox, unaware of the satirically critical intent of the Judas figure.

This covert caricature of their British rulers emerged in part from disappointments with those rulers' own self-representations. When the new British colonists came ashore in 1878, their immediate mission was to safeguard the Mediterranean route to the Suez Canal; their moral mission was to prove the fertilizing, fecund influence of British reason, oriented towards the ever-hastening future and its promised bounty. Snatched from the spiral of Ottoman collapse, Cyprus would be set aright under British rule, its inhabitants taught the proper husbandry of its resources and the sensible economy of time necessary for its prosperity.[4] Attempting to teach by example, the soldiers were immediately set to work in the penetrating July sun to build a pier in the harbor of Larnaca. "The inhabitants were immensely astonished to find our men at work all yesterday," Sir Garnet Wolseley commented in his journal, "and are lost in amazement at the energy with which all our operations are carried on."[5] The inhabitants were perhaps less astonished when the men began to succumb to the "Cyprus fever," a predictable ailment that afflicted those who dared to venture into the middle of a summer day.

These pith-helmeted protectors were greeted on the shore by the clergy and town elites who appeared in their roles as representatives of the order that they did not realize would soon be overturned. Entrenched in the social and legal codes of the Ottoman Empire and accustomed to participation in the provincial life of the sprawling Ottoman state, the Orthodox and Muslim clergy, as well as the doctors, lawyers, and large landowners who supported them, constituted an elite, paternalistic class whose trans-confessional power was consolidated in rights to land and control of resources. In the materialistic worlds of merchants and bureaucrats, there was little to distinguish Orthodox and Muslim elites, so that Greek tithe-farmers could often be seen socializing with the

Turkish aristocracy in salons and luxurious clubs, such as the Yeşil Gazino in Nicosia.[6] So, when the occupying force of the most modern navy in the world came ashore in Larnaca, they were welcomed as representatives of the great Christian empire of which Cyprus would now form a part and in which these elites expected to maintain a leading role.

Though recent nationalist histories have described this initial encounter as one between a colonizer and Greek Orthodox colonized who spoke the same modernist language of national consciousness and rights, it is fairly certain that this is a version of events that emerged much later in the colonial period. In the revisionist account, Wolseley was met on shore by Archbishop Sofronios who, in his flowing beard and robes, raised his arms and blessed the British arrival, proclaiming, "We accept the change of Government inasmuch as we trust that Great Britain will help Cyprus, as it did the Ionian Islands, to be united with Mother Greece, with which it is nationally connected."[7] But as recent work shows, reports of the time made no mention of such a speech; it was not until twenty-five years after the British arrival and the radical changes that it brought that the archbishop was portrayed as uttering such nationalist sentiments.[8]

However, it cannot be doubted that the change of government was a momentous occasion for a province that had long been ignored except as a site of internal exile for religious and political troublemakers.[9] The transfer of power was a neat one on the surface, as the residence of the Ottoman *vali*, or governor, was appropriated for purposes of the new administration, and the *vali* himself and his entourage were shipped back to Istanbul. But it would soon become apparent that the "circle of equity" that was the supposed governing principle of the Ottoman realm did not adapt easily to an administration concerned less with social justice than with justice ruled by law.[10] As we will see in Chapter 2, it soon became apparent that expectations of "paternal" authority could not easily adapt to constitutional law and justice.

What Cypriots had not expected, for example, was that the British would bring with them a promise to pay yearly tribute to Istanbul of the amount of over 90,000 pounds sterling—a staggering sum in a small island of peasant farmers and shepherds where the average annual income in a population of about 140,000 was approximately thirty pounds. Moreover, the tribute itself—while justified as a treaty obligation to the sultan—in fact never reached Istanbul, for it was instead funneled into the hands of waiting bondholders in London, who had financed loans to the sultan in the middle of the century. And British taxation was applied ruthlessly and systematically. After the first collection of taxes, Kyprianos, Bishop of Kition, protested the brutality of the English system, expressing his surprise to Colonel Falk Warren, Commissioner of Limassol:

> If I relate matters in a plain and straightforward manner, it is my character so to do: I used to act similarly toward the former administration, which was not an English administration, and whose officials were not citizens of the most Constitutional state under the Sun …. Excellency, the Cypriotes are the most docile people in the Ottoman Empire, and if any persons have told you otherwise they have deceived You. The rural population of Cyprus, as well as the inhabitants of the cities, are in penury, and they absolutely required some assistance at first so as to enable them to recover. They have been fearfully oppressed, contrary to orders issued by the Imperial Government and in defiance of existing laws, by selfish officials; and I consider that it should be one of the highest duties of the new Administration to shew without any delay the difference which ought to exist between the Turkish rule and the European administration of enlightened Englishmen …. Dear Mr. Warren, I may be mistaken in my appreciation of things, but I will not conceal from you that I think that You treat the Christian population of this district, and their Spiritual Chief, as unmanageable self-willed subjects, a trouble to their late paternal Government, but this is as far from truth as heaven is removed from Earth.[11]

Not only did these first British administrators ignore local expectations of their "civilizing influence," but they also received coldly the seemingly impertinent appeals of Cypriots, who were accustomed to writing to the sultan himself if necessary but who were accused by the new administration of attempting to contravene the law and circumvent the proper authorities. The contrast drawn in the letter between a "paternal" and a "constitutional" government could not be more appropriate to the complaint.

In fact, the immediate result of effective British administration—and the tax collection that was its foundation—was one of the greatest periods of poverty and misery that had been known in the century.[12] The bishop of Kition implicitly compares the new British administration with the extortion of "selfish officials" who had defied orders of the "paternal" Ottoman government. Notably, the bishop does not blame their former "paternal" government or the sultan, but he blames the sultan's officials, who have flagrantly disobeyed existing laws. As in many other cases of the exploitation and oppression of agricultural classes, the bishop protests not against legitimate authority but against that authority's misuse.[13] Hence, he believes that it should be a duty of the new administration "to shew without any delay the difference which ought to exist between the Turkish rule and the European administration of enlightened Englishmen." He focuses on the officials—the "English-men"—themselves, and not on the rule of the queen. He expects those officials to demonstrate that they are not part of a similarly corrupt system that tolerates such abuses.

But what the bishop interpreted as abuse was little more than the systematic taxation applied equally to all. The Cyprus that the British found was a primarily agricultural land of small villages in which, under the Ottoman regime, the village *muhtar*, or headman, had been left to negotiate settlements, administer justice, and collect taxes based on the year's luck or failures of each village family. The loosely woven administrative fabric of the Ottoman regime had allowed for considerable autonomy within—as well as considerable abuse of—bureaucratic roles and jurisdictions. Ottoman governors never attempted, for instance, thoroughly to survey peasant rights to land, trees, and water—a process that would have involved far more complications than their own ends would have justified. But the British penetrated rapidly throughout the island, with a thorough topographical survey led by the young Kitchener and a command that commissioners of the districts visit and assess the state of every village before the year was out.[14] Villagers were issued titles that they could not read for land that they may have had no rights to work.[15] Subjects of an empire had suddenly become the legal, taxable cyphers of a bureaucracy, and they quickly discovered that "equal rights" also meant "equal wrongs."

But what was just as significant was that the demise of "paternal" governance not only affected the people's relationship to the state, it also affected the people's relationship to the clergy and urban elites who had for so long acted as patrons and intercessors. It had not been uncommon, for instance, for the archbishop or a local pasha to go to Istanbul to press a particularly important case. But what was clear from the very beginning of British rule was that all Cypriots—regardless of background or rank—had become equal subjects of the new administration, so that not only the ordinary villager but also the villager's priest, imam, teacher, or elder could be—and often was—charged with the same crime or kept waiting in the same queue as farmer or shepherd.

Overnight, distinctions were erased on all levels, from the villagers who were all taxed equally to the clerics who were suddenly equally accountable under the law. In a particularly scandalous case from 1879, two priests were arrested for grazing their goats in protected forest land and while in prison had their heads and beards shaved. Letters of support addressed to the archbishop and of condemnation of this "vandalous action" addressed to the high commissioner were published in the new newspaper, *Neon Kition*.[16] The administration explained that all prisoners entering the jails had to be shaved. But while newspaper articles and letters to the government did not protest against the sentence, the assault on the bodies and hence on the honor and status of the priests brought fierce condemnation on the over-zealous prison guards and their superiors.[17] In addition, there are numerous cases from this same period of priests and imams appealing to higher religious authorities to intercede on their behalf to have their names removed from the "bad characters' list," a British invention that allowed police the scope to monitor known transgressors, the consequences of which I explore in the next chapter.[18]

In this new, equalized order a division began to emerge between those members of the clergy and elite class who were prepared to manipulate the new forms of representation and to stake their own claims in the political arena, and those who considered it beneath the dignity of their status to engage in party politics. The most important new site for this contest was the new Legislative Council, that body established by the British to give the island some semblance of representative rule. The new administration created the Legislative Council immediately in 1878, with changes to that council's constitution enacted in 1883. This council was ultimately composed of six official members and twelve elected members, the latter divided approximately according to population, with nine Greek Orthodox and three Muslim members, the high commissioner presiding.[19] In concert with the Executive Council, a body of appointed officials, it was the role of the Legislative Council to deal with legal issues that related specifically to the situation in Cyprus. The archbishop and mufti were appointed members, but several bishops and members of the *ulema*—particularly teachers—ran with overwhelming success for seats on the Legislative Council, along with publishers, lawyers, and other members of the professional class. They managed to do so because especially younger, more vibrant members of the elite class found ways to accommodate traditional authority to a new age.

British administrators explained their successes in reductive fashion, seeing the successes of lawyers, publishers, bishops and *ulema* as instances of corruption, vote-rigging, and nepotism. They interpreted those successes in this way primarily because they also saw the local-level rebellions against the authority of priests and against the monetary claims of monasteries, as well as the libel cases so often brought against publishers. Moreover, complaints of fraud and election-rigging were often brought by one faction of the community against another. Archbishop Sofronios, for instance, complained about the bishop of Kition, a particularly radical cleric who in 1884 had won a popularly elected seat in the legislative council and was using it to jockey for power against the "old guard" of conservative clerics, especially by encouraging Orthodox not to pay their tithes. The archbishop complained to the high commissioner, who reports:

> He [the archbishop] also informed me that the Bishop of Kitium had spread a report that it was the intention of the Government to pay the salaries of the Bishops, and that this report had resulted, as he had intended, in throwing the Bishops into embarrassment by causing the people to cease the payment of the usual canonical dues; that the Bishop of Kitium suffered no embarrassment himself, as he had acquired such a position in the Island by the complete subservience to him of the native members of the Legislative Council that he could get his own dues from the people without difficulty .... He added that the Bishop of Kitium gives out to the people that he corresponds with the Queen and that it was owing to his advice to Her Majesty that the tithe on grapes was abolished. I have heard this from other sources.[20]

The archbishop and other clerics used this as an example of the necessity of having their duties and the obligations of the faithful confirmed by law and supported by the state. What it demonstrates most clearly, however, is the new role for traditional leaders in popular politics.

Moreover, a clear division had developed between an "old guard" that sought to maintain the "traditional" source of the clergy's power in its paternal support by the state, and a group of younger, dynamic clergy— and other elites tied to them—that sought to use the new representative politics to create a different kind of power for themselves. While the Orthodox community had always elected its bishops by popular vote, those clergy acquired political power *qua* clergy in a realm where confession was the important political identifier. The bishop of Kition, however, learned to maintain political power in a realm where religion *per se* retained no political force.

Similarly in the Muslim community, the advent of representative politics produced challenges to the aloof, entrenched elites. This first became apparent in 1890, when the mufti of Cyprus, Esseid Efendi, a native of Nicosia born in 1816, died after having served in that post since one year before the British occupation.[21] British bureaucrats, who had spent the previous decade trying to understand Islamic land laws and the Swiss criminal code of the *Legislation ottomane*, were caught unawares when two distinct groups claimed the right *by tradition* to elect the new mufti. Through the kadi, the notables of Nicosia sent their nomination of one Ali Rifki Efendi directly to Istanbul for approval by the *sheikh ul-Islam*, and a copy of the letter went to the high commissioner of Cyprus. But at the same time the chief secretary's office was flooded with hundreds of petitions from the villages with thousands of signatures in support of another candidate, Mehmet Raif Efendi. These petitions asked that the government send its nomination of Mehmet Raif Efendi to Istanbul for approval by the *sheikh ul-Islam*, thus in effect requesting that the government circumvent the leading *ulema*.

The notables felt compelled, under these circumstances, to clarify for the high commissioner the rules for a mufti's appointment, stating that in the past, on the death of a mufti, "the ulemas and notables of Nicosia used to meet at a place and elect one, competent to deal with and manage, questions relating to fetwas," and that approval of their choice was a mere formality.[22] They then charged that the hundreds of seals and thousands of signatures were gathered by less than honest means:

> According to what we now hear some people have sent certain persons, with wages, out to the districts with a lot of memorandas in order to get the Revd. Haji Mussevid Mehmed Raif Effendi elected, who (the persons) are, against the rules current and in force, getting a considerable number of signatures which are being submitted to Your Excellency.[23]

It is difficult to know whether the primary objection was to the solicitation of popular opinion or to the manner in which it was solicited.

The two candidates were both Cypriots with similar backgrounds. The "candidate of the people," Mehmet Raif Efendi, had been the *müssevid*, or scribe, for the mufti's office for approximately thirty years, and it was reported by the late mufti's brother that Raif Efendi had formerly been elected to the office of mufti but had given it up in favor of Esseid Efendi. The candidate of the notables, Ali Rifki Efendi, was a *müderris*, which meant that he was not only a member of the *ulema* but also a teacher. The dispute did not overtly concern qualifications or character but simply the manner of election, as reported by the high commissioner:

> I recently received by request a deputation of Moslems of Nicosia who protested against the appointment of Hadji Ali Rifki Eff. as Mufti and urged that although the final appointment to the office of Mufti rested with the Sheik-ul-Islam the selection was dependent on the election of the Mahomedan inhabitants of the Island and that as Hadji Mehmed Raif Eff. had received the majority of votes he was the proper person to be appointed ... [*Marked out:* Who said that they considered that, in accordance with an ab antiquo rule, the greater number of voices having elected Hadji Mehmed Raif Effendi, that person should be appointed mufti, and expressed the hope that they being in the majority would not be deprived of their right in the matter.][24]

The high commissioner, convinced that the majority had been outwitted by a well-connected minority, communicated with the British ambassador in Istanbul about the matter, urging him to bring to the attention of the *sheikh ul-Islam* the fact that hundreds of petitions had been received in support of the other candidate.

The high commissioner was quite surprised when, several months later, he received from the ambassador a *note verbale*, communicating to him that, in fact, "according to the rule in force the Muftis are elected by the Ulema of the country" and that, as the *ulema* had, in fact, stated, the approval of their choice was a mere matter of formality. The high commissioner remarked that this information differed significantly from what they had been told in the previous year by some of the most respected members of the Muslim community. Then, they had been informed that the election should be a popular one, and that the local authorities should communicate the popular choice to the *sheikh ul-Islam*:

> That was the information which we obtained here last year from the late Chief Cadi and from other persons in the Island, and when I called in question the action that was on that occasion taken by the Porte and the Sheikh-ul-Islam in proceeding, without any reference to this Government and without awaiting any communication from this Government to the appointment of Hadji Ali Rifki Effendi it was mainly because of the way in which the rights (as we understood them to be) of the Mahomedan community here were disregarded.[25]

He also noted that, while the *ulema* sent their choice directly to Istanbul, those who collected signatures had gone through the colonial administration and had their representation entirely ignored.

And so the British administration duly recognized Ali Rifki Efendi, despite resentment of the *ulema*'s circumvention of local authority. It thus remains unclear whether the action of the *ulema* was canonical except in the circumvention of the local government, or whether local Cypriot practice had by tradition come closer to that of their Christian compatriots in requiring a popular election, and the *ulema* were attempting to reassert an orthodox interpretation.[26] Either case would indicate an increasing gap between popular expectations of clerical leaders and the role that those leaders were prepared to fulfill under the new administration. Moreover, when a mufti had to be elected and the popular party claimed the right to elect him *by tradition*, this represented a rather sophisticated understanding both of the ideology of equality and of the construction of "cultures" that underlay much of British colonial rule.

In both communities, then, who *should* lead was suddenly up for grabs. Ultimately, those who were successful would be so by transforming traditional authority to meet the demands of a new age. That new age was not only one of representative politics, but also one of a new role for the bearers of knowledge. The "paternalism" of the previous age had in large part depended upon limited access to knowledge and its power. But at the same time that representative politics developed in Cyprus, so did newspapers and a public sphere. These were interdependent developments, since representative politics depended on newspapers both to instruct and to create an "audience," a "public." Media, in turn, were controlled by the legislators, lawyers, businessmen, and teachers who sought control of the public realm.

These new leaders were, moreover, attempting to describe that public for itself, and the following sections describe the consequences of this. The first consequence was that the division between educated elite and villager came to be described as a division between the leader and his "public." The Villager became a category that represented the Everyman of Cyprus and therefore the Cypriot public—a new category created only in the age of print media. The second consequence was that this new public—despite its presumed ignorance—had to learn to represent itself. This created a paradoxical situation: The "ignorant villager" who constituted the Cypriot public and who needed to be led by his educated leaders still, himself, had at least to know how to sign his name and thereby to form a true representation of himself in the new realm of popular politics. The new requirements of citizenship presupposed an ability to represent oneself both uniquely and categorically, not through a transitory oral declaration but through a form of writing in which one would become uniquely represented and at the same time one would become "only a name." As we will see, becoming "only a name," a representative of "the public," would only be possible when villagers were transformed into citizens and when a new sort of community was created in which one's membership would no longer be determined by the practices and relations of village life but by an identity of equal selves.

The cafe as public platform

With his starched collar, knotted tie, and grey goatee, the Larnaca publisher Christodhoulos Konstantinidhis most closely resembled a German scholar transported to seaside Cyprus. Born in Larnaca in 1847, Konstantinidhis pursued an education that was not unlike the schooling of many of his generation's men. He finished his "Greek lessons" in Larnaca with Chrysanthos Ioannidhis who, by the time of the British occupation, was bishop of Kyrenia. Afterwards, he traveled to Syria to study French, then moved on to Alexandria to study in the Greek high school under the tutelage of—among others—Max Ohnefalsch-Richter, the husband of our ethnographer. Konstantinidhis taught both in Cyprus and in Egypt, employing his spare time to publish the newspaper *Cairo*. From this experience he gained the financial and moral support of the Cypriot Brotherhood in Alexandria to return to Cyprus with the printing equipment to begin the island's first newspaper. In the spring of 1878, he had used his connections in Nicosia to gain publishing permission from the Ottoman governor, so the opening of his new printing office closely coincided with the British arrival.[27]

Like other educated Cypriots—both Christian and Muslim—of his generation, Konstantinidhis navigated his way through the circles of Cypriot emigrants who had established themselves throughout the eastern Mediterranean. For Christians, this meant primarily the communities around the patriarchal seats in Jerusalem and Antioch, as well as the large Greek-speaking communities of Cairo, Alexandria, and Beirut. For Muslims, emigration was usually to the heart of the Ottoman Empire, Istanbul, though many Cypriots were educated in the schools of Beirut, Cairo, and Adana. Strongly aware both of his status identity which linked him to the larger, educated Greek-speaking world and of his Cypriot identity which distinguished him from Greek-speakers elsewhere, Konstantinidhis used the "high" form of modern Greek to publish a newspaper of very local concern, with English translation.

Konstantinidhis' newspaper, *Neon Kition*, initiated a flurry of print activity in the Greek-speaking community that would be followed only much later by similar activity among their Turkish-speaking compatriots. Indeed, immediately upon the arrival of the British, printing presses began to whir, so that a dozen years later seven newspapers in Greek boasted a combined circulation of nearly 3,000 in the island; a "Journal of Cyprian Studies" had been inaugurated, and approximately 450 books had been published.[28] In contrast, the sole Turkish-language weekly, *Saded*, had only sixty-four subscribers.[29] A flourishing Turkish-language press would develop only near the turn of the century with the sudden flight to Cyprus of a number of Young Turks exiled from the capital, who hoped to use the British administration and their strategic position to write critically of the sultan's regime. Early in the 1890s

Zaman and *Kıbrıs* would emerge, the latter published by the Ottoman Club of Nicosia. These local papers would exist alongside others oriented to a world outside the island, such as the pan-Islamic *Dik ul-Sharq*, or "Cock of the East," published in Arabic. Concentric circles of linguistic and social inclusion and exclusion are traced by these literary productions and the audiences that they addressed.

In particular, these newspapers represented the "high" forms of Greek and Turkish, which were at several removes from the Greek and Turkish spoken in the island. *Katharevousa* Greek was an archaized form intended to bring the language closer to that of the ancient Greek ancestors. The archaizing of the language was a nationalist project begun in the late eighteenth century, and *katharevousa* was made the official form of Greek of the new Greek state several decades later.[30] However, *katharevousa* never became the spoken language of the people, who continued to speak what was considered to be a corrupted variant, *dhimotiki*. And so in Greece a diglossia was created that also represented the class divisions created by education.[31] The average Cypriot was at an even further remove from *katharevousa*, since the Cypriot form of Greek was so different as to seem incomprehensible even to *dhimotiki* speakers.[32] Although the Turkish dialect of Cyprus was not at such a far remove from Anatolian varieties, Turkish-speakers in Cyprus still had only limited access to Ottoman Turkish, which was the language created for the bureaucratic needs of the state and which was highly inflected with Arabic and Persian vocabulary and grammar. And in any case, many village Muslims, outnumbered by their Greek-speaking neighbors, spoke Cypriot Greek, rather than Turkish, as their first language.

Moreover, both the Orthodox and Muslim communities of Cyprus were "literate" communities in the sense defined by Goody and others.[33] Not only were both communities heavily reliant upon the written word, but both also believed that the continuity of each community depended upon its preservation through writing. Thus, schoolmasters and other literates were valued and admired not because of simple literacy—not because they had mastered some magical power of words—but because they had been inducted into the mysteries of the long intellectual histories of which each community was proud. To become a fully literate Muslim Ottoman meant that one learned not only Turkish but also Arabic and Persian—the languages of the Qur'an and of poetry. And to become a fully literate Greek Orthodox meant that one learned the languages of Socrates, of the Bible, and of Byzantium.

Thus, literacy had always had the social implications of a "tradition." With the arrival of the British, however, it began to have more and more the social implications of politics. Not coincidentally, publishers were also the lawyers, doctors, and merchant-moneylenders who controlled the legislative council and who were divided amongst themselves over religious issues. What was at stake was the role of religious authority in a new realm of public discourse, where information and opinions were written and widely circulated and where "truth" was no longer referable to an authority on one's metaphysical status. In other words, this new written culture produced innumerable, competing claims to "factuality" with no norms for determining the truth about such facts. The reader— or, rather, auditor, since much of this information was disseminated orally in the cafes—was confronted with news from far-off villages, snippets of poetry in arcane language, gossip about people he didn't know, descriptions of a distant cosmopolitan life, and information about the larger Greek- and Turkish-speaking worlds—those fantastic places where they spoke those strange languages that Cypriots couldn't understand. The very textuality of this information made it fact, and it was in such a context that Cypriot publishers and legislators wished to circumscribe the "facts" of Cypriot culture and to find ways to describe the primarily illiterate villagers who were their public.

Indeed, even until the 1950s in Cyprus aurality continued to play an important role as a means of disseminating information, and the cafe maintains its significance as a public forum even today. As Joyce Coleman notes for medieval England and France, the fact of public reading should not be taken only as a mark of a purported transition from an oral to a literate society.[34] Public reading was often a highly valued practice, and in Cypriot village cafes it provided an opportunity for public debate of issues and discussion of the reliability of printed reports.[35] Oral dissemination of written information was certainly the norm, whether it was the announcements read in the sermons of church or mosque or the legal information distributed through the *muhtars*.

Village schoolmasters not only read the newspapers in the villages, but they also became the medium for party politics. They supported a candidate and explained his "platform;" when villagers did not approve of their schoolmaster's political alliances, they simply got a new schoolmaster. More generally, villages that may never have seen a real Ottoman official were drawn into the web of British bureaucracy and began to be linked through government ties and the new print culture to places they had never imagined before. Taxes and village problems had

before been mediated through the *muhtar*, who had his own networks
and patrons to work for him in the hierarchy of government officials.
But becoming the equal, taxable subject of a "constitutional" empire
meant that one's case was decided not by a co-villager or a co-villager's
patron, but in the impersonal chambers of government "justice" where
the facts and figures of the case were inscribed.

Indeed, within three decades of the British arrival, Cypriots had
learned the importance of paper, and the various ties linking them to the
capital had become a structure of interested middlemen, lawyers, and
scribes who began to reshape politics on the village level. In fact by
1909 the English district commissioners could complain that they never
had time to visit the villages because of paperwork. For instance, the
commissioner of the Nicosia District lamented that

> apart from the work connected with the business of the Capital, there are 211
> villages in the District, all more or less distracted by party quarrels, and the
> amount of office work arising out of the management of their affairs is enor-
> mous. The villagers have now been trained to make their complaints through
> their so-called leaders, and so have little or nothing to say by way of com-
> plaint if approached in their villages; they prefer to send in their complaints
> through advocates in town.[36]

One presumes that, given the commissioner's observations regarding
village party quarrels, the "so-called leaders" were in fact party leaders,
that is, non-elected ones.

In fact, it is clear from police reports of disturbances in the districts
that it was not uncommon for representatives of the Nicosia leadership
to be sent into the villages, where their arrival was often cause for violence. Another indication of such increasing centralization was the close
ties of village schoolmasters to political leaders in Nicosia. During an
election for archbishop, for example, one of the contested villages was
Lefkara, about which the district commissioner reported:

> There was no doubt a disgraceful row at Levkara, but no one was really
> injured, and a prosecution would have led to a crop of perjuries, and much ill
> feeling …. Such rows are sure to recur at Levkara and elsewhere if the school-
> masters are allowed to interfere in village politics. In this case they were found
> with voting tickets already written containing the names of their nominees,
> which they tried to foist on illiterate voters, to the natural indignation of the
> other side.

Moreover, the issue of schoolmasters' political involvements repeatedly
came before the boards of education, but none of the members were in
favor of restraining the teachers. "This is natural," the chief secretary

commented, "for the members it is my belief rely upon these schoolmasters to assist them in their elections for the Legislative Council, Education Committees, Medjliss Idare, etc."[37] In other words, the direct result of this legal-bureaucratic penetration was a form of populist politics.

At least one significant result of this inscription of networks and its use for party politics was the increasing reliance of individuals upon those who could write one's "native" language. Whereas under the Ottoman regime the complaints of a Muslim villager might have been handled by his Orthodox *muhtar*, such a possibility was becoming increasingly unlikely in the highly bureaucratized British administration. While the petitions necessary under British rule may have been written in one's "native language," this was not one's "mother tongue." Scribes, advocates, and other middlemen wrote petitions in *katharevousa* Greek and Ottoman Turkish—languages which were most certainly not those spoken by Cypriot villagers, who for the most part spoke *Kipriaka*—a form of Greek that despite linguistic homogenization is incomprehensible even today to many Greek-speakers in Greece. Thus there came simultaneously to be an increasing dependence of villagers on the "high," written languages for the daily transactions of economic and political life, and a relegation of the "dialect" to the informal transactions that were increasingly undermined by British bureaucracy. In other words, as written transactions became increasingly important, the "serious" business of political life could be conducted only in the high languages of the educated elites, while the dialect forms that could be understood by all Cypriots were relegated to the petty politics of the cafe.

This linguistic separation was also reflected for a short time in the new print media, which for a few years used the dialect to construct an image of the "traditional" villager. Significantly, the publisher Konstantinidhis can be credited not only with opening the island's first newspaper but also with inspiring a new genre of Greek Cypriot publication, the satirical periodical, which flourished at the end of the last century. Large sections of these satirical publications were often written in verse and were strongly influenced by the Cypriot dialect; at least one, *Choriatis* (The Native), was written entirely in dialect.[38] When Konstantinidhis undertook his own satirical writings in 1882 in *Keravnos* (Thunder), it appears that he was consciously imitating the strong and competitive oral poetry tradition that in his time had not yet been monumentalized through study and collection.[39]

Within the decade, his enterprise would inspire ten new satirical jour-
nals—the first two in Larnaca, followed by a proliferation throughout
the island. For instance, from the pen of Vasilis Michaelidhis, one of
Cyprus' great *poiitaridhes,* or oral poets, came *Dhiavolos* (The Devil),
written entirely in fifteen-syllable distychs.[40] Except for the latter enterprise, all the other satirical sheets appeared alongside—and often
inserted within—the "serious" reports written in the high language.
While the "serious" newspapers were supposed to be the voice of
authority, the satirical sheets were supposed to be the voice of the
coffeeshop—a conceit carried farthest by *Choriatis,* whose author was
described in the paper as a straight-speaking villager who had left his
sheep in order to take up the pen.

It is important to note that this efflorescence of rhyming, dialectal sat-
ire did not last beyond the turn of the century. Satirical publications were
a phenomenon of the first twenty years of British rule and quickly vanished during the intracommunal conflicts that racked both communities
at the turn of the century, out of which more strongly and explicitly
nationalistic leaderships emerged.[41] Notably, the satirical publications
appear to have been the only ones intended to be read by the entire Cypriot community, both Christian and Muslim. The only two Turkish-
language satires, *Kokonoz* and *Akbaba,* were short-lived, but the simple,
familiar dialect of the Greek-language satires would have been accessible to Muslim Cypriot readers.[42]

In fact, Muslim readers appear to have been the intended audience of
certain articles and poems, such as the following attack on the constitution of the legislative council, the ratio of which was intended to provide
a balance of Muslim and British to Orthodox members:

> While they know well
> How the ratio falls out
> Thirty Christians
> To five Muslims[43]
>
> And you think maybe they
> Love the Osmanlis,[44]
>
> Maybe the English have
> Ever loved the turban-wearers?
>
> They entrap them with enticements,
> Those efendis and kadis,
> To attack us with deeper
> And more constricting taxes.

People of Cyprus, Christian
Together with Muslim,
You have a common interest,
Work together.
Enough of English
Politics and flattery,
For our common good
We must unite.[45]

There was still, in this period, an obvious ambiguity regarding the boundaries of the community, and even in the next decade, despite the growing politicization of communal life, many of the intellectual class such as Konstantinidhis appeared blithely unaware of the nature of their role in the changes that were taking place.

Benedict Anderson observes that one of the radical breaks created by early print culture—and particularly newspapers—is the emergence of a history of the present in which readers place themselves and imagine themselves as participants.[46] The Cypriot villager for whom the satirical sheets were purportedly the voice was portrayed as jokingly subverting the authorities, at the same time that he confirmed the political agenda of the publisher—who published the "serious," authoritative newspapers in another voice. Notably, this peculiar ventriloquism flourished at the moment of the radical historical break described by Anderson, when a "public opinion" was forming that was defined by its own representation.[47] This self-consciousness of creating a present—peculiar, it seems, to the era known as modern[48]—occurs at the interstices of ideology and hegemony, or of culture thought and culture lived.

Konstantinidhis and others were constructing a "traditional," straight-talking villager who might be both sheep-thief and minstrel. This was their own construction of their public, culled from the "traditions" of village life and the "traditional" political discussions of the village cafe. But these villagers were, at the same time, portrayed as ignorant, and, as we will soon see, they were often harangued for their gullibility in allegedly signing any piece of paper put before them. In such a way, the new print media, rather than widening the scope of political participation, actually served to bolster conservative forms of traditional authority.

Signing for the "simple ones"

In the early spring of 1889, the British administration's chief medical officer sent his assistants into the towns and villages of the districts for the annual register of births and deaths. As in previous years, they went armed with blank forms and filled in these forms with information supplied by the priests and *muhtars*. The assistants' instructions were to collect "the names of the persons as born or dead, the dates on which these events happened, and to note them down on the proper printed form supplied for the purpose."[49] Their task was accomplished by May, and Dr. Heidenstam, the chief medical officer, reported that he heard nothing more of the registration until one of his assistants arrived at the doctor's house one morning in the middle of August. This assistant informed the doctor that he had just been attacked and insulted in the bazaar, and that his attackers had accused him of having collected seals and signatures on behalf of the government and for some nefarious purpose.

In his report, Dr. Heidenstam notes that the assistant's report struck him at first as humorous:

> I confess that at the moment this statement appeared to me so ludicrous that I was inclined to laughter, but seeing the man was serious and that he appeared to be in trouble, I advised him to summon the persons or some of them for having insulted him without any just cause …. A day or two later, however, as I personally witnessed that there was a regular, planned persecution, in the town, not only against this man, but also against the others employed on the same work, and it having been reported to me that it was given out, and generally believed, that I, under the pretext of collecting the returns of births and deaths, had sent out people to collect the seals and signatures of the villagers on blank paper, which was ultimately filled in by the Government and transmitted to the Sec. of State.[50]

The registration of births and deaths had taken place at the very moment that the archbishop and a small deputation were in London for an interview with colonial officials there, in hopes of providing some amelioration of the poverty-stricken state of Cyprus' inhabitants. It was speculated that the seals and signatures would be used in some application against the deputation.

Heidenstam notes that "the matter so filled in, it was asserted, set forth that the people of Cyprus did not recognize the deputation then in England as their representatives, and further that they were not in any way displeased with the taxes." Heidenstam made some investigations into the matter and concluded that the statements were no more than baseless rumor:

> Although perfectly convinced that those assertions were groundless, as no seals or signatures, on other than the printed forms, had reached my office, and the persons employed on the registration of births and deaths assured me

that they had never asked for, or obtained such seals and signatures, and lastly, and not less convincing, the fact that the time when these persons were employed and the registration completed did not correspond with the time, it was stated, that the alleged seals and signatures were obtained. I did my best to ascertain on what grounds the rumours were based and how they had been spread, but unfortunately could not obtain any reliable information. The answers to my questions on the subject were invariably so and so heard it from a peasant and so and so told me of it, but as to the peasant it was not only impossible to trace his name, but even that of the village whence he came was unknown.[51]

Indeed, the rumors spread quickly and, as the story grew over the course of August, it acquired new twists. For example, one version of the rumor insisted that the government officers had misinformed villagers, telling them that one member of the archbishop's deputation had dressed in "Turkish fashion" and was calling himself Mustafa in order to "give the deputation a pan-Cypriote character."[52]

These rumors were not only spread by word of mouth, however. By the middle of August the local papers carried the story, and by the end of the month the Cypriot paper *Alithia* reprinted an article about this alleged trickery that had appeared in the *Metarithmisis* of Alexandria:

> The Cypriots, being most Hellenic in their ideas, could not of course bear that the English, who have occupied their Island as saviours and profess to render its administration a model for the rest of the provinces of the Ottoman Empire, should govern them as a conquered country inhabited by Asiatics or Africans. Therefore, when they were convinced that the Government of their Island does not the least contribute to their material and moral advancement, did not content themselves with a mere manifestation of their complaint in the Legislative Council, with which their Island has been endowed by their new masters and which has a consultative voice only, but went further and took a step, a very important one and the prelude of another more important, that is, they sent to England a deputation consisting of six representatives of the whole island and presided over by the Archbishop of the Autocephalous Church of their Island in order to submit to the Sovereign of their country their complaints and proposed those measures which would tend to ameliorate their condition. This step made a grave impression in Europe and especially in England, but the Government officials in Cyprus endeavoured to weaken this impression by drawing up reports in which the inhabitants of Cyprus are alleged to manifest their satisfaction with the present government of their Island and state that they demand nothing. These reports the Government officials oblige the simpler ones of the agriculturalists to sign.[53]

So, Hellenic pride had led to a deputation, but the government would attempt to use the "simpler ones" for its own purposes.

Indeed, those "simple ones" among the agriculturalists would receive nearly as much criticism as the government that had supposedly deceived them. The newspaper *Salpinks*, in fact, seemed to view them as an interior enemy:

> With that imbecility of our villagers who to everybody who asks for the seal of the village they say at once, "Here it is, efendi!", "Here it is, aga!", any Government could sell us even to the Dervishes of Upper Egypt and, then, say that it is we, the inhabitants, who asked for that.[54]

In more moderate tones, the newspaper *Alithia* urged villagers to be cautious:

> We strongly advise the villagers to be careful not to allow that the seal or signature of the Mukhtar or Azas be affixed on any written or blank paper, presented to them with the content of which they are not acquainted. This advice we give them for their own interest and in order that they may not be rendered victims of their credulity and ignorance, thereby injuring both themselves and their country.[55]

Their very illiteracy meant that their capacity to participate fully in the new forms of politics had to be called into doubt, since that illiteracy implied credulity.

The question of signatures was obviously an important one for British administrators as well, but they also worried about the way in which illiterate villagers appeared to be abused by scribes for whom petition-writing was a profession. By 1891 the commissioner of Nicosia—who received hundreds of petitions each year—observed that these scribes had created a flourishing business as general intermediaries with the government, and that therefore they needed to be controlled:

> It is very necessary that some steps should be taken, if possible, by which these persons should be placed under some measure of control. At present they constitute a class that extort from the public—and particularly the ignorant village public—exorbitant fees for the most trifling services. They do not limit their operation to petition writing, but act as general agents, and were they as a class honest and conscientious, their services would undoubtedly be of advantage both to public, and to the govt. depts. with which they have to deal. But the sole aim of many of these gentlemen appears to be to complicate the matters with which they are entrusted. They make the most exaggerated statements in the petitions they write—in many cases I have found them to be the opposite of what their clients have instructed them to say—and create difficulties at every opportunity, in fact do everything they can to make business from which a fee can be extracted.[56]

The perception of writing as a necessary part of representation before the state made these men all the more powerful. Not only was literacy important for expression of one's opinion, but in the modern bureau-cratic state it is important for the solution of one's problems.

Another incident from only a few years later provides yet another per-spective on this problem of signatures. In a 1900 campaign aimed at culling support for the kadi then in office, representatives of Hacı Hafız Ziyai Efendi circulated through the villages requesting signatures of vil-lagers and seals of their *muhtars* on papers protesting administrative issues. One villager appealed to the government "to take steps to stop what he had reported as it was having a very bad effect, that anything sent out by Haji Hafiz would have great effect in the villages as all the Hodjas [teachers] were his pupils, the Turkish Inspector of Schools was his brother, and the Turkish Judge of Famagusta was his brother in law."[57] While under other circumstances it might have been tempting to interpret this campaign—led by the popular Hacı Hafız Ziyai Efendi—as an incipient democratic movement attempting to undermine the entrenched privileges of the elites, the villager's complaint suggests that voting does not ensure equality.

Indeed, as the villager's plea reveals, one should certainly not confuse the creation of a public sphere with egalitarian ideology; these are sepa-rate, though linked, processes. Indeed, in Cyprus the public sphere was controlled primarily through education, and that education in turn was in the hands of the clergy. The collection of signatures, for example, had become the most significant manner in which to assess and control pub-lic opinion. But in order to be "representative," those signatures had, paradoxically, to be unique. Only a man who could sign his name could be guaranteed full representation; having another sign it was to put that representation into doubt. So, while one's relationships might determine one's political allegiances, it was only as the anonymous member of a linguistic community that one was able to participate in political decision-making.

These incidents provide fascinating commentaries on the problems of representation then facing Cypriots, and they raise questions regarding representation in an age in which literacy appears to be a requirement for that representation. Firstly, literacy, and particularly the ability to sign one's own name, has embedded within it the demand for individual-ism in modern politics—the demand that one present a unique signature at the same time that one becomes "only a name." For very many years, the practice of signing for others continued in Cyprus, and it was only as the category of the "ignorant villager" was created that this practice was discontinued. Significantly, this meant that one's character, one's family, one's fortune, and one's relationships—those extremely political descriptors of identity—are curiously extracted from the realm of the political, or at least from the realm of the individual's participation in politics. Instead, one's uniqueness is represented in script, which is at least in theory available equally to all. But by becoming "only a name," by representing oneself through a unique signature, one also validates a political realm in which all are equal within a community strictly defined by the limits of "high" cultures and languages.

Secondly, the role of newspapers and other publications in this period was still being defined, and rumors remained—and would remain for some decades to come—an important source of information. In many cases, print and other technologies such as the telegraph would be used simply to relay and disseminate rumor faster and wider. There was not, then, a perceived separation between "objective" news and "subjective" word-of-mouth reports. True, in a period in which writing was just beginning to create a "public," the act of publication itself had tremendous influence. Yet in the incident cited above, the primary moving force was rumor, the source of which no one could ascertain. The fiery articles that appeared in the Greek press assured readers that the rumors were true, and villagers began to refuse to participate in any government business that required signatures, including police work. The affair simmered down only when the archbishop returned from London and issued a public announcement to the effect that such baseless rumors only harmed the Church and the nation.

Clearly, newspaper reports and other island publications were intended to create a moral community. In the affair cited above, what is particularly striking is the seemingly irresponsible manner in which newspapers generated rumors. Newspaper accounts were not intended to be objective, and publishers did not see their mission as one of an objective mirroring of events. In the wake of the archbishop's statement, *Alithia* published a retraction, commenting,

> As our programme as publishers is to seek the general interest of the Country, praising as we do the good and reproving the bad acts, we do not hesitate, when injustice is done through bad and erroneous information, to rectify errors and give satisfaction to the injured persons for the sake of their own respectability, ours, and that of our paper.[58]

In this statement of the newspaper's function, no distinction is drawn between "news" and "commentary." Indeed, the newspaper exists not to report objectively but to praise the good and reprove the bad. Similarly, the "publicity" of the early Enlightenment was seen—as Habermas notes—to have a regulatory function that would guarantee the operation of reason in the service of morality. Kant found it to be "the one principle that could guarantee the convergence of politics and morality"[59]—a principle that would have been familiar to those versed in the public discourse of the Islamic world.[60]

Furthermore, it was of the utmost significance that Cypriot print culture was, until nearly the mid-twentieth century, mediated in the villages by schoolmasters and other literates who often had their own political commitments. The British arrival had made possible a particular conjuncture of events: a new program of grants-in-aid to village schools had resulted in an explosion of school openings, while the growth of a popular press had made the role of schoolmasters one of interpreters as well as intermediaries. The schoolmaster reading the weekly news on the porch of the village cafe would have been a familiar sight in Britain at this time, as well as in Cyprus. The difference, however, was that a schoolmaster of Cyprus could not *read* newspapers to his fellow villagers, for most of whom the archaic *katharevousa* Greek or Ottoman Turkish would have been virtually incomprehensible. Instead, according to many accounts of the period, schoolmasters very often *related* events and were thereby given an interpretive authority that also made them subject to criticism and implicated them in the politics of village life.

It is difficult in an age flooded with print to recognize the impact of print technologies without degenerating into discussions of preliterate versus literate, or popular versus learned. Both communities of Cyprus were "literate" in the sense defined by Jack Goody and others. However, writing itself had a more permanent meaning, as part of the ontologies of the Greek Orthodox and Islamic worlds. As a consequence, "news" coming in the form of a high language of the educated did not have meaning as simple information, but only with reference to a higher moral order. Similarly, signatures were not given as an expression of individual opinion but as a validation of authority. Hence, confession shifted from its place as one node of identification for a villager, to having a central part in the construction of the Villager as both public and self-referential witness, one who was always defined as Muslim or Orthodox, Turkish-speaker or Greek-speaker, and for whom the news that purported to be about him also constructed that self in national terms.

In the worlds of early modern monarchical empires, public opinion was seen as *regulatory*, referring to a higher moral order; in contemporary democracies founded on equality, public opinion is *constitutive* of the good. The former is inherently hierarchical, the latter inherently anonymous. What I have attempted to demonstrate here is that Cypriots partook of both of these forms in a somewhat paradoxical way that would only be reconciled through nationalism. On the one hand, the notion of a "public" was founded on new demands for anonymity through literacy. On the other hand, public opinion was also a form of clarification of the truth. But while Kant had seen Enlightenment as the public use of reason leading to greater moral clarity, in Cyprus the increasing clarification of the bounds of morality and the moral community were inherently circumscribed by the linguistic community and the high culture that paradigmatically represented it.

It is in such contexts that Anderson's thesis of "imagined communities" is both most useful and most limited. On the one hand, it is useful as a formula that encapsulates the epistemic shift necessitated by the transition from villager to citizen. On the other hand, it is limited in finding the initial force of such a transition in the print-capitalism of the bourgeois classes. In other words, Anderson relies heavily in his thesis upon print media without questioning the processes by which literacy is evaluated, assimilated, and constructed. And in doing so, he ignores the troubling processes by which the literate citizen emerges.

Conclusion

Almost from the moment of the British arrival in Cyprus, the colonizers' strangeness and harsh justice were excoriated in the local press, their taxes were protested in mass rallies, and their administrators and administration were the subject of coffeehouse gossip. In one of the satirical poems of the period, the bard asks poignantly, "Is there anything that the Englishman loves except his beer?"[61] In fact, British colonial rule in Cyprus suffered from a lack of penetration of British ideas and modes of consciousness, except insofar as those ideas were part of a larger realm of discourse in which many Cypriots already participated before the British arrival. The average Cypriot knew what "equal rights" meant, and he was able immediately to put it to use by refusing to pay burdensome church tithes. That he learned also about "equal wrongs" would ultimately become a source for mobilizing his discontent.

Moreover, the men in pressed suits playing backgammon on the Larnaca wharf were not disempowered, nor did they write of themselves as disempowered. The resistance that they would show to the colonial regime was from a position of considerable power, so that they were able to prohibit proselytizing missions in the island, to retain the administration of their educational systems, and to insist upon retaining substantial control of the affairs of their communities. They experienced crises during this period amongst themselves, but these were crises that would ultimately teach them a new political ballgame. In particular, they would teach them to find newer, more modern ways to describe the political futures of their communities, and how they as leaders would or should realize those futures.

It was within the new, entirely unfamiliar, British imperial framework that forms of authority in Cyprus would be called into question and redefined, and that access to knowledge would no longer be the exclusive domain of a primarily theological elite. The new requirements of citizenship presupposed an ability to represent oneself both uniquely and categorically, not through a transitory oral declaration but through a form of writing in which one would become uniquely represented at the same time that one would become "only a name." And clearly, this required a new sort of community in which one's membership would no longer be determined by practices and relations but by an identity of equal selves. In other words, in order for these subjects to become citizens, they would have to learn to think of themselves differently—not as a Malliote or a Paphiote but as a Villager, not as a man or woman defined by friendships and family ties but as Everyman. They would have to learn to think of themselves as both subjects and creators of a new kind of knowledge about themselves and power over themselves, and thereby to participate in what Anthony Giddens calls "the reflexivity of modern social life."[62] And from this new nexus of truth and power, new and more parochial citizens would emerge.

CHAPTER 2

Bandits and "Bad Characters"

In the handbook for Cypriot police officers published in 1896 by the new colonial administration, there is a passage that appears at first innocuous, but which had important resonances for the development of legal and political statuses in Cyprus of the period. Under the section "Police Duties" and the subheading, "Constables," the handbook notes that "[c]onstables are expected to possess such knowledge of the inhabitants of their District as to enable them readily to recognize them. They are to be instructed to watch unceasingly all persons having no visible means of support, and obtain knowledge of all suspected thieves, idle and disorderly persons, and disorderly houses." This responsibility was reemphasized under the subheading, "Knowledge of Characters," where officers were told that:

> The knowledge of the individual characters of the inhabitants of each District is necessary to the constitution of an efficient Police; it therefore becomes an important duty of the Police quartered in the Town and villages to make themselves as far as possible acquainted with the persons and haunts of all suspected persons therein, in order to their being able to bring them forward without delay in the event of their being charged with the commission of any crime or misdemeanour, or by close observation of their movements deter them from committing depredations or other offences against persons or property.[1]

Moreover, "the names and addresses of all discharged prisoners and suspected persons," the guide says, should be written in the "District Book," which was the responsibility of the Local Commandant.

This list, commonly known as the "bad characters' list" or "blacklist," was an internal mechanism of the police force, and yet clearly those persons whose names appeared on it believed that their reputations had been soiled. The records of the time are full of complaints against this regulation. In one case, a police chief reported that an imam placed on this list "complained pathetically to me in one of my visits to the village of the disgrace of his name being in the police list of bad characters."[2] It is worth noting that according to the report the imam was never actually placed on the list, but he apparently did insist on carrying a gun. What is interesting is the imam's belief that his name had been placed on the list, indicating the extent to which even association with the list brought shame. This can be seen, as well, in the complaint of a number of villagers to the bishop of Kition that as a result of being on this list "they lost their reputation and that even zaptiehs [police] do not consent to associate with them."[3] It was also a device that seemed to require resistance, as when a petitioner in 1909 requested that his name be removed and submitted the statements of his fellow villagers and the *muhtar* to the effect that his character had improved.[4]

This chapter examines the relationship between rules and roles as those rules and roles were being altered in Cyprus around the start of the twentieth century. The implementation in Cyprus of a European governmental rationality and categorization could not be contained within the forms of that rationality itself but instead overflowed those bounds and leaked into seemingly unrelated areas of social life. As a consequence, I ask here what the encounter of Cypriots with that legal-bureaucratic rationality at the turn of the last century may tell us about the sorts of political identities that developed in Cyprus then and after. The focus here is the loose category of the "bad character," a classification used in order to blacklist and shame persons seen as potential or actual troublemakers. The "bad characters" of British reports are very similar to the "rowdy-sheeters" of India: persons who are "known" by the police and the bureaucracy, persons who are observed as troublemakers and often detained in advance of potential disturbances.[5] As in the Indian context, the "bad characters" of Cyprus clearly represent the "other" of the honest, law-abiding citizen-subject.

But while Dhareshwar and Srivatsan describe the rowdy-sheeters of India as the criminals associated with the primarily urban lumpenproletariat, "bad characters" in Cyprus were described as both sheep-thieves and town ruffians, as both illiterate peasants who insisted on carrying guns and hooligans who followed political leaders out to stir up trouble. In colonial records, then, "bad characters" appear both as men with a tendency to criminal activity and as men without agency who were manipulated by local elites to stir up political unrest. That same political unrest, however, was the sort of political unrest that would ultimately find expression in EOKA rebellions of the 1950s. In fact, the category of the "bad character" appears to have been loose enough to encompass all those persons who appeared to threaten the social order, from sheep-thieves to bandits to town youths roused by elite agitators.

In this context, what sheep-thieves and town ruffians have in common is their complete otherness to governmentality, as chaos is to order. Clearly, the category of the "bad character" spilled over the bounds of legal-bureaucratic rationalization, taking on all the changing qualities of the anti-citizen. "Bad characters" were known both for their excess and for their lack: an excess defined by the ways in which they overflow bounds,[6] and a lack defined by their failures to meet basic criteria of the citizen-subject, such as property and literacy. The solution to this problem was not found, however, in the mechanisms of individual discipline described so well by Foucault.[7] Rather, it was found in a corporate discipline that I wish to suggest may have had implications for later politics in the island.

Foucault has argued that European methods of punishment, correction, and discipline derived from a view of human nature reduced to the mechanisms of the body, which could be coercively trained through what he calls a "micro-physics" of power.[8] In colonial legal practice, however, that "nature" was also "culture," in contrast to the presumably non-cultural individualism enjoyed by British subjects themselves.[9] Uday Mehta has argued that liberalism gives "a specifically political significance to human *nature*." It does so, he believes, because "[b]eing born equal, free, and rational, birth—notwithstanding its various uncertain potentialities—becomes the moment of an assured political identity."[10] In colonial practice, only from the presumably non-cultural vantage point of European colonizers was full individualism possible; others were not yet advanced enough to break away from the shackles of their cultural nature.

In British colonial terms, liberal legal practices should lead to the development of democratic institutions that would, in turn, both indicate and promote a people's political maturity. In other words, it was an ideological underpinning of British colonial rule that legal-bureaucratic rationalization—applied to all persons equally—should lead to civilizational and political maturation. This was usually glossed as "teaching people how to be free." The fact that it never seemed to happen in the way that it was supposed to was not counter-evidence to the developmentalist approach, but rather an indication of the strong hold of religion, family, or other elements of "culture" on the manner and extent to which a people was capable of developing. For instance, even as late as 1946, the British chief justice of the island concluded in a report to the governor that the corporatism of Cypriot life meant that jury trials were not suitable for the island, since Cypriots would always show more loyalty to their immediate groups than to abstract ideals of justice.[11] This echoes, of course, John Stuart Mill's observation that certain groups have not yet reached the "civilizational maturity" that would allow them to govern themselves, and that the proper rule for many groups is despotism, as long as its aim is their improvement.[12] Hence, in contrast to the individualistic micro-physics of power that Foucault describes, both the enactment of legislation and the forms of surveillance and punishment in Cyprus were written around the assumption of Cypriots' corporate nature.

This chapter argues, first, that in the early part of the colonial period in Cyprus, the presumed corporatism of Cypriot life was written into law as a popular anthropology of Cypriots' nature. Immediately after the British arrival in the island in 1878, crime appeared to explode despite the rapid penetration of more efficient administrative structures, policing, and judiciary. In the Cypriot popular imagination, this increase in crime was directly linked to a breakdown of the social order and its traditional hierarchies. The attempt by British administrators and Cypriot legislators to combat this crime wave resulted in new legislation aimed at understanding the "real" or "natural" causes of crime in the island. As we will see, the primary result of these new laws was to categorize certain "traditional" practices as "backward," "uncivilized," and in need of correction and punishment. These practices were those of the "backward" villager, the "natural" Mediterranean hot-blood, whose practices needed to be corrected by his superiors.

Secondly, I will claim that it is in the figure of the "bad character" that we find traced most clearly the outlines of the emerging citizen-subject, who is to be the bad character's good twin. In much legislation, crime was not only the crime of villagers, but the crime of villages. Putting people back in their "proper" social places ultimately meant controlling those forces of communal chaos embodied in the "bad character." But it was precisely the new category of citizen-subject, the category defined in Cyprus as both naturally corporate and legally equal, that was in theory responsible for controlling the forces of chaos and bringing about order. I suggest, then, that in contrast to the universalist, Enlightenment figure of "man-as-Machine," the legal image of Cypriots as naturally possessed of corporate characteristics ultimately led to a disciplining of the citizen not as universal individual but as member of his or her ethnic group.

The meanings of equality

Within a few years of the British arrival in the island, colonial adminis-trators were faced with what appeared to be an explosion of crime, and they began to discuss ways to root out what they considered to be the "worst class" of such crimes, namely sheep-stealing and murder. In sta-tistical terms, between the years 1885–86 and 1886–87, the number of cases committed to trial increased by 78 per cent, and by another 46 per cent in the following year. Between 1888 and 1893, arrests rose from 5,724 to 8,543.[13] By 1889, the chief justice commented in his report of crime statistics that "the state of things thus disclosed is little short of appalling, and is deserving the most serious attention. That serious crime should prevail to the extent indicated by these returns in an island with a purely agricultural population, is a very remarkable circumstance, and seems to point out to a widespread demoralisation amongst the people."[14]

This statistical rise is clear, though it is more difficult to say what it indicates, since much of the rise could be attributed to changes in the laws, increased effectiveness of certain branches of the police, and the reclassification of certain practices as criminal offences. For instance, the theft of a sheep or a knife drawn during a cafe brawl were the sorts of "crimes" that were often not reported before the advent of "British justice,"[15] and a consistent complaint of officials was the difficulty in getting people to bring crime to the police rather than settle amongst themselves. At the same time, these sorts of crimes constituted almost all of those brought to trial under the heading "robbery with violence."[16] Sheep-stealing, however, was a common practice among shepherds intent upon proving their wits and manhood, and it obviously resembled in many respects the practice as described by Herzfeld for neighboring Crete.[17]

But there was also clearly a perception amongst Cypriots that a sig-nificant change had taken place. This perception may be attributable both to the clear statistical rise and to the publication of crimes in the local newspapers that began operation in the same year as the British arrival.[18] In 1894, one newspaper, *Foni tis Kiprou*, printed an article titled, "The Moral Situation of the Island," in which it complained,

The newspapers record murders, thefts, rapes, dishonorable acts [atimoseis], vandalism, sacrilege, and all possible sorts of crimes, which were born in the decades of the British occupation. In the pages of these records one sees: on the 1st of January A. is finished with a sword, and on that same day B. is finished with a knife; on the 2nd C. shoots at someone, and on the same day D. strangles someone ....[19]

The newspaper, however, does not associate the perception of a crime wave with its publication. Rather, like many villagers of the time, it associates the island's "moral situation" with the advent of British rule.

Indeed, local officials commented that villagers were in a state of panic, and in 1891 the high commissioner, Henry Bulwer, decided to take a tour of the Limassol and Paphos areas, which were most affected by the crime wave. In every village residents complained of crime— mostly sheep-stealing and murder or assault—and made recommendations about how to put a stop to it. One villager's remarks are typical:

He [the villager] thought the fault was partly due to the education. The schools that have been established teach very little, and their effect has been to weaken the influence of the clergy and of the elder people of the village. Those who go to these schools and learn a little think they are wiser than the priest, and they look down upon their elders. If a priest were to venture now to say anything in church about the thieves he would suffer, and if any elders of the village were to say anything against them they also would suffer .... The people of the district are some of them industrious and some of them idle. Those who are idle make up for their idleness by crime. The old Turkish system was best suited to put a check to crime in the district.[20]

This statement appears at first contradictory, since the villager remarks that education was responsible for this state of affairs, even though the common perception of "bad characters" was that they were ignorant and illiterate.

This appears less contradictory, however, when we notice that the real complaint was of the loss of traditional authority, interpreted by this villager as a result of education. Moreover, this villager echoed the observation of many villagers that only the Ottoman system really could control crime, because only it produced fear and a proper subjection to authority. During this same tour, at the village of Omodhos an address was presented stating that "a sudden transition to a comparatively liberal constitution had let loose the minds of people having a tendency to wickedness, and that taking advantage of the liberty enjoyed by them they engaged openly in crime."[21] Indeed, many villagers appeared to think that prisons were too comfortable, that the formalities of British law were too stringent, and that not enough responsibility was placed on villagers themselves, who always knew the criminals.

Villagers themselves, in other words, attributed the rise in crime to British justice, which appeared to give an excessive liberty and which also appeared to demolish social hierarchies. As I noted in the previous chapter, equality under the law appeared to erase distinctions on all levels, leading to a breakdown, or perceived breakdown, of social order. In 1891, High Commissioner Bulwer described the breakdown of authority in the villages and the disorder that appeared to prevail in areas with no police to patrol them. Bulwer added, "The influence of the elders of a village and of others whose position ought to carry weight, is no longer sufficiently regarded by those disposed to disorder and lawless conduct."[22] Indeed, the sudden divorce of religious and political authority was causing a crisis of representation that manifested itself as an apparent crisis of morality. For instance, *Foni tis Kiprou* reported in 1895 that it had received letters from several villages describing vandalism and a breakdown of order: "During the evening the doors of priests and honest heads of families were sprayed with human excreta, and large stones were hurled against the houses of decent people."[23] The control previously exercised by priests and elders was not only called into question but also challenged.

And clearly, many villagers thought that an assertion of authority was what was needed to bring things back under control. An 1897 petition of residents of Omodhos, for example, reveals many of the prevalent village concerns, since their request appears to be based on a rumor that circulated throughout the district. The police chief, Mr. Greenwood, reported,

> From what I hear the Omodos villagers wish that their village be transferred to the Paphos District because they are under the impression that Mr. Mavrogordato has authority from Govt. to use the whip; several villagers of Omodos, Arsos, Tokhnou, Ayios Therapou, Pano Kividhes, Kandar, and Episkopi seem to be under the same impression as on different occasions asked me why I do not get permission from the Govt. to use the whip like Mr. Mavrogordato, they all agree that the use of the whip is the only means of stopping crime, and that Mr. Mavrogordato has been able to put a stop to crime by making use of it.[24]

It should be noted that the whip—used on horses and dogs and in Greek legend by Ottoman officials on their Christian subjects—was not only an instrument of violence but also an instrument of humiliation.[25] Crime could be controlled, these villagers thought, by putting people back in their appropriate social places.

Clearly, ordinary people of the period perceived a direct link between the breakdown of traditional hierarchies and the breakdown of social order. Moreover, they encouraged British administrators to use systems that had been in place under Ottoman rule, such as making entire villages responsible for crimes committed in them, or simply taking the word of villagers that someone was a "bad character." Bulwer commented,

> The old Turkish system of punishment, many people declare, was far more effective than the present in dealing with offenders. The old administration often left things alone for a long while, but when it moved it came down with a heavy hand on the offenders. It did not stop for many formalities or for great preciseness in the evidence. It was enough that a man was known as an evildoer to the people generally, and that there was reasonable cause to believe him guilty of certain offences.[26]

In an interesting variation on this, the bishop of Kition reported that "the people wish restrictions to be put on persons of bad character, on persons whom the Mukhtar and Ayas of a village may say are of bad character. Such persons might be restricted by being confined to certain localities."[27] The latter suggestion clearly offered a very interesting compromise between the British desire for legal codification and the local understanding of the most effective means of social control.

The Ottoman criminal legal system in force when British administrators arrived in the island was one that those administrators complained was too centralized and which they entirely altered within the first five years of the British administration. In the system in place when the British arrived, each of the five *kaymakamlık*s, or districts, of the island had its own district court, while a central, "supreme" court in Nicosia tried more important criminal cases and sometimes admitted appeals. The court of a *kaymakamlık* (known as the *meclis-i daavi*), consisted of two Muslim and two Christian members, all of whom were elected by the people, with the kadi or the *kaymakam* presiding. The central court of Nicosia (*meclis-i temyiz* or *meclis-i tahkik*) was similarly structured, but with three Muslim and three Christian members. The kadi presiding over the Nicosia court was also considered to be the supreme authority on legal matters in the island. District courts tried both civil and criminal cases, while important criminal cases were sent to the capital.[28] The shari'a court (*mahkeme-i şeriye*) dealt with civil cases of marriage, divorce, inheritance, or any other such cases that might fall under Islamic law.[29]

British administrators complained that the system was too centralized; that elected judges were prone to graft; and that aside from the
kadis, other judges had no legal training. Administrators claimed, as
well, that the kadis were trained in shari'a law rather than in the full
workings of the Ottoman legislative system that was put in place in the
decades of reform in the middle of the nineteenth century and based on
the Code Napoléon.[30] As a result, within a few months of the British
arrival a Court of Justice for the queen in Cyprus was established, con-
sisting of the high commissioner, a judicial commissioner, and deputy
commissioners. And as noted in the previous chapter, the Legislative
Council was established immediately in 1878, with the task of dealing
with legal issues that related specifically to Cyprus.

Within two more years, a complete overhaul of the system resulted in
a unified organization of courts that administered a dual system of law:
British subjects were subject to the laws of England as modified by local
legislation, while Ottoman subjects were subject to Ottoman law. All
cases were tried in the same courts, however, which continued to be
divided into six districts, now with sixteen subdistricts. A supreme court
was established that had jurisdiction over all cases and consisted of two
English judges. In the district courts, one English judge presided and
judged non-Ottoman cases, while in cases under Ottoman law two Cypriot members—one Muslim and one Christian—who had been
appointed by the government assisted. Small civil cases and some criminal were tried in the subdistricts by village judges, who were either
Muslim or Christian and were, again, appointed by the government. In
many cases, Muslim judges were replaced with British judges, with the
previous judges acting as interpreters, while the British judges issued
verdicts.[31] And at the level of enforcement the changes were equally significant. While a large proportion of the Ottoman *zaptiye*—or police
force—was retained, significant numbers of British troops were also
employed in law enforcement. This extended force, and the new rules
that governed it, meant that more suspects were taken into custody, and
more cases came to trial.

For British administrators, this new system was intended to correct
what they believed to be the corruption and rapacity of the old regime.
Under that regime, elected judges were ill-paid or not paid at all, and so
according to British officials most cases were decided by bribery, which
they believed to be endemic to the Ottoman system. In 1880, for
instance, High Commissioner Biddulph wrote to the Colonial Office that
the kadi of Paphos District had been tried on the charge of accepting

bribes from suitors in the local court. He was sentenced to prison, a sentence that Biddulph ordered be carried out in the fortress of Famagusta. "Although the punishment is not severe according to our notions," Biddulph commented, "yet it will create some sensation amongst the people; for although the Cadis, like other officials, are almost universally corrupt, I believe the trial and conviction of a Cadi for accepting bribes is an absolutely unprecedented occurrence."[32]

British officers believed, in other words, that teaching "the Turk" how to rule meant the implementation of fair and impartial justice guaranteed by an efficient police force. Cypriots, however, perceived this same system as the cause, in large part, of the apparent wave of crime that swept the island in those decades. The comfort of life in the British-administered prisons, as well as the formalities of British law, meant that few "bad characters" were deterred from evil deeds and that many, in fact, were encouraged by the new system to criminality. The assumption, in both British and Cypriot assessments of the situation, is that those "bad characters" always existed in the island, but that the new system had "let loose the minds of people having a tendency to wickedness." It was the very equality of the new system that had supposedly accomplished this, and it was with this new equality that both Cypriot legislators and average villagers would have to contend.

Putting people in their places

Two of the changes in the legal system against which villagers consistently complained and which they persistently resisted were structural ones that were unavoidable under this new form of justice. The first was the elimination of what we might call "character witnesses" and the institution of evidence-based justice. It was reported in many instances that under the Ottoman system it was enough that someone was known as a "bad character" to those of good reputation in the village or district. More consonant with practices elsewhere, however, was the general agreement that the testimony of two credible witnesses had been enough to convict. Messick has noted that in Yemen the definition of a credible witness was someone of irreproachable character, a definition which he says is concerned "not so much with absolutes as with deviations from local societal or even personal norms, which are taken as indicative of an instability of character thought to bear on one's capacity as a truthful witness."[33] For instance, someone of high social standing engaged in a lowly occupation would be suspect. The request that restrictions be put on persons whom "the Mukhtars and Ayas of a village say are of bad character" is clearly a local use of the validity of the testimony of credible witnesses.

Under the British administration, however, judgment was based on collected evidence and on sworn statements by eyewitnesses; all else was considered to be hearsay. Because of the nature of many crimes (such as sheep-stealing, which often took place at night and in remote locales), gathering evidence or eyewitnesses was difficult, so that villagers were discouraged from reporting crimes. Many saw that those accused often went free and returned to take revenge on those who had reported them. Moreover, the clear shift from witness-based to evidentiary-based justice meant a decline in the power of elders in villages to control "evil-doers." As we saw above, this was also interpreted as an effect of education, which appeared to undermine traditional authority.

To many British officials, however, it seemed clear that the failure of villagers to report crimes was related to the system of village adjudication. "Under Turkish administration," reported the chief commandant of military police in 1882, "the police were not in the habit of prosecuting, this duty being left to the injured party or his friends. There was grave reason to believe that this system led to compromises and condonements of offences against the public peace."[34] And so the second problem for many villagers was the attempted elimination of village adjudication, which British officials tended to interpret as complicity. This was also sometimes seen as encouraging the "kidnapping" of herd animals, which were the most common reasons for such adjudication:

> [W]hen an animal was lost the owner knowing or suspecting who had stolen it would employ a third person who would put himself in communication with one of the associates of the supposed thief and come to terms with him. The principals in the transaction, namely the person who has been robbed and the thief, never appear personally in the negotiation, which is carried on by agents on both sides. A sum of money being agreed upon, a place is named by the associate of the thief where the stolen animal will be found at such and such a time.[35]

This was clearly the common practice amongst shepherds themselves, often extended to what one British witness of the period calls the "perpetual feud between the owners of flocks and the tillers of the soil."[36] In the latter case, however, the "tillers of the soil" clearly wished to use the new justice system not only to prevent crime but to eliminate pastoralists.

Where British officials saw the best way of dealing with crime to be increased efficiency in the collection of evidence and its prosecution, many Cypriots themselves believed that the real solution lay in an adaption of local practice to the new legal system. Villagers and legislators alike suggested on many occasions that the most effective way of dealing with crime would be simply to confine the "bad characters," or those who were known by others to be "bad characters." In other cases, villagers suggested that villagers be made responsible for crime in the villages. In 1881, for instance, the commissioner of the Paphos District reported that "[i]t is not very long ago since I received petitions asking that the Mukhtar and Azas of the village from whence the robbery had taken place might be imprisoned, as they know who the thieves were. Villages, too, have sent down a paper saying that so and so are the bad characters of their village, and requesting that they be imprisoned."[37] In other words, many villagers believed that local practice should be enshrined in legal code. Controlling crime was not just a matter of policing but of putting crime in its proper social context.

In terms of legislation, this meant that Cypriot legislators called upon by British colonial rulers to deal with crime had to undertake an anthropology of village life that attempted to understand the social origins of crime. Legislation such as "The Field Watchmen's Law" and the "Malicious Injury to Property Law" had a profound impact on the structure of village life and on the capacity of the administration to penetrate it. The former provided for village police, requiring each village to appoint one of its own to patrol the fields at night and prevent sheep-theft and injury to property. The latter ordered that remuneration for damaged property would be paid to the victim by the village as a whole if no arrest was made, and that the *muhtar* would be responsible for collecting the required amounts. It is notable that both these laws require the active participation of villagers and place the responsibility for any single villager's actions on the village as a whole.

The manifest goal of these and other laws was to identify "criminal elements" and to pressure their fellow villagers to use the legal system over which the British administration had control. Clearly, this form of pressure was based on the perceived communal nature of Cypriot identity, in which destroying reputation and public shaming were considered to be some of the most effective means of social and crime control. Another aim, of course, was to eliminate pastoralists, who were too difficult to assess and tax, and to encourage the stability and calculability of agriculture. It was not difficult to enlist Cypriot members of the

Legislative Council for this purpose, since most, at least, of the Greek Cypriot members were moneylenders with a vested interest in the stable continuation of agricultural production. In fact, one of these elected members proposed in 1897 an amendment to the "Malicious Injury to Property Law" that would expedite the collection of compensation, since, as the bill stated, "In some parts of the Island the Mukhtars have been unable or unwilling to collect the compensation."[38]

At the same time, there were important disagreements in the manner in which British officials and Cypriot legislators interpreted the "nature" of Cypriots. In their many discussions of such matters, British officials clearly attributed culture to nature, seeing crime as a result of the "nature" of the Mediterranean hot-blood, who was also controllable only by corporate means. On the other hand, most Cypriots—both legislators and villagers alike—clearly saw "nature" as something subordinate to, rather than productive of, society. One sees this difference quite clearly in the persistent conflict between Cypriot legislators and British officials over the desire of British administrators to outlaw knives in public places and to control firearms. In 1911, the government proposed a new knives law that would have allowed for their seizure by the police. The Cypriot members of the council would not agree to this law but would agree to increase significantly the fines on persons caught carrying daggers at weddings, fairs, brothels, or licensed premises—significantly, virtually the only places where villagers and townspeople met. In commenting on this bill, the king's advocate noted, "It is a pity that the unofficial members of the Council could not be persuaded to carry the matter a little further but it is a fact and well known to them of course that to the uneducated Cypriots just as to other Mediterranean people the knife naturally takes the place of the fist or less dangerous weapon of other European nationalities."[39] Knives were not just a convenient tool but a characteristic of the Mediterranean and its people.

In contrast, bills proposed by Cypriot legislators emphasized the ways in which "bad characters" should be reined in by society—how nature should be controlled by culture. In 1909, for instance, a Greek Cypriot member of the Legislative Council proposed to draw up a law that would have allowed anyone to bring a charge against anyone else saying that he is a dangerous person and should be incarcerated. "And if," the proposed bill stated,

> after the issue of such an order against a certain person, the two thirds of the towns and villages commissions lying within thirty or forty miles from his usual place of abode seal and sign a petition to His Excellency the High Com-

missioner that such person must be confined, then this person to be arrested at once and confined and such a person to be set free, when the two thirds of the commissions aforesaid of such towns and villages seal and sign a petition to His Excellency the High Commissioner that the same person must get rid of such a confinement.[40]

This merely reflects in proposed legislation the persistent demand of many villagers for the confinement of "bad characters."

Moreover, those "bad characters" were both an intrinsic part of and a poison in village life. One instance of this is a bill that was brought forward on several occasions between 1911 and 1913 and eventually incorporated into another law. This bill, proposed by the Muslim members of the council, was cited as "The Dancing-Girls at Moslem Feasts Law, 1914," and its aim was to prevent women from singing and dancing at feasts, though it was aimed specifically at prostitutes and women who sang and danced professionally. In support of the bill, the legislators gathered letters of support from the elders of numerous villages, all of which cited dancing-girls as the major source of evil and crime in Muslim villages. Said one,

> Our local Government is aware of a great deal of troubles and crimes that take place on account of prostitutes going out to the villages during the course of a wedding. It is being witnessed with regret that the harm and devastation brought about by these ill famed women in material and virtual points such as health, morality and peace, are prevalent. We, therefore, pray for the kind assistance of the Government in reducing to law the Bill precluding the dancing-girls from attending weddings.[41]

Dancing-girls, like "bad characters," poisoned the otherwise innocent villagers, who at the same time were all classified as equally susceptible to that same poison. While British administrators wanted villagers to report crimes to the police and to become more individually responsible as legal citizens, Cypriot legislators wanted moral codes committed to law.

Hence, the response of British administrators and Cypriot legislators alike to the increase in crime was to pass more laws, the effect of which was to classify the crime *in* villages as the crime *of* villages. Like most anthropologists studying the Mediterranean, both Cypriot legislators and British administrators saw violence in the villages as a matter of honor and shame,[42] and they tried to obviate the expected problems of perjury and complicity through increased police penetration and penalties against the villages as a whole. Where they differed, however, was in their assessments of what this meant. As I remarked at the beginning of

the chapter, even as late as 1946, the chief justice concluded that jury trials were not suitable for Cyprus. He explained,

> Racial and religious divisions among the population are extremely sharp. So
> are the divisions between different political parties and other factions, even
> when formed for an apparently common object. The grouping of people
> resulting from these various divisions and ties attracts a far stronger loyalty to
> a group from its members than they could at present be expected to show,
> either to the public interest or to justice to an individual not belonging to the
> group or between two or more individuals belonging to different groups.[43]

Mired in what anthropologists have called "amoral familism," Cypriots
were just not ready for impartial justice that was not socially relative.

However, we can see that while British administrators emphasized
the possibility of correction, to be enacted on persons as individuals in
possession of certain rights and capacities, Cypriot legislators and villagers alike emphasized control, to be enacted on persons as members of
communities and bearers of honor. Peter Berger has noted that the concept of honor "implies that identity is essentially, or at least importantly,
linked to institutional roles."[44] Berger's assertion is that honor is linked
to others' view of one's capacity to fulfill what is expected of one in a
particular institutional role. This seems to be what was at stake when
certain villagers suggested to Bulwer in 1891 that "if a system of jury
trial were introduced crime would be put down."[45] This was not because
these villagers thought that jury trials would be impartial; it seems clear
that they did not. Rather, if the goal was social control, then partiality
might actually be more effective than impartiality.

For British officials, it was important that the nature of Cypriots be
controlled and submitted to an impartial justice, which would ultimately
teach them the values of equality and individualism. For Cypriots, it was
important that forces of chaos within the community be controlled. As
such, lawlessness was not the breaking of abstract moral rules but a dis-
engagement from the ethical control of society. As Messick noted in the
passage quoted earlier, an irreproachable character was linked not to a
universalized, abstract morality but to one's capacity to fulfill one's
proper social role. In summary, then, what one finds in this period is an
effort to control crime through a codification of an "essential" Cypriot
identity that did not conform to standards of individualism. For British
administrators, this presumed lack was something to be overcome if
Cypriots could only break away from the ties of culture and custom. For
Cypriot legislators, it was precisely those customs that should be
enshrined in law.

Corporate but equal

We see, then, that the equality of British justice, which led on the one hand to a breakdown of traditional authority, was enshrined in law as a reflection of Cypriots' corporate nature. Whereas initially and in theory that corporate nature was the corporatism of the extended family and the village, at the same time the immediate breakdown of traditional authority was accompanied by the growth of a new form of corporatism: that of one's linguistic/ethnic group. The bad character was no longer the outcast and outlier of the village community but came—in both British and Cypriot imaginings—to represent the anti-citizen. Cypriots' continuing ambiguous relationship to that anti-citizen reveals, I believe, much ambivalence about their own transformation into citizens represented not by *muhtars* and *ağas* but by "ethnic" leaders.

In order further to understand what the political consequences of these changes may have been, it is helpful to focus on the difference in British and local interpretations of what I have called here "corporatism." Clearly, this difference centered on the meaning of institutional roles and of what it meant to be "known" as a character within the community. It was precisely at this juncture of "knowing" that we can find the difference between British and Cypriot understandings of what it meant to be a person and a legal subject. For British officials, "bad characters" were any transgressors of public order, encompassing persons with "no visible means of support" as well as bandits. This category included, as well, town youths and members of the elite classes who stirred up trouble in protests against the administration. They were, in other words, all those who opposed the laws of the state. In the case of British officials, *knowing* the "bad characters" meant the capacity for surveillance—the capacity to "watch unceasingly" all those who might stir up trouble, as the officers' handbook makes clear. This is, I believe, a paradigmatic example of the type of surveillance that Foucault locates at the heart of Western governmentality.[46]

This form of governmentality was tempered, however, by Cypriot villagers' often blatant refusal to subject "their" bad characters to the mechanisms of British justice. Their "knowledge" of bad characters was a relational knowledge, embedded also in mechanisms of social control. One of the best examples of such relational knowledge was villagers' "knowledge" of bandits, the ultimate "bad characters." Paul Sant Cassia, for instance, puzzles over the popularity of banditry in Cyprus during this period and concludes that "bandit morals are embedded in, and indistinguishable from, the general morality of society."[47] This certainly corresponds to the common anthropological view of the Mediterranean area that has tended to look on violent crime as endemic to Mediterranean village life, and on certain kinds of crime as not only acceptable but necessary to maintain the social order. "Bad characters," then, were those who threatened the social order; as a sign of the anti-citizen, it was important that "bad characters" were both excluded from and an integral part of their society. It was precisely the bad characters' violent presence that marked the boundaries of the civilized community.

Who would be included in and who excluded from that community was being redefined in this same period. The relational nature of identity clearly began to change during this period, indicated in the manner in which the discourse with regard to persons also began to change. This change is seen most clearly in such areas as intercommunal sexual relations and marriage, "conversion," and the status of the *linovamvakoi*, a group of professed Muslims who practiced Christian rites. Until approximately the turn of the century, intimate relations between Muslims and Christians appear to have been a fairly common, if not unproblematic, feature of life between the communities.

There are no estimates of the numbers of such relations, but in British reports of the time one often finds conversions for the purpose of establishing relations: a girl who converted to Islam to become the second wife of her father's friend, a policeman; or another, much younger girl who wished to convert to Islam after being sent by her family to work as a servant in a wealthy, Muslim household in Nicosia. These were cases that appeared in the legal reports only because the parents complained, and the incidents were investigated. Other incidents were more problematic, though also amusing for their descriptions of conversion (and seduction) gone awry: the Muslim boy of Lefkara who pinched a Christian girl's cheek at a well and caused a general riot; the Christian girl who was seduced by a Muslim "procuress" and deflowered by a young Muslim man; or a riot during a wedding between a bride and groom of Episkopi and Kolossi, supposedly begun by the Muslims of Episkopi because one of their girls was living with a Christian boy in Kolossi. Claude Delaval Cobham, the commissioner of Larnaca, reported numerous instances during the same period:

> A Youth of about 20 named Halil Aziz, of Levkara, came to my house here and said he wished to become a Christian. I asked him why, he said he did not know. He did not know what Islam was or what Christianity was. He could not read or write. He seemed to me a person of weak intellect. I told him it was no

business of mine: if he really wished to become a Christian he had better go to
the Archimandrite. He went: the Archimandrite found him absolutely ignorant
of the rudiments of any belief, and refused to baptise him, but told him to put
himself under instruction, either here or with the Papas [priest] of his Village.
It seems he stayed there some days, lived with Christians and ate pork with
them.[48]

Cobham goes on to conclude that the boy's motivation for conversion
was his infatuation with a Christian girl, with whom he had already had
relations.

Such reports increased towards the turn of the century—probably a
product of increased police penetration—before suddenly disappearing
entirely. In the first decade of the twentieth century, both communities
were racked by intracommunal political disputes from which they
emerged with much more clearly defined outlines of the constitution of
community. This is seen in the fact that straddlers on the borderline had,
by this time, been forced to declare their allegiance, and reports of conversion absolutely disappear from the historical record. Even the
linovamvakoi, who had for centuries straddled communal boundaries,
were pressured to declare their communal affiliation. In 1880, Esme
Stevenson, the wife of a British officer, had described the *linovamvakoi*
as follows:

There is another sect in Cyprus, the members of which go by the name of
"Linobambaki," or "linen and cotton." They are thus called from belonging
neither to the Christian nor Moslem faith; though in outward appearance they
resemble Turks. They are in reality members of the Greek Church …. They
are poor and industrious, but not held in much respect by either Turk or
Christian.[49]

These *linovamvakoi* were the descendants of Greek Orthodox men who
had converted to Islam, taking Muslim names, and had married Muslim
women during the Ottoman period; they had continued to practice the
Greek Orthodox rites—supposedly secretly but in fact quite openly.
Mrs. Stevenson estimated their number at about 1,200 and claimed that
they lived primarily in a small corner of the northeastern portion of the
island, though evidence from police reports and censuses suggests that
their number was about twice that and that they were scattered throughout the island, mostly in villages.

By the beginning of the twentieth century, however, numerous Greek
Orthodox proselytizing missions pressured the *linovamvakoi* to convert
as a reflection of the "truth" about their identity. The success of this
pressure can be seen in the number of village disturbances resulting

from spectacular "conversions"—or, rather, returns to the faith. Cobham
described such an incident in Lefkara:

> Ibrahim Yusuf a man of 45, a "linobambakos," declared himself a Christian
> and was baptised. He was paraded about the village streets very late one
> evening and passed through the Moslem Quarter, accompanied by a great
> crowd, and holding in his hand a piece of pork, from which he ate. The whole
> affair was in the highest degree unseemly, but there was no breach of the
> peace.

It became standard practice upon a "conversion" for church bells to be
rung and guns fired in the middle of the night, for a baptism to take
place, and for the man (for it was typically a man) to be paraded through
the village eating a large chunk of pork. Afterwards, his wife was often
pressured to go and sleep with her newly Christianized husband. Before
this time, the *linovamvakoi* had occupied a marginal position, negotiat-
ing their way among the various types of affiliation possible to them in
the two communities. The first of these spectacular conversions were
condemned as unseemly by the archbishop, who recommended that the
government take steps against the provocateur, a non-Cypriot doctor
who had misled the people by his "charlatanism."[50] But at the beginning
of the century, such an indefinable position was no longer possible, and
the *linovamvakoi* were socially pressured either to "redeem themselves"
as Greek or to "turn Turk."[51]

In similar fashion and at the same moment, intercommunal marriage—and even attempts at intercommunal marriage—entirely
disappeared from the record. What is significant about such incidents is
that before this period the *linovamvakoi* had not been ascribed some
"underlying" identity, some "true" identity that was hidden behind name
or outward signs of confession. Their identity was in their practice,
which was both Christian and Muslim, and in their kinship networks and
friendships. They were marginal and ignored. They became important
only in a period in which it was considered important for them to declare
their "true" Greek identity through professing their "true" faith. Hence,
religion became a part of a fixed, ascribed identity.

Bandits and bad characters

From these examples, I believe that we can begin to understand the
importance of the ambiguous *knowledge* of "bad characters." The most
spectacular example of this ambiguous knowledge is villagers'

responses to the activities of a particularly audacious bandit gang that roamed the island in the same period, known to all and yet betrayed by none. These bandits became the subject of a popular literature that alternately portrayed them as hooligans and heroes. They were the epitome of the anti-citizen, subject to no laws but their own, their popularity revealing the ambiguities in Cypriots' own definitions of what it meant to be both a "bad character" and a "good citizen." Many of those ambiguities appear to have turned in the Ottoman period on the relational nature of one's legal subjecthood, based less on the notion of a unitary subject than on the notion of roles—as a father or mother, a Christian or a Muslim, a *muhtar* or priest, a trader or a craftsman. This clearly changed as a result of British legal-bureaucratic practice, and understanding this change is important as background to an analysis of the ambiguous popularity of bandits and other bad characters in the period.

We saw that villagers complained of the destructive effects of education. It should be noted, however, that although education spread in the island during the period as a result of grants-in-aid for the establishment of schools, this education was not significantly different from what had been in place before the British arrival. Rather, the explosion of print in these years, as well as the new status of writing, gave a novel power to those who had learned to command the languages of status, namely the written word. In turn, the citizen came increasingly to be defined as a Greek-speaking Greek Orthodox or Turkish-speaking Muslim legal subject. Indeed, changes in legal status were directly associated with a new sort of clientelism based on writing rather than on traditional authority.

"Bad characters," then, came to represent that part of the social self that was to be both remembered and forgotten, that part of identity that Michael Herzfeld terms "cultural intimacy:" "the recognition of those aspects of a cultural identity that are considered a source of external embarrassment but that nevertheless provide insiders with their assurance of a common sociality."[52] This appears to have been the primary reason for the popular fascination and titillation caused by the famous bandit gang known as the Hassanpoulia. While much of the literature on banditry has suggested that bandits are "primitive rebels" or are possessed of an inchoate political agenda,[53] I wish to focus instead on the titillation of banditry and what I believe it indicated: the pursuit of freedom expressed in a conservative idiom.[54]

In order to see the relationship between banditry and identity, it may be useful to look at the close parallel in Greece. Koliopoulos has noted that in the Greece of the nineteenth century there were two parallel discourses regarding bandits: one asserted that bandits operating within the Greek state were not Greeks but were "Albanians, Vlachs, and residents of Turkey."[55] Under this formulation, banditry in Greece itself was a foreign and transient phenomenon, while "the 'ethnos' was 'innocent'" and "had no reasons to fear the sullying of its honor."[56] The second discourse, however, saw the bandits as heroes, associated both with the founding of the modern Greek state and with the attempt to reclaim "unredeemed" Greek territories from the Ottomans. In both state discourse and popular literature, it was said that these bandits "punished 'the crimes of the Ottomans' as well as 'traitors and Christians who were accomplices of the Ottomans'."[57] In this discourse, bandits were described as brave, handsome, patriotic, and haters of Turks (*misotourkos*).

The case in Cyprus was different, however. The most notorious gang of bandits, the Hassanpoulia, was dominated by Muslims, gained the support of wealthy Christian flock-owners, and became a part of a popular literature written in Cypriot Greek.[58] One such poem described the bandits as masters of disguise:

> Hassanpoulia, Hassanpoulia, flying like birds,
> dressed in different clothes everyday,
> Greek today and Turkish tomorrow.[59]

The gang was so popular and well-supported that a special law, the Outlaws Proclamation Act of 1895, was passed by the Legislative Council to facilitate their capture, "extraordinary powers being given to the Executive to remove from the disturbed districts, persons suspected of assisting and harbouring the outlaws." The result was the arrest and imprisonment of the principal flock-owners of the districts of Paphos and Limassol.[60] When eventually captured, the gang was tried in another district to protect the witnesses, and when eventually executed, they were buried within the prison walls to avoid public displays.

In a special police report of 1896, it was noted that "they [the bandits] were responsible for 12 of the 17 murders reported in excess of last year together with many cases of attempts, wounding, rape, highway robbery, and animal stealing." Furthermore, "bad characters taking advantage of the temporary withdrawal of the Police for special services added to the list by going about armed and representing themselves to be the Poulis."[61] The police themselves credited the law, rather than public support, for the gang's capture:

Until the Outlaws Proclamation Act was passed in 1895, it was found impossible to check the support afforded by the villagers, or to control the bad characters who made use of the Poulis for their own designs, but as soon as the law was in operation it did not take long to remove those persons who supplied the outlaws with food, clothing, arms, ammunition and money.[62]

What I believe particularly noteworthy here is not only the widespread public support but even the discussion in the police record of the manner in which "bad characters" took up arms and posed as members of the bandit gang.

In no discussions of these criminals has any significance been attached to the fact that they and their supporters were both Muslim and Christian, and that they were seen as changing their identity as they changed their clothes.[63] Moreover, these bandits were very clearly identified with a certain age category known in Greek as the *pallikari* and in Turkish as *delikanlı*. In one popular poem, for instance, the poet wishes his audience "to listen to how Hassanpoulis [the leader of the gang] was a *pallikari*."[64] In general, the *pallikari* or *delikanlı* is seen as a young man whose transgression of boundaries is permissible, because he is testing his manly strength. However, *pallikari* also came to have the meaning of fighter or soldier, as one can see in the fact that this is how *pallikarya* has entered Turkish: to mean both a Greek ruffian and a Greek soldier.

This tension between the ruffian or criminal and the freedom-fighter had a different valence in Cyprus to the one it had in Greece, at least at the start of the twentieth century. At that moment, unlike in Greece, it appears that the titillation caused by banditry expressed in popular literature was related to a fluidity of identity that resisted legal-bureaucratic rationalization and expressed a "tradition" of transgression. This is symbolically very distinct from the later Greek Cypriot invocation of the *pallikari* in the nationalist movement of the 1950s aimed at evicting the colonizers and uniting Cyprus with Greece. Symbolically, there were many resemblances in the later anti-colonial struggle to the *kleftes*, or bandits, such as the fact that it was one of the first modern guerilla wars, in which very young men followed their leaders into the mountains, often living for extended periods in caves.[65] In both cases, an appeal to "tradition" was used to justify violence: in the case of bandits, this was a living tradition of testing one's manhood through sheep-theft and controlled lawlessness of the sort that British officials wished to root out. In the case of the anti-colonial fighters, this was an appeal to a glorified tradition of guerilla warfare that had also contributed to the independence of Greece.

The knowledge of "bad characters," then, was also a form of social solidarity and a way in which the bad character's opposite, the respectable citizen, was defined. This also meant, however, that knowledge of bad characters was relational insofar as the "bad character" was a social role that embodied a "tradition" of transgression. Committing the relational nature of this role to law and submitting it to evidentiary proceedings also entailed, I have argued, an inscription of the corporate nature of Cypriot identity. That corporate nature, moreover, was legally expressed in the script languages of two separate linguistic groups—Greek and Turkish—and ultimately dependent upon a new form of clientelism defined not by traditional authority but by writing. It is a longing for that traditional authority, I have suggested, that may have produced the extraordinary support for and popularity of a gang that so clearly defied inscription in the new legal categories. And yet it was those new legal categories that would contribute to the popular understanding of a new, and nationalist, *pallikari* who aimed not at the restoration of traditional authority but at the "restoration" of the invented traditions of the nation-state.

Conclusion

As in other colonized areas, the practices of law under British rule in Cyprus were neither fully liberal nor fully equal. However, the ideals of liberalism and equality under the law led both to a disintegration of traditional structures of authority and to new legal-political structures in which "equal" subjects were represented as "naturally" members of communities. This happened, I have argued, both because of local legislation that cast Cypriots as "naturally" possessed of certain traits or tendencies that were in need of correction, and also because the new structures of legal bureaucracy required that villagers depended upon the middlemen who linked them to elites in the towns. However, if equality under the law is codified not on an assumption of individualism but on an assumption of partiality and corporatism, what are the political results?

The corporatism of Cypriot political life throughout the twentieth century is a subject that has been much discussed in the literature on Cyprus.[66] Indeed, one sociologist claims that "[t]his corporatization of political and civic life poses serious obstacles to the rationalization and modernization of the political culture and ethos of the Republic of

Cyprus."[67] Moreover, the same scholar argues that "[t]here appears to be a general reluctance to question accepted dogmas and to express individual opinions, with an implicit acceptance that only social groups or organized actors are legitimate sociopolitical actors."[68] A similar phenomenon clearly exists in the Turkish community of Cyprus, as well, and in both cases is expressed in a unifying ideology of nationalism.

However, implicit in the analysis I have presented here is the suggestion that the uses of "corporatism" as an analytical category need to be problematized if we are to understand the strength of nationalism for the formation of identities in the island. The disappearance of the *linovamvakoi* became necessary at a particular moment when authority, and the constitution of the community that authority was to represent, were called into question. At this moment, villages were being more closely connected to the towns through bureaucracy and middlemen, who were able to maintain face-to-face ties while satisfying the bureaucratic requirements of representation through writing and the uniqueness of the signature. A new print culture was describing linguistic worlds in which "serious" politics and the politics of the cafe were represented in different languages. And the increase in crime—or perceived increase in crime—seemed to result from all this ferment, so that villagers admired the bandits who eluded British forces, even though those same villagers demanded stricter implementation of the punishments that should put people back in their "proper" social places. And so legislators and publishers could construct a "traditional" villager who was a template to receive the discriminatory wrongs of the community. Thus, the new identity of equal selves could be interpreted in communal terms, allowing for new interpretations of structural inequalities that explained them not through the failures of particular, corrupt officials, but through the divisions that suddenly seemed to be inherent in things.

The ambiguities produced by this legal-bureaucratic experience can be seen in the figure of the "bad character," who defines the citizen by defining the anti-citizen. The simultaneous attribution of corporate responsibility and expansion of forms of linguistic, bureaucratic representation ultimately had the effect of inscribing persons as members of linguistic groups. And it was in such a context that bandits might represent a dangerous, but titillating, form of freedom from the constraints of categories.

PART TWO

Movements

Introduction

In a corner of the main square of Nicosia, a commemorative bust perches on an Ionic pedestal, around which lounge taxi drivers sipping coffee and twirling prayer beads. In the noon light, the white glare on the marble obscures the features, but one can still discern the strong forehead and voluminous mustaches. The bulbous statue eyes watch the town hall across the street and the hurry of high-heeled women who rush between the shops. Few know that the bust's model, Nikolaos Katalanos, was one of the most powerful and puzzling figures in modern Cypriot history. The life-sized bust hardly does justice to a man who was a captivating orator, penetrating writer, and tireless nationalist, both cultured and charismatic, royalist and populist. No history indicates that he ever married, yet his manhood was unquestioned by followers who accepted his complete devotion to "the cause." He had arrived in Cyprus as a teacher of the Nicosia Gymnasium and had been dismissed for insubordination.[1] He remained for almost thirty years as a journalist, agitator, and politician, and when his visa was revoked and he finally returned to Athens, he proudly distributed calling cards reading, "N. Katalanos: Professor—Journalist—First Political Exile from Cyprus (11 April 1921)."[2]

As early as 1895, a teacher whom Katalanos allegedly attempted to kill in a dispute implored the archbishop to punish Katalanos and to protect the teacher from him.[3] The mufti complained on several occasions that Katalanos was canvassing the village coffeeshops and rousing a few drunken Christians to violence against their Muslim neighbors. Certainly, Katalanos almost single-handedly raised close to 1,000 volunteers—mostly young boys—to be sent off in 1897 to the war in Crete.[4] He published the newspaper *Evaghoras* until it was closed for libel violations in 1905, when he became a writer for other papers.[5] And despite his immigrant status he was elected numerous times and by handy margins to the Legislative Council. Indeed, it is all too easy to see Katalanos as an influential ideologue representative of that intellectual

class so often blamed for diffusing a homogenized, nationalist high culture.[6] Alternatively, one might see him as an Hegelian "great man," the
voice of forces that he deludes himself in believing he controls. Here,
we want to see him as a heroic leader whose heroism was defined by the
times and by what history has made of him. The truths that he spoke res-
onated with Cypriots of the period, who recognized in his articulation of
their culture a truth that was already being lived.

Katalanos led a radical nationalist following, drawn primarily from
the lower classes; at the same time he was a staunch royalist whose loyalty to King Constantine has been blamed for his exile.[7] As we will see,
in his very contradictoriness Katalanos was representative of a particular
strain of Greek Cypriot thought that would eventually be triumphant: the
demand for leaders who were not only representatives but also representations, whose authority was constituted not only by equality but by the
immortal truths that that equality appeared to represent. A curious combination of eternal truth and present necessity would imbue Katalanos
with an authority both modern and timeless.

Kierkegaard noted that the dialectic of antiquity tended toward leadership; that the dialectic of Christendom tends toward representation;
and that the dialectic of the present age tends toward equality.[8] In his
venomous attack on the equalizing abstraction called "the public," this
eccentric but perceptive philosopher described the strange dialectic of
representativeness, and his comments are worth examining at length:

> In order that everything should be reduced to the same level it is first of all
> necessary to procure a phantom, a spirit, a monstrous abstraction, an all-
> embracing something which is nothing, a mirage—and that phantom is *the
> public*. It is only in an age which is without passion, yet reflective, that such a
> phantom can develop itself with the help of the Press which itself becomes an
> abstraction. In times of passion and tumult and enthusiasm, even when a peo-
> ple desire to realize a fruitless idea and lay waste and destroy everything—
> even then there is no such thing as a public. There are parties and they are con-
> crete. The Press, in times such as those, takes on a concrete character
> according to the division of parties. But just as sedentary professional people
> are the first to take up any fantastic illusion which comes their way, so a pas-
> sionless, sedentary, reflective age, in which only the Press exhibits a vague
> sort of life, fosters this phantom …. The public is a concept which could not
> have occurred in antiquity because the people *en masse in corpore* took part in
> any situation which arose and were responsible for the actions of the individ-
> ual, and, moreover, the individual was personally present and had to submit at
> once to applause or disapproval for his decision. Only when the sense of asso-
> ciation in society is no longer strong enough to give life to concrete realities is
> the Press able to create that abstraction, "the public," consisting of unreal indi-

viduals who never are and never can be united in an actual situation or organization—and yet are held together as a whole.[9]

What if, however, the people participate both *en masse in corpore* and as a phantom public? What if a party quarreler such as Katalanos claims through the press to represent public opinion?

We need authority, wrote the fourteenth-century philosopher Ibn Khaldun, to subdue the violence that pulses in all of us. This eternally returning theme, like the comet that appears to portend a new era, curves and arcs through the centuries, striking those philosophers who seek a renovation of their times through a science of human life. The philosopher was later revived by Ottoman historians, and his themes were echoed in early modern Europe, where similar crises of authority threatened.[10] Agreeing with Aristotle, Ibn Khaldun derives authority from the political nature of humans, which demands social organization. He and other philosophers of the premodern era derive the king's authority from God, and believe that a people is created by that authority. In the modern era, as we know, authority supposedly comes from the people, from an authorizing public. Or, as Camus so trenchantly put it, "Power is no longer what is, but what should be."[11]

The significant difference between the moderns and their predecessors is that ponderers such as Hobbes—on the cusp of the modern era—grappled with the seeming magic of the authority that controlled that surging violence. "The word of God delivered by the prophets is the main principle of Christian politics," wrote Hobbes in *Leviathan*. He goes on to discuss how one knows a prophet, or how a true prophet can be distinguished by the faculties of reason.[12] As Ibn Khaldun noted, the philosopher of the human sciences must address the question of prophecy, for the true prophet is also a politician with the power to persuade, while the best leader is the prophet with the power to penetrate the veil that hides the ultimate truth from ordinary eyes.[13] The philosopher-king is not only an ideal but also a problem, for he embodies the circularity of an authority validated by claims to truth and truth imposed through authority.

Obviously, to say with our Enlightenment predecessors that the "real" authority lies with the people is to miss the point. Cyprus at the turn of the century suffered what was called in the last chapters a "crisis of authority." There, we examined the crisis; here, we will witness the decline of a divinely inspired authority and the rise of a "public." But rather than accept that this was the abstract, homogeneous, passionless public described by Kierkegaard, we will see how the public defined its "publicness." For in Cyprus, even the abstract could not be faceless, and men such as Katalanos who represented "the Press" were also powerful speakers who moved their audiences with direct, even visceral, orations. This would seem in most ways to confirm Bruce Lincoln's claim that authority is performative and ultimately rests on the effect produced by a speaker or performer within particular, authorizing circumstances.[14] Lincoln's argument, however, does not address the idea of authority as an abstraction—a necessary enterprise in an era in which the authorizing arena is an abstract "public." For in a place such as Cyprus the self-consciousness of one's role in creating the authorizing public created a role for "truth" that was at the same moment ideologic and hegemonic—both consciously thought and unconsciously lived—and of an authority that was both representative and representational. And as Christian and Muslim diverged on these issues, we have the real roots of cultural difference in the contemporary era.

CHAPTER 3

Tactics and Truths

On a bright Nicosia day in the spring of 1900, Archbishop Sofronios was borne in state to the next world, carried aloft in his throne through the chapel near where he had passed much of his life. In that life, the prelate was a virile, fatherly man, and he appeared in his pontifical robes like a gentle farmer grown wise. Reigning from his worn, wooden compound that Cypriots called the "archiepiscopal palace," Sofronios and his predecessors on the Cypriot throne had been the only Orthodox archbishops since the fall of Byzantium to wear the royal purple, carry the imperial scepter, and sign in the crimson ink of the Byzantine kings.[1] He was thickset, with smooth, olive skin under the requisite flowing beard, with the hands of an athlete and the spectacles of a scholar. During his thirty-five years in office, this soft-spoken man had achieved a precarious balance amongst various parties, sympathizing with the growing leftist tendencies of the peasant farmers, manipulating the two imperial powers that governed the island, and maintaining his dignity among the clerical elites of the Orthodox world. A former gymnasium headmaster educated in Athens, Sofronios had grown weary of the petty political intrigues that engulfed the latter years of his reign.

Those factions that had exhausted him were also prepared for the moment of his death. The chapel doors had barely clicked shut on the ceremony when supporters of the factions scurried to their respective coffeehouses to plot the strategy that they hoped would propel them to power. Sofronios had borne the brunt of the paradoxical situation in which the Church had been placed by the British arrival: while the clergy were chosen *ab antiquo* by popular election, their authority also needed the support of the state, which it lost under the British administration. How could the clergy be the voice of the people, if their decisions were not enforced by the will of the people, embodied in the authority of the state? Indeed, Sofronios struggled against an increasing impotence to control his flock and preserve his church, and the newspapers complained that bishops were forced to canvass the villages and extort dues in order to survive, closing the churches when no money was paid.[2]

This chapter examines why the struggle for power that began with Sofronios' death and that engulfed the first decade of the twentieth century eventually resulted in the triumph of nationalist politics. The delicate balance amongst various parties that had been achieved during Sofronios' thirty-five-year reign was shattered with his death, throwing the Greek Orthodox community into what would become a turbulent, decade-long dispute over his successor. The two candidates for his position—the bishop of Kition and the bishop of Kyrenia, both named Kyrillos—were opposites in character, temper, and appearance, as well as in their preparedness for a long, wearying political battle that appeared to have no normative constraints. The bishop of Kition (Kyrillos Papadhopoulos) drew his support from a populist swell in the districts caused by recent droughts; his core followers were journalists, lawyers, politicians, and moneylenders who hoped to use a more politically minded archbishop as leverage to gain greater power from the British colonial government. In contrast, the bishop of Kyrenia (Kyrillos Vasileiou) was supported by the older elite of urban merchants, as well as by that minority which saw the position of archbishop as a religious rather than political position. The campaigns on both sides were filled with lies, liars, scoundrels, and rogues, and the ridiculous could often become the hilarious when factional supporters encountered each other at church services and caused the candlesticks to fly.

The opposition between the two parties could be broadly described as that between populism and paternalism. Even more, however, the dispute between them was about a new role for religion in politics, and politics in religion. By this time enosis had already become the avowed desire of those writing in the media and speaking in public spaces. The outcome of this tumultuous decade, however, would determine what that movement was to mean. The "paternalist" faction struggled to maintain the dignity of the church, and through that dignity, their power. The populist faction accused them of elitism, ignorance, and indulging in "Oriental" vices. The "populist" faction, on the other hand, appropriated discourses of race and nation that allowed them to incorporate Orthodoxy—and their role as its representatives—as an essential, defining element of the political community. The paternalist faction accused them of introducing violence into Cypriot politics, as well as of adhering to freemasonry, that product of the revolutionary West. As we will see, the contest over who was to become archbishop was also a contest between East and West, Romeic and Hellenic, played out at the very local, and very political level.

This chapter explores, then, the triumph of the populist faction and their agenda of political redemption. I will describe the division between the two factions as one between prophetic power—represented by the bishop of Kyrenia—and evocation, or "calling forth," of a latent ethnic potential. The latter also entailed representing for the people their "real" nature, at the same time representing the solution to their most basic problems as a freedom that could only be realized through union of the island with Greece. While prophetic power was based on a belief in a basic separation between elites and masses in their access to knowledge and truth, a populist "evocation" implied, in a Platonic way, that relevant truths were latent in the person and only needed to be called forth. Paternalism and populism, then, were not only political strategies but were, more importantly, ways in which each party defined what constituted relevant knowledge in a new age.

Historically speaking, knowledge in Cyprus had never been apolitical: religion in Cyprus was immanently political, and religion and education were inextricably entwined. Earlier in the nineteenth century, induction into the esoteric knowledge of religion had required a knowledge of letters, while the acquisition of that knowledge had been undertaken primarily as a means of entering a closed circle that had access to the divine—as well as to other forms of power. Yet, the ecclesiastical monopoly of education among the Greek Orthodox was never separated from politics, while the monopoly in the Ottoman Islamic contexts was never independent of the state but was integrated into the state's most basic structures. Greek Orthodox clergy acted as political representatives under the Ottoman regime, while the *ulema* exercised various political functions in a state in which the sultan periodically proclaimed himself caliph. I would suggest that at this most fundamental historical level there was no basis for the illusion of an intellectual class that could be seen as independent of the power structures of which it formed an intimate part.[3]

Bishops and battles

The fight that erupted in 1900 between supporters of the wan, ascetic bishop of Kyrenia and the rough, somewhat brutal, bishop of Kition quickly overflowed Cyprus to involve much of the Greek Orthodox world. By tradition, the archbishop was to be elected by sixty representatives of the people—thirty from the archiepiscopal see and thirty from the other districts. These general representatives were to be elected by parish representatives, the numbers of which were determined by the census of 1891. But when many more parish representatives than were authorized showed up to elect the general representatives, the vote was called into question:

> It is said that in some villages no voting at all took place but that certificates were drawn up at a subsequent date stating that so and so had been elected; in others influence was brought to bear by money lenders and merchants, and in others people from the towns tore up the voters' tickets after they had been placed in the ballot box and compelled the voters to hold a new election and to elect them as their representatives.[4]

Of the general representatives elected, twenty-three were said to be in favor of the bishop of Kyrenia, while twenty-one supported the bishop of Kition. The election of the other sixteen was called into question, and an examination was ordered by the Holy Synod, causing the resignation of its president, the bishop of Kition. Thus began the campaign that would rend the community for a decade.

The bishop of Kition, Kyrillos Papadhopoulos, was not a typical metropolitan. He was certainly no scholar, and he was something more of a political brawler with a mesmerizing control over his followers and a desire to reassert the absolute authority of the archbishop. He was only about thirty-five years old in 1900, having graduated in 1880 from one of the lesser middle schools. Afterwards, he taught the alphabet in a primary school for eight years, while at the same time acting as a priest and living in the archiepiscopal palace. He was, in rapid succession, elected bishop of Kyrenia, then bishop of Kition, and finally competed with his older rival for the archiepiscopal throne. Ohnefalsch-Richter, who knew him around 1910, gave a priceless description:

> He has an elevated and impressive bearing and … a long, black and thick beard, and a lot of hair that is hidden with difficulty under his *kalimafchi* [headgear of an Orthodox priest]. In his face that's pale like wax, two sparkling eyes with thick lashes dominate, and his well-formed lips close energetically and with sweetness, depending on the circumstances. Between

them projects a hawklike nose, which despite its position, length, and angle, suits the face. He belongs to those who tread on the dead. With these idiosyncratic physical and spiritual characteristics, he enjoys, both among the natives and the English, greater authority than his late predecessor Sofronios. The High Commissioner, when he wants to bring off something that pertains to the Greeks, behaves graciously towards him, and suddenly it's done.[5]

Unlike the gentle, bookish Sofronios, Kyrillos Papadhopoulos was both despised and feared by British administrators, who recognized his charisma though swore that they could not understand it.

So in the course of less than twenty years Kyrillos Papadhopoulos rose from "teacher of sacred history" to become archbishop. Along the way, aside from his religious offices, he also became one of the most popular, vocal, and intransigent elected members of the Legislative Council. Kyrillos Papadhopoulos was one of a new breed of vocal—even vociferous—religious leaders-cum-politicians who were learning to transform and reappropriate the formerly political dimension of their clerical role. The bishop's personality produced a passionate following, as well as intense hatred among his opponents. From the beginning of his clerical career, his behavior was unlike that of any of the older generation of clerics, who always attempted to assuage the government and the feelings of their Muslim compatriots. This bishop and future archbishop did not take those things into account and concentrated instead on his Orthodox following. For example, the following 1890 petition to the high commissioner from a village of Morphou district could never have been written about Archbishop Sofronios or his cohort:

> Your humble petitioners are the inhabitants and agriculturalists of the village of Avlona in Morpho natice. They are in the habit of paying their taxes and tithes to the Govt. regularly and they do not in any way act against the laws and thus, under the protection of Her Majesty the Queen, they keep up their reputation. On the 25 August last the Bishop of Kyrenia came to their village and while they were sitting at the cafe in the village the Bishop passed by them to visit their (Greek) cemetery near the church. Because they did not get up to salute him he used lot of bad words and injured their reputations. Although it is a known fact that Govt would not allow him to use such words, unjustly and although they desire to prosecute him but as he is the chief of religion, they do not know which court they have to apply to and therefore they have been obliged to lay the matter before Your Excellency's consideration and request that Your Excellency may be pleased to give them permission to prosecute the Bishop and to let them know which Court they are to apply to.[6]

This occurred only a year after the election that put the bishop into office in the see. As we will see, it was precisely those abilities as a brawler that would later confirm the bishop's support by worshipful followers.

Kyrillos Vasileiou, the bishop of Kyrenia, was in contrast a faded figure who knew well the rules and regulations of the system within which
he had been raised and educated, but who would not have deemed it
proper to engage in the same sort of populist appeal as his rival. The
power that he possessed and would ultimately exercise much later
derived from the fear accorded holy men. One theologian and historian
comments that the people, "in spite of regarding him as comically thin
and sallow, venerated him as a saint and wonder-worker."[7] He sought to
uphold the dignity and traditions of the church, even if it entailed the
increasing interference of the laity. Indeed, one of the primary objections raised to the initial election was that, on the previous day, the
bishop of Kition had campaigned in the district governed by the archiepiscopal see and where voters tended to be more conservative. This
was seen as scandalously improper, and the bishop of Kyrenia himself
discreetly remained in the archiepiscopal palace.

The battle to elect an archbishop that ensued upon Sofronios' death
began the first political campaign in Cyprus that might be called "modern." Until that time, elections to seats in the Legislative Council—the
only island-wide representative body—were the only contests that
required any sort of campaigning. But because these were district elections, campaigning was minimal: the incumbents were re-elected time
after time, and they were almost always moneylenders, lawyers, newspaper publishers, or all of the above. Since many of these men had
already played the role of patron and intermediary between villagers and
the government in their districts, there was little contest for election to a
government seat. The attempted election that began in 1900, however,
was a mud-slinging, highly publicized battle to claim public opinion—
not to win it, but to claim that they already controlled it. Each side
claimed to be the representative not of a faction of Greek Cypriots or
even of a majority of Greek Cypriots, but of all Greek Cypriots.

Furthermore, since the election process had stalled on charges of vote
fraud, "the truth" about the election remained in dispute, allowing both
sides to claim and trumpet a victory. In large part this contest was
between groups of elites who claimed particular followings and who
used their privileged positions as middlemen to carry on a dual campaign: on the one hand, they disputed the legality of elections in the
chambers of the colonial administration, while on the other hand they
kept their own forces in the districts mobilized for action against the
other party. However, this was also a popular election of a "national"
sort in which virtually every male adult voter participated. Previous
archbishops had also been elected by popular vote, but there is every

indication that the favorite of the elites had hardly ever been contested. Recognizing villagers' increased involvement and interest, the candidates had to reflect a "national" consensus and their themes had to be popular ones, indicating that times had changed. The very different ways in which the two candidates responded to this challenge indicates, firstly, that this was a crucial turning-point in Cypriot political history for which not everyone was prepared, and, secondly, that the political future of Cyprus was still being contested.

The issue that had excited these men and their followers for fifteen years was not only the question of populism and authority, but also its more practical manifestation in the question of church finances. The loss of authority and the loss of revenue were inextricably linked, and as the new form of government was itself supposed to be representative of the people, those people, before granting renewed authority to the church, wanted more voice in its expenditures. Interestingly, their demand was essentially to turn church properties and sources of revenue into endowments to be used for communal purposes, much like the *vakıf* properties of Islamic regimes.

These issues were already well-formulated in the decade before Sofronios' death, and he was frequently pestered to resolve the issues. Numerous articles appeared in newspapers such as *Salpinks*, which explained that the problem was a dual one of the relations of the church to the state, and the relations of the church to the people. By the former was meant that the church should be supported in its authority by the government:

> Why then is the bishop called an ecclesiastical authority, since he exercises no authority over the priests, his decisions carry no weight, he has no power to restrain them within the circle of their sacred duties, no authority to protect and insist upon the observance of the sacred canons and ecclesiastical ordinances? Why then, indeed, are there bishops at all when their admonitions dissolve into the air, their censures are despised, and their penalties are derided? Do they exist that they may ordain priests only, i.e., that they may increase the ranks of anarchy, insubordination and scandals?[8]

The powers of the church, they insisted, should be written into law, just as "the rights which it possesses over the people, and the duties which it ought to perform towards it, should be equally defined by law."[9] The only way to accomplish this, they claimed, was to assign fixed salaries to the clerics and expend the rest of church funds on public works, especially education.

Similarly, during Kyrillos Papadhopoulos' initial election to the see of Kyrenia in 1889, one group so strongly opposed his election that they absented themselves from the proceedings and formally protested against the election. "But in the end," the commissioner of Kyrenia writes,

> the new Bishop was duly elected by a majority and the discontents since purposed to prevent him being installed in his diocese or taking possession of the property of the See. I understand that they even proposed to do without a Bishop considering that if that were done, they could administer the revenues more advantageously while they would derive direct benefit from the control of that portion of the funds available or devoted to educational purposes, by employing it in sending their nominees to Athens.[10]

In other words, the dispute centered at least in part on the question of the disposal of church funds, which the new and considerably stronger bishop could be expected to—and, in fact, did—use to consolidate his power.

But in their campaigns for archbishop, the candidates differed not so much in regard to issues but in regard to claims to represent the "truth" about Orthodox Cypriots. Early in the campaign the supporters of the bishop of Kition claimed that the followers of the bishop of Kyrenia cared only for their class interests and would work with the British rather than for enosis. The newspaper *Foni tis Kiprou*, which generally supported the bishop of Kyrenia, responded with an editorial which ran:

> The Cypriot people always distinguishes itself by patriotism in the true meaning of the word, patriotism pure, sincere, and brotherly .... They never permit themselves to be used by representatives as the means of their advancement. It is from such signs that it is possible to be certain in saying that the entire orthodox population of the island remains in complete harmony, and no one would dare to be exploited for other reasons, so that a child of Cyprus would not blame his brother for lacking patriotism. In other words, in this question all have lived as brothers, because they have but one goal, one single desire, their physical restoration through enosis with Greece.[11]

It was here, then, that the line was drawn: one's reputation could be defended, but patriotism defined one's right to *have* a reputation. It was not permitted to challenge one's patriotism, because without it one was placed outside the moral order. A consensus had been reached, then, concerning enosis, even if enosis was not the fervent desire of all Greek Cypriots that the newspapers and elites often claimed that it was.

Where the parties differed was in what they asserted that this meant; their assertions were also claims to define the truth about Orthodox Cypriots and their capacity to represent them. Since few of their voters read and most were influenced by news filtering to the villages through their party leaders or schoolmasters, there were certain key representations evoked by what we would now call "buzz-words." The bishop of Kition, for instance, was accused of participating in the rites of freemasonry, and the newspapers examined freemasonry in all its detail over several years. On the other hand, the bishop of Kyrenia was described as being surrounded by a "gang" (*simmoria*), most of them brutish and immoral. How these representations differed is of particular concern here, since it demonstrates the deep class divisions that perpetuated the dispute over a decade. It demonstrates, as well, a clear use of the rhetoric of Romeic versus Hellenic cultures that would later determine the form taken by Hellenism in Cyprus.

Accusations of freemasonry against the bishop of Kition were rarely made directly; instead, most accusations were made either against the bishop of Kition's closest followers or in a manner which cast doubt on the bishop, both because of the mystification associated with this supposed sect, and because, without a direct charge, the bishop could hardly deny it. Hence, an editorial in the *Foni tis Kiprou* described a Nicosia demonstration in which shouts of "down with Orthodoxy and long live freemasonry" were heard. Says the writer,

> But what has made a horrible impression upon us is the mixing up in those shouts for Masonry of the name of one of the candidates for the Archiepiscopal throne. If the persons who did so are really working for the success of the Bishop of Kition, they are rendering him a very bad service and the Bishop of Kition could rightly say: "When I have such friends, what for me if I have enemies."[12]

The author signed himself "an Orthodox," using the reactionary "Orthodoxy" slogan adopted by the bishop of Kyrenia's party. In addition, the author vituperated not only the demonstrators themselves but those whom he hinted were behind the demonstration: namely, those who, for a number of years, "have abused everything, i.e., the people and clergy, the heads of the society and every holy and high establishment." The campaign was one directed at the mystification of freemasonry as opposed to the revelation of Orthodoxy—in other words, against the secrecy of things learned as opposed to the clarity of cultural givens.

Freemasonry, though, was both a secret rite and a revolutionary movement, and accusations of association with freemasonry were often lodged against those with a clearly revolutionary agenda. It would later be rumored, for instance, that many Young Turks were freemasons.[13] Also by this time, Leo Taxil, a French journalist who began his career avidly against Catholicism but later embraced the Church, had published numerous books and tracts that associated masonry with Satanism in the European popular imagination.[14] It was assumed that freemasons were atheists and their rites un-Christian, and so the charge seems an unsurprising one to lodge against a clergyman whose agenda was clearly the revival of Hellenic glory as opposed to Orthodox unity.

One of the most outspoken supporters of the Hellenic agenda was Katalanos, who was one of the bishop of Kition's right-hand men and who was accused by the opposition—with considerable justification—of having introduced libels, slander, and the violent settlement of disputes into Cyprus.[15] In his newspaper *Evaghoras* he indulged himself in various misrepresentations that cost him not only his newspaper but his freedom. The slander which resulted in a jail sentence was directed against the Pancyprian Gymnasium, which was funded by the archbishopric, then under the direction of supporters of the bishop of Kyrenia. In it, he described a bacchanalian excursion of gymnasium boys with their masters, claiming that unspeakable acts had been performed with the guidance of the gymnasium teachers:

> Disorder and dissoluteness, confusion and loud noise, bacchanalian frenzies and indecencies prevailed from morning to evening and called forth the astonishment and indignation of the simple villagers. Especially, the two Baccanalians whom the boys call, in an expressive manner, the one by the name of Zivania [a Cypriot alcoholic drink] and the other by the name of Cognac, lost all decency and decorum and set a very bad example to the school youth .... Groups of boys dispersed here and there far from any supervision and were led by their youthful ardour to an improper vivacity and we are unable to reduce to writing all that is narrated to us and, however much we may discount for exaggerations, then again what remains calls forth a blush.[16]

This was certainly not the first such attack on the gymnasium "professors," who universally supported the bishop of Kyrenia.[17]

In response to the charges of freemasonry, Katalanos attempted to portray the bishop of Kyrenia and the gymnasium teachers who were his supporters as ignorant, immoral, and consumed by party hatred. In December 1901 he described the bishop of Kyrenia as follows:

> It has been shown on many occasions and in the present one also that there is no Christian virtue in this entirely unworthy Bishop, and that emaciated and very pale bit of flesh that is preserved in life by pus and bile only, is filled of such personal and party animosity and wickedness as rarely happens even to vulgar men ...[18]

He continues by claiming to describe the practices of the Orthodoxia Club, directed by the bishop of Kyrenia:

> Among many other things in the conventicle that is near the theatre, the Dervishes that went in it exchanged with the lector or with the preacher, before the prayer, the following dialogue: "Dost thou renounce Satan?" "I renounce him!" they reply in a chorus, repeating the same answer thrice, when the lector

or the preacher says: "and spit upon him!" Phtou, phtou, phtou, phtou rustles in the chamber from mouths smelling of onion, garlic, coriander, leeks, and other smelling vegetables. And satan having nowhere to go in order to flee from the smells jumps on the shoulders of the preacher or of the lector, and then commences the satanology of the preacher who transports the blessed auditors to all the departments of hell. The auditors are of the lowest social riffraff, they are illiterate and unlettered, and they are full of superstitions and presumptions which are strengthened by such deeds, they becoming maniacs and bigots.[19]

Those who accused the bishop of Kition of elitism through freemasonry got their own through charges of bigotry stemming from ignorance and superstition.

Even more than that, however, Katalanos' descriptions of the bacchanalian excursion and of the satanic rites performed by the bishop of Kyrenia and his supporters employ key terms of an Orientalizing discourse. As Michael Herzfeld and others have noted, Greece has teetered for more than a century and a half on the ideological divide between the Romeic (defined by Orthodoxy and the Eastern Roman Empire) and the Hellenic (defined by a Western European fascination with Ancient Greece). The Romeic and Eastern defines those qualities that are, in Herzfeld's terms, "culturally intimate"—i.e., constitutive of self but at the same time represented only to insiders. The Hellenic, on the other hand, circumscribes a history that has political and ideological salience in the West and so is something in which one *should* take pride. The Hellenic attaches one to the West, while the Romeic ties one to the East. Hence, in Katalanos' description, dervishes, garlic, and hints of homosexuality are not simple caricatures, but are caricatures framed in a language that points the reader to the lingering influences of the "Oriental" Turks.

Moreover, the ideological terms in which the dispute was played out were no doubt known to and discussed by most Greek Orthodox in the land. Weekly newspapers published hardly any other news during the decade, and they published it with bold headlines. It is unlikely that future voters in the rural areas kept abreast of all events in the campaign, since the most generous estimate of total circulation for all Greek newspapers in the island was only equal to 1.3 per cent of the Greek population. However, they were certainly aware of the more spectacular aspects of the dispute, if not from newspapers then from rumors circulating the village coffeehouses and telegrams transmitted to the districts. They were aware, for example, of the scenes described by the Holy Synod in a 1901 memorandum to the three patriarchs and the Metropolitan of Athens. There, the Synod disapproved of the bishop of Kition's decision to bring a suit for slander against a person who had charged him with freemasonry, and to do so immediately before the election:

He brought the matter into court on the eve of the elections of representatives, although the defamation had taken place a considerable time previously. He went to the town of Varosha, situated in the Archbishop's Province, in a tumultuous manner, provocative of demonstrations and counter-demonstrations on the part of the Christian folk, the consequence whereof might have been very serious, had the police not been present in force. He was escorted on his journey by a train of persons of the lowest class, and by harangues openly delivered to meetings of the populace he kindled the fires of passion amongst Christian men .... The Bishop's progress was a scene of tumultuous display, evoking a great concourse of people, in consequence of which an unfortunate Christian boy met a miserable death under the wheels of a carriage in the Bishop's retinue.[20]

They would also have been aware of the assault on Katalanos by a Kyrenia supporter; the counter-assaults by supporters of the bishop of Kition; the fracases in several churches in which supporters of the two parties beat each other with candlesticks; and the riots that erupted throughout the island when news was telegraphed that Kition supporters had attacked the archbishopric, which the police had in consequence closed.

The government finally decided that it had to intervene to settle the affair when Nicosia had reached such a state of bedlam that reinforcements of police and mounted infantry had to be called into the town from Famagusta, Kyrenia, and Larnaca. In April of 1908, the town exploded:

A large body of the Kyrenia party had come into Nicosia from the surrounding villages and collected opposite the Kitium Cafe of Saripoglou where a large number of Kitiumites were assembled inside. It appears from information received that stones were first thrown from the windows, the upper story and roof of Boulgaros's hotel, and the Kyrenia party then attacked the Kitium Cafe with stones, sticks, and revolvers, the stones were large river stones. The Kyrenia party also attacked the hotel, the windows and doors of the Cafe were completely demolished and everything smashed inside the hotel, and all the knives, forks and spoons were stolen. The Kyreniates also smashed nearly all the windows and did other damage to Mr. Theodotou's (MLC) [Member of Legislative Council] house. The adjoining houses of Mr. Derbi and Mr. Mavrogordato also suffered damage. Shots were fired by Mr. Zenon Zacharides, and he will be prosecuted .... During the afternoon, on the same date, the Police took away from both parties about 200 sticks, iron bars and bludgeons.

That same night, the police chief reported, revolvers appeared, and for quite a long time a gun battle near and from the houses of several members of the legislative council interrupted the Nicosia night.[21]

Not surprisingly, the bishop of Kition and his populist following eventually triumphed, and with an overwhelming majority of votes. If this was a surprise to the bishop of Kyrenia and elites of Nicosia, it was, I would argue, because their conservative appeal did not recognize that the printed word had begun to move from the privileged realm of the clergy into the public sphere. While literacy was far from universal, by 1910 virtually every large village in Cyprus was equipped with a school and a master. Moreover, in the drive towards centralization villagers were no doubt at least aware of the attempt to smooth out differences of language and culture through education, making it possible to imagine a community that was *not* divided by village or united only by religious leaders. In other words, there was little room for revealed knowledge in an egalitarian age.

The bishop of Kition and his cohort claimed new truths, truths rooted in a political economy of oppression and in the idealisms of ethnic imaginings. These were portrayed as eternal truths that had only to be evoked, brought to light. Katalanos, for instance, declaimed to Cypriot villagers:

> Formerly Crete was our property, afterwards it came into possession of the cruel Turks, and now Greece got it back. We, the brave Hellenes, should form an alliance, being united in one, and let us make turn round the doggish and infidel Turks like a kebab on a spit. I will unite Cyprus, like Crete, with Greece by making myself a bridge between Cyprus and Greece.[22]

Katalanos represented himself in a new public arena, claiming that public as his authorizing voice. Heidegger noted that "to glorify, to attribute regard to, and disclose regard means in Greek: to place in the light and thus endow with appearance, being. For the Greeks glory was not something additional which one might or might not obtain; it was the mode of the highest being."[23] Similarly, Katalanos "stood for" the people in a dual sense: both as their representative, and as a representation who "brought into the light" the reality of their being. One indication of how successful this must have been is the statue of Katalanos that now graces the main square of Nicosia, dedicated by his students, who remembered him as a national hero.

The politics of redemption

Only two years after the bishop of Kition's election, Cyprus experienced one of the bloodiest riots in its history. The riot began with fifty students of the Pancyprian Gymnasium, who were returning from a field trip late at night and marched through a Muslim village on the outskirts of Nicosia singing patriotic songs. In the dark, they were set upon and chased away by the Muslim villagers, whose patience had been sorely tried by months of Greek agitation, by a recent Nicosia meeting of nearly 10,000 Greeks to demand union with Greece, and by Greek taunts for the recent

Ottoman losses to the Italians. Two of the boys were lost in the fields and did not return home that night, and telegraphs shot to all points of the island announcing their murder. The riot ended two days later during the festival of Kataklysmos in Limassol, with five dead, 123 wounded, and thirty-seven taken into custody, six charged with "intent to massacre."

The year was 1912, and the island was shaken by its first large-scale intercommunal conflict. Kataklysmos—also known as the festival of Aphrodite—had barely begun in Limassol and Larnaca when news of the Nicosia events reached the coastal towns. Both Greeks and Turks had come from the villages for the fair, and in the tense atmosphere that had prevailed for several months, a few insults were enough to spark an inferno. In the preceding months, Greek Cypriot legislative council members had resigned their positions in protest against the tribute and the continuing British refusal to consider the question of union with Greece. Moreover, each Greek petition for enosis was met with an equally heartfelt petition on the part of the Muslims for continuing British rule or a return of the island to the sovereignty of the sultan. Greek Cypriots were encouraged to boycott Muslim businesses, and they were led in their efforts by their legislative council members, who refused to attend government social gatherings or the "at homes" of the high commissioner's wife.

The violence began in the area of Djoumada outside Limassol, where Greeks threw stones at two Muslim carriages that were passing by on their way to the fair. One of the Muslims inside drew a knife and stabbed two of their assailants, and within minutes the bells of the Katholiji Street Church began ringing to collect the crowds. The commission of Muslims and Christians that was assembled some months later to inquire into the incident decided that the church bore a heavy responsibility for the melee that followed. Women and children were caught in the rush, and in the midst of the confusion the mosque was defiled. During the next days, Greek papers were filled with horror-struck stories about the new Turkish terrors, particularly since many of the police on the scene were Muslims. British troops had to be ordered from Egypt to quell the panic of many villagers, who began to chase the Muslim *zaptiye*s away from their villages. Yet, it was the Muslims who began the first of what would be a series of emigrations: Within a few months, twenty-three families had left Limassol to live under the protection of the sultan.

By the time of Archbishop Sofronios' death, religion had already been politicized. We saw this in the last chapter in the case of the *lino-vamvakoi* and the demand that they declare their "true" allegiance. At the turn of the century, at a time when Greece was still expanding, this meant that the rhetoric of Greek "restoration"—especially the recapture of Istanbul, the old Constantinople and Byzantine imperial capital—was employed as an expression of the desire for freedom that had as its necessary concomitant the defeat of their Muslim rulers. This was a rhetoric of race and regeneration, in which the "eternal enemy" was always the Turk—a theme whose consequences I will take up again in Chapter 8.

Katalanos, for example, canvassed the villages just before the turn of the century, urging villagers that "the time to turn these irreligious doggish Turks on spits like kebabs has come."[24] The newspaper *Kiprios*, which would support the bishop of Kyrenia, accused Katalanos of introducing brawling and assaults into Cypriot politics, remarking that "it is very regrettable that the action and teaching in Cyprus of Mr. Katalanos have born fruit."[25] While both sides of the dispute would ultimately lay claim to the honor of Greekness, and while both sides would claim to desire union with Greece, it was the bishop of Kition and his coterie who turned the question into an ethnic matter, with that hallmark of ethnic consciousness, an eternal enemy.

And in a time of poverty, the rhetoric of redemption and restoration and all that it implied had tremendous appeal. As early as 1895, for instance, the streets of Nicosia had been filled with surging crowds battling in the name of their communal rights, calling for abolition of the tribute and its overwhelming tax burden. On Greek Independence Day, and again on Easter Sunday, Orthodox Nicosians had marched through the streets and insulted their Muslim neighbors, inflamed by a rhetoric of freedom that had as its necessary concomitant the call for the union of Cyprus with Greece. These crowds demanded that Cyprus be ceded to Greece or that the tribute be abolished, along the way insulting Muslim women and *ulema*, crying "boom, boom" to indicate that they would be shot. One schoolmaster composed a song which ended each verse with the refrain, "Let us kill the Turks with a swift sword and have our revenge."[26] The magistrate of Nicosia commented that

> For three days past I have heard what I thought to be idle gossip, relative to the feeling, religious in a sense, now existing in this town, between Greek and Turk—from what I can gather—this hostile feeling has arisen, through the torchlight procession which paraded through town on the night of the anniversary of the Declaration of Greek Independence. This procession happened to go through the Tekakhale Quarter of Nicosia, a quarter mostly inhabited by Turks, whilst parading through this quarter, the Greeks—schoolchildren for the most part—had the bad taste, to sing songs which referred to the slaughter of the hated Moslems. This has given serious offence to the Turks, and also, alarm.[27]

That these sentiments were pervasive cannot be doubted; their interpretation, however, is more problematic. The colonial secretary reported, for instance, that the mufti had complained that

> At Tochni on the road to Limassol there was a disturbance lately between Moslems and Christians; this bad feeling between the two races has spread to the women of the two creeds; they are insulting one another showing that race feeling runs high and is being talked about in private houses.

The commissioner further commented that,

> Public houses and brothels are open till the morning and are the cause in a great measure of disturbances. Greeks in the market place are calling Moslems "dogs and donkeys" but the Moslems have not to the present retaliated. At Larnaca the police have been assaulted.[28]

Much of this change was summarized by Muslim observers, who registered their surprise at the behavior of their Christian neighbors:

> Our Christian compatriots, who for centuries have been living under the blessed protection of the great Sovereign [i.e., the sultan] ... have during several years that is to say since the change of the administration, gradually and without any reason changed their tongues and manners, and commenced to show strange and surprising manners .... As long as the indifference and apathy of the Government, and the patience and mildness of the Moslems are continuing, our Christian compatriots taking advantage of every opportunity do not abstain from showing demonstrations which are considered to be an insult to the Moslems, they carry it on in such degree that in their places of worship, in their meetings, and in the streets they are openly making such speeches, and showing such demonstration, which no conscience can bear, and which causes great excitement and anger.

The author ended this commentary with a rather ominous warning:

> The Moslem inhabitants are registering with iron pens on the page of their conscience the events of the past sixteen years. But when that page is filled up, and there is left no space or extent to register more events, then they will be in the necessity of practically putting a stop to the events of daily occurrence.[29]

This was obviously a novel mode of behavior, unknown in the memories of those living during the period—something not only written about in newspapers, but also something fought over in the cafes.

Despite the anti-Turkish rhetoric, however, it is worth noting that the bishop of Kition often worked closely with Derviş Paşa and other Muslim members of the Legislative Council, as we will see in Chapter 4. Unlike the bishop of Kyrenia, who appears to have made no such alliances, the bishop of Kition seems to have united with his Muslim colleagues over opposition to the "old guard" in Cyprus, as well as to the Ottoman state.

They could also unite in a rhetoric of regeneration, even if that rhetoric by necessity implied different futures for the two communities.

It is clear that by this time the processes of identity inscription outlined in Chapter 1 had already become a point of rupture between the two communities. As we have seen, the idea of a public—and hence of an anonymous citizen—differed significantly between the two communities, as did the developing goals of education. Thus, the mufti complained as early as 1895 of the change that had overtaken their Greek compatriots:

> The change of the administration has converted the population into a different mould by the promulgation, all at once, of an excessive liberty, and has driven and incited the Christian (Greek) population to a lot of unsound and nonsensical thoughts, as if that change was designed to bring about a revolution in morals and usages. The Moslem population have however faced all the aggressive and right impairing proceedings and demonstrations of the Christian Community with perfect endurance and firmness, looking forward with hope for the measures and action to be taken by the local Government.[30]

In 1895, the mufti could still interpret the problem as one of government, which had allowed an "excessive freedom" to its subjects.

By the time of the Limassol riots, however, both communities had begun to use the language of race, vaunting the "natural" virtues of one's own group and vituperating the "natural" faults of the other's group. Hence, the polite letters sent by Muslim leaders to High Commissioner Adams requesting that the Greek demands for enosis be ignored were interpreted in a Greek newspaper as a natural disposition to trickery and flattery:

> Adams should have come to us that we should have been brought back to the times of Turkish tyranny and despotism, to the times when the Christians used, unsuspiciously, to fall into Turkish ambushes or used to be killed in the streets and when the houses used to be shut up from sunset; that the Turks, who by nature and by position, are presumptious and disposed to flatter, should have been encouraged by his well-known attitude towards the majority of the inhabitants, i.e. the Greek population.[31]

Similarly, the argument of race began to serve as a stronger pretext for asserting one's "natural" rights. After the Limassol riots, in a large gathering of Muslims at Nicosia, speakers condemned the increasing tendency to blindness on the part of their Greek compatriots:

> Both the speakers spoke in the same strain, as follows:—"The Christian Cypriotes were under the Sultan of Turkey & this Island was handed over to England to administer under a Convention. Ever since the English Occupation the

Christian Cypriotes had been agitating for their ideals forgetting altogether that
another race in the Island, the Turks, were also human beings & had rights."[32]

Contrary to the mufti's assumption, that "revolution in morals and
usages" was hardly limited to the Greek community. Rather, it arose
from a more fundamental revolution of imagination that would occur in
both communities, but at a different pace and in a different manner.

In the Greek Cypriot community, as I emphasized above, this meant
that "the public" became a contested space for claiming consensus.
What I have described here as "populism" was a mode of politics that
was essentially performative and hence rhetorical, though this was rhetoric in the ancient sense, as something that was seen to represent the full
flowering of cultural achievement. I discuss this in detail in Chapter 5,
but for now it is worth noting that this rhetoric was more than persuasion; it was a claim to define the real. This is clear in the ways that, for
instance, Ancient Greek often appeared in the public arena as a means of
influencing the public through an impressive performance which they
could not understand rather than through content. For example, one
police report of 1906 reported that a speech in the ancient language
made by the schoolmaster of Dhroushia "aroused the suspicions of the
Moslems who appear to have concluded that the speech was intended to
excite the feelings of the villagers and to incite them to acts of violence."[33] Populist leaders such as Katalanos claimed authority not
through prophetic power but through a claim to represent an underlying
"truth" about their constituency.

There are clearly interesting parallels that may be drawn here with
modes of rhetoric and public performance in ancient Greece. I would
like to point to such parallels without suggesting that they indicate cultural continuity; it is precisely Greek nationalism's dependence on a
thesis of continuity that has bedevilled the study of contemporary
Greece. In fact, in few other fields is the question of historical comparison, continuity, and change so fraught and so over-determined by the
claims of modern nationalism. In response to that thesis of continuity,
Michael Herzfeld, among others, has passionately argued that the concern with the ancients is really about the present of Europe and
categories created by European concerns.

Even Herzfeld's own *Poetics of Manhood* (1985), however, draws
attention to the modes of self-representation and performance that define
the selfhood of Cretan villagers and that appear to mirror similar forms
of representation that find their roots in the classical past. In particular,
Herzfeld's important study demonstrates that "Glendiot" villagers col-

lapse the modern distinctions between being and appearance, which we so often take to mean the distinction between the real and the unreal, the authentic and the inauthentic, the permanent and the transitory. This they share with their ancient predecessors, for whom, as Heidegger notes, "Being means appearing. Appearing is not something subsequent that happens to being. Appearing is the very essence of being".[34]

The populist rhetoric of the bishop of Kition and his cohort made them representative in the dual sense mentioned above: both as the people's representatives, and as those capable of representing them by "bringing to light" their true nature, as when they gave speeches in Ancient Greek. Hence, the claims of a Hellenic identity were accompanied by new modes of performance and rhetoric—what the mufti called a "revolution in morals and usages." Whereas the call for renewed devotion to Orthodoxy reproduced the paternal politics of an earlier era, the populist leaders of the bishop of Kition's movement announced themselves as representatives of the race and its redemption. Moreover, they claimed to evoke "eternal truths"; that the "eternal truths" that they claimed to represent were also exclusive ones that attempted to expunge an "Oriental" history is one of the primary tragedies of Cyprus' modern history.

Conclusion

The triumph of the bishop of Kition and his "nationalist," populist politics did not bring a Hellenic identity to Cyprus, but it laid the groundwork for a broader understanding of that identity not simply as political strategy and route to freedom, but as an expression of truths always already present. The bishop of Kyrenia appears to have seen himself as being as "Greek" as any other Greek-speaking Orthodox, and he appears to have believed in the unity of Greek Orthodoxy and therefore that it would have been right for Cypriots to join with their Orthodox brethren in the Greek kingdom. However, it was the discourse of race and regeneration employed by the bishop of Kition that eventually would triumph. Moreover, that language of race and regeneration was also a language from which the "Oriental" Romeic had to be expunged, and in which only the glories of Hellenism could triumph.

Orthodoxy *per se*, then, could not be a movement of the masses; that could be accomplished only through the rhetoric of race and regeneration. Furthermore, the rhetoric of an eternal enemy that is the hallmark of ethnic consciousness was easily employed to mobilize the dispossessed masses, who found in it the necessary concomitant of a Hellenic history that had been oppressed but not defeated. The redemption of the race meant, by necessity, the defeat of the Turks. It is not clear to what extent Greek Cypriots who spoke the language of race associated "the Turks" that they deprecated with "the Turks" who were their neighbors—although it *is* clear that Muslim Cypriots feared those threats and responded to them. It is also clear that anonymous violence became possible in Cyprus at the same time that a public emerged that described itself as ethnic, anonymous, and unanimous.

I do not want to discount the role in Cypriot politics played by events external to Cyprus, such as the continuing antagonisms between Greece and the Ottoman Empire. However, the 1897 war in Crete—which was close to home and increasingly bloody—caused only isolated coffeehouse fights, much the way a football match might today. It was not until 1912, when relatively distant events unrelated to Cyprus were combined with increasing poverty and internal political disputes, that real ethnic violence—i.e., violence enacted upon unknown others simply because they belong to a particular ethnic or religious category—created a danger of rupture between the two communities. Indeed, the triumph of the bishop of Kition meant that the language of race, redemption, and the defeat of eternal enemies would be the language in which politics would be conducted for many decades to come.

CHAPTER 4

Pashas and Protests

In his grainy photograph, the pasha wears a fez and a gold-embroidered jacket, and around his neck hangs the medal of his rank. He has the beard of an *âlim*, and his black, piercing eyes stare down at the camera from behind his thick mustache. Little is known about the person of Tüccarbaşı Hacı Ahmet Derviş Paşa, but much is known about his public persona. Around the start of the twentieth century, he was the proprietor of the Turkish-language weekly *Zaman*; an ally of the kadi, Vecih Efendi; a rabblerouser who canvassed the villages making speeches and spreading gossip; and for several years was the most influential politician in the Muslim community. In 1900 the kadi and his retinue caused a riot in the St. Sofia Mosque that came to be known as the mosque "uprising;" just a week before, Derviş Paşa had circulated through the villages around Kyrenia, collecting seals from the *muhtars* in protest against the administration of education and the *evkaf*—the issues about which the riot took place. It would probably be most accurate to describe Derviş as a Young Ottoman, or one of that group of educated, nineteenth-century reformers who sought modernization and Westernization from within the framework of an Islamic world empire.

This chapter explores a moment in Cyprus' history when a new "public" was being constituted amidst challenges to traditional authority. It was in this context that the populist rhetoric and rabblerousing activities of Derviş Paşa gained significance, as well as incurred censorship. In 1901, many of the *ulema* of Nicosia gathered to write a *mazbata*, or official report, to the sultan regarding Derviş Paşa's activities. In writing the report, these notables knew quite well that they were condemning Derviş Paşa to a trial from which he had no hope of emerging unscathed. And while the official judgment transmitted from Istanbul to the British government in Cyprus has many humorous elements, those same elements were obviously taken very seriously by those who had drawn up the *mazbata*:

The local mazbata, ... bearing the seals of the leading inhabitants, states that he [Derviş Paşa] stained the honour of the State by publishing numerous malicious articles, offensively against the person of His Imperial Majesty the Caliph, and expressly against the loyal ministry and the great governors of Provinces; that, driven by folly, he made a number of stupid publications against the local government also, in consequence of which he was made an object of all sorts of insult and mockery before the (local) Criminal Court publicly, he having thereby trodden under foot the dignity of the high rank possessed by him; that he not only scattered sedition among the Moslem Community, but, some months since, during the election of a successor to the deceased Archbishop, he went to the Nahieh of Karpas and instigated the Christian population to elect for a successor the clergyman called "Kyrillos" whose election was not consented to by the Christian notables, when the Greeks treated him [Derviş Paşa] with insolence face to face, and exposed him in their newspapers; that, taking no warning even by this, on Wednesday, the 1st of September 1316 (13th Sept. 1900), at about 4 o'clock at night (4 hours after sunset), the voices of "Zito Greece! Zito Kyrillos!" ["Long live Greece! Long live Kyrillos!"] were raised to the skies by five or six hundred Christians, partisans of Kyrillos, in the market places and streets, he being with them, under the Greek flag, when a great riot would have taken place between the two parties had not the Police reached in time; and that he was always the cause of such things, and ever inclined to sedition.[1]

Because Derviş Paşa failed to appear for his trial in Istanbul, he was sentenced—according to the Ottoman penal code—to imprisonment in a fortress for life and deprivation of all civil rights, on charges of sedition and failure to appreciate the high rank of *mir-i miran*, or pasha. While the local government chose to ignore the sentence of imprisonment, they thenceforth ceased to use the title of pasha in reference to Derviş.

What is interesting about the case is, first, that Derviş Paşa was sentenced for the dual crime of seditious activities and unbecoming behavior; this will be discussed at some length below. He was sentenced not only for his actions, but equally importantly for the form that those actions took, which allowed Greeks to treat him "with insolence face to face" and to "expose" him in their newspapers. The second interesting feature of the *mazbata* is its mention of Derviş Paşa's frequent associations with that faction of the Greek Cypriot community that was most vocally demanding union with Greece. The accusation lodged against him, however, was not that he had conspired with Greeks generally, but that he had conspired with Kyrillos (Papadhopoulos), "whose election was not consented to by the Christian notables." He had, furthermore, participated in a raucous public demonstration that almost resulted in a riot.

In fact, Derviş Paşa appears to have been on very close personal terms with the bishop of Kition, and they often worked together in the legislative council on issues such as community control of education.[2] Derviş apparently was significantly involved in the increasingly violent struggle for power that tore at the political and religious foundations of the Orthodox community. It is, indeed, significant that Derviş supported the young, charismatic bishop of Kition against his older, more conservative-minded rival.

Derviş was fluent in Greek, as was the kadi Vecih Efendi, a native of Ioannina and formerly kadi of Aleppo.[3] They and their supporters allied themselves in opposition to the primarily pro-British supporters of the mufti, Ali Rıfkı Efendi. Supporters of the mufti included Mehmet Sadık Efendi, who was the Turkish Delegate of Evkaf, a position created with the 1878 convention with the sultan. Derviş's opposition to the representatives of *evkaf* revenues continued with Sadık Efendi's successor, İrfan Musa Efendi, whom British administrators often described as the "most able Turk in the island." In fact, the single issue that perpetuated struggles within the community for more than five decades was the question of the care of and control of the Muslim religious foundations. In the villages of the plains and seaside, minarets spear the horizon, and small tombs or tumble-down mudbrick buildings are, by tradition, respected as religious devotions. Fields, workshops, and stores were called *vakıf* (pl. *evkaf*), or religious endowment, and their profits were dedicated to religious purposes small and large. After three centuries of Ottoman ownership, Cyprus was permeated with the signs of an Islamic empire, in which the religious and the economic, the spiritual and the secular, were not only intertwined but were one.

The gradual untangling of the financial and the spiritual was the work and the project of the British in Cyprus, who agreed with the sultan to administer Cyprus' *evkaf*, all of which they counted, categorized, and inspected within three years of their arrival. Some 100 of these were *mazbuta*, or administered by the state, while at least 220 others were *mülhaka*, or controlled by a trustee who was usually an heir of the *vakıf* founder. Prior to the British arrival, the Department of Evkaf in Istanbul had had at least nominal control of the *mazbuta* revenues, which had been redistributed throughout the empire. Derviş and his friends objected precisely to the control outlined in the convention, which put the management of *evkaf* revenues in the hands of one Turkish and one British delegate, with the approval of the High Commissioner. This, they claimed, was entirely un-Islamic, since it gave responsibility for the management of their most sacred religious and educational affairs to non-Muslims.

The question also acquired acute relevance with regard to the problem of education, since the British arrival in the island had signaled hard times and poverty for many Muslim Cypriots, who could not afford adequately to support education. Men such as Derviş claimed that these endowments belonged to the people and were intended as supports for the Muslim community, referring to the spirit rather than the letter of the rules regarding them. In other words, those who wanted education to become a means of progress and change insisted that the new relations of religion and state justified the conversion of *evkaf* revenues into community funds that could be diverted to the support of education. While the mufti accepted the state that supported his own authority, Derviş Paşa and others were rethinking the authority structure that the mufti took for granted. It seems that for this very reason Derviş worked well with the populist, anti-British faction of the Greek community: both the bishop of Kition and Derviş Paşa strove for the reestablishment of unquestioned authority, but with a populist base.

As we will see here, the controversy surrounding Derviş Paşa and his cohort centered on the role of the "enlightened" individual, who was the representative of "truth" or orthodoxy, and who was able to make truth claims on the basis of his behavior or comportment. In the first section, we will discuss this in terms of the distinction drawn at this time between "revelation" and "enlightenment" as descriptions of the type of authority that the modern state should have. In the second section, we will discuss what these two truth-claims have in common—namely, an understanding of truth as something that should be "revealed" or "laid bare"—and of the implications of this for leadership. We will argue there that leaders had visibly to embody the truth-claims that supported their authority, so that it was precisely on the basis of behavior that leaders such as Derviş Paşa could be stripped of their authority.

Enlightenment and revelation

One morning in early July 1900, the kadi ran in his nightshirt into the middle of the Larnaca streets crying for a beautiful girl. Only a few days before, he had roused the crowds in the St. Sofia Mosque and had vigorously insulted his enemies. Several Turkish notables from Nicosia followed and seized him, hauling him back to the seaside hotel where he had installed himself the night before. Though he had been recalled to Istanbul, the kadi never made it there. Instead, he was sent off to Lapithos, on the northern coast, where he remained until he was sent home to his family.

Interestingly, the kadi had been exhibiting symptoms of madness for months, but his seeming abnormalities did not prevent him from becoming a charismatic leader with worshipful followers. While it would be difficult to speculate on its causes, one of the most fascinating elements of the kadi's madness was his obsession with conversion and transgression. While he thrashed about in the Larnaca hotel, his servant could persuade him to take his medication only by telling him that it had been sent by "his friend, the bishop." And when a French doctor arrived with an Armenian translator, he immediately insisted that the pair convert to Islam. The translator protested that the French doctor knew no Arabic; the kadi ordered that he translate the profession of faith into French (a doctrinally incorrect, if not sacrilegious, order), then announced that they both were Turks.[4] This hint of the prophetic secured authority, at least until it caused its collapse.

Although the actors in this dispute consistently changed, the fundamental divide in the Muslim community until the establishment of the Turkish Republic was between those who believed that a revived Islam was the key to modernization, and those who called for a Western-style modernization that could only be implemented from the top. And so, at precisely the same moment that the Greek Orthodox community was rent by the first failure to elect a successor to Archbishop Sofronios, the Muslim community was similarly divided between the kadi, with his populist following, and the mufti, with his support by the elites and the British administration. The former used Islam to appeal to the masses and apparently believed that it was only an Islamic identity—the identity of the masses—that could be the basis for a modern state. An Ottoman identity was available only to a few and so could not form the basis for a populist movement. In contrast, the mufti and his followers believed strongly in the need for leadership and argued that it was only through "enlightenment" that the state would be saved.

The controversy began earlier, in 1899, over the conduct of the summer midday prayers. Two years before, the veranda of the St. Sofia Mosque had been enclosed at the request of the mufti, and he had since ordered that summer prayers be allowed there, where it was cooler. The Department of Evkaf, or religious foundations, had granted the mufti's request, only to find itself in direct confrontation with the kadi and his supporters, most notably Derviş Paşa and Hacı Hafız Ziyai Efendi. They strongly animadverted the performance of holy services in "the place of shoes" and insisted on its doctrinal incorrectness and disrespect. The delegates of *evkaf* suggested, in return, that "it should be courteously hinted to these gentlemen, who seem to have lost their heads, that they are interfering with matters which do not concern them."[5]

Within six months, however, such a furor had erupted in the Muslim community that the government could no longer state with such assurance which matters concerned whom. By the year 1900, supporters of the two parties could not attend the mosque together, and the kadi issued severe warnings against certain *müezzin*s performing their functions in the mosques. The kadi sent criers through the town changing the time of afternoon prayers, used police to control those who entered the St. Sofia mosque, and ordered the faithful to attend speeches regarding education and the *evkaf* revenues. In the middle of that year, members of the mufti's party transmitted a telegram to the high commissioner asking for government intervention. It ran in full:

The Hakim (Kadi) had the Chief Secretary's telegram, dated the 7th July 1900, printed at the "Zaman" printing office, and as if his conduct and behaviour, in conjunction with Dervish Pasha, at a public place such as the Saray Square, in vituperating a number of imams and muezzins of consideration and of rank, and his actions in dismissing and appointing some of them (imams and muezzins) so as to bring the blood of everybody to a boiling point, were not sufficient, he [kadi] proceeded to the Saint Sophia mosque together with persons such as Haci Mustafa Khanci, Mustafa Kafeci, Ali Faik, the Clerk Ahmet Muhieddin [kadi's clerk], and Imam Salahi, whom he uses as tools for incitement and for calling and bringing together the public, and with a large number of coffee-house people collected by him at the Mahkeme, the people going on foot, and he, together with Ali Riza, editor of the *Zaman*, in a carriage with utmost deliberateness; and while thus proceeding they uttered insults and allusive censures with one voice saying "May God overpower the enemies of the Hakim Effendi; may they become blind; may their children never be happy!" and they pronounced extraordinary and terrific imprecations before the houses of persons of honour and rank raising the voices of "amen" to heaven with intent to make themselves heard by the families of the latter. They announced through criers that speeches were to be delivered by the Hakim Effendi at the mosque with regard to education and to the Evkaf. He [kadi] gave orders to the police officer publicly and audibly, respecting certain people, saying "Drive away these pigs; throw them out! I am the commandant of the mosque, it is under my orders, even the Vali [Governor] cannot interfere!" and Bakkal Ali, and others of his [kadi's] assistants, rising up and committing acts of insolence such as giving out shouts, the people became confused; and the naib [kadi] has really been the cause of the prevention of today's religious ceremony. Besides the children dripping with blood under feet in consequence of the confusion of the people while the riot was taking place, women shouted saying "Mercy, our husbands and children will be torn into pieces!" and thus the Police even were driven to a state of confusion, and though but a moment remained for the bloodshed the affair has, through the good measures of the Police, been stopped for the present; but nevertheless want of security and excitement still continues in a very bad way. We apply for the immediate measures of the Government, and call its protection and attention, and we persons of honour petition Your Excellency for the preven-tion of Hakim from his aggressive conduct still continuing as if he were a second Government as witnessed by the Police.[6]

When asked to report on the incident, the commissioner of Nicosia, Arthur Cade, replied that there had really been very little excitement, just a few women letting out cries because of the crowding. He noted, however, that "on the departure of the Chief Cadi a number of his fol-lowers removed the horses from the carriage and dragged it themselves." He further remarked that the excitement appeared to have been too much for the kadi, whose health had since broken down.[7]

It was later that same month that the kadi was hauled from the Lar-naca hotel. Despite his discreet removal from the island, the campaign continued, as representatives of the kadi's supporters were sent into the villages to gain signatures on papers protesting the administration of *evkaf* and the organization of the *i'dadî*, or secondary, school. In the meantime, the mufti and his supporters stood aside from the rabble, appealing to the administration for reasoned intervention. In the end, the high commissioner wrote to Istanbul at the appeal of the Muslim com-munity, asking for a ruling about whether the kadi's or the mufti's judgment should be binding on questions of worship.[8]

It might be possible to see this ferment as a sketch in miniature of the turmoil of the late Ottoman Empire, but for the striking parallel with the dispute that was erupting at the same time among Orthodox Cypriots. Both the bishop of Kition and the kadi made themselves conspicuous through heated public displays in which appeals were made to and through the masses. And both closely allied themselves to the most vocal members of the legislative council, such as Derviş Paşa and Kata-lanos, who "managed" these public displays from behind the scenes. The religious was being consciously and conspicuously realloyed with the political, within the new framework of popular politics.

Furthermore, the mufti recognized that the kadi was making claims to a different kind of political authority "as if he were a second Govern-ment." In fact, the kadi had often called himself the sole ruler of the island, and his friend Derviş Paşa consistently described himself as the people's representative. Under their direction, the Muslim Cypriot community was first mobilized *en masse* in political demonstrations of support or condemnation. Moreover, Derviş and his supporters were known to circulate through the villages, discussing issues with the villagers and spreading rumors. And his was for many years the only Turkish-language newspaper of local concern, since the others were published by exiles from Istanbul who opened their publishing houses in order to criticize the sultan. It is significant that, unlike in the Orthodox community, there is no indication that the "party" of the elites ever had or attempted to have a public voice.

These two very different understandings of the public and its representation primarily conflicted over issues of public writings and public speech. Derviş seems to have been an all-round rabblerouser with a tendency to florid exaggeration, and (as the *mazbata* implies) he was often the object of legal suits over his publications. In fact, many leaders of the Turkish Cypriot community began to demand a censorship of that community's newspapers that became the primary cause of the death of a flourishing local press. Indeed, the desire to suppress opposing opinions led to the dissolution of all Turkish newspapers during World War I; they would not reappear again until the early 1920s.[9]

It is important to stress that censorship was not an accepted part of life for Orthodox Cypriots; it was an accepted part of life only for Muslim Cypriots. Certainly, the *ulema* in Cyprus saw their duty to control what Timothy Mitchell calls the "spreading of words,"[10] and they frequently appealed to the British government to ban newspapers that published articles that might be seen as provocative or critical of the government. The mufti himself wrote such a letter protesting the rumored application of Ali Rıza Efendi, headmaster of the *i'dadî* school, for permission to publish a newspaper by taking over Derviş Paşa's printing-house and type:

> As it is manifest that the object of such men is spite and sedition, and that he (Ali Riza Efendi) will make publications against the Government of Her Majesty the Queen, and against the Ottoman Government, a thing which Your Excellency would, of course, not consent to; and whereas Your Excellency has promised to grant no permission for the publication of any paper, either an application by fugitives from abroad, or by persons in the Island, without first referring the matter to me, Your Excellency's humble well-wisher, in order to ascertain whether it would be proper to grant such permission; and whereas the object of publishing a paper ought to be the rendering of service to the State and to the public, I request most pressingly that no permission may be granted to such spiteful and seditious persons.[11]

Similarly, the mufti had complained of the newspapers *Kıbrıs* and *Ak Baba*, published by Derviş Paşa, calling for the revocation of their license:

> It being evident that Your Excellency does not approve, and Her Majesty the Queen does not consent that papers like the "Kybris" and "Akbaba" should, by relying on the position in which they are found, dare to be so impudent as to make such imputations and calumniations against the august person of such an unequaled Monarch as is His Imperial Majesty the Sultan—the illustrious sovereign of the Moslems, who, as it is a fact admitted by all the great Powers, giving up sleep and comfort, always thinks of the welfare and prosperity of all his subjects; and it being manifest that Your Excellency, being in charge of the Government of the Island, has, by law, the power of chastising such insolent persons [as the proprietors of the papers in question], I pray, in the name of the Moslem community, that Your Excellency may be pleased to inflict the necessary punishment upon them.[12]

The mufti regarded it as his sworn duty to protect the interests and authority of the state.

Furthermore, the two groups disputed the other's right to speak in the mosque, as well as the right to control the appointment and dismissal of *müezzin*s and imams, or those responsible for mosque services and sermons. In fact, one might say that the supporters of the kadi and the mufti no longer spoke the same political language. It is clear that in such a dispute we witness an attempt at a definition of orthodoxy, what Talal Asad calls "a (re)ordering of knowledge that governs the 'correct' form of Islamic practices."[13] It would be far too easy—as Asad suggests—to see disputes of this sort as a "manipulation" or "negotiation" of religious signs and symbols in an attempt to assert or maintain authority. While "authority" was, no doubt, the central issue, it was an authority that was, ideally, defined by consensus and demonstrated, in the case of the kadi, by the crowds who pulled his carriage through the Nicosia streets.

Certainly, when the mufti appealed to the colonial government to prevent public speeches in the mosques, he did so with an evident incomprehension of the event against which he protested:

> The man called Salahi, who does not possess the least qualification for such teaching, did last year ascend the pulpit at the sacred St. Sophia mosque, quite of his own accord, giving rise to disorder among the people through his utterances contrary to religion, and he was consequently prevented from that action. This year, the attendants (of the mosque) were ordered not to provide a pulpit for him, and although he attempted to commit no such action up to the present yesterday I was an eye-witness when he possessed himself of a platform in the same sacred mosque and began to tell stories and speak nonsense, having behind him Bakkal Ali [a grocer], the katip [clerk] of the Sheri Court,

and others; and considering that the proper place for story-tellers is a coffee-
house, or some other [similar] place, such action in a sacred mosque being
utterly unlawful under the Sheri, and it being anticipated that in case of my
preventing him, in pursuance of my duties, from such action his supporters
may bring about a disorder in the sacred mosque this year also; and the giving
of advice by such ignorant and intriguing persons in a sacred mosque, contra-
rily to religion, is in nowise admissible, I request in the name of religion that
orders may be issued for the prevention through the Police authorities.[14]

The supporters of the kadi had claimed the mosque as a public space for
the Muslim community in which issues regarding that community
should be addressed. The mufti, on the other hand, expected the colonial
authorities to protect the mosque against secular intrusions.

There are two conclusions to be drawn here. Firstly, those who
defined a public sphere through their words—whether in print or in public spaces—did not speak *to* the people; rather, they used those fora in
order to speak *for* the people. But this did not mean expressing public
opinion; rather, it meant representing that opinion in a way that the
speaker himself deemed to be truthful. Even Derviş the rabblerouser and
populist apparently saw his role not as the people's voice but as a voice
that "stood for" the people. Not long after the riot in the St. Sofia
Mosque, Derviş himself wrote directly to the sultan about his role in it,
claiming that

> Thanks to me the rising which occurred in the Mosque was suppressed. A few
> young Turks have been arrested. Your Majesty is acquainted with them. It is to
> be feared that a further disturbance will occur, if an Imperial Order does not
> arrive. The newspaper *Zaman* has given publicity to the event in a special sup-
> plement. The Naib [kadi], your faithful servant, who has laid bare the secrets,
> was about to acquaint Your Majesty with the occurrence, but for the last
> eleven months Memduh Pasha has not paid him his salary. The Naib awaits
> your orders.

The kadi was responsible for a further telegram in which he claimed to
have suppressed the "revolutionary chiefs."[15]

As Derviş remarked in the paragraph above, such exaggerated
accounts of events were also being printed as news in Derviş's paper,
echoing a similar tendency in the Greek community to use the press for
the dissemination of rumor and hyperbole. But while Nikolaos Katalanos endured libel suits in response to his slanderous articles, the
punishment decreed for Derviş Paşa was a much harsher one, suggesting
that such articles were even more problematic for their readers. Giving
"publicity" to an event was to make it public, to make it known, to bring
it to light. Similarly, the kadi had "laid bare the secrets." It appears, in

fact, that for Muslim Cypriots the "public" was not an anonymous body of homogeneous opinion—what Kierkegaard called a "third party" which always observed our actions and subjected them to its judgment. Rather, the "public" was by its nature *all possible opinions* and all possible interpretations. Authority, then, is the claim to the *true* interpretation, to a transparent representation of the truth that's hidden by the clamor of false opinion.

This was, in fact, a consistent theme throughout the British period—a demand for authoritative interpretation—a demand for "the truth"—that would provide the support for political power. By 1912, many of the actors in the dispute had changed, but the issues remained consistently the same. At that time, the newspaper *Seyf*, published by members of the Liberty and Progress Club whose offices overlooked the religious court of Nicosia, deplored the lack of unanimity among the population, blamed it for the community's ruin, and scathingly attacked the community leaders who had allowed this disunity to occur:

> O Representatives and Heads of the nation! It is you who should pull us back and save us from that valley of decay. The matter of furthering our Education and saving us from ignorance, of urging the people to follow arts and trade and do good things with harmony and concert in matters concerning the public, and of teaching and encouraging them is a human duty that entirely belongs to you .... If, from the point of interests of the nation and country, we speak and write about those actions done to the nation, and about the calamity the nation was subjected to by those actions, they are, unscrupulously and without feeling the slightest shame, falsely accusing us of spite and selfish end, and misleading the people by sophistry.[16]

The article demands, on the one hand, that leaders act in a manner that accords with their duty, while it accuses them, on the other hand, of sophistry—or rather, of presenting false opinion as truth.

Secondly, as we will see more fully in the next section, the ideological divide was between those who appealed to the masses as Muslims and those who maintained their elite status as Ottomans. Furthermore, this division between Muslim and Ottoman represented a fundamental epistemological divide. A Muslim identity was achieved through accepting revealed prophecy, while an Ottoman identity was achieved through a process of "enlightenment." Revelation was available to anyone, enlightenment only to a few. But what both of these conceptions share is an idea of a truth to be accessed and "laid bare." Indeed, it seems that these are two poles of the abiding tension between consensus and truth that lay at the heart of issues of authority in the Muslim community. For while problems of interpretation should ideally be resolved by consensus of the community, the ultimate truth is that revealed to the true believer and therefore not subject to interpretation. In his study of Yemeni texts and contexts, Brinkley Messick succinctly describes this tension between *homo equalis* and *homo hierarchicus* implicit in much of the practice of Islam. In particular, the right to speak as a witness that is theoretically granted to all Muslims is in practice qualified by conditions requiring that that witness be a free Muslim of "irreproachable character."[17] The witness, then, must be shown to conform to certain cultural norms—thus demonstrating that his character is not unstable—before he can be authorized to speak.

Both revelation and enlightenment were theoretically available to anyone but practically available only to a few. The difference, then, had become one of political identity, in which Islam represented the masses and things Ottoman represented the elites. At this time, then, it appeared that Islam and its implications of revelation and prophecy could form the only basis for a progressive nation-state of equal citizens. Hence, when the kadi's worshipful followers pulled his carriage, they did so in the name of their own communal rights. It is significant, then, that it was ultimately the notion of "enlightenment" that would be deployed by Atatürk in his constitution of the Turkish Republic.

Muslim and Ottoman

Derviş Paşa's close ally, the bearded, respected *âlim* Hacı Hafız Ziyai Efendi, was eased from his position at the *rüştiye*—or junior high—school in 1896, after sixteen years as its headmaster. Some members of the Muslim educational board thought that, on "educational grounds," there could be no place for him in the new *i'dadî*—or senior high—school that they were creating, precisely because he had been trained at the prestigious university, al-Azhar, in Cairo.[18] Others wanted to keep him on to teach religious classes and Arabic, particularly since he was still only in his forties, with a large following that had already given him a seat in the legislative council. While his ties with the school would gradually be severed, he would become acting kadi in 1909 and mufti in 1912, and would serve in the latter post as *ex officio* president of the Muslim educational board until 1936. A Cypriot historian comments regarding Hafız Ziyai Efendi that "he served until 1928 as both an educationalist and as mufti, expending great effort for the progress of the

Turkish Cypriot Community, going everywhere in the island to investigate the problems of the people, to boost their morale, and to intervene for them in his position with the English administration."[19]

Although they greatly respected Hafız Ziyai Efendi, the mufti and Muslim educational board used strategies to force his retirement from the *rüştiye* school during its reorganization in 1896. Because they wanted to bring it in line with other schools of the Ottoman Empire, there was no room for a religious scholar as its head. Derviş Paşa and his companions, on the other hand, wrote of the Ottoman regime as "the sick man of Europe" and believed that a close association with its decaying body had led to their own decline. Within a very short time, they would wave the banner of religious rejuvenation as the best means to real recovery, and they would fight against the secularizing reforms of the *i'dadî* school.

However, Hacı Hafız Ziyai Efendi had also become associated with the decline of this school of higher learning. Two years before his dismissal, the building housing the school had become so dilapidated that it had to be demolished. In various British reports, the indignity of its demolition and the incapacity of the Muslim community to reorganize the school become metonyms for what was seen as the more general dependence, subservience, and fatality of Turkish culture. Indeed, from 1894 until 1897, classes were held in a hired house simply because no agreement could be reached within the community about the proper course of action. Moreover, enrollment had dropped from 141 boys in 1891 to only eighty in 1895.[20] Finally, the British administration took the extraordinary step of demanding a complete reform of the school that would bring it into line with other schools of the Ottoman Empire. A new building was built, and the school's reorganization was effected by Ali Rıza Efendi, former headmaster of the *i'dadî* school of Beirut.

Previously, young Muslim men had traveled outside the island for higher education, and they might subsequently be placed anywhere within the service of the Ottoman Empire. One of the eventual effects of reforming and opening Cypriot Muslim higher education was to keep young men within the island and to funnel them back to the village schools. The reforms had the unwavering support of the mufti, who ultimately opposed Hafız Ziyai Efendi's appointment even as a teacher of religion and Arabic, because the new style of public instruction followed—as in the Greek schools—a revised version of the Lancaster model. The new teachers supplied by the Ottoman government came equipped with voluminous regulations regarding classroom size, the color of desks, equipment to be used, and punishments to be enacted. This new concept of *ma'arif*, or public instruction, of which the *i'dadî* school was supposed to be the exemplar has been described by Berkes as "the learning of unfamiliar things."[21] Certainly, no other school of this sort existed in the island.

With a new building and new curriculum, the school advanced from the class of *rüştiye* to *i'dadî*—basically a difference between a middle school and a high school. It had been thirty years since the establishment of the first *i'dadî* school in Istanbul, and now the school in Cyprus would offer appropriate selections from the general curriculum, which included Turkish literary prose and composition, French, Ottoman law, logic, international economics, geography, world history, algebra, natural sciences (*ilm-i mevalid*), accounting, geometry, physical science, chemistry, and drawing.[22] For Cyprus, Greek became mandatory rather than French, which was taught only to the two higher classes.[23] The new headmaster made significant changes which ended only with his death less than a year later and the subsequent fight that erupted to control the appointment of a new headmaster and hence the future of Muslim education in the island.

The party of Derviş Paşa and Vecih Efendi tried at this time to force upon the school a new Ali Rıza Efendi, this one from Adana. The mufti, in response, wrote to the high commissioner, Walter Sendall, praising the recent reforms that had been made through Sendall's "kind, and education-diffusing assistance." Sendall, it was claimed, "having witnessed with his own eyes, during that period, the daily decay of the Moslem education has rightly had pity on our neglectful, and heedless condition," had built the new school, brought new masters, and put the curriculum in a "perfect condition." However, the appointment of the new Ali Rıza could, he laments, destroy all that had been done:

> The character of the teacher appointed being doubtful, his ability consisting only of Arabic and religious sciences, and he being unacquainted with the new science, and industry, we are convinced that he will destroy from the foundation the expected, and desirous progress, and we consider his presence, not only as Headmaster, but even as assistant master, to be a most dangerous thing.[24]

The mufti and his followers, then, were strongly supportive of the modernizing reforms, which were seen as one of the last hopes for maintaining the integration of Cypriot Muslims into the Ottoman Empire.

Literacy had always been the one essential requirement for entry into government service in the Ottoman state, and such literacy did not necessarily imply any further education beyond the ability to read and write in the various, appropriate calligraphic traditions.[25] Disappointment with—and, indeed, fear of—the perceived decline of the Ottoman state had led, during the Tanzimat period in the early nineteenth century, to a renovation of the educational system, beginning with the higher education from which were recruited the officials and functionaries of the state. Ottoman historians have often referred to this as the period of "Westernization," though I would prefer temporarily to suspend such labeling. Certainly, it was a period during which the state and its requirements were being reconsidered, and the *rüştiye*, *i'dadî*, and *sultani* schools (the latter being a particular type of high school) were created to provide a secular higher education that would be an alternative to the religious *medrese*. To call it "Westernization," however, implies that it was something more than an attempt to reproduce in the Ottoman domains the kind of education in which many officials had already participated in France and England and which was seen as appropriate for a state that was beginning to reconsider its religious foundations.

The literature on modernization in the Ottoman Empire and in the Islamic world more generally usually presents an unsatisfying antithesis between those who sought wholeheartedly to adopt a Western modernity and those who wanted either to accommodate it to Islam or to reject it entirely. In both cases, it is asserted that Muslims perceived their situation as one of backwardness, and that this was taught to them by military losses to technically superior Western countries; by the dissolution of the Ottoman Empire through the efflorescence of freedom-seeking nationalists among the minority populations; and by incursions of Western colonial powers into historically Muslim territories.

In such analyses, then, Muslims are always said to be reacting to the power of the West, whether by accepting it, rejecting it, or finding its ultimate roots in the traditions of Islam. Any of these choices assumes two complete, and possibly incompatible, systems of belief that must either be reconciled or destroyed. Analyses of the problem further assume an underlying intellectual unity of a putative "Islamic world" and hence usually fail to address problems of modernization as they appeared in practice. I want to propose here that the central intellectual problem encountered by Turkish modernizers at the turn of the century was the notion of "progress"—of a time that moved towards an open, ever-expanding future—and of the moral discipline that it implied. I

would like to suggest, furthermore, that many of the difficulties encountered by students of "Islamic modernization"—especially in the
Ottoman Empire—derive from the fact that their own analyses of ideology presuppose a unitary, "modern" subject, and in particular one
appropriately placed in a fixed system of classes.

The mufti who supported the "new science and industry" did so not
because he was a radical modernizer but because that "science" was
already an established part of the intellectual sphere that he inhabited. In
fact, the average, ambitious Muslim Cypriot parent had similar expectations from the higher education of his child. This became quickly
apparent to the new Ali Rıza when he appeared in the island and was
appointed. Within a few months, the new Ali Rıza complained that six
of the nine boys who had been awarded scholarships to attend English
classes at the i'dadî had left the school, and the inspector of schools
reported that four of these had gone to the Greek Orthodox Pancyprian
Gymnasium, where they hoped to get a more useful education.[26]

In fact, the first British reports assessing the state of the island's education indicate that lack of resources rather than lack of desire had kept
the "leading Moslem gentlemen" from bringing their schools into con-
formity with the new school system in the Ottoman Empire:

> The remaining schools in the town are all more or less poorly attended, and
> the less said about them at present the better. I must, however, add that many
> of the leading Moslem gentlemen, Fuad Effendi, Hilmi Effendi, and many
> others have spoken to me on the state of their schools, and one and all are anx-
> ious that they should be thoroughly reorganized, and brought on to an equality
> with other schools in Europe. They are desirous that really useful subjects
> should be taught, and the moral standard raised. This, I believe, is the general
> desire of most of the Moslem population of Nicosia.[27]

This "moral and material" reformation continued to be the expressed
desire of many of the ulema and elites of the Muslim community.

It was, paradoxically, the radical modernizers who supported a headmaster who—it was claimed—was trained only in religious sciences and
Arabic. And when controversy forced him to resign and another master,
Halil Bey, was appointed by the Ministry of Education in Istanbul in his
stead, complaints against Halil Bey by men such as Derviş Paşa were
always presented on religious grounds. When, for nearly a month one
spring, Halil Bey failed to escort the i'dadî boys to the afternoon and
Friday prayers, he was ordered to do so by the inspector of schools after
complaints from Derviş Paşa and others.[28] The custom—unique in
Cyprus to the i'dadî school—of the boys attending prayers together dur-

ing the Friday holiday indicates that the concern was not only with the boys' religious education but also with the singularity of their privileged position as future leaders.

The return to a simple, purified Islam that was demanded at this time by Derviş Paşa and other "progressives" was certainly not a reaction *against* modernization; rather, it was a *means to* modernization. Indeed, for educated Muslim Cypriots of all stripes, *kalkınma*—"progress" or "recovery"—depended on renovating the Ottoman state, and they were divided simply over the form that this should take. This reflected, firstly, a desire to return to the vibrant heyday of Ottoman sovereignty—nostalgia for an idealized past best reflected in current American demands for a return to "traditional" family values. Just as the corrosion of "family values" is, for some, the perceived source of America's moral and material decay, so a return to the values of traditional Muslim, Ottoman society was perceived by someone like Derviş Paşa as the only road to recovery. Secondly, the empire's decline had resulted in a soul-searching that compared the empire with those—such as the British—that expanded at its expense. Interestingly, many Muslims in Cyprus believed that they saw in the British Empire qualities—such as justice and strong government—that needed to be revived in their own. Finally, and most importantly, Derviş Paşa and his supporters saw that a Muslim identity was the closest approach to something that could be seen as a national identity. In contrast, an "Ottoman" identity was also an exclusive category accessible only to a few, who would represent the masses—a problem that would be only partially resolved with the Turkish nationalism of the republic.

While Muslims were created through accepting revealed prophecy, "Ottomans" could be created only through education. What these two sources of authority shared was their common lack of "modernity." The first proposed a religious, rather than a secular, basis for the communal identity that should legitimate state authority. The second, renovating the idea of "the Ottoman," involved an attempt to modernize a category that was distinctly unmodern—unmodern because it posited a hierarchical rather than shared past as the basis upon which the state could be renovated. It was not an ascribed but an achieved status—not a category of birth but a category of cultural attainments. That past was contained, furthermore, in books rather than in bodies; it was an identity that could be acquired through work rather than through birth.

In fact, it appears that it was precisely this immanently modern notion of *individualistic* equality—in which what makes us deserving of equality is somehow possessed by us and inalienable from us—that was most difficult for late-Ottoman elites. Individuals were culture-, religion-, and kinship-bearers whose identity depended not on "inalienable rights" but on attainments. In other words, whether one believed in revelation or in enlightenment, one still posited a type of knowledge that was not inalienable and that was, in practice, available only to the few who would lead.

Rather, we witness a different sort of transformation, succinctly described by Şerif Mardin as a cultural one:

> Since the beginning of the Tanzimat, we see a new characteristic emerge, that the "enlightened" individual came from a younger generation, and that the expectation was that the state would be saved by them. This expectation is the sort of idea that runs entirely opposite to Ottoman cultural expectations. In traditional Ottoman society, the person who was expected to rescue the state was experienced.[29]

Mardin goes on to explain that it was precisely the idea of an historical evolution leading towards a better future that made the new generation so important in Ottoman cultural life.

Hence, when allies of the kadi and mufti fought over control of *evkaf* revenues and education, they did so not only in the name of "progress," but more specifically in the name of a progress that would define and legitimate their own claims to authority. The alterations in the curriculum and the systematization of education were designed precisely to create an "enlightened" individual who could lead. This, I would claim, was the common assumption that united Derviş Paşa and his opponents: both sought to control the education that would produce future leaders, and they did so with the knowledge that both revelation and enlightenment implied privileged access available only to a few.

The importance of appearance

This unity of knowledge and personhood is seen quite clearly in the dual charge of seditious activities and unbecoming behavior lodged against Derviş Paşa. One could dismiss the dual charge as coincidental, yet the fact that a large group of Nicosia notables brought the charge suggests otherwise. In similar fashion, the activities of Greek agitators such as Katalanos became the subject of complaint by their Muslim counterparts only when the methods were offensive. A 1910 editorial, for instance, complained not of Katalanos' activities but of his words:

Katalanos is free to collect subscriptions for the Hellenic navy, nobody can prevent him from doing so, but he should not, in every speech he makes for that purpose, curse and swear at the Turkish Government and the Turks. We also are collecting subscriptions for the Ottoman navy, but no Turk is heard of to have defamed the Greeks, or the Greek Government, for the good breeding of Turks prohibits such defamations, and they never condescend to do such low things. Katalanos, who cost his own people very dear, is now trying in the villages he goes about to alienate our Greek compatriots from the Turks with whom they have been for years on good and friendly terms, to open a deep precipice between them, and in so doing, he is become the cause, as a natural consequence, of the occurrence of many evil things, which form an important matter the Government should take into serious consideration.[30]

While one's beliefs were the private affairs of the heart known only to God, those beliefs did not always coincide with what it was possible publicly to say.

More importantly, however, what the two conceptions of truth as "revelation" or "enlightenment" have in common is that they both see truth as something to be accessed and "laid bare." Derviş, in his controversial telegram to the sultan, claimed that the kadi had "laid bare the secrets." But, furthermore, those secrets are ones of an underlying order, and one's comportment should reflect one's access to that order. This is a somewhat unusual understanding of "representation:" word, gesture, and action do not "stand for" the truth, they *reveal* it. In other words, when Derviş Paşa was accused of seditious activities and unbecoming behavior, he was accused of making claims to truth that could not be supported by his comportment.

These links between truth-claims and comportment could be seen most clearly in the types of persons produced through education. There, the discipline in manners and comportment that was seen as an integral part of that education acquires a new significance as it is reduced to rules and gradations of transgression. Firstly, it should be noted that higher education—the education that would result in leadership—was seen as a privilege that should not be and could not be open to everyone. Canon Frank Newham, the inspector of schools from 1900 to 1930, remarked in 1904 that the number of Muslims enrolled in his English School had risen dramatically. This, he thought, was because admittance was so difficult:

They come because the payment of fees keeps the school more select, and also because I am exceedingly strict in enquiring into the character of boys before admitting them. It is known that I have refused as many as I have accepted, and this has done the school a lot of good among the Moslems.[31]

For similar reasons, the Muslim educational board had requested that the government reform the *i'dadî* school and would request in 1904 that similar steps be taken for the Victoria Girls' School.

Secondly, because a particular kind of breeding and Turkish discipline were expected to result from higher education, the control exercised by the teachers within their schoolrooms was absolute. When several boys from the *i'dadî* school presented a petition to the government protesting against the indiscipline of the school under the third headmaster, Halil Bey, the kadi deplored the action, remarking that it "is contrary to all good manners taught to Turkish boys."[32] Moreover, Mehmet Hacı Velizâde, who had submitted one of the complaints about Ali Rıza Efendi, roused the antipathy of Halil Bey when he ascended the *mihrab* of the St. Sophia mosque and preached that under the English government, "morals, considered to be the most important subjects of teaching, are not taught in the school." Yet, as Halil Bey pointed out in his complaint to the government, books were taught in all classes that included sections concerning the boys' moral duties; the book for the fifth form was, in fact, called "Laudable Moral Qualities" and began with a tradition of the Prophet, "I have been sent in order to complete the noble qualities of character."[33]

Such laudable qualities are reflected in the regulations regarding rewards and punishments, which were laid out in great detail in the official instructions for control of *i'dadî* schools, which were also adopted in Cyprus.[34] There, we find several gradations of punishment—some of them cumulative—for offences ranging from inattention in lessons to disobedience and disrespect towards teachers, to being seen outside the school in improper circumstances. The rules are intended as a complete guide to the schoolboy's daily life, both inside and outside the classroom.

Also, the punishments are designed to disgrace the offender publicly: One of the more serious punishments, the *tekdir-i aleni*, or public punishment, consists simply of "the public reading before the staff and the boys of the report setting forth the reasons why it is necessary to punish the boy, and the registration of the event in the general register."[35] And in the children's reading books, passages explain the heinous nature of such punishments: "Such boys as get 'Tevkif' punishments pass into the ranks of bad pupils and it makes his teacher extremely grieved," explained one. Another, explaining a somewhat more serious punishment, the *izinsizlik*, or withdrawal of leave, remarked,

Not only the teacher but also the father and mother of a pupil who is always getting an "Izinsizlik" punishment like this will be unhappy, and every one will find fault with him. And at school his companions will call him a very naughty and badly behaved boy. So long as a boy is at school he must strive to get no punishment.[36]

Silence, unquestioning obedience, and good manners were the characteristics expected and enforced by the regulations.

There are several conclusions that can be drawn here. First, one had to be "qualified" to lead, and one became qualified by demonstrating one's knowledge, one's "enlightenment." That demonstration, furthermore, was through certain accepted forms of behavior and comportment. Second, while leaders clearly had to be representatives of the "will of the people," their role as representatives was supported not by their popularity but by their transparent *iconicity*. Leaders had visibly to embody the truth-claims that supported their authority, so that it was precisely on the basis of behavior that leaders such as Derviş Paşa could be stripped of their authority. While those who supported the claims of revelation were themselves supported by prophecy and hence popularity, those who supported the claims of enlightenment were themselves supported by an elite status that revealed a closer and closer approach to truth.

Conclusion

Derviş claimed to reveal a truth about his community and to "lay bare" its secrets which had otherwise been hidden through sophistry. The challenge to Derviş's claims was in large part a challenge to his behavior, or his ability to represent truth through what I have called here a transparent iconicity. It appears, in fact, that the attempt to redefine orthodoxy took place as an attempt to redefine what could be accepted as representation. Because of the perceived problems of interpretation, it was necessary for representation—whether verbal or political—to be transparently *iconic*, i.e., transparently to reveal an underlying, unseeable truth. Moreover, the truth transparently revealed should be proven by the unanimity with which that truth would be lauded and supported. In other words, the ideal of the prophetic ruler was transferred with difficulty into representative politics.

The differences are subtle but important between what I call the demand for transparent iconicity in the Muslim community and authority based on fame in the Greek community. The similarity is that both

Katalanos and Derviş recognized the new authorizing circumstances
created by the new political arena and by the new uses of words. When
Katalanos declaimed in a remote Paphiote village that through himself
he brought the truth into the light and made apparent Greek Cypriots'
own true nature, it was a statement that depended at once on his display
of strength before an audience that already knew him and on that audience's ability to imagine itself as the abstraction that he described.
Derviş, on the other hand, found that he was both the writer and the pro-
tagonist of a history that was constantly being remade.

It should be no surprise, then, that within both communities there
came to be an increasing pressure for consensus and an increasing suppression of debate. In the Muslim community, the possibilities for
challenge to authority led to a need for suppression of those challenges
to prevent the perceived immanent dissolution of the community into
chaos. The two claims of revelation and enlightenment would only
finally be worked out with the Atatürk revolution, when "enlightenment" was utilized in the project of creating citizens for the new nation-
state. Ultimately, only the enlightenment project could succeed, for it
implies a closer and closer approach to truth that could be welded to
nationalist ideas of progress.

For Greek Cypriots, on the other hand, it became clear that debate is
fostered in arenas where truth is contestable, but not in those where one
is defined by reputation. Furthermore, it is reputation that defines the
person, in a manner quite different from that employed in Western
Europe. J. G. Peristiany has commented, for example, that to disregard
one's social evaluation by others is to place oneself outside the moral
order.[37] Epistemologically, the subject is not defined by the gaze of the
self at the world but by the world's gaze at the self—at one's place, family, position. It seems, in fact, that transmission of a so-called "high
culture" is probably fairly unproblematic in a society in which politics is
not necessarily based in egalitarianism but may depend upon revised
notions of hierarchy. But it is the definition of that learned culture as
"high" which deserves further exploration.

PART THREE

Revolutions

Introduction

From the high fortress walls of Nicosia, a wide boulevard leads inward to the gates of the archbishopric and to the square that has been and remains the center for Greek Orthodox life in Cyprus. On many days, the cantors' songs echo in the narrow streets, and the bustle of ecclesiastical business fills the neighborhood with black-robed priests, marriage applicants and their sponsors, the cry of children brought to be sanctified. Across the square and shadowed by bristling palms, the columns of the neoclassical Pancyprian Gymnasium stand serene, cerebral, and solid. The modern history of Greek Cypriot spiritual and intellectual life is encapsulated in one square block, which today is also graced by a thirty-foot black marble statue of the late Archbishop Makarios—ethnic father, underground revolutionary, and former president of the republic.

When the gymnasium was built in 1893, the streets emanating from the square were also home to the lawyers, doctors, merchants, and publishers who were patrons of the middle class, friends of the bishops, and English-speaking intermediaries with the government. At the time, several of them pressured the archbishop through anonymous newspaper articles to accept the funds that the Cypriot Brotherhood in Egypt was offering for the establishment of the higher school, which was to be the clean, ordered, disciplined organ of the nascent nationalist movement. From their cafes, they could have heard the construction, which involved considerable cutting of stone—an unusual and expensive practice in Cyprus. Over the next several years, they kept careful track of the Greek-born "professors"—among them Katalanos—who were imported to impart a higher, classical education to the best and brightest Christian youths of the island. And when these men began their fight to control the archbishopric, the school was torn asunder by their venom, like the child that Solomon offered to cut in half.

The central organizing principle of the Pancyprian Gymnasium was the creation of Hellenic citizens who could parse their Ancient Greek verbs, recite Homeric verse, prattle about ancient Greek history, and still be prepared to take an active part in commerce, in the professions, and in the intellectual life of the Greek kingdom that it was believed Cyprus would eventually join. Most importantly, the gymnasium became the training center for teachers of village schools, soon obviating the need to import Greek teachers or to send young Cypriots to Athens. Along with its much smaller counterpart, the Phaneromeni Girls' School, the gymnasium became the site in which Cypriots attuned to peculiarly Cypriot needs could be trained to address those needs while still imparting an Hellenic education. Only in such a way, it was believed, could the movement for union with Greece become a movement of the masses.

Education was one arena in which the British government, despite its efforts, would never gain full control. British administrators recognized quite early that the education imparted could never be sufficiently described by the documentary evidence that they collected—the books, the analytic programs, the inspectors' reports. They recognized that the real effects of education were in the teacher's voice, the ephemeral marks on a blackboard, and the near-magical powers attributed to the educated. Even until the mid-twentieth century, all the men in a village coffeeshop would rise when the schoolmaster entered. Although, under the British system of grants-in-aid to schools, masters were bought and sold between villages like cattle at auction, this observation belies the real problem of a village teacher: His power had to be wielded or destroyed, and the masters who successfully remained in one village were those who controlled village politics.

Moreover, resistance to government intervention was always strong, particularly since education in both communities was a sacred rather than a secular practice. The real control of communal education was never among the musty papers of the government offices or the "native" inspectors with their string ties and impeccable English accents. Rather, it was in the solemn, gilded halls of the archbishopric and in the nearby, smoke-filled chambers of the mufti. Within the first three years, British administrators recognized that little could be done in any area of education without the cooperation of the archbishop and the mufti, who controlled the priests and imams who—at least in the first years of the administration—were also the teachers of the village schools. Moreover, the financially-strapped administration could provide little economic support for what were essentially community projects and so had no grounds to demand increased control. And even when such control was successfully asserted in, for example, new legislation, it became clear that the system in place was highly resistant to change of the sort that the British wanted.

While there certainly were overt political, national intents in the content and teaching of education, we will examine here the culturally specific uses of that education in Cyprus, as well as the point at which and the manner in which an ideology became a practice. In particular, we will look at formal education as a valued tradition, something *always already* representative of community continuity, and at the implications of that tradition's dissemination to a wider audience. This analysis is, in fact, a direct attempt considerably to complicate the ultimately oversimplified analysis of education as "symbolic violence" by examining in detail what it means for education to be "the privileged locus of the illusion of consensus."[1] In particular, we will examine communities in which the practice of pedagogy necessarily contains a recognition of its arbitrariness that Bourdieu and Passeron want to claim must always remain unrecognized.

In both communities of Cyprus, education was explicitly described and debated as an ideological practice. This became quite clear in the first decade of this century, when debates over words and authority found their most crucial manifestation in the struggle to control education. As early as 1881, the English director of education, Josiah Spencer, had written regarding the role of the teachers and the importance of their words:

> I may be permitted to remark that of all things the most to be deprecated at the present time is the importation of Masters from the Hellenic Kingdom to spread sedition and discontent amongst the people. This is the avowed object of certain persons. And their pretended anxiety for superior scholastic training is a mere cloak for what I am told is in some cases an organized plan for weakening the people's confidence in the British Government and making them everywhere disaffected and disloyal.[2]

Spencer's concerns arose from the well-known policy of Greek nationalists within Greece to use the Greek schools of Anatolia and Cyprus to cultivate the *meghali idhea*, or the irredentist ideal of uniting all Greek-speaking peoples in what were seen as historically Greek lands. Through this policy, the Ottomans became pawns in their own destruction: Paradoxically, the liberalizing reforms of the Tanzimat aimed at quelling disquiet among minority populations gave considerable scope for the development of nationalist programs. For Greek Cypriots, freedom was to mean enosis—an ethnic union in which the Greek soul would finally find its full flowering in the liberation of political sovereignty.

It becomes clear in such discussions that in their education Greek Cypriots experienced none of the illusions of autonomy or indifferent objectivity that Bourdieu and Passeron claim are so essential for the functioning of pedagogic authority. As we will see, even the differences of social and economic class that have been shown to produce contradiction at the heart of the supposed universality of so much of modern education must operate differently in a closed, agrarian society in which education is both explicitly hierarchical and explicitly ideological. Similarly, the push for modernization in the Turkish Cypriot community led to an explicit emphasis on education as the appropriate means for altering patterns of thought. Both emphasized the consciously ideological and reproductive nature of education, describing the training of the young not only as the privileged locus of consensus but also as the site in which that consensus is defined as truth. Hence, British attempts to reform pedagogic practice always met strong resistance, since such attempts sought to reform that practice from an emphasis upon rote memorization to an emphasis on reasoning and problem-solving. Whereas the British sought to create citizens who understood what was right, Cypriots of both communities sought to train their children to know what was true.

In Cyprus, literacy and education had always had the social implications of a "tradition." Both the Orthodox and Muslim communities of Cyprus were "literate" communities in the sense defined by Goody and others.[3] To become a fully literate Muslim Ottoman meant that one learned not only Turkish but also Arabic and Persian—the languages of the Qur'an and of poetry. And to become a fully literate Greek Orthodox meant that one learned the languages of Socrates, of the Bible, and of Byzantium. Thus, schoolmasters and other literates received status, deference, and admiration not because of simple literacy—not because they had mastered some magical power of words—but because they had been inducted into the long intellectual histories of which each community was proud. The ritual spaces of church or mosque and school, and the persons of priest or imam and schoolmaster, received equal veneration and were often, in fact, the same. Just as a dilapidated chapel was sacred, so a dank, cramped village schoolhouse was a venerable site of learning.[4]

Similarly, education maintained its sacredness, even as it became increasingly secularized. Until the end of the nineteenth century, elementary education was a necessary part of becoming a full member of the religious community, someone who could engage in its rites and recite its texts. Paradoxically, the increasing secularization of education in fact led to more vehement attempts to represent education as a sacred part of community reproduction. Even by the beginning of this century, the archbishop protected education from British meddling with the proclaimed goal of maintaining it as the national space for the training of Greek citizens.[5]

Hence, while one cannot deny that education for its own sake was highly valued by Cypriots, or that educated persons obtained significant amounts of "cultural capital," I want to argue here that the ethnic experience of education was considerably more than that: that through education one became more fully what one was, in ethnic terms. Becoming a "true" Greek or a "true" Ottoman (and later a "true" Turk) was something achieved through education. As we will see, even in primordialist descriptions of ethnic identities in Cyprus, those were identities of "high" civilization, cultivation, and therefore education. Educated persons, then, were not only endowed with something that could be converted into status; they were, in experiential fact, *better* persons than their uneducated peers. In prenationalist terms, the fundamental goodness of education was inextricably intertwined with the roles that educated persons played: in the Greek community primarily as priests, and in the Ottoman Turkish community primarily as imams, judges, and members of the ruling class. In nationalist terms, that goodness was diffused. Succinctly, one might say that ethnic ideals were also ideals of civilization and civility; those ideals of civilization and civility required education, which would make one a *better* Greek or a *better* Turk. Therefore, by *modus ponens*, to become a better representative of one's ethnic group through education was to become a better person.

The next two chapters, then, explore the role of traditional education in the modernity of nationalism. Chapter 5 examines education not as propaganda but as practice, an institution in which Cypriots learned not how to *think* nationally but how to *be* nationally. Chapter 6 then looks at the moral discipline of the patriot, and at how that moral discipline differed for each community. For while one may have learned to become a better person through education, one learned to become a better person of a particular type. Education was seen as a necessary part of one's growth to full humanity insofar as that humanity was understood as being specifically Greek or Turkish. One might learn from one's father how to be good at being a man, but to learn how to be good at being a Greek or a Turk—i.e., how to be a good Greek or Turk—one needed education. But clearly the conception of a communal or ethnic humanity, and of educated persons as bearers of that social tradition, contained within it the seeds of potential conflict. One might, in fact, aspire to an identity that was exclusive by necessity. It was this, I wish to argue, that was in fact what occurred in the case of Cyprus.

CHAPTER FIVE

Educating Ethnicity

One brisk October night, flames licked and lit the sky of Nicosia as policemen battled against a barrage of stones hurled by young boys. The colonial governor had been writing a confidential dispatch on the seditious activities of the bishop of Kition when news of a speech given by that same bishop to an unprecedentedly large crowd in Limassol was telegraphed to his followers in Nicosia, who rang the church bells to gather the people. Shortly afterwards, a crowd of almost 5,000, mostly ruffians, criminals, and students, was whipped to a frenzy by the priest Dionysios Kykkotis and marched on Government House in the gathering dark. The pretext for the demonstration was a new tax law, even though most of the demonstrators were too young to pay taxes. After a siege of nearly four hours in which the youngest of the students formed a phalanx against policemen while the older students hurled stones through the windows, the old wooden structure was set alight. Within half an hour, this symbol and site of British colonial power had been reduced to ashes.

The year was 1931, and the reprisals that this action incurred would affect the entirety of the island until the end of World War II. For the next sixteen years, the colonial government would censor the press, ban demonstrations, enforce curfews, and acquire significant control of the schools, within which they believed much sedition was born. In his report on the events of 1931, Sir Robert Storrs, then governor of the island, noted that "in the towns the movement had in the process of time continued to make headway." It had done so because "fresh generations of youth sedulously indoctrinated with disloyalty had been launched by the secondary schools (in Cyprus non-Governmental) on all the professions; and, outside the Government service and the realm of Government influence and activity, every branch of public life in the Orthodox community was in some way allied to the cause of Union."[1]

Indeed, by the time of that eruption, every force in the Greek Cypriot community had been mobilized in the cause of union with Greece and had been oriented across the sea, to the mainland "mother." By 1922, the National Assembly was formed with much fanfare—though at first with little support—with the specific goal of using all means possible to achieve enosis. It claimed as members "all adult male Cypriot Greeks and all Cypriot Greeks living abroad;" the archbishop was its president, while the bishops were the leaders of the district committees. They established "national" youth clubs in the villages and an office in London, and they proclaimed that thenceforth the members of the Legislative Council would be answerable to the Assembly. Money came from the Church, from subscriptions, and from organizations like the Patriotic Committee of Cypriots in Egypt. Through the organization of the Church, they encouraged and supported the involvement of villagers, and many of their representatives were sent into the rural areas to deliver speeches explaining their position. In 1930, an election year, police reported 555 speeches delivered in villages, while police had on record 246 speeches in 1931 prior to the riots.[2] In fact, by the time of the riot, enosis had become the theme and substance of every social undertaking in the community. Athletic events, social clubs, reading rooms, clubs of retired servicemen, boy scout troops—all used their organization (and in some cases their quasi-military character) to rally for union with Greece. Not only in Cyprus, but also in London, Athens, Cairo, and many other foreign capitals, Cypriots were organizing in a campaign that for many would be their life's work.

The year 1931 marked a period of subtler rebellion for the Turkish subjects of Cyprus, as in May of that year they formed a "national congress" to assess the problems afflicting the community and to unite under a banner of opposition to government policy. Only recently, they had followed the Turkish Republic in a reform that in many ways marked the culmination of the traumatic changes of the Atatürk regime: Turkish Cypriots had changed their alphabet. Newspapers began to print in the Latin script, and night classes were established to teach the new alphabet to the already literate and to educate the illiterate in the simpler language of the new Republic. A group that had only recently defined itself as ethnic was reaching into the pre-Islamic, pre-imperial past in an attempt to characterize that ethnicity. Rupture thus became as much a part of the new Turkish identity as a putative cultural continuity characterized the Greek *ethnos*.

It was the belief of British administrators in Cyprus that much sedition in the island was born in the schools. Colonial administrators frequently accused schoolmasters of instilling nationalist sentiments in the young and of stirring up trouble in the villages, often by political rallying. It is easy to take such accusations at face value, especially since they accord so well with our own "common-sense" notions about the ways in which education has been used in nationalist projects to disseminate elite-derived nationalist histories and sentiments. But when one looks more carefully at the position of schools, pupils, and masters within the social structure of the island, contradictions in this thesis immediately become apparent. When such a small proportion of children was receiving an education beyond basic reading and writing, how could nationalism be disseminated through the schools? How did young people who set themselves apart from the community through education manage to become not only leaders but representatives and articulators of the desires and needs of the communities? How could the chaotic and *ad hoc* nature of education result in something as systematic as patriotism?

This chapter takes up this question by examining the relationship between education and nationalist selves, contending that the relationship was not one based on "propaganda" but on perceived tradition, and that it relied not on "inculcation" but on mastery. I have argued elsewhere that education in Cyprus was necessary for nationalism because education already embodied community traditions and represented communal continuity.[3] As I noted in the Introduction to Part Three, both the Greek Orthodox and Muslim communities of Cyprus were literate in the sense that they considered the best, most representative, and indeed most virtuous aspects of the communities to be embodied in the texts and traditions learned through formal schooling. Education was something that was supposed to create better persons, persons who embodied communal understandings of virtue or worth. In Cyprus, in both the Greek and Turkish communities, it has been common to say that one went to school to "become a person" (Turkish: *insan olmak*; Greek: *na ghinei anthropos*). Certainly, students became—in a very fundamental sense—different persons through education.

This chapter first examines the vexed issue of "propaganda" in the schools, arguing that schooling should in fact be assimilated to the much wider practice of apprenticeship, in which one makes oneself into a master of a body of knowledge. I then argue that this form of schooling resulted in considerably different conceptions of what could be seen as a "master" of those bodies of knowledge. For Greek Cypriots, the intellectual created through the schools was a rabblerouser, a speechmaker, even a show-off and poseur. This was the case, I want to argue, because persons, in the Greek conception, were always already ethnic beings, and the fuller realization of that through education entailed a comportment that iconically represented the evocation of his Greekness. For Turkish Cypriots, on the other hand, the teacher, leader, and scholar were to be grave and respectful, iconically representing the seriousness of the traditions of truth that they embodied. This was the case, I will argue, because persons, in the Turkish conception, were bearers of a culture into which one was born but about the nature of which one needed to be "enlightened." In other words, as educated members of each community fashioned themselves into persons better capable of realizing the ideals represented by "high" culture, they also came to embody very different ideals, and ones that would ultimately come into conflict.

The formation of an aesthetic

In photographs striving to capture Cypriot life near the beginning of the twentieth century, pretty Cypriot girls stare shyly and wistfully into the camera or avert their faces. In some photos, they self-consciously pose in party clothes that they have embroidered, while in others one sees them shaping pottery, weaving cotton cloth, stitching exquisite lace creations, or working in the fields. Muslim women are caught only as a blur of black in the background, but one sometimes finds their young, unveiled daughters in these photos—brown, bashful, and indistinguishable from their Greek neighbors except by their clothes. Boys pose with their sheep in imitation of their audacious shepherd fathers or shoulder their way into the photos of factories and marketplace. In one photograph from a dye factory, men stand side-by-side with equal numbers of boys who barely reach their chests.

Most children in Cyprus were workers, cherished not for their sweet faces and play but for their silence, obedience, and labor value. In these circumstances, the school was a world apart, entered through considerable self-denial and struggle. The largest villages in the island—of which there were only a handful—contained no more than a few hundred inhabitants, yet these were virtually the only villages able to raise enough funds to build separate schoolrooms, or to provide desks, chairs, boards, and books. In such villages, two or perhaps three masters might teach upwards of 200 pupils of varying ages from surrounding villages, often in the same room amidst a terrific cacophony. In the smaller villages, one master handled all the classes, often teaching in his house or in whatever old building could be spared. Children scribbled their lessons on boards, in the dirt, and even on their persons, and it was not uncommon for them to work in unlit rooms without adequate windows as their peers grazed sheep in the poppy-covered fields or worked with their families in the orchards.

Apprenticeship and servitude of children were common for most poor rural families, and it was a lucky family that owned enough land to provide for the children's futures without sending them to work in the towns. It was an even luckier and rarer family that could send its children to school beyond the age at which they could begin to work. Only the family truly blessed by fortune or determined on advancement at all costs could educate all its children or send one or more of them to secondary school. In many circumstances, however, at least one boy of a rural family would be apprenticed at around the age of seven to a master for whom he would act for some years as a servant before gradually learning a trade. Girls of especially poor families were often sent into domestic service in the towns at about the same age, essentially acting as indentured servants for a number of years, after which the family for whom the girl worked would ideally provide her with a dowry and either find her a husband or place her in another line of work. "Family life" was attenuated along the lines of economic advancement or survival, and the romantic ideals of home and hearth so dearly cherished by the British rulers of Cyprus found little scope in this world of work.[4]

Needless to say, the ideals of practical education and childhood labor rarely matched the reality. It was a common complaint, for instance, that too many of the girls sold into domestic service entered a type of concubinage that often ended in prostitution. Attempts to legislate against it usually failed, since such girls were rarely seen in public until after their release from servitude. Even as late as 1931 the practice was clearly common, since a Nicosia hostel opened three years earlier to house such girls reported that seventy-one from that town alone had passed through its doors during the year.[5] The treatment of boys tended to be rough but practically rewarding, since they learned skills and trades that would secure their futures. One man who had been apprenticed to a Famagusta carpenter in the 1920s laughingly recalled that the carpenter had always brought his apprentices in from their chores and offered them plenty of water before their meals, hoping to fill the boys' stomachs before having to feed them. It was not until rather later that the apprenticeship of girls was given attention: a Nicosia seamstress, for example, kept a houseful of young teenage girls in the 1960s and 1970s, teaching them the art in return for small payments by their families and for the girls' manual labor.

In these circumstances, the school was a world apart, though not because it was part of a "public" world that children entered outside the "private" world of the home. What set the school apart and provided it with an unbroken rhythm of its own was not the distinction between public and private life but a more fundamental epistemological association of word and power. Cypriots were poor and primarily illiterate, and it had been in most cases at the initiative of unlettered parents that schools had been founded—organized would be too strong a word—for the village children. They would scrabble together the money to build or lease a room, hire a teacher at a competitive rate, and periodically spare their children to attend the classes and learn reading and writing. Education was certainly an *ad hoc* affair, engaged in when time and work permitted. One of the great incentives for poor Cypriots to give their children even a very basic education was the promise that they would learn the rudiments of their religion, especially since priests and imams very often acted as village schoolmasters.

In social terms, the teacher was granted absolute power in the classroom at the same time that he was virtually powerless within the community. The teacher had absolute authority to control his students— who knew the terrible punishments that could await them—and was encouraged by parents to use it. Usually this simply involved beating the child with sticks, but it could also mean forbidding him to have his lunch, forcing him to carry heavy rocks, or confining him, perhaps in a dark place. Another frequent punishment used a crude type of stock to pin the boy's feet while the teacher beat the soles with rods. In any case, the parents relinquished the child to the teacher's control and expected that such punishments would follow. Parents would leave their children with the teacher, saying in Greek, "*Dhaskale, kreas dhiko su, kokkala dhika mu*" or in Turkish, "*Deri senin, kemikler benim*"—"Teacher, the flesh is yours, the bones are mine."[6] Historian Yeorghios Prodhomou describes how such terror was a central part of the teacher's authority and how mothers often controlled their disobedient children by threatening, "I'll send you to school to learn!" He reports how one teacher nailed a student's ear to the wall, while another accidentally killed a pupil while punishing him for an error in recitation. The latter became known by the nickname Kannettin (from the Turkish word *kan*, or blood), and lenient teachers would often hear the rebuke, "Ach, now *Kannettin* was a *teacher*!"[7]

Given the respect of Cypriots for education and the educated, and the absolute control exercised in the classroom, it seems paradoxical, then, that schoolmasters during this period were abused, maligned, libeled, victimized, and traded between villages like horses at auction. School committee elections became occasions for terrible, slanderous fights in which the teacher would have to ally himself with a person or a faction, often promising parts of his salary in advance so that votes could be bought. In response, the opposing faction would often accuse the teacher of indecent or immoral behavior and would not infrequently demand government intervention. Those teachers who were not politically committed would often be forced repeatedly to sell themselves to the highest bidder, and would move each year from village to village, from district to district.

All sides could agree that the education of the children suffered from the chaos caused by such rivalries, in particular because of the resulting inability or refusal of village committees to pay teachers a decent wage.[8] The first "inspector of schools," the Reverend Josiah Spencer, commented that in these early decades of British rule, "In more than one of the most important Christian villages rival committees and rival schools of a temporary character have been found, preventing until lately the establishment of good and permanent schools in those places." Most newspapers agreed with Spencer, though they framed their remarks in even more negative terms:

> Neither the state nor the society is justified in remaining apathetic spectators, as we have entrusted to these people the education of our children .... If in the home one gives the first moral lessons, the teacher is he who cultivates those and roots them in the soul of the child. Thus, when we are indifferent to these individuals and when they are not recompensed or are recompensed inadequately, discouragement naturally occurs, the teacher becomes discouraged and from disinterest does not manage or fails in the fulfillment of his duties.[9]

The writer felt it necessary to articulate the problems of non-payment, since the social status of masters in fact required them to teach, whether they were paid or not. It should be noted that the problems outlined by the newspapers were not the concerns for continuity articulated by Spencer and others. Rather, they were concerned for the teachers' dignity and expressed worry that they would not be able to fulfill their expected role.

All of this seems to undermine the usual story told by scholars about Cyprus, in which a new, ideologized, intellectual class used the schools and the newspapers to hammer home nationalist propaganda that eventually became part of daily life in the island. Throughout the period of British rule in the island, administrators constantly decried the "propagandizing" and "troublemaking" role of elites, and especially of teachers. Administrators were particularly concerned about Hellenic propaganda, and the British director of education suggested as early as 1881 that

> exceeding care must be taken to prevent the employment as masters in any schools assisted by the Government of political agents who might think it their duty to stir up in the hearts of the otherwise contented and loyal villagers, those aspirations and longings which have been so often shown to be unreasonable and hopeless, and which can produce no other result than discontent and unhappiness.[10]

Indeed, whenever confronted with "discontent" or "agitation," British administrators in the island primarily blamed an elite group of nationalist agitators, particularly in the Greek community, whose attempts to rouse the "patriotic" sentiments of their compatriots occasionally produced results.

Despite this, though, administrators consistently complained of the ineffectiveness of education in Cyprus and repeatedly battled with Cypriot leaders to try to change it. Among other changes, one of the most important that British administrators wished to see was instruction in students' "native" languages. Cypriot resistance to such change worried the administration throughout the colonial period, since it presented a problem—the problem of understanding the apparent emotional efficacy of forms of language that Cypriots did not easily understand. It is well known that the Greek spoken in Cyprus, *Kipriaka*, is different enough from the Greek of Greece as to be often incomprehensible to other Greek-speakers. It is also common knowledge that a large number of Muslim Cypriots spoke *Kipriaka* as their first language, and that those with Turkish as a first language spoke a form of Turkish highly influenced by their *Kipriaka*-speaking neighbors. But the languages of education were "high" languages—the reconstructed *katharevousa* Greek taught in the schools of Greece, along with the ancient language; or in Muslim schools the languages were first Arabic as the language of the Qur'an, then Persian as the language of poetry, and finally Ottoman as the language of bureaucracy. None of these forms resembled the languages spoken in the "mainlands" of Greece and Anatolia, and certainly they bore little resemblance to the forms of Greek and Turkish spoken in Cyprus.

And so from the moment of their arrival and for many decades following, British colonial administrators complained that young students spent incredible amounts of time memorizing languages that they did not understand while learning nothing of the language that they actually spoke. The first inspector of schools commented in 1881, for instance, that Muslim village schools spent too much time on Arabic, first, and then on Persian:

> They begin at the wrong end in their teaching, and as most of the children are taken away at an early age to work with their parents, the result is that many of them never arrive at the beginning, never learn to read and write Turkish at all .... I have pointed out everywhere that to spend a portion of the day in learning to read and write their own language would be a help and not a hindrance to the children in mastering the lessons which at present occupy all their time. The task of committing to memory words which convey no meaning to their minds is too prolonged and severe, and would itself be more quickly accomplished if they had from time to time the relief of a lesson that they could understand, and which would interest them.[11]

He made similar remarks about the Greek schools:

> Grammar has always been the great forte in the Greek schools; but in the villages they did not learn to speak or write much the better for it .... The village children are not long enough at school to learn the ancient Greek Grammar to any purpose. They have hitherto generally gone to their work in the fields, in spite of all the grammar they have said by heart, unable to speak or write the simplest sentence of modern Greek correctly.[12]

Other observers, such as C. D. Cobham, commissioner of Larnaca, made similar remarks for the teaching of history:

> The other day I found in a large hill village a class, wholly ignorant of the elements of hygiene or rural economy, pattering details from the history of the Hyksos and of Sicyon. Naturally their streets were filthy, and their modes of cultivation pre-historic.[13]

If we leave aside the remarks about Cypriots' hygiene, we are left with a general picture of a "knowledge" that is learned but presumed not to be understood.

The idea of the efficacy of a language that one cannot understand was echoed by Muslims in 1906, when several petitions were sent to the government, praying for the protection of the rights of Muslims in the island. The commissioner of Paphos, C. G. Wodehouse, wrote to the chief secretary to say that the Muslims' sense of being threatened had arisen because of a speech given in their village:

> I believe the whole trouble to have arisen through an ill judged speech delivered by the school master of Droushia, on the occasion of the anniversary of the Independence of Greece on the 25th of March. The speech was made in *Classic Greek* this aroused the suspicions of the Moslems who appear to have concluded that the speech was intended to excite the feelings of the villagers and to incite them to acts of violence.[14]

There is no implication that the ancient language was comprehended by villagers, but it appears nevertheless to have been emotionally efficacious.

One of the great difficulties encountered by administrators who wished to reform the schools was language-teaching and its relationship to religion. In both communities, education had long been a sacred, rather than a secular, practice, and schoolmasters at the beginning of the British colonial period were usually priests and imams. Colonial officials requested and soon required that the Muslim schools first teach the children to read and write Turkish before forcing upon them the difficulties of Qur'anic Arabic and literary Persian, the relevant parts of which languages they seemed only to memorize, in any case. They could do less in the wealthier Greek schools—which were less dependent upon government aid—but still required those funded by the government to teach the children to read and write modern Greek, i.e., *katharevousa*.

Despite their need, village committees followed the lead of church leaders in rejecting government grants when it became known to them that Spencer had recommended in 1880 that English become the language of instruction throughout the island. This he recommended "from no political motive but on purely educational grounds," and his remarks were printed in the Cyprus Blue Book reports, which were readily available in the island. The agitation against Spencer's comments was such as to force an apology from the Earl of Kimberley, then Secretary of State for the Colonies, who asseverated that Greek, "regarded as a vehicle of education affords ample means not only for an ordinary education but for the attainment of a high degree of mental culture."[15] Spencer himself wrote a further memorandum in which he claimed to have been misunderstood:

> As to the teaching of English in native schools, it has only been provided where it has been earnestly desired by the people; and the introduction of this

study into the curriculum of these schools has not been regarded as in any way superseding or disparaging the native languages.

He did not include in the official memorandum a further remark that "the real value of [the native languages] (especially of Ancient Greek) for mental culture, the people may by *this very means* be brought to understand."[16] The means to which he referred were higher instruction, which he believed to be available only in English.

The goal of British administrators in their reforms was clear: in the first instance, to teach the children to read and write the languages that they spoke and to sum for business purposes. For those children able to progress past elementary school, they sought to establish schools and curricula that would teach pupils the modern "mental culture" of which both Spencer and Lord Kimberley wrote. When two "educational experts" reported on the island schools as late as 1912, they commented regarding the Muslim schools that

> it is as much as the inspectors can do, even in the better schools, to suggest that the children should be trained to rely more upon their own common sense and less on mere learning by rote, that they should be taught to read books with some understanding of their contents, and to express their own thoughts with fair readiness, both in speaking and in writing.[17]

Although praising of the attempts at reform in the Orthodox schools, very similar comments were applied to them, as well:

> Too little stress seems to be laid on training the children from the earliest stage to describe their own ideas and experience in their own words. On the other hand, the Programme gives undue prominence to transcription and other mechanical exercises, valuable enough in their way provided they are not employed, as they so often are where the teacher has several classes to manage, merely as the most convenient means of keeping the children out of mischief.[18]

The transformation of Cypriot education into a system which produced thinking, reasoning, expressing individuals was one which preoccupied colonial administrators throughout the British period. The project of "thoroughly modernizing" their Cypriot subjects would even lead colonial administrators somewhat later to an attempt to supersede the apprenticeship system by providing further, practical education, such as woodworking and horticulture, or "domestic sciences" for girls.

The significant difficulties for British educators in reorganizing the Cypriot educational systems, as well as the resistance with which their efforts were met, provide some indication of the very different goals of the communities themselves for their educational systems. The primary hope of those acquiring more than an elementary education was an appointment to a government position, which was considered to be the best and most secure career path. This would suggest that Cypriots saw education as a practical means of advancement, and one might expect that they would be only too ready to approach education more "practically." Yet it is clear that the decision to give a child a secondary education was not a pragmatic one, since there were often shortages of the government jobs that these men sought. Furthermore, these young men could become a financial burden on their families, since any secondary school graduate would not be expected to engage in manual labor, even when he could find no other employment. Instead, he would often grow the fingernails of his pinky fingers long to indicate his more educated status and would spend his days debating politics in the coffeeshops.

Furthermore, it would always be difficult to reform organization and curricula when pedagogy focused, not on the systematic training and disciplining of the mind, but on memorization and recitation. Although the Greek schools of Cyprus had supposedly adopted the much-vaunted and much-discussed Lancaster method as early as 1859,[19] the schools of Cyprus were hardly disciplinary machines of the sort described by Foucault.[20] The schools were not ordered but chaotic, were not quiet centers of monastic discipline but cacophonous centers of arbitrary punishment. And it was unnecessary for them to be Lancaster copies, since the embodiment of written materials meant that those materials rather than the person were the focus of training. One became a person who had mastered literatures rather than one who had mastered a technique.

While the fetishization of language is an infamous part of the nationalization process,[21] its role in creating an imagined community is not enough to explain the process at work here. For British administrators, what was puzzling about Cypriot education was that it appeared to produce people who were better ethnic representatives of their communities, but it did so through an education that students appeared not to understand. Clearly, the assumption at work, derived from Western social theory, was that education is supposed to be about *learning how to think*. The concomitant idea that nationalist "propaganda" taught in the schools produces nationalist subjects also relies on a very similar view of the role of education: supposedly, education teaches us how to *think* nationally, rather than how to *be*.

In contrast to this, I believe that education in Cyprus must be seen as something much more akin to apprenticeship, in which the pupil becomes the master of a body of knowledge, which he or she at the same time embodies. Indeed, in the techniques of learning, in the master's relationship with his pupils, and in the pupil's relationship to the knowledge learned, there was virtually no substantial difference between the school and the workshop. This comparison, I believe, helps to resolve one of the significant problems in thinking about the relationship between education and nationalism: namely, how certain kinds of teaching supposedly *produce* nationalist subjects. Rather than looking at schools as sites of *production* (or even of reproduction), I believe that they should be seen as sites of very specific kinds of socialization. One did not *acquire* (skills, knowledge, etc.), one *became* (a type of person capable of doing X). Through schooling, one became a master of certain bodies of knowledge and a particular type of person. That type of person, I wish to claim, was the master of a body of knowledge that had come to represent the traditions of the community. It is in this way that the "high culture" of schooling could be converted into nationalism.

Indeed, it was over the implicit assumption that education is about learning *how to think* that Cypriots and their colonial rulers consistently conflicted. For example, both Orthodox and Muslim communities in Cyprus clung to rote memorization and the learning of "useless" things despite British administrators' attempts to teach them the error of their ways.[22] Dale Eickelman has described the rote memorization that characterized Islamic learning, suggesting that subsequent changes in pedagogy indicate "a major transformation in the nature of knowledge and its carriers."[23] Eickelman and others[24] see the embodiment of the Qur'an through memorization as a feature uniquely Islamic, and one which has shaped both education and Islamic societies' encounters with Western powers. Interestingly, however, the rote memorization and extreme discipline of Greek Orthodox education differed little from that of their Muslim counterparts. The most significant difference was not in pedagogy but in content: Muslim children spent years learning proper Qur'anic recitation while understanding almost nothing of what they learned; Orthodox children spent years learning to recite Ancient Greek while comprehending virtually nothing of what they memorized.

Rather than seeing this rote memorization as a feature particularly "Islamic," it seems to me more useful to see it as a type of apprenticeship in which one not only masters a body of knowledge but also embodies those marks of mastery that indicate one's status. Adeeb Khalid draws a similar conclusion for *madrasa* education in Central Asia, remarking that "[r]ather than being an institution of higher learning in the modern sense of the word, the madrasa was the site for the reproduction of one class of professionals, those concerned with various aspects of Islamic law."[25] It is as a person shaped by that body of knowledge that one works, lives, and innovates. And it is one's being as a person who has mastered that knowledge that one displays in one's comportment, gestures, and speech. In such ways, one can see the differences between forms of knowledge in the Greek and Turkish communities of Cyprus as they were mastered by persons in those communities.

The ethnic fantasy

In early 1912, an article appeared in the *Kipriakos Filaks* that greatly agitated many of the Muslims in the island. The kadi wrote a letter of complaint about the presumed writer, Nikolaos Katalanos, and his "Solution to the Anatolian Question." The author of the article asserts that the Ottoman Empire—which he calls "Turkey" (*Tourkia*), following European usage—would have vanished from the face of the earth a long time before if it had not been buttressed by European powers with an interest in its survival. As a solution to the "Anatolian Question"—the rather presumptious "problem" of the division of Anatolia—the writer proposes a Darwinian competition of races, in which the outcome will be determined by "the racial superiority of the Greeks as they reclaim their paternal inheritance, without injury from neighboring and utterly enslaved nations." After a eulogy about the probable benefits to humanity and to Anatolia of Greek rule, the writer concludes that, "the Greek race, if it does not contain its national virtue in the peaceful antagonism towards other races, will find it possible to impose its spiritual nation-state on the thousands of inhabitants of these nations and to enlighten them with faith, and to restore the cross to the dome of Aghia Sophia [in Istanbul] and to return the [Byzantine] Two-Headed Eagle to the battlements of the Kingdom."[26]

Such was the rhetoric which, by the turn of the century, filled Greek newspapers, was recited by Greek schoolchildren, and flowed from the mouths of Greek politicians. As I remark in Chapter 3, it was a rhetoric of race and regeneration, and one which obviously partook of the familiar, idealized motifs of nationalism at the turn of the century. It was also a rhetoric that by necessity had as its central demand the call for the realization of a dream and ethnic ideal that, more than any other single idea, would determine the future of the island: enosis, or union, which for

Greeks meant freedom and for Turks meant fear. The union of Cyprus with Greece was a desire expressed during even the earliest days of British rule, and Greek Cypriot historians usually refer to it as the free expression of a long-cherished hope.[27] Turkish Cypriot historians also find early references to the idea of enosis, though they do so to demonstrate that Turkish Cypriots always reacted immediately against this aspiration.[28] In contrast to both, contemporary foreign observers often complained of the trouble-making elites who tried to rouse the contented villagers to fruitless action.

What Greek Cypriots saw as a primordial inheritance, British administrators saw as troublemaking propaganda. What is interesting is that Greek Cypriots, while admitting that much of the inheritance to which they laid claim was learned, appear to have seen no contradiction between a primordial and an articulated identity, or between ethnicity learned and ethnicity lived. In the dispute over the nature of Greek Cypriot education it is obvious that the repeated claim of Greek Cypriots that "there is no such thing as Greek propaganda in Cyprus" is not only a political one. It reveals, more than anything else, an epistemology in the critical sense, i.e., the articulation of a theoretical mastery of the world. Propaganda—deliberate, second-order, and purposeful—was not separated by its nature from the forms of enacted ethnic identity.

Put another way, the fact that teachers overtly attempted to instruct their pupils to nationalist action did not make that instruction any less hegemonic, any less a part of those practices that John and Jean Comaroff remark "are so habituated, so deeply inscribed in everyday routine, that they may no longer be seen as forms of control."[29] The dispute over the nature of Greek education hinged, then, on two very different notions of the educational process. In particular, British administrators saw the overt efforts of schoolteachers to "inflame the minds of the pupils against other races resident in the Island" as a directly political attempt to disturb the status quo. The inspector of schools observed in 1911 that he had found

> some rather strong expressions in certain school books, but the majority of village children do not reach to that point (i.e. the higher classes) or they are too young to understand it. I think there is little or no anti-Turkish or anti-English teaching in the *Elementary* schools—what there is is in the secondary schools to pupils who are of an age to take it in—and this does not depend on set lessons or books but on what the teacher *says* on the thousand occasions when he can introduce his sentiments into *any* lesson, without any check.[30]

This kind of education was, in other words, not a discipline but a deception, not culture but cant.

For their part, Greek Cypriot spokesmen recognized the British fears of nationalist agitation and often asked, when various educational schemes were offered, "Will the Government attempt to control the teaching of 'Greek national history' in the schools? If so, it were better to repudiate government assistance altogether."[31] Moreover, Greek Cypriots agreed that education was explicitly political and believed that it should be. I would argue, in fact, that it is only in arenas in which one attempts to maintain the illusion of non-political objectivity in education that the political is seen as propaganda. Students of the Pancyprian Gymnasium were told, for instance, that they were being prepared to take up their political duties:

> We have had and always have the idea that the Pancyprian Gymnasium excellently fulfilled its purpose, that it not only transmits the light of education throughout the island, but it also prepares young, vibrant youths .... It educates men of wisdom and full of self-denial, true defenders of Faith and Fatherland .... To you, noble adolescents of today, tomorrow the fatherland will entrust her future. You will govern her fate, you will be the labourers who will guide her reestablishment, the apostles of the Great Idea.[32]

For Greek Cypriots, then, education was indeed a discipline not unlike that known by their British rulers. The significant difference was in the type of citizen produced.

The use of language is an important key to this. Interestingly, the rhetoric of nationalism was not even fully available to everyone, since it was almost always spoken in *katharevousa* or even in Ancient Greek, giving a breath of the Parthenon to each syllable. This was the language of the learned or at least of the literate, the language of "national" celebrations and political speeches. The villagers to whom such speeches were directed were not expected to understand them, only to have a visceral response of pride. Instead, in speeches given in Ancient Greek, the content of such speeches was ontologically inseparable from the archaized language; dreams of recapturing Byzantium could only be expressed in the language that was also the historically continuous and consistent spirit of the race. "Christian Hellenism cannot be fully understood without its original kingly language," explained one newspaper article, "The new Hellenism is so closely connected with the ancient, that it is not possible to understand how the second can exist without the first, the belief of which is still symbolized by language."[33] The all-conquering Greek language was the ultimate proof that the Greek spirit was timeless but historical, unchanging but adaptable, continuous but malleable. For these reasons, instruction in the language was much like military training: One did not need to understand the mechanics of the training to understand that the goal was to become a disciplined soldier.

Foucault writes of the "great book of Man-the-Machine," the modernist project begun by Descartes and finished by those faceless functionaries of the new sort of governmentality which regulated the body.[34] The disciplined body of the modern soldier demonstrates in its comportment the ideal regulation of that controllable, manipulable, and perfectible machine. In a strangely similar way, the Greek Cypriot image of "man the ethnic subject" demanded a discipline that could only be accomplished through the regulation of education, while simultaneously denying the *necessity* of that education for the creation of ethnic subjects. In other words, philosophers of the French Enlightenment would have said that man *is*, by his nature, mechanical, but that education was required to achieve his *telos*. Similarly, Greek Cypriots would have said that a human is, by nature, an ethnic subject, a member of his or her race, but that education was required to achieve his or her higher end.

I would suggest, in fact, that much as repetitive military drills train the soldier to respond without thought to commands, so the rote memorization of passages in Ancient Greek or of the distance from Athens to Sparta was intended to domesticate and control an identity seen as already ethnic. Indeed, articles about education made it abundantly clear that the primary goal was to create ethnic subjects trained in a moral discipline that could best be learned by becoming literate. One 1912 article claimed, for example, that

> Education and the school are foundations and institutions Greek for ages, because first and foremost our nation, in the cultivation of a spiritual and moral man, marks out as special and indispensable the attributes and signs of civilization, of freedom, and of good-citizenship.[35]

Education had begun only within the writer's lifetime to mean more than reading, writing, and basic arithmetic, so the writer could have had few illusions regarding any kind of "higher" education. Moreover, folktales regarding the "secret schools" that supposedly kept Hellenism alive through the ages never suggest that those schools did more than teach children the basics of their language. Rather, they suggest that the mere fact of linguistic continuity symbolizes a racial continuity.

Benedict Anderson has suggested that print capitalism created bourgeois communities defined by vernacular languages, and that these first

imagined communities would become the basis for nationalist imaginings.[36] The Greek Cypriot case presents a peculiar instance of a local
community finding commonalities through a new print network that was
written in a nationalist language to which they aspired. In other words,
the farmer sitting in the coffeeshop listening to the news being read by
the teacher or the *muhtar* was simultaneously incorporated into several
concentric circles of community—Paphiote, Cypriot, Greek, Greek
Orthodox—while finding those identities idealized through a language
from which he was excluded. The language was only as "naturally" his
as any other inheritance, and was therefore something that he would
have to earn and fight for.

In Marrou's examination of the centrality of rhetoric in the education
of antiquity, he makes an important remark about the value of rhetoric
that could just as well be applied to our Greek Cypriot villagers:

> Learning to speak properly meant learning to think properly, and even to live
> properly: in the eyes of the Ancients eloquence had a truly human value tran-
> scending any practical applications that might develop as a result of historical
> circumstances; it was the one means for handing on everything that made man
> man, the whole cultural heritage that distinguished civilized men from
> barbarians.[37]

The ideal man was eloquent, but eloquence was also inseparable from
ethnicity. To acquire the "kingly language" and to use it properly was
also to become a true Greek, a truly civilized man.

Indeed, it is abundantly clear in discussions of education that the realization of ethnic identity through education was the realization of an
unquestionable good, the realization of one's full humanity. This is so
much a part of Greek Cypriot discourse that I can pick an example only
somewhat at random. It is certainly well expressed in the words of Leontios, bishop of Paphos during the 1930s, who defended the need for a
purely Greek education by saying,

> Here, however, it is a question of an historically Greek island, having a history
> of five thousand years, a history of a glorious civilization, occupied during
> these times by a population purely Greek, noble, and Christian .... For this
> reason the official and systematic attempt to anglicize the Greek Cypriots is
> reprehensible ... [Greek education] consists in its teaching not only of the
> Greek language, but also of Greek history, the history of the *ethnos*, about
> which the wise men of all nations have not ceased, and will not cease, their
> praise .... It is a truth scientifically proven that the Greeks—the ancestors—
> became the first creators of education, and in this way they became the edu-
> cated people of humanity .... The Greek spirit approaches the universal

meaning of "human," and Greek education (*morphosis*) means human education.[38]

To deny Greek Cypriots a Greek education was not just to deprive them of their rights but to deny them full humanity, since humanity directly corresponds to Hellenism.

There are a few conclusions that I would like to draw from this. Firstly, Greek Cypriot history is inevitable, unchangeable, and irreplaceable. Secondly, many Greek Cypriots believed that nationalist pedagogy and what might be seen by others as nationalist propaganda were directly successful. However, they were successful because the work of education was a somewhat Platonic evocation of a Greek spirit, a Greek potential, already present in the child. As early as 1916, this was expressed in a eulogy addressed to the first contingent of Boy Scouts in the island:

> These youths, by being taught under the liberal status quo of Cyprus their duties towards their motherland, will, when the moment will come that they should be called up to the colours and that they should continue the interrupted work, be the most enthusiastic and most disciplined soldiers of Him. Likewise, when, directly, they will be swearing by this sacred flag of the fatherland, the scouts' oath, a thrill of emotion will run through their bodies, and the whole long and glorious history of the great race to which they belong will, in that moment, pass through their mind, and they will remember, yes, they will remember the sacred oath which, thousands of years ago, the Athenian youths used to swear at the same age, the oath, that is, that they would defend the fatherland both when found by themselves and when found in company with others, that they would not abandon the sacred arms and that they would not hand back the country smaller. They will remember that those who, about a century ago, fell at the Dragatrani as the heroic victims of the Hellenic liberty were, like them, still in their youthful age, in their very boyhood. They will remember all that and how much more will they not remember! The whole history of the race will pass before them as an immaterial power and will strengthen them and will dictate to their souls the creed "I believe in a great Hellas", and, in a frenzied emotion, they will, with the hand upon this sacred flag and with the soul knelt down, give all of us here the assurance that it will not be they who will disgrace the history of their fatherland, but they will be those who, either as citizens or as soldiers or either here or anywhere else shall be nothing else than the observers of the historical traditions of the nation, and the continuators of a history a more glorious of which no race can shew.[39]

The "immaterial power" that is the history of their race would be evoked as an orgasmic thrill, an organic shudder, that would leave them spiritually prostrate before the glory contained in the Greek flag. "They will remember all that and how much more will they not remember!"

exclaimed the speaker, arousing in his audience all the ideas of ethnic history already imprinted in the mind.

Thirdly, Greek Cypriots described their own history as the inevitable and inescapable history of humanity, in which their own role was already largely predetermined. Their duty was to be, either as citizens or soldiers, "nothing else than the observers of the historical traditions of the nation." Hence, the ultimate human goal accords with the ultimate national goal.

And fourthly, this enactment, this self-conscious achievement of an aesthetic ideal, was in fact the achievement of an Hellenic ideal. The movement for enosis was the villagers' movement, yet it could never be led by them; its ideals were communal ones, but they could never be represented by the common villager. I would insist, however, that this did not make those ideals any less their own, any less of a shared, cultural inheritance. Indeed, education was cultivation precisely because it evoked the inheritance that could be shaped to true humanity. The average villager could not aspire to that ideal, but it did not make it any less *his* ideal. Put simply, the dream of "progress" through education, of a "better future" that demanded the molding of young minds and bodies, was, for Greek Cypriots, the fulfillment of an ethnic fantasy. Man is, prior to cultivation, an ethnic subject, but only through cultivation could he blossom to achieve the aesthetic paradigm that the colonizers saw as propaganda. "Progress," then, was the fulfillment of an immanent potentiality. Progress becomes predestination, and education becomes evocation.

The dream of enlightenment

Barely a decade after Katalanos asserted the eternal rights of Greeks to "reclaim" Istanbul, Mustafa Kemal Paşa—also known as Atatürk, or "father of the Turks"—solved the infamous "Anatolian Question" by routing the Greek forces then advancing through Anatolia, dissolving the sultanate, and establishing the Turkish nation out of the ruins of the Ottoman Empire. By 1923, Atatürk had firmly consolidated power in the new capital, Ankara, and in the new ideology of Turkish nationalism, of which he was the greatest articulator. By 1937, one year before Atatürk's death, the six founding principles of the republic had been enshrined in the constitution: republicanism, nationalism, populism, revolutionism, secularism, and statism (*cumhuriyetçilik, milliyetçilik, halkçılık, inkilâpçılık, layiklik, etatism*).[40] Atatürk himself was both the *gazi*, or religious warrior, and the ethnic father, so highly revered that he could be referred to in writing by a capitalized third-person pronoun, which in English we reserve for reference to God.

Within a matter of a few years, Muslim Cypriots became Turks, taking upon themselves an identity forged in the crucible of nationalism. Atatürk's reforms were adopted with speed and vigor: the Arabic alphabet was discarded and a Roman alphabet instituted in its place; European hats were donned when Atatürk demanded that they be; women appeared in public unveiled at the command of their fathers; and young nationalists opened night schools to teach the new reforms. The entire project was predicated on an orientation towards the future, and a perceived need for self-remaking, indicated both by repeated cries of Turks' backwardness, and by the common understanding of salvation as something that would come from above.

Certainly, Turkish Cypriots were at a distinct disadvantage with regard to their Greek neighbors. However, in almost every case the source of this disadvantage was seen not through the lens of political economy, but as a weakness of the self, a weakness internal to the society, and something in need of remaking. In one study of the history of Turkish Cypriot education, the author quotes the remarks of a medical doctor who was educated in the last decades of Ottoman rule, became a member of the Young Turk movement in Istanbul, and escaped exile by fleeing to his native Cyprus, by then under British rule. He also taught French for some years at the *i'dadî*, published the newspaper *İslâm*, and opened his own industrial training school until forced by Nicosia elites to close it. In this teacher's memoirs he explains

> that because in the villages there were fewer Turks than Greeks; because they spoke Greek, and because without schools, or imams, or mosques, or teachers they were in a pitiable situation, under the influence of clever priests a portion of them were Grecified. He says that in the Ottoman period because not only in the villages but even in the towns not even a speck of importance was given to education, the future of up to forty villages was dark.[41]

However, a teacher educated in a *medrese* in Istanbul, "by founding a large medrese in Paphos, and by preaching sermons in the mosques and villages to warn and awaken the people, and thanks to the students that he distributed to the villages, the villager was saved from becoming Greek."[42] The "darkness" of custom and ignorance—represented here by the "Grecified" Muslim villager—was overcome by the "enlightenment" of civilization represented by the traditionally educated intellectual who, despite his religious education, was able to "warn and awaken the people." This, indeed, was one of the primary responsibilities of those known as the *aydınlar*, a word that literally means "lights" or "enlightened ones" but which refers to all those who have "knowledge." In this vision, intellectuals would preserve "the people" from the calamities to which they would otherwise be led by custom and ignorance.

In Cyprus, their own backwardness was clear in comparison with their Greek neighbors, who appeared to succeed at Muslims' expense. Moreover, this self-criticism extended even to the heart of the society, namely to its dealings with women. One Turkish Cypriot teacher whom I interviewed was born in 1919 in a small village in the Paphos area of Cyprus. Both his father and elder brother were teachers, so his family's association with education stretches into the early Hamidian period. When discussing his own family, he noted that "although my father was a teacher, he didn't send the girls to school. He said they could go to primary school, but he only sent one sister. My elder brother, oooh, he finished primary school, he finished *rüştiye*, he became a teacher. My elder brother. But my father didn't send my sisters who came after him, not even to elementary school." While this was no doubt a common practice, in actual fact Muslim schools in the island for many decades compared favorably with Greek schools in regards to primary education for girls. One reason for this is indicated in observations regarding girls' education by the first British inspector of schools, Josiah Spencer, who wrote in 1881 that,

> The condition of the Masters of the Christian village schools has generally been hitherto such as to prevent parents from sending their girls, except a few very small ones, to School. The Moslem village Masters being generally older men, and religious Teachers, there is not the same difficulty, and their Schools are usually more mixed than the Christian village schools.[43]

Even as late as a 1913 report on the state of Cypriot education, Muslim girls constituted 37 per cent of the total 5,692 children enrolled in elementary classes, while girls in the Christian schools made up only 30 per cent of the total of 25,854.[44]

Despite this, however, the same teacher clearly believed that the opposite was the case, and he made a direct association between the perceived backwardness of Muslim education and the lack of education for girls. In our interview, I had noted that, beginning from the early Hamidian period and continuing until Cyprus' independence in 1960, there had been complaints lodged with the British administration about the deficient nature of Muslim/Turkish education, especially in contrast to their Greek neighbors. When I asked this retired teacher about the problem, he remarked:

> This was true. Theirs was much better. And in any case they gave much more importance to education than we did. They definitely sent their Greek children to school. It should also be good for the girls. Because with us, boys and girls couldn't ever be together, that is. At twelve years old they [the girls] were completely covering themselves (*çarşaf örtüsünü giyerlerdi*). The Greeks weren't like that. The Greeks were always in love, always going to the church together, our girls didn't go to the mosque, the women. Of course there were those who went, but they had a separate place. But not like the Greeks, the Greeks on Sunday all went to the church, all together, there was mingling (*kaynaşma vardı*), girl, girl-boy mingling happened. That's why, if a girl goes to school, if a Turkish girl goes to school, and if she learns reading and writing, she writes a letter to her lover. That's why families didn't send them! Greeks weren't like that, the Greeks were different. And they gave much more importance to education, that was the reality.

While my question had concerned the perception of a backwardness in comparison to Greek education, his answer focused very clearly on the relationship between that backwardness and traditional practices and perceptions with regard to girls.

Indeed, one of the more puzzling features of Turkish modernity has been the use of women in Turkish modernizing endeavors.[45] What are often considered to be the "paradoxes" of Turkish modernity are clearly exhibited in the early republican demand that women be "modern yet modest." Although Atatürk is, in nationalist discourse, usually credited with freeing women from the yoke of a slavish religious backwardness, one sees both in family histories and in writings of the late imperial period a tendency within the *memur*, or civil servant, class to educate and "enlighten" its women. In literature, in memoirs, and in recollections of persons educated in the late Ottoman and early republic periods, there is a direct association made between freedom for women and being *medeni*, or civilized.[46]

The association of women with the traditional, the national "inside," and hence with an essential identity is a common theme in many nationalist imaginations.[47] What is fascinating in the Turkish case is the clear popular association of the traditional with the backward, where the backward is perceived to be a danger within the society, something to be fought, altered, or repressed. It was a danger because it was a weight on the society, something holding up its progress. For Turkish Cypriots, this was perceived most clearly in contrast with their Greek neighbors, who both gave more importance to education and allowed the education of their daughters. And finally, there was clearly a perception of the possibility of change and self-remaking.

Correcting the "backwardness" within the society came to depend, in turn, on the *aydınlar*, who should teach one the error of one's ways. The concept of "enlightenment" (*aydınlatmak*) was certainly central to the the speed and ease with which Atatürk's reforms were accepted in Cyprus, where he was often called the *ikinci peygamber*, or second prophet, and the "savior" (*kurtarıcı*) of the Turks. He was called the latter certainly because of his military triumphs, but even more importantly because of his renovation of Turkish society, which supposedly pointed them on the way to "truth."

Many Turkish Cypriots felt that, while Atatürk had given them an identity, they were in need of their own local "savior" to rescue them from their backwardness as a minority ignored by their Greek neighbors. In the crucial period following the Turkish War of Independence, for example, an important Turkish Cypriot doctor and member of the legislative council wrote of what he saw as the *malaise* of his people. "In this century of perfections in which we are living," he wrote, his people are "obliged to be subject to its enlightened and civilized currents" at a time "when nations that have determined to become holders of word and position" have taken control of their destinies. In his own country, however, it is different:

> Protection of property and family; maintenance of fame and prosperity! let a handful of young folk be as much vigilant and cautious as they can. Let a party of enlightened persons cry out with all their power: this is the way of truth! I wonder in how many hearts and in how many intellects will this cry of truth find an echo.

Indeed, the ideal cultural type to be molded in Turkish schools was the "enlightened" individual, and the aesthetics of self-fashioning was one of "enlightenment." While the goal of education was *kalkınma*—recovery or progress—pedagogy itself was described by the verb *aydınlatmak*—to illuminate, to clarify, to enlighten. Unlike the European Enlightenment, whose articulators described their task as one of bringing light to the darkness of religious orthodoxy and prejudice, those who called for *aydınlatmak* saw its knowledge as literal clarification. The *aydınlar*—the intellectuals—were presumed to be "enlightened" and possessed of the clear knowledge necessary for leadership.

Moreover, their fitness to lead could be seen in their possession of certain types of knowledge, and one most often criticized one's political opponents for being "ignorant" or "lacking learning." In 1919, for instance, several young men called together Muslims from throughout the island in an attempt to organize in protest both against Greek agitation for enosis and against what they claimed was the deprivation of their rights by the colonial administration. A highly admired English teacher, Necmi Potamyalızâde—who was a frequent contributor to the magazine *Near East* and an even more frequent correspondent with the government—claimed that the meeting was an attempt to disprove one of his articles, in which he had argued that the British Empire should retain Cyprus in the face of Greek protests precisely because of the loyalty of the Muslim population. Those who organized the meeting, he asseverated, were acting on their own, and "none of them had the credentials of the people authorizing them to decide and act as their representative." Furthermore, in the published article that described the meeting, Potamyalızâde found evidence of their inability to lead:

> Many mistakes in that article, even in the composition of the language, may convince that these persons, whoever they may be, were not of good education, except perhaps in their own businesses, and therefore lacking much both in knowledge and in judgment.
>
> That they were devoid of such standard feelings of nationality and patriotism, which they declare to be their impulse, it is proof enough that they did never show material symptoms of their feelings, even when their duties called upon them. The education and the civilization of the Muslims of Cyprus are in a deplorable condition; they are already in the clutches of the most awful enemies of humanity and civilization, it requires little foresight to see the grim face of Destruction lying in ambush in the way of Muslims a few decades further, and what efforts have they made to save these poor men? On the contrary, there are instances that some of them did not hesitate to injure Muslims in different ways. If they had any feelings of nationality, first of all they would learn their own language, and not display such inability in connecting two passages with each other.[48]

It is clear that Potamyalızâde saw a direct relationship between their "lack of credentials" and their lack of eloquence.

It is the lack of leaders who can show the "truth" that results, it was believed, in the decadence and despair of the Muslim community. In contrast, they see only unanimity among their Greek compatriots:

> In order to secure their future, they, the Greeks, are unanimously and with one accord doing their best by embracing willingly all sorts of trouble and hardship and sacrificing almost their moneys and lives, and in view of that activity and sacrifice their success is, we are sorry to say, certain and beyond doubt.

One envies the Greeks, saying "would that it were so for the Muslims!", and cannot help crying bitterly for our abasement and lack of proper spirit in face of manliness of the Greeks .... There shall come a day when the known persons, who for the decadence of the nation sell their conscience in return for a salary and present of a few paras [coins], shall not be allowed to utter untrue words, as they do now in the coffee houses, for the purpose of deceiving the people, and the young men of enlightened ideas will inflict condign punishment upon them, and their benefactor, and they shall be looked upon by the people as "Traitors of the Country."[49]

The "young men of enlightened ideas," the men blessed with the enlightenment of progress, would one day achieve their rightful status and punish those who had led the community astray through "untrue words."

Even—perhaps especially—those who slandered each other in their newspapers and in public addresses complained that "our life is taken up with factions, enmity, revenge." An article published by the opponents of *Seyf* complained that the two primary problems in the Muslim community were the organization of education, which could not satisfy the needs of the country, and a second disease:

Our second and most dreadful disease is lack of character. What a great number of important nations that have been sovereigns of the world and masters of arts and knowledge have been buried and lost for lack of character. There is no society, no tribute that has disappeared for anything else but lack of character.[50]

We see, then, that not only is power directly linked to the mastery of arts and knowledge, but also that that mastery is linked in some amorphous sense to "character," to the unanimity that would bring progress.[51]

There is, then, a linked complex of ideas: the "young men of enlightened ideas" should possess "word and power" secured through the unanimity of the community—which unanimity would "qualify" them for their position. Transparency, clarity, and enlightenment were the ideals that continued to be reflected in educational practice. The ideal of transparency helps us, I believe, to understand the links between a school discipline that emphasizes obedience, politeness, self-effacement, and duplication (discussed in Chapter 4), and a mode of political behavior whose ideal is unanimity. Discipline in the Muslim community taught one to become *as iconic as possible*, not by possessing qualities such as honor but by embodying those qualities—i.e., becoming honorable. It is, in fact, a rather different notion of agency, defined not by what one *does* but by what one *is*. Hence, identity was always something *to be achieved*, always something to be made through the self-conscious striving for a transparent iconicity. Once one acquired the "character" of the "young men of enlightened ideas," this would be reflected in the unanimity of the community.

Moreover, the ideal of "enlightenment" emphasized education as truth, and becoming educated as an approach to truthfulness. Hence, leaders were educated, and the educated were leaders. But, furthermore, it was precisely the idea of *approaching* truthfulness, of always striving to achieve greater truthfulness, that made the ideal of enlightenment seem immanently progressive. As a result, these same young men would serve as the guides into Atatürk's future.

Conclusion

Briefly, I have attempted to show one possible way of problematizing and rethinking the historical role of education in creating nationalist subjects. I argue that the status of learning in the Orthodox and Muslim—later Greek and Turkish—communities of Cyprus meant that it was always already a system whereby one transformed the self into a master of those bodies of knowledge. This, I have suggested, might be most easily seen as a form of apprenticeship in which one shapes oneself in the mold of traditional knowledge and thereby becomes the type of person capable of calling upon that knowledge.

Furthermore, I have sketched two alternative ways in which this might be realized. In the Greek Orthodox case, education's task was a cultivation or evocation of a latent potential of the ethnic subject, while in the Muslim case it was a form of enlightenment in which the intellectual occupied the role of physician whose task it was to guide and heal. I wish to suggest in conclusion that it was these two alternative understandings of the social role of knowledge that in fact proved divisive for the two communities. For as education was, indeed, transformed into a vehicle for nationalism, it acquired force in uniting Turkish- or Greek-speakers across the divides of class, village, and genealogy because of the fact that it had always united Muslims and Orthodox in similar ways. Hence, the "high cultures" of nationalism were not an imposition but an aspiration.

CHAPTER 6

An Education in Honor

One day at the height of the shortages and hunger that afflicted even Cyprus during World War II, a young boy from the Pancyprian Gymnasium left his house in the afternoon and went outside the city walls to cut oranges from one of his family's fields, planning to give them to some of his friends the next day. As always, he wore his school uniform and cap, with the initials "ΠΓ" and his student number on each, so he was easily recognizable to the Turkish trooper who stopped him on the road back to his home. The trooper scolded him for carrying a pocketknife in a public place, took down his number, and sent him on his way. The next day, however, the headmaster of the gymnasium entered one of the boy's classes, read the trooper's report to all present, and sternly reprimanded the boy for having brought embarrassment to his school. The man who was this boy described the strictness of the school with a wistful note of nostalgia in his voice, and he explained to me the various methods of surveillance, including the infamous *paidhonomos* or after-school disciplinarian—an institution that only a few years ago one Minister of Education suggested reinstituting.

Such surveillance and discipline became particularly important less than a decade later, when in 1955 Archbishop Makarios III and General Ghiorgos Grivas Dhighenis[1] called for armed struggle that would bring down British rule and unite the island with Greece. Photographs and news clips from the time show teenage girls in their school uniforms marching through the Nicosia streets under the uplifted Greek flag, or young boys of nine and ten years old being caught by the scruff of the neck and dragged away by British soldiers. Guns in violin cases, weapons in schoolbags, coded instructions hidden in notebooks—these became familiar parts of the EOKA guerilla campaign. Many of the rebellion's actors were of fighting age; many others were students of the elementary schools. While their parents hesitated to join the fight,

3. Village schoolchildren pose with the Greek flag in the 1950s.

students were successfully organized *en masse* by priests and teachers who had worked closely for years to prepare the groundwork for such an uprising. It was the moral discipline described by my informant, the willingness to sacrifice and obey, which many Cypriots have claimed made Greek students the most powerful weapon in the hands of EOKA.

Similarly, Turkish schools became training grounds after 1963, when the *Türk Müdafaa Teşkilatı* (TMT), or Turkish Defense Organization, followed the prior example of their Greek compatriots and began organizing for the impending armed conflict that would divide the island. Both EOKA and TMT had as their goals a violence that would shatter history and lead them towards freedom. While such violence is enacted in the name of the past, it is always oriented toward the future. Furthermore, insofar as patriotism is a moral discipline that orients us towards future action, it is a discipline that has an ethical aim. As we will see, Greek and Turkish Cypriots both believed schools to be necessary parts of their nationalist futures, not because of the nationalist histories that the schools taught but because of the way in which those histories were oriented towards the future through the moral discipline of a patriotic life.

It was not until the post-World War II period that Greek nationalism in its Cypriot phase was able to claim popular support for violent revolt;[2] not coincidentally, it was only in the postwar period that education could genuinely be claimed to be universal.[3] This chapter will examine, firstly, the role of the schools in implementing the moral discipline of nationalist ideology and in the creation of "patriots" for the struggle. Greek Cypriot educators and politicians perceived and repeatedly claimed a direct correspondence between the transmission of nationalist ideology and the creation of young Greek nationalists. For Turkish Cypriots, in contrast, the moral discipline of nationalism would come about through a process of self-improvement made possible by "culture" and "enlightened education."

As Durkheim observed, both regularity and submission to authority are necessary components of a "spirit of discipline," which is the foundation of a moral temperament.[4] This "spirit of discipline" has a slightly different formulation in Bourdieu's habitus, or "the internalization of the principles of a cultural arbitrary capable of perpetuating itself after [pedagogic action] has ceased and thereby of perpetuating in practice the principles of the internalized arbitrary."[5] Even more than an internalized "nationalist identity"—which must, like all identity, alter its form in changed circumstances—Cypriot educators were concerned with creating the moral discipline of a patriotic life.

This chapter addresses, secondly, the role of morality in the dialectic of imagination and experience, or how a history that excludes one's neighbors can become the basis for action. In creating "truths," discourse also creates horizons of imagination—those points beyond which one cannot see. At least since Plato, we have known that the true is inseparable from the good and the beautiful. Here, too, truth orients us towards an ethical aim—an aim that for Greek Cypriots was defined in terms of justice and that for Turkish Cypriots was defined in terms of respect. While Greek Cypriots fought for the reconstitution of an imagined former order, Turkish Cypriots struggled to create something entirely new, something that had never existed before.

Furthermore, we will see that it was the very immanence of the future that gave to education its immediate effectiveness. "Educating the youth" was also a task of creating a new world, which could be immediately realized. Not only did one become encultured in the history and goals of the nationalist enterprise, but there was a complete congruence between those goals and the possibility of their fulfillment. It is in this realm of action that the distinction between education as evocation and education as enlightenment finds its full force, for here we will recognize most fully the vast difference between fulfilling a destiny and creating one.

Also, it should be noted that the discipline discussed here is not a discipline in the avoidance of certain behaviors but a discipline in the regimentation of behavior, the latter undoubtedly involving—as Foucault notes—an orientation towards the future.[6] As a former teacher of the Paphos Gymnasium described, discipline itself was never a problem in a society in which children could not escape observation. But the apprenticeship in adult life undertaken in the Greek schools of Cyprus was always explicitly aimed at an anticipated future and was, therefore, explicitly nationalist. All were trained to fight for an ideal: not simply an ideal of justice, or of freedom, or of a better life, but an ideal of enosis, which encompassed all of these. The students who fought and died with EOKA did so not only to gain their freedom from colonial rule, and certainly not to gain Cyprus' independence. They fought not for the freedom defined by individual, human rights but for a freedom of the *ethnos*, which could only be accomplished by the union of Cyprus with Greece.

Hence, it is this relationship between discipline and nationalism that will be discussed briefly here, first by exploring ideas of progress as these were taught in Greek Cypriot schools and by exploring how disciplinary mechanisms were oriented toward such expectations of the future; secondly, by examining the Turkish Cypriot demand for a progressive "culture" and its relationship to structures of authority; and finally by considering the more specific and realizable goals that subsumed individual histories under nationalist ones. This will be an examination, then, of the relationship between the moral discipline which defines the patriot and the type of freedom for which that patriot was taught to fight.

The inevitable progress of freedom

In the last two years of the EOKA struggle, a fascinating periodical was published for students of elementary schools. In simple and repetitive patriotic language, *The Training of the Young* vividly described heroic martyrdom, the proud history of the Greeks, and the responsibilities of the Greek youth. In one of its first articles, titled "We will acquire our freedom," the anonymous writers describe their cause:

> The history of Hellenism from the first years until today must make us optimistic for the future. Because it shows us clearly the strength of Hellenism and its immortality. Do you understand what [history] will say after so many raids, so many conquests, so many vicissitudes will not erase us from the face of the earth, as have been so many other peoples, but we will continue to exist as Greeks, to speak the same language that our great forefathers spoke?[7]

The repetition of this theme in each issue of the periodical is an echo from the past of the same words so often spoken to me today by former members of EOKA, both teachers and students. Not a single one failed to remark that the struggle of EOKA was not simply a struggle born of the insults, condescension and mismanagement of the British, but was a struggle rooted in a past which made their victory inevitable.

Not long before the start of the struggle, protests were begun against what were seen as the "dehellenizing" measures of the British.[8] Even though British policy in the early 1950s was in fact more liberal than it had been a decade before, political and religious leaders sent missives of varying length to the United Nations and other international agencies, protesting against British measures curbing expression of Greek nationalist sentiment, particularly in the schools. In 1935, the government had attempted to set intercommunal standards for education, hoping to quell the rising fervor of nationalism both by the elimination of symbols and subjects of nationalist histories and by economic growth anticipated as a consequence of increased numbers of university graduates. Furthermore, the British system was adapted to Cypriot schools, and regional, nationalist histories and literatures were replaced by world histories and European literatures. The culmination of British schemes was seen to be the Teachers' Training College of Morphou, where Greek and Turkish teachers were taught together. The Greek Cypriot leadership claimed that future educators graduated without a proper understanding of their own language and history.[9]

As has been noted previously, the conflagration of 1931 and the ten-day period of rebellion that followed it had not only resulted in a period of extreme mistrust between Cypriots and their foreign governors, but it had also given to those governors an opportunity to accomplish many repressive tasks that had often tempted them as easy solutions to the political ferment—but which they had previously been unable to justify. Previously, even a law as seemingly beneficial as the 1929 Elementary Education Law had provoked the irate condemnation of politicians and much controversy within the two communities. That law had taken the appointment, dismissal, transfer, and replacement of elementary school teachers away from the village committees and had placed it in the hands of the government. Although the primary aim had been to provide some continuity and stability for the elementary schools, many Cypriots had interpreted it as a move in the direction of full government control.[10]

The riots, then, provided an opportunity to gain even fuller control of the workings of education. Indeed, education had been a near-obsession of the British governors since their arrival in the island, not only because an English-speaking elite was necessary for the workings of the bureaucracy, but more importantly because those governors suspected that there was something that smacked of sedition going on there. Even though, until the final rebellion that would loose the British grasp, government agents repeatedly concluded that the majority of the people was, in their own time, loyal, they saw education as a long-term project aimed at altering the character of the people and hence the future of the island.

Less than a year after the 1931 riots, Governor Robert Storrs transferred from the island and the former colonial secretary, H. Henniker-Heaton, acted in his place. Henniker-Heaton observed then that the reforms that had taken place in the elementary schools could hardly be considered sufficient:

> The secondary schools are very far from being all right. Astonishing as it may seem the curriculum in the Lycees or Gymnasiums is laid down by the Ministries of Public Instruction in Greece or Turkey. Comment is needless by me saying that the results are deplorable. These schools furnish practically all the schoolmasters for the elementary schools. I may as well say at once that I am not very deeply concerned in the effect of the teaching given from a political aspect as I do not consider the ages of 7–14 as being very formative, but I do attach great weight to the effect of these raw intellectuals on a population which is largely illiterate. Every village has its one or two schoolmasters or dismissed masters to read the news and propound meanings. Neither the training nor the atmosphere in the Gymnasiums have a breath of British ideals.[11]

Henniker-Heaton's concern, then, was mostly with the wider effects of the secondary school graduates on their illiterate fellow-villagers— hardly an unimportant concern, but not entirely in accord with the concerns repeatedly expressed by his compatriots. The previous governor, Storrs, made lengthy remarks regarding education and its allegedly seditious character not long after his arrival in the island and his first full tour of the districts:

> It cannot be said that there is any definitely Anti-British Curriculum in the Schools, but they are all actively Hellenising. All Greek Elementary Schools use the "Analytical Programme" as published in Greece, definitely adopted by the Board of Education. No reading books are allowed in these schools except those that have been approved by the "Critical Committee" in Athens. The Gymnasium of each town and the Teachers Training School are recognized by the Greek Ministry of Education, and work under Regulations issued there from. Portraits of King Constantine and Queen Sophie, of Venizelos and other worthies adorn the walls of the class-rooms together with elaborate maps of Modern Greece, while that of Cyprus, if to be found at all, is as a rule small, out of date, worn out and frequently thrust behind the black board. I have from the first made a practice of asking one or two questions in each form of the schools in the towns and villages I have visited, and discovered during the first few weeks (until my methods became known through the Press) a ludicrous difference between the home and abroad knowledge of the best pupils who, always exactly informed as to the distance between Athens and Thebes, and usually as to the capital of Norway or of Japan, would hazard guesses varying from 20 to 1500 miles as to the length or breadth of Cyprus .... I am advised, and on the whole believe, that ninety per cent of the population would, if a fair plebiscite were taken, vote for the closest union with Great Britain. But I incline to doubt how far the young generation brought up under the present Pan Hellenic curriculum would continue so to vote. And the curriculum could hardly be modified unless Government were in a position, which it is not, to assume entire financial responsibility.[12]

I quote this at length for the manner in which it strikingly emphasizes the relationship between immediate, factual knowledge and a purported disloyalty to the British Empire and desire for a more radical political solution.

Certainly, the British governors of Cyprus believed that the troubles stirred up by a nascent nationalism were created by the political leaders and that the average Cypriot would not, under other circumstances, be concerned with such matters, occupied as he supposedly was with his own quotidian affairs. The goal, then, became a severing of this seditious communication, whether in the schools, in speeches, or in the press. Furthermore, the colonial governors could easily find indications of this policy's effectiveness. Henniker-Heaton, touring the island approximately a year after the 1931 riots, observed what he believed to be an instance that justified his own belief in this policy:

> The Mayor of Polis, the second town in Paphos, who is a man of some character was illuminating. He said that the people bore no ill-will towards the Government now but they had certainly been oppressed before. When asked how, he replied by instancing the Education Law which brought the schoolmasters under the Government. The fact that it is still in full operation did not disturb his conviction that there had been a change. It is outstandingly clear that now that the people are not being told daily from the platform and by the newspapers that they are being oppressed they fail to feel the alleged oppression.[13]

Simply by severing the links with those seditious interpreters of events, the colonial government could prevent (to paraphrase Gellner) the conquest of nationalism through the imposition of high culture.

Now, what were these measures that the British implemented or attempted to implement? Firstly, it should be noted that in all explanations by Greek Cypriot teachers and the ethnarchy of the actions of the British administration in regards to education, a consistency of policy is attributed to the British which denies the possibility that the fate of Cyprus could be contingent either upon changes in British personnel or upon events taking place in other parts of the Empire. For example, it is claimed in various memoranda sent to international agencies that the British "always" wanted to eliminate Greek and replace it with English.[14] It is worth noting, however, that the consistency of policy attributed to the British evidences a forgetfulness of events and debates within the memories of the writers themselves. For example, it was only after Government House was burned in the riots of 1931 that the government instituted controls on curriculum and administration. And even these—as one Greek Cypriot author observes—were only applied when there was provocation; usually the government simply tried to attract students to its own schools by charging lower fees.[15]

Secondly, and related, the teachers and clergy who were the writers of these memoranda objected to island-wide, intercommunal standardization. For them, the Morphou Teachers' Training College was a great danger to the future of Greek nationalism in the island, since future Greek and Turkish teachers were taught together, and many of the classes were conducted in English. Furthermore, the Secondary Education Law of 1935 had instituted a common curriculum in the schools of both communities of the island in which, as the memorialists put it, "The teaching of Greek was defined as simply the teaching of a language without its being stated that it was the pupils' mother tongue." Moreover, between 1935 and 1949, Greek history was taught as part of the general history of the Balkans and not, as the memorialists phrased it, "as the history of the Greek world to which Cyprus belongs historically and ethnologically."[16]

Then, thirdly, there were complaints about the depoliticizing measures of the British, such as the prohibition of Greek maps which included Cyprus; pictures of the Greek royal family or other Greek personalities; the teaching of the Greek national anthem; the celebration of Greek independence day; the use of the Greek flag; and the use generally of anything which bore the blue and white colors of Greece and could be construed as symbolic of Greek nationalism.

Now, each of these things, and particularly all of them taken together, was seen as an attempt to "dehellenize" the Greek youth. My informants, in talking of the period, deny that the schools were necessary for the creation and transmission of an Hellenic identity, yet they discuss these British measures as attempts to "dehellenize." In particular, they argued that these measures "aimed, among other things, at bringing into realization the idea systematically propounded by British propaganda that there was a distinct Cypriot nationality unconnected with the Greek and Turkish inhabitants of the island who were called simply Cypriots."[17] This leads us, I believe, to what could be considered to be the central paradox of nationalism: namely, that ethnic, supposedly blood ties could be created and taught. This was a problem explicitly discussed in both communities in Cyprus, who resolved the tension in strikingly different ways.

For Greek Cypriots, "dehellenization" was, on the one hand, a rallying point: while the triumph of Greeks was inevitable, many feared that the British could eventually win by the implementation of ruthless tactics aimed at Anglicizing the youth—or, even worse, Cypriotizing them. In other words, if one's own history is one of inevitable triumph, the only means of victory available to the enemy is the erasure of that identity and hence of the history still to be unfolded. On the other hand, it was believed that, because such efforts were "unnatural," they represented a pedagogy with limited effectiveness. This position has been succinctly expressed by Michalakis Maratheftis, who, in describing the revolt of students against opportunities offered to them by the British, remarks, "This is proof that education which expresses the timeless ideals of a people influences more the shaping of their ethnic identity than does school teaching, when it opposes the feelings and values of the whole populus."[18] As I note in Chapter 5, Greek Cypriot pedagogic ideology actually takes on a rather Platonic character: one is Greek by blood, and education should be but a reminder of that.

Underlying these contrasts is the marked distinction discussed in Chapter 5 between the types of nationalist histories propounded by the two communities. For, while Greek Cypriots described ties of blood and historical inevitability and claimed that the island was 3,000 years Greek, Turkish Cypriots invoked rivers of blood spilled in the conquest, saying that "every inch of the land of Cyprus is soaked with the blood of sixty thousand of our forefathers." For Greek Cypriots, their right to rule the island is decided by a history that reveals an ineluctable movement towards the island's union with the greater Greek world. In contrast, Turkish Cypriots have claimed their right to rule the island through the contingencies of conquest, citing the Ottoman capture and rule of Cyprus and the thousands of Turkish lives lost in pursuit of the island's possession.

Within the context of the EOKA struggle, it is particularly important to note that a contingent history is much closer to human life than a history that overtakes one as inevitable. In other words, a contingent history provides a future that is achievable, while in an inevitable history one is merely part of a grander scheme. Within this framework, the measures of the British could be seen as "dehellenizing" in a logical sense: they attempted to present a Greek history, and particularly a history of Cyprus, that was not one of inevitable and consistent movement but was instead one describing Cyprus as the subject of numerous conquests and a very small part of world history. In contrast, such measures were not seen as "deturkicizing", since even that small minority of Turkish

Cypriots who dared to say that "Cyprus is Turkish" did so in terms of the contingencies of conquest.

It is now easier to understand why many of my Greek Cypriot informants replied with indignation when I asked them what they had hoped to gain from the EOKA struggle and from enosis: it was not a struggle, they claimed, for increased rights and opportunities, but for union with their mother Greece, for which all of their history had prepared them. Progress was not the opening up of the great unknown, a future to be made, but the closure of aeons. Hence, freedom meant enosis, because freedom was the realization of an already imagined, inevitable future.

Discipline and freedom

On Sundays when he was a boy, one Turkish Cypriot teacher told me, he and his family were afraid to leave their houses. It was the Greek "national day," he said, and Turks feared to go into the streets because of the readiness for conflict with which their Greek neighbors would emerge from church services. He struggled to understand this strange and sudden change that allowed neighbors to turn into enemies, but he began to understand it better later, when he entered the Teachers' Training College at Morphou. There, he said, he was taught Turkish songs by a Greek teacher, and, in contrast to what the Greek leadership was saying, he always sensed that the Greeks enrolled there were proud to be there, since the competition for the school made acceptance an honor. At the same time, he rode the bus each day with Markos Dhrakos, who was to become one of the young heroes of EOKA. They always chatted, he said, and liked each other quite a lot, until one morning when the Turkish Cypriot's greeting of "Merhaba" was met with the reply, "Enosis."

This is what I consider to be the true result of the disciplinary mechanisms of the Greek community, of which the schools are the strongest, most important and most influential—though I would hardly claim to be the only—example. In the name of nationalism a censorship occurs of one's own behavior in regard to others—and in regard to others one may have considered to be friends. This discipline was not achieved by corporal punishment or other less violent means of classroom control; rather, it was achieved by a careful penetration of the schools into every facet of the child's life. The Greek schools of Cyprus entered into the arena of what many of us would consider to be "family discipline" and in fact intruded upon and attempted to control what many of us today would consider to be the realm of the family. The role of the *paidhono-mos*, or after-school disciplinarian, for instance, was to patrol the streets, cafes, and cinemas to be sure that the 5 p.m. curfew had not been broken and that the students were not wasting their time in the cafes or corrupting their minds in the movie theaters. The fact that most secondary schools required their students always to wear their uniforms and hence readily to be distinguishable from their non-enrolled counterparts aided the *paidhonomos* in his task. In the conflict between family and school, the school invariably won the day, and won it with the strong support of the Church leaders.

One former teacher has commented to me that the discipline of the schools was no different from discipline in other countries and was, indeed, more lax than that of British schools. And so it was, at least in the classroom. Rarely did one find within the schools themselves the phenomena described by Foucault and familiar to many of us, at least in myth: the gradations of punishment for various omissions or commissions, the strict limitations imposed upon time and its use, the general emphasis upon training and correction. In fact, inspectors of the village schools often complained that students were allowed to run wild and that the uproar was fantastic. Furthermore, the active role of teachers in village schools was minimized, since older students were trained to teach the younger ones. But what is peculiar about the Greek Cypriot schools is, firstly, their penetration into the sphere of the family—something that was still allowed by parents in an age in which education was a privilege and something for which one struggled. Maratheftis has commented that the "ethnic work" of education during the British period was simple: "It was to instill in students the love of Greece and the desire for enosis. And in this work the school had the cooperation of almost all the community, except for the few Anglophiles."[19] Because of the status ascribed to and the visibility of the uniformed secondary-school students and their families, the range of actions permitted to them was highly circumscribed.

Secondly, with the archbishop at least tacitly presiding over the secondary schools, the schools' interference in all aspects of children's lives took on what one might call a religious character. Secondary schools were pressured to reject government monies which would allow for government control, and in the early 1950s only the Commercial Lyceum of Polemi accepted a government grant. Furthermore, the Church leaders defined a classical education as the only patriotic sort, since it was closely tied both to the curriculum of Greek schools and to the traditional education of which the Church had formerly been the bearer. Despite Cyprus' growing industries of the postwar period, technical and commercial education was strongly discouraged by the ethnarchy. In 1952, for example, the headmaster of the Pancyprian Commercial Lyceum in Larnaca wrote to the archbishop complaining of the pittance that had been granted by the Church to a school that boasted 733 male and female pupils. The headmaster comments,

> Do you perhaps deem it absolutely necessary for our school, as well, the only completely recognized Commercial School, to convert to a classical school? However, it is well known to Your Grace that up to now there has been no graduate of the Pancyprian Commercial Lyceum who has diverged from the path of belief in the national ideals.[20]

He goes on to accuse the archbishop of prejudice in the matter of educational content, arguing that his school has also nourished the pupils on religion, morality, and the ideals of human freedom.

Supporters of a "practical" education were often accused of being socialists or communists, and almost the only letters of complaint against Church educational policy had a primarily communistic and anti-clerical—if not anti-religious—bent. Proof of the effectiveness of the Church's policy was the number of students enrolled in classical academies as opposed to technical or commercial lycea. Although the attendance of the Larnaca school was quite large, the technical schools established by the British suffered more, to the extent that a Famagusta teacher suggested in 1958 that the Church consider opening its own technical schools. The Turks were taking advantage of this education, he said, and were beginning to prosper. If Greek students were not similarly educated, he feared that "even if enosis should happen tomorrow, the Turks would remain a thorn in our side."[21]

Finally, a "choicelessness" was created that was echoed in the political arena, where nationalism had become the unquestioned driving force of politics. Not only were the schools themselves under financial pressure from the government on one side and the Church on the other, but students were also taught the political nature of knowledge. They were instructed, for instance, that learning English was destructive to the national cause. In contrast to other colonies where the colonized so often absorbed, subverted, and reinvented the cultures of the colonizers in order to use them as weapons, Greek Cypriot leaders objected that knowledge of the English language was detrimental to their political aims. By 1936, English was introduced into the two highest classes of

the largest elementary schools of the island. Archbishop Leontios initially protested this move on pedagogical grounds, but then wrote that

> As by the Orthodox Christian religion the Archbishop has preserved the unity
> of belief with the other Orthodox Christians of the world, so through national
> education he has kept the Greeks of Cyprus united with fellow Greeks in
> whatever country.[22]

In various protests, the recurrent objections to English teaching indicated that it was not enough that students should learn their own
language; they also should not learn another. But Persianis notes that,
despite Church opposition, English had become an economic necessity,
and the increasing desire of parents that their children learn the language
forced the Church to accept the situation.[23] During the EOKA period,
however, English again became a target, as students burned their
English textbooks to demonstrate their hatred of the colonial
government.

The politics of knowledge extended to after-school activities, as well.
The Boy Scouts were taught to give an oath to the king of the Hellenes,
while theatrical and musical performances and football games became
opportunities to display one's loyalty to the cause of enosis. More
importantly, freedom of speech within the Greek community only
extended to those who spoke in support of union with Greece. In 1954,
for instance, the government began an intercommunal periodical for students. After its first issue appeared, the governing board of the Greek
schools issued a circular warning the schools against further participation in the publication. "The goal of this publication," they claimed," is
to furnish the Greek children of the island with free reading materials
that are odourless, colourless, and completely devoid of the Greek
spirit."[24] Their proof of this was that the word "Greece" was mentioned
only once, and then on page 26. A further circular used its opposition to
the magazine to argue the inseparability of education and ethnicity:

> [S]chool administrators and teachers are exhorted carefully to consider this
> serious problem and to protect their schools from this publication, which
> removes education from its natural ethnic foundation and leads the youth in
> dangerous paths.[25]

The aims of pedagogy were ethnic rather than scientific, just as the goal
of the impending struggle was enosis rather than the freedom of
independence.

During the infamous school closings of 1955–57, when five-sixths of
the Greek Cypriot students had their schools shut by the British

administration, the main justification given by the British was the indiscipline not only allowed by but actually encouraged and fostered by the schools. The government, in fact, accused the schools of having become "centres for the organisation of lawlessness, riot and violence."[26] This discipline—or antidiscipline—required the strict implementation of a code of honor that was a code of rebellion. The schools, in taking over the disciplinary role of the family, substituted for it a larger family and hence a higher authority to whom the students owed allegiance and of which the schools were the representatives. It is no wonder that in Greek Cypriot textbooks of the period one hardly ever finds references to Greece that are not couched in familial terms. This did not only include the rather distant term "motherland," but more importantly the image of a Mother Greece, living and breathing through the soil of Greek land, waiting to embrace her lost child as she had so many other lost island children. And in the name of this family and for this marvelous reunion with the mother from whom they were kept apart, these children—and many of them were very young children—planted bombs, killed English soldiers, and generally led the fight in which their parents were often reluctant to take an active part.

Regarding this antidiscipline, it should be noted, firstly, that the goals of EOKA were essentially non-democratic in nature, even though many of its supporters cry that EOKA had the backing of the vast majority of the Greek population of the island. Indeed, in the Church-sponsored plebiscite of 1950, nearly 96 per cent of eligible voters cast their ballots in favor of enosis. This would appear at first glance to be a sterling example of the Tocquevillian definition of democracy, in which public opinion—the opinion of the masses—is master. As Tocqueville makes clear, however, true democracy is not defined by the vote but by a consensus that ensures the individual's right to freedom of thought and expression, of which the right to choose one's representatives is a part. In Cyprus, however, the situation was considerably different. To turn again to the periodical published for elementary schools, one finds an interesting article on discipline, discouraging the children from buying English products. Rather than arguing, however, that the consumption of English products had been roundly condemned by the Greek Cypriot public, it argues the following:

> Since, therefore, discipline is that which can bring happiness to a family, progress to a society, and can secure the victory of a fighting people, soldiers of the good, of Christ, and of country must be obedient to our one legendary leader. All must obey only that one. And that one is none other than the voice

of Church and Country. We didn't expect, though, Church and Country to speak. Their representatives speak, however. The two heroes speak who are deeply engraved in the souls of every Cypriot child. Two names, which have so much to say to us, two names which close the history of a fighting people: Makarios—Dhighenis.[27]

It is important to note that while this hardly represents an appeal to public opinion, neither is it a call for blind obedience to the persons themselves. Rather, it is a call for obedience to a consensus seen as timeless, ahistorical, understood, of which the two leaders are the voices.

The most effective result of the ideological discipline of Greek Cypriot schools was, without doubt, the suppression of debate, since debate is only possible in arenas where truth is contestable. As a result, many who participated in the enosis struggle have described it as an ineluctable event, one whose inevitable realization could not be doubted. A particularly poignant instance of this "choicelessness" was related to me by a Turkish Cypriot who was teaching in the English School in Nicosia during the period of the EOKA struggle. As a natural sciences teacher, he taught both Greek and Turkish Cypriot students, all of whom, he said, were always respectful to him in the classroom, even though many of his Greek students were known members of EOKA. One day, however, a group of Greek Cypriot students came to him after class and asked to speak to him. The one who had been appointed as their spokesman asked him straightaway what he thought of the EOKA struggle. When the teacher refrained from answering, the boy proceeded to lecture him on the history of Cyprus that made it a Greek island. The teacher then told them something that apparently they had not considered before: that the implication of their statement was that the Turks who were their friends and neighbors and teachers did not belong in the island. This training in blindness is one way in which the paradox of a "taught" ethnicity is resolved, and in the Greek Cypriot case this is most often done by an exclusion of other histories, which makes one's own history inevitable.

In this case, moreover, what is most striking is the attempt to create consensus, to create "choicelessness," by silencing those voices which might question the island's supposed thousands of years of pure Greekness and hence call into question the obligations and duties imposed by blood, as one finds in the case of supposed "dehellenization." The erasure of the Turkish Cypriots is one example of this, but there are hundreds of others: the expulsion of communist teachers from the schools by the archbishop; the letters one finds from students reporting on the thoughts and behavior of their fellow students; and in general the official censorship, such as the condemnation of and marginalization of those students who took British scholarships for their studies, or the previously mentioned prohibition on participation in the intercommunal student periodical, which the archbishop described as anti-hellenic, for it made no mention of "the idea of the Greek nation, Greek values, Greek virtue, and the Greek traditions of this land."[28]

It should be clear by now that enosis was not only a goal but a right, and its fulfillment was to be not the realization of a dream but the actualization of justice. So it was described in every United Nations memorandum, in every organization's constitution, and more generally in every document—any newspaper article, speech, private letter—that dealt with the question of enosis. The acting ethnarch called upon UNESCO to work "in the name of Liberty, Justice, and Humanity" for the abolition of the "dehellenizing" measures of the British government.[29] Another such memorandum spoke of those dehellenizing measures as a violation of "the racial, ethnic, and linguistic rights of the different communities."[30] And when the Association of Greek Cypriot Intellectuals—university graduates—met in 1954, its members declared their intention to work for those rights in their capacities as community leaders:

> They declare their insistence on the one and only claim of the Greek people of Cyprus for union with motherland Greece, which is the only rightful solution of the Cyprus Question and through which alone the National Restoration of Cyprus can be effected, and that they, in their capacity as intellectual leaders of the Greek people of Cyprus, will not only continue supporting its struggle for Union with Greece, but being conscious of their obligations to it, they will intensify their activities together with its natural leadership, the Ethnarchic Church, in order that this claim of the Greek people of Cyprus may soon become a reality.[31]

Liberty, justice, and humanity were eternal truths toward which Greek Cypriots struggled in their attempts to realize the destiny of enosis.

When translated into the realm of action, such an antipodean cosmology—rooted, as well, in the complexities of village politics—cannot but lead to violence. Hence, EOKA took it as its task not only to defeat the British, but also to censor Greek Cypriot thought and behavior. In 1958, after punishing a Greek teacher of English from the village of Agros because he allegedly insulted Archbishop Makarios, EOKA distributed a leaflet, demanding the following:

We call upon all those who had the audacity to express their sympathy with a man who disrespected the Ethnarch and the heroes who fell for the most sacred ideal, freedom, and who did not repent or admit his error, to say whether they are real Greek Cypriots who love their fatherland, and ask them to stop this treacherous behaviour before we force them to.[32]

For Greek Cypriot nationalists, freedom was not a right but a duty, and enosis was not a future to be made, but a future to which one should concede.

The discipline of culture

On the northern outskirts of Nicosia as one approaches the mountain road to Kyrenia, the village of Gönyeli nestles amidst rolling terrain. In the summer, the land around the village is scorched and empty, treeless and brown. It was somewhere in this parched landscape that, in the early summer of 1958, British forces abandoned eight Greek Cypriots in the middle of the night, far from any Greek village. Their murder that night at the hands of Turks is hardly discussed in Turkish Cypriot history, but the name "Gönyeli" has come to mean for Greek Cypriots the beginning of the slow and bloody unraveling of their dreams. Only a few months before, TMT had succeeded its smaller predecessor *Volkan* (Volcano) in organizing to fight against the Greek rebellion. Greek Cypriots generally believe that TMT had colluded with British forces in the murders outside Gönyeli, and they hold TMT responsible for the following months of death and random destruction. Certainly, they believe that TMT was to blame for the first flights from mixed villages, and that it was TMT's policy to provoke violence in order to separate the communities even further. It is true that those flights from mixed villages would be an ominous precursor of the enclavement of Turkish Cypriots in the independence period and of the eventual division of the island.

The resistance seemed to have come from nowhere; but it should be clear by now that the shock of that campaign was in no way the fault of Turkish Cypriots, who had opposed enosis since the first murmurings of support for it among their Greek compatriots. That opposition, however, was framed in terms that Greek Cypriots simply could not take seriously. They laughed at the Kıbrıs Türktür Partisi (Cyprus is Turkish Party), even though now they see in it the first manifestations of "Turkey's eternal imperialistic aspirations." It was ludicrous, they would say, for a minority to claim sovereignty over the island. But Turkish Cypriots knew well and responded to the fact that the claims that "Cyprus is

Greek" were not made because the majority of the population was
Greek-speaking, but because the Greeks in Cyprus truly believed that
the island itself was Greek soil, and that their majority status could
allow them to do something about that.

As we will see in Chapter 8, the Greek Cypriot demand for "justice"
was met with a demand for "respect"—a demand that by its very nature
caused disrespect. This was why, in the postindependence period, it was
not enough for Turkish Cypriots to be equal under the law; they wanted
to be recognized as equal by their Greek compatriots. It was certainly
plausible under such conditions for British administrators and Greek
Cypriot antagonists to assert that the average Turkish Cypriot had no
understanding of community or nation, and that any supposedly nationalistic action taken was "stirred up" by troublemakers in their
leadership. At the same time, Turkish Cypriots claimed that their
"nationalistic impulses," or desires for modernization and progress,
never found a voice. Clearly, the Greek Cypriot demand for "justice"—
perceived as a universal and timeless moral attitude towards their
claims—ignored the Turkish Cypriot demand for "respect," which was
rooted in the contingencies of daily life and the humiliations that Turkish Cypriots recall with such vividness and feeling today. It was by
finding a voice, by speaking as "one man," that Turkish Cypriots hoped
to wrest from their Greek neighbors the respect that they had, until then,
refused to grant.

It is within this context that one must interpret the growing demand
among Turkish Cypriots for something that they called "culture" that
was supposed to improve the community and lead them into a brighter
future. In this regard, education was supposed to make the children
proud, even though the discipline of a nationalist education was not, for
Turkish Cypriots, the life-changing event that it came to be for their
Greek compatriots. According to one former teacher, Turkish Cypriot
schoolchildren of the 1940s were taught about "the Assyrian Turks, the
Hittite Turks, the Persian Turks." Many of the glories of Middle Eastern
history were claimed for Turkish ancestors. But this attempt to subsume
world history under Turkish history was unsystematic, and it was
dropped from the curriculum by the 1950s. What emerged in its stead
was an increased value given to "culture," which would improve the
community, unite it, and give it a voice that could command respect.

It is, indeed, interesting that while Turkish Cypriot education was
under the same constraints as that of Greek Cypriots, there were no complaints of "deturkicization." The teaching of English, the teaching of

Turkish language and history as part of world rather than national history, and the training of teachers at the intercommunal school at Morphou were all part of Turkish Cypriot education. But protests against these measures were limited, and Turkish Cypriot newspapers called, instead, for "progress" or "advancement," particularly in the villages. An English education would not "deturkicize" the youth; it would simply prove ineffective as a means of progress.

Indeed, the sociological foundation of Turkish nationalism appeared to imply that the best education was a cultural one that gave pride of place to the cultural lenses through which individuals inevitably see the world. Hence, Turkish nationalists in Cyprus would often argue on pedagogic grounds that any Anglicization of the school was educationally pointless. One member of the legislative council, Zekia Bey, commented that an English headmaster, being a foreigner to the "habits and inclination" of the children, would not know how to lead them or how to converse with their parents. He prophetically remarked that "to endeavour to change by force the character of one race into that of another race does not result in anything but prepares the ground for reaction."[33] The only road forward was the road of nationalism, and a nationalist education was not only a political but also a pedagogical necessity. Hence the resentment against the first English headmaster of the Lyceum, who invariably followed a policy of depoliticization. When he refused to allow students to celebrate Turkish Independence Day, newspapers lambasted him: "This was a disrespectful action on the part of Grant, and was a threat and a tendency on the road to extinguishing national feelings in the pupils."[34]

Much was written in response to colonial authority, and a savvy use was made of the colonial rhetoric of culture and tradition. For instance, Turkish nationalists often argued that alterations in the schools implemented by the colonial government contradicted that government's avowed aim of maintaining the traditions of its subjects. When the English headmaster decided to introduce commercial studies into the Turkish Lyceum to aid those students who would not proceed to Istanbul University, it produced a political firestorm. The governor reported that "these classes, known as 'College' classes, had formed the subject of much political opposition on the ground that they were opposed to the traditions of the Turkish race."[35]

Aside from demonstrating Turkish Cypriot politicians' simultaneous savviness and powerlessness under the colonial regime, these discussions of education are quite interesting because of the manner in which

Turkish Cypriot nationalists expected to "awaken" the villagers, and what they expected to happen as a result. Most crudely, education was to be the motor for a process of evolution. The progressive function of education was expressed as early as 1926, when a committee formed to reconsider Turkish elementary education stated its belief that since it was an "undeniable and self-evident truth"

> that education, like every other walk of life in progressive communities, must necessarily attain perfect regularity and harmony by the gradual process of evolution, and that a community should be converted from an incoherent mass into a society of mutual support, we feel convinced that by dealing with our present subject-matter, viz. our elementary education, we shall be speaking for the Moslem community which, owing to neglect and indifference, is behind-hand in everything.[36]

Similarly, the newspaper *Söz* urged in 1931 that "For us, a national education system is necessary before everything. This truth we will seek in the motherland, in the great Turkish spirit. An educational system will come from Turkey. This is how it must be …. This is the path that for us is the path of life, the path that will be our salvation."[37]

These demands were echoed in the 1950s, when it was generally believed that "culture" or "civilization" was what the villagers needed in order to awaken them to their political plight. As a result, there were numerous proposals to provide villagers with traveling lecturers and theaters, libraries, and various kinds of training. The youth magazine *Gençlik*, for instance, urged that,

> In order for the Turkish community of the island to progress, the cultured youths are obliged to use their learning. Especially in our villages, we can be certain that the day that the cultural level of the Turkish villager rises, the level of everything else will rise.[38]

Given the nature of Atatürk's reforms, it should not be surprising that there was, in fact, an underlying association of nationalism with modernization, progress, and "enlightened culture."

As has been noted earlier, Turkish nationalists in Cyprus followed Atatürk in drawing a separation between civilization, which represented material progress, and culture in the anthropological sense, which also represented a moral and spiritual progress. But the use of these terms is not always consistent. Thus, it is often very difficult to disentangle the various meanings of culture (*kültür*) that are deployed by commentators on the Turkish community's contemporary state. One writer, for instance, used "culture" in what appears to be the sense of "high culture":

Culture plays the greatest role in a community's progress and in orienting it towards the good, the beautiful, the positive, the future. A society's need for culture is as great as the need of individuals for water, bread, and air. Just as it is not possible for a person to live without air and water, so, in these times, it is outside the realm of possibility for a society to live without culture.

It can be said that culture is the real element in a society recovering, maturing, and advancing. A society without this is like a lifeless corpse. Culture directs a group of people towards the lighted path, and it gives to groups and individuals a feeling of presentiment; and it increases their capacity for understanding.[39]

A clue to how one might disentangle this use of "culture" from the more common anthropological use out of which it grew is provided by another article that explicitly attempts to delineate the proper use of the terms:

The meaning and nature of culture and civilization are generally confused, and these two words are frequently misused. We say, a cultured or civilized man, or a civilized country, a cultured country. In truth, the intended meanings of these two words are entirely different from each other. We know the difference in general between civilization and culture: civilization is a materialist accomplishment; it occurs to us that in the way that we use "culture", it is a religious, academic, and artistic accomplishment .... Some people are of the opinion that the relationship between civilization and culture is fortuitous. According to them, civilization is a ripe fruit, and culture is a flower added to the fruit.

The author goes on to remark that civilization and culture are not necessarily related and that a civilization that is not very advanced can have a culture, while a culture that is highly developed can be without the material advantages of a civilization.[40]

Turkish Cypriot education, then, was a process of "enlightenment," or *aydınlatmak*. But as I want to outline here, this was not a scientific enlightenment but rather an enlightenment of self—a clarification, if you will, of one's environment, traditions, and culture. This became clearer to me one October day when I went to one of the shoddily constructed government offices of Northern Cyprus to interview a former director of Turkish Cypriot education. He had been an inspector of schools in the 1950s, and among other things I wanted to ask him why, during that same period, Turkish Cypriots didn't complain along with their Greek counterparts of "deturkicization." He laughed heartily, then said that Turkish Cypriots weren't obsessed, like their Greek neighbors, with some idea of "pure" culture. He characterized it as "a lot of demagogy," then went on to say that it was this idea that was responsible for mistrust. "Otherwise," he says, "you could find Greeks and Turks living contentedly with each other individually, but when it came to communally, the Greeks would always try to look down at the Turks, not because they thought they were the majority here, but because they thought they belonged to a high culture …. Every race has their own characteristic; this is their characteristic."

Rather, he said, it was well-known that, pedagogically speaking, children learn best by learning first about their own environment. In this regard, education was supposed to make the children proud—proud of their inheritance, proud of their traditions. So while Greek Cypriots spoke of an *Elliniki* or *ethniki psychi*—a Greek or ethnic spirit—Turkish Cypriots spoke of *milli hisler*, or national emotions. And in complaints of problems in the schools, Turkish Cypriots would often say that their "national life" (*milli hayat*) or national feelings were in danger of being extinguished, like a flame.[41]

Indeed, the Durkheimian sociology that was the foundation of Turkish nationalism appeared to imply that the best education was a cultural one that gave pride of place to the cultural lenses through which individuals inevitably see the world.[42] But the implication of this is that those lenses should also be crafted, and possibly crafted differently.[43] The anthropological idea that persons think, feel, and see their world through culture was widely accepted. But there were certain implications of this in the Turkish nationalist context that I want to draw out here.

The first is that persons are dependent upon culture, but that *for that very reason* the nature of that culture needs to be clarified. In order to work together as a community, we all have to look through the same lenses. This is a theme that emerged repeatedly in discussions of education in Cyprus, where it was generally believed that the community had fallen behind because of disunity and lack of clear articulation of its nature and goals. As early as 1926, a committee formed to reconsider Turkish elementary education stated its belief that since it was an

> undeniable and self-evident truth that education … must necessarily attain perfect regularity and harmony by the gradual process of evolution, and that a community should be converted from an incoherent mass into a society of mutual support, we feel convinced that by dealing with our present subject-matter, viz. our elementary education, we shall be speaking for the Moslem community which, owing to neglect and indifference, is behindhand in everything.[44]

These concerns were echoed in the 1950s and 1960s, when parties and newspapers organized conferences about culture and proposed providing libraries and theaters to villagers. Those same publications repeatedly emphasized that "especially in the villages a great obligation falls on our intellectuals and cultured youths."[45]

The function of culture is particularly clear in the debates over its meaning and use, in which one journalist remarked:

> Our cultural needs have not been fully satisfied. On the day that our great need for culture can be satisfied, our future will become clear. For this reason, it is necessary for the people to appreciate this truth and to make self-sacrifices for cultural institutions, to bring up educated children, and to increase their zeal in this regard in the present.[46]

"Culture" is indeed meant here in its anthropological sense, but it takes on the overtones of "high culture." The reason for this, I would propose, is that in Turkey as well as in Cyprus the articulators and clarifiers of that culture were a group known as the *aydınlar*, or intellectuals, who in the nationalist period attempted to describe what the "true" Turkish culture had been and should be. As I noted earlier, the word *aydın* literally means "clear" or "enlightened," and when applied to a person is usually translated as "intellectual," replacing the older *münevver*, which literally means "enlightened." The *aydınlar* can include not only what we mean by intellectuals but also novelists, essayists, journalists, and poets.[47] It was their responsibility to separate the "true" Turkish culture from the false, searching, for instance, for the *öz Türkçe*, or pure Turkish, hidden underneath the useless accretions of Persian and Arabic.[48] In Cyprus, the *aydınlar* were expected to instruct "the people" in things such as religious practices, since too many villagers still clung to the syncretistic practices that borrowed from their Christian neighbors.[49] Thus culture, for all of its anthropological undertones, was still something accessible primarily through education and "enlightenment," and through a clarification made possible by the *aydınlar*.

Second, it is clear that this notion of a "culture" clarified through education also represents a form of progress. During these same debates in the 1950s, it was repeatedly stated that the only way for villagers to progress was "education (*tahsil*), education, and again education," and that "without educated youths, the villages that are behind in the cultural realm cannot progress."[50] Indeed, it was clear in such debates that culture provides the ethical aim that will direct the community into the future. The reason for this, I believe, is that Turkish nationalists in Cyprus followed Atatürk in drawing a separation between civilization, which represents material progress, and culture in the anthropological sense, though in this instance it also represented a moral and spiritual progress, *in contrast to* material progress.[51] Culture, then, was meant in its anthropological sense, but it also had a positive, even progressive value.

This equation of a fully articulated culture with a moral progress was possible, it seems, because of a fusion of Durkheimian sociology with older understandings of culture and moral progress, by which was clearly meant something quite similar to the old Kantian notion that the human race was slowly developing towards civilization and morality, and that this should make us more and more capable of being responsible citizens. Obviously, given that this progress should make us more responsible citizens, this notion of human moral progress is inseparable from the polity. There is, then, an inference to be drawn from this idea that in its more popular or Romantic forms certainly was drawn: namely, that human civilization and moral progress would be realized in particular cultural and political forms. So for Turkish Cypriots, "becoming cultured" became a moral imperative and the failure to do so a moral failing. "Progress" was a closer and closer approach to truth achieved through the *aydınlar* and resulting in an overall improvement of the community.

Conclusion

An education in nationalism must be an education oriented towards the future and thus is primarily a moral discipline that produces the habits of a patriotic life. Foucault has outlined an extremely influential analysis of modern European disciplinary measures, arguing that they arise from the emergence of the individual as an instrument of power.[52] According to Foucault's argument, modernity has produced new relations between the individual and the state, not because of the essence of modern government, but because of the methods of modern governance. Moreover, Foucault describes an ideology of government that assigns it an omniscience or omnipresence that demands an individual discipline meticulous in its attention to the details of control. He emphasizes the calculable, manipulable individual, disciplined in the linear time of state ideology where "progress" is cumulative.

In contrast to the Western European educational model analyzed by Foucault, the schools of Cyprus did not practice a discipline that was a process of objectification of the individual and the body, but one of subjectification, one in which the individual is not calculable but malleable, in which the student is not exhorted to control himself in relation to himself, but to control himself in relation to others. To put it another way, the discipline described by Foucault is one in which the notion of "evolutive," linear progress calls for an indefinite segmentation of time and control of it. However, the Greek Cypriot notion of progress, being inevitable, was in fact static: it was not a history that could be made. One finds, then, not a control exercised over time and one's disposal of it, but a control exercised over individual experience in a history which is timeless—a minute delimitation of the boundaries of the individual in relation to society rather than a micro-control of development. History cannot change, and one's experiences must conform to it, even in the future.

And for their Turkish Cypriot counterparts, the struggle for the "culture" that education would bring was fundamentally a struggle for enlightened clarity in the face of an ever-achievable future. This orientation of nationalist discipline would only be realized in the postindependence and post-1974 periods, when educated leaders who "wrote" Turkish Cypriot history also became claimants to power who "made" that history. Thus the circularity of claims to truth and claims to authority could dissolve in the rupture of violence that would recreate history itself.

From this analysis of patriotic discipline it should be clear that the two sides of nationalist violence—namely, sacrifice and aggression—are irreducible to secondary explanations that describe war not as killing for one's country but as dying for one's country. Anderson argues that "the great wars of this century are extraordinary not so much in the unprecedented scale on which they permitted people to kill, as in the colossal numbers persuaded to lay down their lives."[53] But this is hardly enough. In the conflict that erupted in Cyprus—as in most conflicts of this century—sacrifice and aggression, love and hate, freeing the land and vanquishing the enemy cannot be separated through a simple sleight of hand that substitutes epic narrative for emotional agency. Instead, we must ask how the epic becomes the emotional, and how the death of another by one's own hand becomes a patriotic act.

PART FOUR

Aftermath

Introduction

In his study just off the entryway, we sit in low, cushioned chairs as I am questioned about my ancestry. I speak in a stilted, *katharevousa*-inflected Greek as both a sign of respect and a proof of my abilities in the language. Also, I am aware that this kind of speech is politically marked, and that for men of my interlocutor's generation it is like a whisper from the mainland that they had striven so hard to reach.

My informant, whom I will call here Kostas, was one of that disgruntled group of former fighters who felt that Archbishop Makarios, long-time president of the republic, had betrayed and unjustly marginalized them after Cyprus achieved its independence in 1960. He had been close to General Ghiorgos Grivas during the anti-British struggle, and he was available, as well, when Grivas founded EOKA B' with the goal of forcing union with Greece. Nicosia is replete with signs of that struggle, and of the Turkish intervention that defused EOKA B's 1974 coup and subsequently rent the island. There are, of course, the decaying buildings and sandbags along the Green Line that divides Nicosia, as well as the ancient slogans scrawled on the walls. Greek Cypriots will often pronounce on which signs of machine gun fire are remnants of the coup, and which are mementoes of the Turkish army. Just across a narrow street from my own home in Nicosia, I could see a building riddled with bullet holes, which friends assured me were from the 1974 coup, when Kostas' companions stormed the archiepiscopal palace nearby. Almost any Greek Cypriot will blame their fate on such men, and on Turkey's eternal imperialistic aspirations. Turkey always wanted the island, they say, and these men gave Turkey a pretext to take it when they overthrew the government and began killings of Turks and their Greek Cypriot opposition. Yet these men walk free and live their lives punished only by the damning certainty of defeat.

These men walk free, one must surmise, because so much blood has been shed and so much lost that to punish them would seem superfluous. After all, their goal was an understandable—and almost an attainable—

one. They wanted to unite Cyprus with its mainland mother and to evoke in Cyprus all the glories of Greek civilization. For such men, an independent republic was ignoble, an affront to the purity of Cyprus' Greek history and the result only of petty, pragmatic politics that forced them to take the Turks into account. Although these men were a very small minority and so have become an appropriate scapegoat, their sentiments are only an extreme version of the average Greek Cypriot insistence that the island is 3,000 years Greek, that the soil, sea, and sky are Greek.[1] But these men, unlike many others, had little to lose.

The numbers of Turkish Cypriots who had little to lose is much larger. My EOKA B' informant has expressed for me his distaste for Turks, claiming that he has never met a good one, and that they are all *atakta paidhia*, or unruly children—implying that their misbehavior upset more serious plans and hence deserved to be punished. He is clearly an extreme case, and yet his words and actions, and the consequences of those words and actions, are formed within a cultural milieu that shapes and accepts them, allowing that some fundamental aspect of his claims may have some truth. It is the fundamentals of nationalist logic, I will claim in Part Four, that give scope and possibly reward to violent action and that create the conditions under which conflict, once begun, is difficult to halt.

Anthropologists and sociologists have long acknowledged that one of the things that holds us all together is the very thing that tears us apart. Part of being human, they say, is dehumanizing others. Georg Simmel's analysis of "the stranger" almost a hundred years ago has hardly been surpassed as a succinct encapsulation of the exquisite tension between nearness and remoteness that allows that barbarization of the other to take place. According to Simmel, strangers are others that we know; if we do not know them, they simply are not in our consciousness and so are not categorized. But knowing them makes them strangers to us, not part of us. They are those people with whom we have "merely universal human similarities."[2] Hence, we emphasize difference at whatever level we find it; what we stress are not the individual qualities of the stranger but the stranger's alienness, whether it be in terms of nationality or merely being from another village. "For this reason," says Simmel, "strangers are not really perceived as individuals, but as strangers of a certain type. Their remoteness is no less general than their nearness."

In Part Four I would like to ask how what we might call "ethnic estrangement" has been and is still constructed in Cyprus and how those categories of strangeness might be overcome. Living together does not necessarily create sameness, and the search for sameness is not the only and not necessarily the best way to begin a debate over the possibilities for a multicultural Cyprus. This analysis asks for a rethinking of the recent past, and in doing so places a certain burden of responsibility on Cypriots themselves. As such, it is certain to irritate those who prefer to believe that Cypriots are *only* victims—whether victims of international conspiracies,[3] victims of British colonial policy,[4] victims of the "mother countries,"[5] or victims of their own leaders.[6] The last of these explanations is perhaps the most pernicious, because it acknowledges the role played by Cypriots in creating the misfortunes of the island, but says that those Cypriots were few and that the overwhelming majority was without agency. And none of these explanations takes into account that "victims" of the sort of which they speak can be and sometimes are complicit in their own victimization. To take an extreme example, one could argue that the average German in Nazi Germany was terrorized and victimized by Hitler's regime; yet abundant evidence indicates that large numbers of Germans were actively acquiescent in the crimes perpetrated during the period.[7] Leaders are not uniformly tyrants, and even tyrants often intuit the will of the people.

The two chapters of this section, then, assert that while Cypriots have certainly been victims, they have not *only* been victims. They also assert that seeing Cypriots *only* as victims denies rather than resolves the crucial problem. And that crucial problem, I claim here, is one of ethnic estrangement that has taken a vehement and sometimes violent form in the nationalist era. The ambiguity is that not all Cypriots have been nationalists. But that, I argue here, is not fundamentally the point. Neither have all Cypriots at all times felt the strength of ethnic estrangement; it would peak in times of trouble and wane in times of calm. So it is no doubt true, as many leftists claim, that villagers got along well together and had few problems. But—as I have attempted to show—villagers were still divided by religion, and religion became ambiguously and increasingly frequently linked to ethnic nationalism during the British period. This was not a strategy of the British but a seemingly inevitable result of Cyprus' entry into modernity. So, as Peter Loizos has eloquently shown, the pathologies of a few could be shaped by the unarticulated imaginings of the many.[8]

The category of "the stranger" is poignant because he is someone with whom one lives, whom one knows at least superficially, but in whose life one does not fully participate. When older Cypriots say today that "we always got along together, they used to attend our weddings,

and we attended theirs," one can certainly interpret this hopefully with
Vassos Argyrou, who calls this a "period of peaceful co-existence" indicated by the fact that weddings were "occasions that renewed old
friendships and established new ones."[9] Certainly, it appears unambiguously true that, until some point in this century, the vast majority of
Cypriots would have found their own identities at the level of the family,
or the village, or confession, or possibly profession. And insofar as difference was constructed and the communities that we now categorize as
"Greek" and "Turkish" were divided, it was primarily through religion.
Yet it would simply be historically inaccurate to say that villagers
"always" got along together, that there were no significant perceived
differences between the communities, or that the changes in communal
self-definition associated with nationalism had not penetrated the
villages.

On the most benign level, this was represented by a polite, even
friendly, but hardly intimate form of social interaction made necessary
by the physical closeness of city neighborhoods or the economic depen-
dency within villages. One Turkish Cypriot informant who came from a
wealthy Nicosia family grew up in the 1940s in a mixed area of the
town, a map of which he drew for me on a piece of scrap paper. "It's
true," he claimed,

> we were good neighbors. If one was sick, the other would come and say hello
> …. But we wouldn't go with a Greek family to the cinema. They would go to
> see a Greek film, we would go to see a Turkish film. On Sunday morning, they
> would all go to the church, here [indicating on the map], and on Fridays we
> would go to the mosque. And in the evenings, they would not come to our
> house as guests, and we would not go to their house as guests—never. But you
> know on some afternoons and evenings, Turkish Cypriots at the time—and I
> think now, too, in Nicosia, in the walled area—people would sit in front of
> their houses, and if you had *molohiya*[10] … people would come together and do
> it [i.e., pick the leaves from the stems]. But other than that, I don't know of
> any mixing up …. Whatever relation we had, it was more an act of necessity,
> and not an act of affection.

This act of necessity would have been a basic part of life for many, but
for my informant it acted to bridge a gap that already existed.

In an important and strongly-felt assessment of the state of scholarship and writing about Cyprus, Peter Loizos employs the term "invasive
ethnicity," which he defines as "ways of thinking and acting about
nation, state, ethnic and personal identity which tend to dominate the
contexts in which they are called forth."[11] Loizos persuasively argues
that a rewriting of Cypriot history from a non-nationalist perspective

would see complications such as the class allegiances that have pro-
moted intercommunal cooperation. This assessment represents a much-
needed call to awareness of the ways in which ethnic concerns inform
and deform scholarship. But I believe that we must do more than this.

These chapters take up nationalist logics in Cyprus through a comparative prism, demonstrating the ways in which they conflict at the levels
of discourse, history, politics, and even nature. In this way, I explore
some of the ways in which ethnic estrangement may have made the
cooperation that my informant called an "act of necessity" a less and
less likely possibility. In Chapter 7, I examine ways in which ideology is
naturalized in Cyprus, how this at the same time naturalizes claims on
the land, and how such naturalization results in what I call "nationalist
logic." Chapter 8 then looks at the political impasse that results from
these differing logics and how that impasse has played out in Cyprus'
recent history. There, I interpret the demands for "justice" and "respect"
that I claim frame political discourse in the Greek Cypriot and Turkish
Cypriot communities, respectively. In fact, I will argue, it is the very
closeness of the island, the sense of entanglement with and intimate
knowledge of the other, that has made moral discipline—patriotism—all
the more compelling, binding, and blinding.

CHAPTER 7

The Purity of Spirit and the Power of Blood

Nationalism notoriously naturalizes, most often through taking the "natural" units of body and kinship as its metaphorical models. In such a way, sameness and difference may also be inscribed onto the body of the other. In this chapter I will explore that structure of differences by examining some of the ways in which nationalisms are naturalized, especially in bodies: the human body, the family as organic unit, the body of the land, and the body politic.

Much recent literature on the nation-state suggests that "natural" kinship relations are transposed onto the nation, creating images of a motherland (or fatherland) in which citizens become children with duties of loyalty to the family.[1] Here, I partially accept such claims while also arguing that kinship relations are significantly transformed in the nation insofar as they must also accommodate a kinship with the land. The national "family" is never only people but also always invokes some gendered image of the land as a member of that family. The land "belongs" to the national family, just as people do. In Cyprus, taking account of a kinship with the land has entailed a transformation of kinship relations that also partakes of religious imagery. What is centrally important in such images, I will claim, is the common substance that land and people are imagined to share. Moreover, this common substance is regarded as so 'natural' that it forms an important axiom that is central to understanding the logic of nationalisms. In the case of Cyprus, understanding the differing ways in which nationalism is naturalized is also, I claim, central to understanding the ethnonationalist conflict that has divided the island.

This chapter, then, explores the naturalization of nationalist ideologies in Cyprus, and through that naturalization, both the assimilation of land into the communal body, and the logic of histories that explain that assimilation. In discussing the transformed kinship images that result, I also wish to address what appear to me to be two inadequacies in the feminist focus on gendered images of the nation. The first is the tendency, when making comparisons, to see what is alike rather than what is different: father/mother, public/private, outside/inside, and culture/nature distinctions seem to repeat themselves in many nationalist imaginations.[2] Many argue, for instance, that "[i]n a complex play, the state is often gendered male, and the nation gendered female—the mother country—and the citizens/children become kin."[3] In this way, Pettman and others note, women become symbols of the nation and men its agents, while such symbols create a plausible belief in nationalism as a form of kinship. It appears, in such descriptions, that all forms of national gendering bear some resemblance to each other simply because of their capacity to represent the reproduction of the nation. Yet, as we will see, even images that resemble each other can have strikingly different implications. For instance, the Greek Cypriot image of Archbishop Makarios as a national, spiritual father was quite different from the Turkish Cypriot reverence for Mustafa Kemal Atatürk: the former was a presumably celibate priest dedicated to the Church, while the latter was a conquering war hero. Both can be seen as father figures, yet of very different sorts.

The second problem is the tendency, when looking at specific cases, to ignore the fact that gendered images themselves are often contradictory: the "motherland" is also often the "fatherland," just as the state may be a patriarchal figure or a nurturing mother.[4] Unraveling these various loose and contradictory metaphorical threads leads only to further description, and a vain search for consistency. Instead, I wish to argue that in Cyprus, at least, what are centrally important and generally coherent within these sets of metaphors are descriptions of what land and people share in common. Gendered images are employed to tie a specific land to a specific people in a description of relatedness. In order to do so, they must imagine that land and people share a common substance—some medium through which their relationship can continue into the indefinite future.

David Schneider has argued that in American kinship terms, relatedness is seen as something that is passed in the blood. Furthermore, he argues, "a blood relationship is a relationship of identity. People who are blood relatives share a common identity, they believe. This is expressed as 'being of the same flesh and blood.'"[5] Schneider goes on to claim that the relationship is believed to be one of material, genetic substance, and it is on the basis of this that kinship appears to be unavoidable, unchangeable, and natural. The sexual, reproductive relationship between men and women is supposed to be an affair of nature just as kinship is, even if there are specific rules surrounding it.

In examining gendered images of the nation, I believe that Schneider's analytical categories provide a useful starting point, and I am going to try to push those categories to their theoretical limits. I will argue, first, that Cypriot genderings of the nation are based on some idea of a shared substance that makes a relationship possible, though the substances that I will describe here are considerably different from Americans' images of kinship as something passed in the blood. As we will see, the Greek Cypriot community has tended to use metaphors of "soul" or "spirit" (*psychi*, or sometimes *pneuma*) to represent their kinship with the land, along with accompanying attributes of spiritual purity. In contrast, the Turkish Cypriot community has used metaphors of "blood" (*kan*), though the Turkish Cypriot use of blood is quite different from the American usage described by Schneider and is accompanied by attributes of power.

It is not a novel observation that these two metaphors have occupied central positions in the communal imaginations of Cypriots.[6] What I wish to do here, however, is to demonstrate the ways in which these very different metaphors, in fact, circumscribe the same domain insofar as both of them describe that substance through which a relationship of land and people is possible. Furthermore, by making this comparison, I also wish to draw out contrast. In other words, Greek Cypriots use the word *aima*, or blood, metaphorically, but their use of it is not the same as the Turkish Cypriot use of *kan*. Similarly, Turkish Cypriots use the word *ruh*, or soul, but with more limited scope than the Greek *psychi*. Instead, as I hope to show, the equivalence is actually between *psychi* and *kan*, between soul and blood.

The equivalence is also, ultimately, between purity and power—those essential characteristics that regulate what are perceived to be the "natural" relationships between people and land. In Schneider's argument, there is a direct correspondence between what are perceived to be biological, blood ties and consequent notions of "natural" sexual relations. Taking this analogy to its limit, I wish to show that the ruling metaphors of spirit and blood in Cyprus have essential characteristics that describe and regulate "natural," national relations. In the Greek Cypriot case, I wish to show, the union of land and people is of a rather spiritual sort, partaking of a purity that highly resembles the immaculate conception. In the Turkish Cypriot case, on the other hand, that relationship is a more literal one, stamped on the land by power. The substances of spirit and blood, and the relations of purity and power, are not Cypriots' notions of family relations transposed onto a national scale. Rather, these images take models of local relations and enlarge them in culturally plausible ways that also take into account kinship with the land.

Of course, metaphors governing the relations of the "imagined community" are more diffuse than those regulating kinship relations on the ground. With that in mind, I wish also to describe how I believe that these metaphors are naturalized in practice. Just as Americans believe that the blood relationship is an objective fact of nature, so metaphors of a kinship between people and land appear to be part of an objective, historical reality. This becomes most apparent, I believe, through cultural reason embedded in forms of historical proof. I will argue here that the "facts" of history and the apparently natural forms of proof that govern them also create a seeming reality for the "natural" relations of purity and power that regulate the relationship of people and land. And it is this, I hope to show, that makes for two very different conceptions of naturalized history divided, in Cyprus, by an abyss that has been difficult to cross.

Kan and psychi

In discussing the EOKA campaign against the British and its aim of uniting the island with Greece, one older man who had been involved in the organization of the rebellion claimed that, after the Cypriot victory over British forces, one of the British leaders had said that "we were defeated by Greek history." What did he mean by that? my informant rhetorically asked.

> He meant to say that the people of Cyprus, all the Greek people of Cyprus who are taught Greek history and are worshippers of Greece, they were filled with this great spirit (*pneuma*)—the Greek, the Greek-Christian spirit.

The word that he used—*pneuma*—means not only soul or spirit, but also the "breath of life." It is, as well, the word used to refer to the Holy Spirit. The use of spiritual metaphors is ubiquitous in nationalist discussions of the EOKA struggle, as in the opening paragraph of a book dedicated to heroes of EOKA, in which the author notes:

The spirit (*psychi*) was especially tested during the Cypriot Struggle against the English, of the period 1955–59 .... And in the end, in the midst of so much blood and so many tears, the Christian and Greek spirit of Cyprus was victorious.[7]

And yet those spiritual metaphors are even more pervasive than this context, since they are the primary means of understanding the presumably eternal Greekness of the island. Another informant, for instance, recited the lists of various conquerors of Cyprus before proclaiming that "Cyprus is still Greek. Its spirit is Greek."

Indeed, for many decades Greek Cypriot discourse has been filled with references to the eternal manner in which spirit links land and people. In the passage quoted in Chapter 5 by Bishop Leontios of Paphos, the bishop argued against government measures to alter education, claiming that Cyprus is "an historically Greek island, having a history of five thousand years, a history of a glorious civilization, occupied during these times by a population purely Greek, noble, and Christian." Moreover, he notes, it is well known that their Greek ancestors were the source of knowledge and beauty, so that "the Greek spirit (*i Elliniki psychi*) approaches the universal meaning of 'human.'"[8] Or, to take a more recent example, one Greek Cypriot textbook for students at middle schools is devoted entirely to "our occupied lands"—i.e., those lands occupied in 1974 by the Turkish army and now declared part of the Turkish Republic of Northern Cyprus—and proclaims in its introduction that:

This world lives deeply rooted within us. We stubbornly hold onto it and transmit it to our children. The longing increases with desire; we will keep the flame of tradition inextinguishable in our souls in order to transport it to where it belongs, in order to continue a march that began thousands of years ago.[9]

It is clear that in this vision "the ancestors" are linked to the present through an all-powerful, unchanging "Greek spirit."

I would like to contrast this with a Turkish version of Cypriot history. Within my first few weeks in Cyprus I had already begun to notice that a tremendous stress was laid on fighting and martyrdom, so that many friends thought it necessary to take me to former hideouts of Turkish Cypriot fighters and to areas where important battles had taken place. Soon, it became clear to me that martyrdom was a central theme in understanding Turkish Cypriots' explanation of their attachment to Cyprus, and that martyrdom was important in understanding both the meaning of the Ottoman conquest of the island and the meaning of violent events in living memory.

4. "Direniş" (Resistance) by Güner Pir, courtesy of the Turkish Republic of Northern Cyprus National Struggle Museum. To the right of the painting is a list of dates on which significant attacks against Turkish Cypriots occurred.

Indeed, blood spilled in Cyprus was not only a legitimation of Turks' presence there but also expressed a spiritual kinship with the land. For instance, in the early 1950s the newspaper of the Cyprus is Turkish Party began explaining the party's position in numerous articles that emphasized the precedence of blood spilled in the Ottoman conquest. "Take ear," said one of the more literary versions,

> the Cypriot rivers ring with Turkish warcries, and in the emerald-flowered fields nightingales sing in the fluency and refinement of the Turkish tongue. And the soil is kneaded with the blood of thousands of Turks and filled with the bones of martyrs …. Turkish Cyprus, standing like a shining rock in the deep and limpid waters of that old Turkish sea, the Mediterranean, is the possessor of such a history. For Cyprus thousands of Turks shed blood, and if necessary thousands of Turks will give their lives.[10]

Or, more recently, in the poem by Mehmet Levent that won the Turkish Republic of North Cyprus "National March" contest, the poet declaims, "Hail to the martyr's blood that gushes from this land!" (*Selam bu topraklardan fışkıran şehit kana!* [sic]).[11] Here, the link to the ancestors is quite visceral, uniting various Turkish conquests of Cypriot soil. It does not imply a lack of change, but it implies a moment of change. In other words, one is linked through the land to the ancestors not by an unchanging, immortal soul, but through what blood—and the shedding of blood—has created.

The "immortal Greek soul" of Greek Cypriot discourse is, I would argue, inseparable from the Greek Cypriot discourse of freedom. The idea that the body is enslaved and forced into allegiance to foreign rulers but that the soul remains free and Greek was one of the most central rhetorical points leading up to the period of independence. It has been perhaps best described as "the politics of waiting" (*i politiki tis anamonis*) which one Greek Cypriot teacher, scholar, and former EOKA leader defines as, "the politics in which the body is compelled to kneel but the soul remains intact and erect."[12] In fact, Greek Cypriot discourse leading up to the period of independence was filled at all levels with a division between the enslaved, corrupted body and the pure, free, and entirely Greek soul. For example, in a poem written for elementary school children during the period of the EOKA rebellion the writer asked, "What shall freedom mean?" and answered, "It's the soul in the body, it's the life in the person" and went on to opine, "The Greek may be trapped and enslaved, but his soul lives free" (*O Ellin sklavos ki'an piasti zi eleftheri i psychi tou*).[13] In this vision, the unseen but ever-present soul or spirit is timeless, eternal, unchanging, always consistent with itself. Hence, *psy-*

chi provides an internal continuity, something that is always there despite the buffeting of life and fate.

Of course, *psychi* in this sense refers both to the soul of the individual and to the spirit of the nation. Hence, this same periodical for elementary schoolchildren could talk both about the enslaved Cyprus "whose soul still cries for freedom"[14] and could often subtitle itself "the periodical of the [spiritually] pure Cypriot child" (*to periodhiko tou aghnou Kipriopoulou*). Furthermore, the extent to which the notion of an unchanging, eternal spirit had penetrated Greek Cypriot self-conceptions is perhaps best revealed in the use of the language of purity and spirituality. For instance, one 1930 protest against government measures did not explicitly use the word *psychi* but still made its claims on the basis of a spiritual continuity: "Every step of the Cypriot land (*kathe vima tis Kipriakis ghis*) demonstrates that the people is one of the most historical peoples with the same civilization, the pure, chaste Greek civilization."[15] Here the writers use the adjectives *akraifnis* and *aghnos*, each having a different connotation of purity.

The primary attribute of soul, then, is purity. And indeed, metaphors of spiritual purity were at least as common as metaphors of spirit themselves. Greek Cypriots describe their national identity in terms of cleanliness, holiness, elevatedness, even nobility. In a negative sense this purity entails a lack of mixing, of stains, of sin, of abnormalities or defects, even of experience. Purity is fundamentally consanguinal—"of the same blood," brothers. Purity is also exclusive: it excludes, by definition, anything that is not part of itself.

And here we arrive at the link between such metaphors and the gendered body of the nation. In the Cypriot case *psychi* as something internal, pure, and natural (as opposed to imposed) also entailed femininity and the honor of protecting the feminine. Hence, the physical body of the nation—the land—enslaved for centuries, had maintained a pure and chaste Greek soul. In this sense, it was not only that the earth is described as a mother, but also that the purity and chastity of the land as body of the nation were equated with femininity. So Greece was always portrayed as "the mother," while Cyprus was alternately portrayed as a mother or a chaste maiden.[16]

This symbolism for several decades imbued all aspects of Cypriot life and was present not only in speech but also in poetry, in graphic art, and even in the theater: there are dozens of reports in the British files of school performances in which a schoolgirl fettered in chains represented Cyprus struggling to join her Dodecanese sisters in the arms of her mother Greece. The importance of this motherly symbolism may be best seen in the repeated use during the 1950s of the rather awkward phrase, "*i Mitera Patridha Elladha*"—"the Mother Fatherland Greece." It appears here that *patridha*, or fatherland, had evocative limitations when used on its own.

It is not surprising, in fact, that in this period of pre-independence nationalist agitation Cyprus could be depicted as both mother and maiden. Virgins are pure, while mothers are the providers of continuity. This would be especially true if we apply to Cyprus many of the observations made for Greece that mothers provide the spiritual center of the family.[17] Moreover, it has been repeatedly observed that the *Panaghia*, or Virgin Mary, "has often played a special role as the protectress of the Greek nation."[18] The *Panaghia* also has very local manifestations so that "different" *panaghia*s are associated very strongly with localities, even villages.[19] Whether mother or maiden, one could argue, is immaterial to the case, if one takes seriously the assessment of John Peristiany, who claimed that in Cyprus "if it were possible to combine the concepts of virginity and motherhood the ideal married woman would be a married mother virginal in sensations and mind."[20] Whichever feminine metaphor one chose, one's motives with regard to her were pure ones, involving her protection and the task of freeing her from the degrading enslavement of foreigners.[21]

Moreover, I believe that this is where we find the significance and strength of the church; in fact, it appears that here we may find some effective resolution of the oft-noted peculiarity of the Orthodox Church's involvement in a nationalism that appealed to the pre-Christian past.[22] The notion of a "Greek spirit" could elide the distinction between the ancient, heathen past and the more recent Christian one by connoting spiritual purity and continuity. Moreover, Iossifides notes that in the Greek village where she worked, many of the villagers believed in a common kinship uniting Orthodoxy through time, secured by the Virgin Mary, who unites the family of humans with the family of the Divine. "Through the Panayia," she claims, "humans are, so to speak, in an affinal relationship with the Divine."[23] When transposed to the plane of the nation, it appears that there is a circular move at work that links *psychi* and its purity to the land as mother, that the mother is conceived as the body of the Church, and the Church as the soul of the nation.[24] Hence, priests could also represent Christ protecting the virginal body of the Church, namely the land. This certainly appeared to be at work in the images of Archbishop Makarios as spiritual father and the land of Greece as spiritual mother.

Since the 1974 invasion of Turkish troops and division of the island, the gendering of the nation has not significantly changed, but now the nation is represented as a mourning mother in black.[25] Here, land and people are joined in the pure tears of the mother crying for her missing—whether missing persons or lost lands. In this symbolism, the women themselves become iconic, crying at the ceasefire line in periodic protests in which they hold the photos of their missing sons and husbands. Moreover, in another extension of this symbolism, features of the land are sometimes individualized and represented as lost children. Hence, a poem by a female author is able to represent the Pentadhaktylos Mountains as "The Pentadhaktylos, My Son" and to individualize its five peaks with the names of former heroes of the anti-colonial rebellion.[26] And both the missing lands and missing men can be represented in paintings as the martyred Christ and their mothers as the Virgin Mary left behind to mourn.[27]

In direct contrast to this, I want to pose the Turkish Cypriot use of *kan*, or blood. Although this metaphor was mobilized to support a political cause only in the 1950s, its evocative power to define the community was demonstrated much earlier. After the first intercommunal riots in 1912, many Turkish Cypriot families began emigrating to Anatolia. In that year, a meeting was held to protest the court's judgment regarding the rioters, and one of the speakers ordered the following:

> We must remember that our Moslem Forebears shed their blood and lost sixty thousand souls in this island. The ground we stand on contains the blood and remains of our Forebears. We hear that a good many of you intend leaving the island, but you are not to do so. You are to stay here and assert your rights and die.[28]

But this was not only the language of rhetoric, even in this early period. Indeed, it had become a common way of encapsulating the Turkish Cypriot community's links to their native land. For instance, one Turkish Cypriot woman recalled that when she entered school in 1919, her mother taught her the following poem to recite to her teachers:

> *Toprakları sıksam çıkar Türk kanı,*
> *Yerleri kazsam çıkar Türk kemiği.*
> *Nedir bu Türklerin çektiği!*
>
> If I squeeze this soil, Turkish blood comes out,
> If I excavate this land, Turkish bones come out.
> Oh, what these Turks have endured![29]

In such images, blood imbues the land and becomes consubstantial with it.

Furthermore, the blood soaking the land through martyrdom is clearly masculine, achieved through conquest, while the land itself is connoted as feminine, especially in relationship to the image of an *Anavatan*, or motherland. Indeed, Samuel Kaplan reports from southern Turkey that "[b]lood as vital life essence finds resonance with popular notions of virility."[30] Kaplan notes that many village men believe that blood and sperm are interchangeable, and that sperm flows in a man's veins. Furthermore, the red of the Turkish flag is clearly associated both with territory and with blood, so that "[a]s soldiers shed blood for the flag, the banner becomes one with the collective body. Flag and soil are interchangeable surfaces."[31]

Carol Delaney has proposed for Turkey that this is a part of the monogenetic "seed and soil" metaphors that she believes are shared in the Abrahamic traditions, in which procreation is explained as the active male seed planted into the passive female soil.[32] This, she believes, also applies to and explains nationalist images of conception of the nation, in which "what is emphasized ... is not just gender, but gender in the context of reproduction."[33] She extends this to the images of *Devlet Baba* (Father State) and *Anavatan* (Motherland), which she believes were manipulated in the early nationalist period to symbolize the control of state over a land uniting a people.[34]

However, in the descriptions above it is clear that the creative act is the joining together of these two entities in a form of matrimony. Blood and bones would lose their force if not joined in the land and sanctified in the remembrance of those for whom they constitute "the ancestors." Indeed, such images appear to be ones of a type of marriage—a marriage of Turkish power and conquered land from which one claims one's lineal descent. This can be seen, as well, in the contested designation of Cyprus as the *Yavru Vatan*, or "Baby Homeland," in contrast to the *Anavatan*, which is Anatolia. In Turkey this association is quite common, clearly implying that Cyprus is the offspring of the Anatolian mother and the Turkish blood shed in the island.[35] While many Turkish Cypriots now resent the belittling implications of this designation, many also find it difficult to resist the cultural logic that leads to it without rejecting Turkish nationalism altogether.

Hence, blood is a life force, containing the potential for creativity. In this sense, blood's primary attribute is power, implying strength, vigor, energy, force. In social terms, power is amoral—it is neither good nor bad. In political terms, power is creative, authoritative. So, Turkish blood shed in Cyprus was foundational, authoritative, incontrovertible. There are no questions of mixing here: power can incorporate all into itself. If anything, power is expansive and therefore, I would argue, affinal in the anthropological sense, so that it is corporative and incorporative. I should also note that while one can have varying degrees of power, one cannot have varying degrees of purity. Purity is all or nothing, white or black. Power, on the other hand, is negotiable and tameable, as well as, at times, uncontrollable.

This is not to say that Turkish Cypriots were not concerned with mixing; indeed, metaphors of blood seem invariably to elide with notions of racial purity.[36] But what I want to propose is that this was a purity of power—that mixing did not entail defilement but loss of strength.[37] In practice, the concern with blood and bloodlines did not emphasize the unnaturalness of mixing, but rather its immanent possibility, and the possibility that it would dilute the strength of the community. Hence, one of the greatest fears in the middle part of the century was that Greek Cypriots would seduce Turkish girls. One Turkish Cypriot woman recalled such a "kidnapping," or "elopement" (the Turkish *kaçırmak* is ambiguous in this situation) in the late 1940s, which she claimed was provoked by Greek "propaganda." "In the Greek churches," she claimed, "they had started to make propaganda saying, 'You should marry Turkish girls.'"[38] Although the verity of the accusation is doubtful, I heard many similar recollections about this period, themselves descriptive of Turkish Cypriot fears of powerlessness and assimilation.

Such fears also go far to explain the 1950 Turkish Cypriot family law, which retained religious aspects of marriage in order to outlaw the marriage of Turkish girls and Greek boys.[39] While the law itself was ultimately expressed as a prohibition of marriage between a Muslim woman and a non-Muslim man, the intent of the prohibition was clear in public discussions of it. One group associated with the newspaper *İstiklal* wanted the wholesale adoption of the Turkish law in opposition to the larger, better supported group around the newspaper *Halkın Sesi*. The latter used the example of intercommunal marriage as the most compelling reason for wishing to adapt the law to Cypriot circumstances:

> There's also a point that is added to the Turkish law: "Turkish girls are not to marry Greeks." The commission put this in with the intention of protecting our most important of rights amongst the Greek majority. Because we are in a foreign country (*ecnebi bir memlekette olduğumuz için*) this was seen as a

need. This is part of our religious ethics. What will you say, dear *İstiklalcı*s, if
we remove this clause? Should we remove this saying that the Turkish Civil
Law should be brought to Cyprus to the letter?[40]

At the same time, marriage amongst Turkish Cypriot youths was
strongly encouraged, though in the proper and "civilized" (*medeni*) way:
through a controlled form of love.[41] "According to the opinions of sociologists," said one newspaper article, "the most suitable thing is
marriage by meeting with the knowledge and approval of the family."[42]

Indeed, there appears to be a close similarity between the manner in
which the sociological bases of marriage were rethought in the early
Turkish nationalist period, and the emotive connotations of an image of
Turkish blood and bones spilling into and mingling with the soil. Both
nation and family, I would suggest, were being rethought as created,
contingent centers of emotion that depended for their existence on the
"proper" devotion of their members. Hence, the nation was almost
invariably discussed in affective terms: *milli hisler*, national emotions or
sentiments; *millet sevgisi*, nation love; *bayrak sevgisi*, flag love; *Atatürk
aşkı* or *Atatürk sevgisi*, Atatürk love. In similar ways, I believe, images
such as blood spilled indicate not only a relatedness to the land through
consubstantiality, but also a singular love for the land metaphorically
encapsulated in the notion of blood. As in romantic love, there is something here of what Simmel calls the rejection of generalization in the
enjoyment of the seeming uniqueness of intimate, erotic relations.[43]
Love, in this sense, appears ineluctable, unchosen. And so love itself
becomes a duty, and the emotions of family and nation circumscribe a
seemingly unchosen and unavoidable relation of nearness.

Blood, then, contains what is essential, which is life or power. Furthermore, while the power of blood is explicitly linked to the masculine
realm, the land is linked to the feminine, but as wife rather than as
maiden or mother. It is the *marriage* of the masculine and feminine
realms—their erotic union—that is productive. This is particularly
apparent in the fact that it was the *marriage* of Greek boys and Turkish
girls that was at issue in the mid-century—not the girls' violation, but
their seduction and incorporation into the other community. So, in the
Greek Cypriot case the ideal is of a virgin mother protected by a celibate, spiritual father, and the mother (like the Virgin Mary) can be
productive and provide continuity on her own. In the Turkish Cypriot
case, however, it is the marriage of land and blood—of fertility and
power—that produces descendants. It is in this sense, then, that the warrior, Mustafa Kemal, could be called Atatürk, or "father of the Turks,"

5. A Turkish Cypriot village under attack, artist's name withheld. Courtesy of the Turkish Republic of Northern Cyprus National Struggle Museum.

6. Awaiting the return of the missing. From the Church of the Missing, Republic of Cyprus.

while his chief commander could be depicted in a quasi-marital relationship with the *Anavatan*, or motherland.[44] Moreover, such images make self-conscious reference to the Muslim idea of the *gazi*, or holy warrior fighting for the faith. Indeed, Mustafa Kemal himself was awarded the title of *gazi* in 1921, since his rise to power was part and parcel of cleansing the land of invaders.[45]

In the post-1974 period, this symbolism is most clearly seen in the status of the new *şehitler*, or martyrs, who are invariably portrayed as those fallen in the battle that divided the island. The symbolism is uniformly masculine and triumphant, perhaps best represented by the enormous monument to the *şehitler* that today projects from the Kyrenia coast in Northern Cyprus. Though dedicated to those who were slain, it was placed at the site of one of the 1974 Turkish landings and is most obviously interpretable as a giant modernist hand rising from the sea. Also, in posters used during the 1974 Turkish military campaign and which Greek Cypriots often use today in their own propaganda, the images clearly glorify the violence of conquest.

Spirit or blood, then, are imagined as the common substance shared between land and people, and it is within this framework that imagined kinship ties of the nation acquire their rhetorical force. Male and female images may be employed at various moments to express different things—for example, the Greek image of land is usually that of the mother or virginal girl; however, in the post-1974 depictions of lost lands, the comparison drawn between missing lands and missing men leads often to a depiction of the land as male, kept in the memory of a weeping woman. Alternatively, one may find a powerful contrast in the reverence by Greek Cypriots of the presumably spiritual and ascetic Archbishop Makarios,[46] also first president of the Republic of Cyprus, and that by Turkish Cypriots for the warrior-hero Mustafa Kemal Atatürk.[47] If one wants gendered consistency, one will not find it here, or in any such images. What is consistent, however, is the image of a medium through which land and people are related, and of the "natural" relations of purity and power that govern their intercourse.

Finally, I should note that while images of land or people may not be consistently gendered, there is a relatively consistent gender representation of the purity of spirit and the power of blood: the former is predominantly represented by feminine imagery, while the latter is in almost all cases represented as masculine. This fact cannot, I believe, be fully understood without placing it in the context of that which explains this substance shared between land and people: namely, differing theories of history. As we will see, the purity of spirit also clearly represents the natural order, something outside human intervention, something which always has been and always will be. The power of blood, on the other hand, represents a creative potential and the possibility for human, cultural intervention in the progress of nature. In other words, these gendered representations appear to depict an order of things in which, in Sherry Ortner's terms, "female is to male as nature is to culture."[48] But it is only, I believe, by understanding local theories of history that we can see why the substance linking land and people should be gendered along a nature/culture divide.

The historians and the nature of history

Having outlined two different versions of kinship between land and people, I will now argue that it is not gender or kinship *per se* that gives these images their apparently naturalized force. In Schneider's terms, American kinship depends upon a prior belief in the biological "facts" that appear to define and determine relations of kinship and family. This belief is so strong, says Schneider, "that it is quite difficult, often impossible, in fact, for Americans to see this as a set of cultural constructs and not the biological facts themselves."[49] Schneider utilizes a distinction between reproduction as a biological fact and the cultural construction of reproduction as a biological fact, noting that the cultural construction of reproduction as biological fact derives its force from the belief that it is purely natural.

Again stretching Schneider's analytical framework, I want to argue that in similar ways, the nationalist kinship of people and land is seen as a part of the historical "facts." Clearly, the relationship of land and people is not biological but historical, and so history replaces biology as a natural force, though again history is culturally constructed in the same way that biology is. Just as shared genetic substance derives from a theory of a natural, biological order of things, so shared spirit and blood derive from theories of a natural, historical order of things. In other words, twisting one of Schneider's phrases to my own purposes, we could say that nationalist kinship is not a theory about history; but history serves to formulate a theory about nationalist kinship.

This is easiest to see when one looks at what are taken to be naturally convincing forms of historical proof in the two communities of Cyprus. "Proof" always implies certain culturally accepted axioms that can be taken to be true ("the earth is round"), as well as culturally accepted logical forms to constitute sufficient proof. In other words, as well as axiomatic statements, the apparent transparency of logical proof also relies upon certain ideas of "natural" relations: P, $P—>Q$, therefore Q. I wish to argue here that the "natural," "genealogical" relations inscribed in gendered imaginings of the nation represent a naturalization of the meaning of particular relations in history. Just as any statement that we make about history relies upon the relationship between "before" and "after," so other statements about the meaning and movement of history must be inscribed in the nature of things. Spirit and blood, I hope to show, in fact represent and derive from culturally specific ideas about the "natural" historical order.

As we will see, Turkish Cypriots speak of their history in terms of contingency, and forms of historical proof exist within what I will call here an "archaeological" discourse, attempting to secure truth by tracing causation. Their Greek Cypriot compatriots, on the other hand, construct an ineluctable history discussed within the framework of what I will call a "genealogical" discourse in which historical proof is aimed at demonstrating truths that are taken to be self-evident. In genealogical discourse, one traces links between persons and events whose relationship to each other is already presupposed. In archaeological discourse, in contrast, one attempts to construct a causative sequence that will explain events. In the first, one validates truth; in the second, one uncovers truth.

In his own work of comparison of the two Cypriot communities, Yiannis Papadakis has analyzed a number of the ways in which what Paschalis Kitromilides calls the "dialectic of intolerance" has worked further to separate the two communities by leading to extreme positions in situations of conflict.[50] In a relatively recent article, Papadakis analyzes what he calls the "mythical realities" in each community: the common Greek Cypriot belief in Turkish expansionism and the common Turkish Cypriot belief in a continuing push for enosis.[51] These are, according to Papadakis, mirrors of each other in that the purveyors of these ideas find confirmation for them wherever they look. Moreover, by finding "evidence" of the enemy's alleged actions and motives, one gains justification for one's own communal "autobiographical narrative."[52] Papadakis furthermore notes that there are certain fundamental similarities in the nationalist projects pursued by both communities, particularly in those projects' extreme forms. Among those is the fact that national groupings engage in historical myth-making that justifies present actions.

While Papadakis makes a number of important observations, he appears unwilling to consider the possibility that these nationalisms are not mere reflections of each other but in fact are constituted by fundamental differences. The perceived threats of Turkish expansionism and enosis are not, I wish to argue, parts of the same framework of nationalist discourse, but rather constitute a pair of "antithetical assumptions about being-in-the-world," in the words of John Comaroff.[53] The ways in which Greek and Turkish Cypriots "prove" the continuing threat of Turkish expansionism or enosis are based upon certain fundamental assumptions about self and other rooted in "natural" notions of conception and genealogy.

Many Greek Cypriots expressed the belief to me that Turkish Cypriots are Greeks "by blood," but that they had converted to Islam in the early years of Ottoman rule. Or, as one young professional expressed it to me, "Even if my brother goes astray [i.e., becomes a Muslim], he's still my brother." Proof of such an idea is taken from many aspects of the syncretistic history of the island. One older man who had once been a teacher and who had fought with EOKA explained to me that

> The Turkish Cypriots whom one sees now … a large part of them are Greeks who left their religion. One proof [*apodheiksi*] of this is that there are plenty of Turkish villages with the names of saints—Aghios Vasileios, it's a Turkish village; Aghia Varvara, it's a Turkish village. And what this is is an indication that these areas during the Lusignan period [i.e., before the arrival of the Ottomans] were occupied by Greeks and they were Islamicized with the Tourkokratia [Ottoman rule].

In other words, in this older man's view, the fact that Turkish villages retained Greek names was a sure indication that its inhabitants were "really" Greeks.

While this idea of underlying blood ties is a common belief, it has taken different tones in different periods of the island's history. For instance, in two articles from 1964, the historian Theodoros Papadhopoulos attempts to demonstrate "the importance of Islamization as the demographic source of the Turkish Cypriot community."[54] Indeed, he claims, at the time that the British left Cyprus in 1959, there were "only" 45,458 persons who could claim to be "true" Turks, but one can only understand this demographic fact by "uncovering from under the cloak of Muslim character their Christian origins."[55] In another publication, the same author argues that this changes the entire character of the "ethnological problem" in Cyprus and by implication should change diplomatic policy. This is clearly a use of "real" blood ties to exclude from political consideration the claims of a minority that by Papadhopoulos' demographic magic is virtually eliminated.[56]

Yet this same argument is reflected quite differently in the post-1974 period by Kyriakos Chatziioannos. Using many of the same statistics, he also takes the fact that many Muslim Cypriots spoke Greek and practiced religious rituals of a syncretistic nature as an indication of their "true" Greek nature. From this he claims to have demonstrated "the fact that the Turkish Cypriots are our brothers, ancient and new victims of the Turks of Turkey, just as we are."[57] He further claims that the Republic of Cyprus needs to make clear to the United Nations and to all its friends that

> the Turks of Turkey are strangers to the Turkish Cypriots. That they [the Turks] are of a different ethnological composition than the others [Turkish Cypriots], who are our kinsmen [*pou einai dikoi mas syngeneis*]. That with the Turkish Cypriots we lived peacefully and like brothers and that Turkey, knowing this, undertook to turkify them and to uproot them from their hearths.[58]

Moreover, this concern with a purity and continuity that underlies external appearances is reflected in what I have called a "genealogical" discourse, by which I mean one that merely attempts to trace links that are already assumed. This is a very prevalent form of "proof," expressed, for instance, in opening remarks given in a 1993 international archaeological symposium by the then minister of education, who stated that:

> The goddess of love emerged from our sea shores, and the depths of our soil have shed light on 3,000 years of Greek history and civilization because the heart of the island, since the time of the Trojan war, beats along a Greek frequency despite the Laestrygons and the Cyclops encountered in the flux of time.[59]

The symposium itself was supposed to be a proof of what was already known, just as various moves of the Turkish state are taken as "proof" of Turkey's eternal imperialistic aspirations.

In contrast to this genealogical discourse and distinctly ethnic notion of genealogical blood ties, I want to suggest that, despite Turkish Cypriots' uses of blood as a metaphor for historical power, it is blood without genealogy—it is simply blood shed, or an inert historical fact, something that one uncovers archaeologically. As in the Greek Cypriot case, this is perhaps best understood through the ways in which Turkish

Cypriots attempt to explain the other community. One old teacher remarked that "we were never obsessed, like the Greeks, with some idea of a 'pure culture.'" Rather, he argued, the Greeks have fantastic notions about the nature of descent:

> You see they have this utopia. For instance, this business about the island of Aphrodite. They think that Aphrodite *really* came out of the sea in Paphos, and then went up to our village and took a bath in the spring near Latchi .... Of course this is a myth and so on. But to believe that this island is *the island of Aphrodite*—Aphrodite's something mythical. Very strange to me, anyway—to make it a political thing. Some things which came from the walls of Troy say that some of the men who escaped from there established some colonies here, but there were no Greeks here. But all these things which we have ... show that either the culture was connected mainly with Anatolia because it's closer, to Syria, and then to Egypt. The Greeks came later, and they never dominated the island as such.

Like the few Turkish Cypriot works that deal directly with the issue of Greek Cypriot culture, the concern here is with heterogeneity, factuality, and mixture.

An interesting example of this comes from Necmi Potamyalızâde, whom I mention in Chapter 5 as a teacher and self-proclaimed defender of the Turkish Cypriot community. He was also an ardent Anglophile who used his excellent command of English to write volumes to whomever would read them. He continued for over two decades to write long and often unprintable letters to the editors of the *Morning Post* and the *Near East* in which he used Homer, Herodotus, and other ancient sources to undermine Greek Cypriots' claims. These sources, he believed,

> clearly proved that the Greek Christians of Cyprus are not Greek by origin and descent, that their language is not the language of Homer, but "only a dialect of the ordinary commercial language of the Eastern Mediterranean which has gradually superseded the Italian," that Cyprus had never been a Helline island, that the permanent retention of Cyprus by Great Britain is most just, honourable, necessary and a sacred moral obligation, that it can never be just or reasonable to allow a plebiscite in Cyprus about the political status of the island.[60]

He cited his own ancestors' arrival in the island during the conquest of 1571 in an attempt to "disprove" the claim that Turkish Cypriots were in fact converted Greeks and hence Greek by blood.

Indeed, Necmi was only one of the most learned representatives of that "archaeological" discourse that soon became the most common way in which Turkish Cypriots discussed their own history in their island.

This even included citing the geological fact that the island itself had, aeons ago, broken away from mainland Anatolia and still shared its shelf. One of the more interesting examples of this type of work is that by Mahmut İslâmoğlu, who, in his book *Cypriot Turkish Culture and Art*, begins the work by saying that it is "dedicated to all our martyrs who made Cyprus a homeland for us" (*Kıbrıs'ı bizler için vatan yapan tüm şehitlerimize ithaf olunur*). Then sandwiched between chapters that deal with handicrafts and food (including recipes) and those that deal with wedding customs and sayings is a chapter called "Cypriot Turks' origins, blood groups and resemblances to the blood of neighbors." Yet the conclusion that he draws appears to prove nothing about what Turkish Cypriots *are* and only to show what they are *not*, in defense against attempts to claim them as Greeks by blood. So after a comparison of blood groups he summarizes by saying that "it can be seen that the Cypriot Turk is not a convert but is of Anatolian Turkish origin."[61] He then proceeds to devote the rest of his work to an in-depth demonstration of the ways in which Greek Cypriot culture is mixed with and influenced by that of the Turkish Cypriots—in other words, to show its lack of purity, its heterogeneity, and the power of factuality.

Turkish Cypriot "archaeological" discourse appears to present an odd and significant contrast to Anderson's claim that in the nationalist imagination the Unknown Soldier must remain unidentified. "To feel the force of this modernity," Anderson notes, "one has only to imagine the general reaction to the busybody who 'discovered' the Unknown Soldier's name or insisted on filling the cenotaph with some real bones."[62] Yet, it was precisely the "reality" and specificity of the imaginations of conquest that gave to Turkish Cypriot history its discursive force. Potamyalızâde himself wrote a poem in 1943 addressed to "all our martyrs and those who love them," meaning those who had died in the conquest of 1571. In it, he addressed the "martyr" in the second person singular, calling,

> Hello, oh great martyr, oh great soldier!
> Hello, oh undying soul, oh immortal guide!
> Your tomb: not this transitory dome, but the heavens,
> Your light: time lit by moon and stars:
> Birds do not fly over this fortress, but you flew,
> Steel cannot penetrate these walls, but you did.[63]

The poem derives its discursive power precisely from the imagined recreation of conquest and specificity of lives.

Moreover, the "reality" of this corporeal union with land is not only poetic; it is commonly invoked as an expression of viscerality. The commonplace aspect of it may be seen, for example, in a recent newspaper editorial that berated an unnamed citizen for allegedly attempting to sell his property over the internet to a Greek Cypriot. The writer exclaims, "You caused the bones of the martyrs to ache in the native land" (*Şehitlerin kemiklerini sızlattınız memlekette*).[64] Like the images of those killed between 1963 and 1974 that one finds throughout Northern Cyprus, this invocation of "martyrs" is not anonymous but is given specificity through the names and faces of not only Turkish soldiers but also one's family members, co-villagers, and friends.

These common, naturalized understandings of national conception and descent are also, clearly, expressions of the nature of history. Greek Cypriot versions of history consistently demonstrate purity and continuity, while Turkish Cypriot versions consistently emphasize brute factuality and heterogeneity. This is why, I believe, forms of historical proof used in the Greek Cypriot community tend only to reiterate and validate truths that are already given, while forms of historical proof used in the Turkish Cypriot community tend to be used to affirm the truth of their experience not only through the constant citation of the remembered past but also through a compilation of "truths" about the contingent nature of Cypriot history.

To return to Papadakis' article, one can see this in the ways in which Greek and Turkish Cypriots "prove" the continuing threats of Turkish expansionism and enosis. Perhaps the key lies in one of Papadakis' own observations, when he notes that although Turkey had clearly made contingency plans regarding Cyprus, "to argue that the problem is simply one of Turkish Expansionism is to ignore the rather striking contingency of the 1974 coup and amounts to a projection of current problems into a distant past."[65] Conversely, although clearly enosis had been an important part of Greek Cypriot community life even into the 1960s, "projecting this into the present suggests an effort to justify a problematic—certainly by UN standards—*status quo*."[66]

While Papadakis wishes to see these two sets of imaginings as reflective of each other, clearly the accusations lodged and the proof mobilized in their service take place at considerably different levels of abstraction. Greek Cypriots "demonstrate" the eternal imperialistic aspirations and plans of an entity of which they have no direct knowledge except as a military machine. In such discussions, "Ankara" becomes the seat of an evil empire whose primary goal is and always has been to expand and crush all those surrounding it. Furthermore, this discourse almost always links present-day Turkey's supposed barbaric irredentism in a sweeping arc through several centuries into the Ottoman past. Turkish Cypriots, however, "demonstrate" the continuing aspirations of those whose names and faces they know quite well. They discuss the alleged plans of people with whom they grew up and went to school.

Indeed, not all myths are the same, and the difference in content and form of those myths reflects not only a superficial difference but also a more fundamental difference regarding what constitutes a convincing narrative or sufficient proof. John Comaroff has noted that, at least in ideal-typical terms, nationalisms tend to dissolve into two types, which he terms Euronationalism and ethnonationalism. The first might be seen as a "constructed" type, one which gives itself a historical origin and places emphasis on chronologies and the process of homogenization. The second might be seen as primordialist and essentialist, "[i]ts genesis may be ascribed to superhuman intervention, and its past, whether or not it is told in the manner of a narrative, is often condensed, authoritatively, as tradition or heritage."[67] Clearly, the emergence of these types of historical construction depends itself upon history, and in particular on one's position in an unequal political-economic relationship, as Comaroff demonstrates elsewhere.[68]

What is interesting in the Cypriot case is both the extent to which the nationalisms present in Cyprus appear to conform to these ideal-typical models, and the manner in which they invoke ideas about forms of "natural" relations that can constitute the basis for forms of historical proof. The Turkish Cypriot version has been constructivist, capable of incorporating change into its account. It is, in that sense, based on a contingent understanding of history that particularly emphasizes conquest—the Ottoman conquest, the 1974 "conquest"—and does not claim an ineluctable destiny either for themselves or for the island. This is why Turkish Cypriots were capable of taking on a Turkish identity that was self-consciously constructed for them by Atatürk in the republican period. The Greek Cypriot version, in contrast, has been primordialist and has emphasized ethnic continuity ("Cyprus is 3,000 years Greek") and the pure Greek identity of the island. This contrast is partly seen in claims of awareness: Turkish Cypriots make no claims to awareness of an ethnic identity before the Atatürk period, whereas Greek Cypriots claim "always" to have had an awareness of their ethnic bond. This is also most strongly expressed in the metaphors of birth discussed above: while Greek Cypriots claim a spiritual birth through the unity of history, religion, and land, Turkish Cypriot nationalists claim a more literal birth through the conquest of Cyprus by Turkish warriors whose blood spilled into and fertilized the land.

These rather different forms of nationalist logic clearly represent the historical "facts," and it is on the basis of these historical "facts" that one understands the kinship of land and people through spirit or blood. When looked at in this way, I believe, we come to a more complex understanding of the nature of nationalist kinship than that which proposes a more direct correspondence between family and nation. For instance, what I have outlined here appears directly to contradict the claims of Carol Delaney, who has discussed the parallels between relations of family and nation within the context of Turkey,[69] and more broadly for the Abrahamic religions. As noted before, Delaney's central thesis is that all relations of authority in the West stem from what she calls a "monogenetic" theory of procreation, in which the creative "seed" of the man is planted in the passive "soil" of the woman. Her suggestion is that all nationalisms stemming from the Abrahamic traditions should be the same with regard to notions of conception and their production of gendered relations of authority. Moreover, she believes that it is through similar notions of the national family—seen especially in descriptions of national conception—that one can find the source of attachment to the nation, presumably shared in all nationalisms stemming from the Abrahamic tradition.[70]

However, if what I have outlined above can be seen as convincing, then her proposal of a similarity in nationalisms derived from the Abrahamic tradition appears to be distinctly misguided. And it is misguided, I have argued, precisely because of an attachment to a direct parallel between understandings of family and constructions of national kinship. Moreover, the difference that I have outlined is not one that is peculiar to Cyprus and its history; interesting parallels can be drawn between Bosnia-Herzegovina and Israel/Palestine, at least. In the former case, Tone Bringa argues that "the Muslims understood and communicated their identity in a different idiom from both Serbs and Croats."[71] While their Christian (Orthodox and Catholic) neighbors emphasized blood, descent, and the naturalness of their ethnic identity, "the Muslims, on the other hand, referred to their collective identity in an idiom which de-emphasized descent ('ethnicity') and focused instead on a shared environment, cultural practices, a shared sentiment, and common experiences."[72] In somewhat similar fashion, Israelis have emphasized the remote past and their eternal attachment to the land of Israel, seeing

Palestinian history-making as a false attempt to make claims on a land to which the Jews have a holy, historical promise.[73]

The purity of spirit and the power of blood, because naturalized as axiomatic principles and structured as forms of natural relations, also appear to work transparently. Comaroff has summarized a similar process by noting that

> [f]rom the perspective of Euronationalism, all ethnonationalisms appear primitive, irrational, magical, and, above all, threatening; in the eyes of ethnonationalism—which appears perfectly rational from within …—Euronationalism remains inherently colonizing, lacking in humanity, and bereft of social conscience.[74]

Comaroff goes on to remark that "[b]ecause they are founded on antithetical assumptions about the very nature of being-in-the-world, each appears to the other to belong to a different time and space."[75] I have attempted here to take Comaroff's analysis a step further, by uncovering some of the ways in which these antithetical assumptions may be naturalized as forms of rational thought. In short, cultural constructions of the "natural" historical facts give a factuality to the purity of spirit and the power of blood as understandings of the "natural" relations of people and land. In other words, it is not only that nationalism enlarges the "natural" relations of family, but that nationalism transforms those relations in particular ways that not only make the cultural into something natural, but that make a naturalized history into a form of cultural reason.

Conclusion

There is a coherent connection, then, between notions of the natural and the cultural logics that form the basis for ideology. The seeming reality of a substance shared between land and people derives from cultural notions of the natural, historical "facts," seen most clearly in forms of proof, which themselves depend upon culturally determined understandings of naturalness. We see at work, then, cultural logics and the instantiation of those logics in notions of substance that constitute what Bruce Kapferer defines as an ontology: "the fundamental principles of a being in the world and the orientation of such a being toward the horizons of its experience."[76]

As Kapferer notes, at any given moment, for any given person, different, and even conflicting, ontologies may be at work—individualistic capitalism alongside a religious worldview that emphasizes selflessness, for instance. Where those ontologies are articulated as ideology, one may become dominant because of its overriding capacity to explain the real of the everyday and to predict the future. If the analysis of the previous chapters is convincing, it should be clear by now how and why ontologies rooted in Christian and Muslim traditions were articulated in a new era as the ideologies of nationalism. The difference between the two has often appeared as part of the "dialectic of intolerance," or the tendency for extreme versions of these forms of thought to emerge in situations of conflict. It is certainly that, but I believe that it is more than that, and that indeed the inability to bridge the abyss between these forms of nationalist logic has remained hidden because of the tendency to see these nationalisms as reflections of each other—to subsume them into the same cultural logics or religious traditions. However, it should be clear by now why, to the contrary, the articulation of these logics as ideology set Cypriots on an ideological course that was destined to drive them farther and farther apart.

CHAPTER 8

Justice or Respect?

In the summer of 1996 one of the worst post-1974 flare-ups of violence occurred on the ceasefire line that divides the Greek and Turkish areas of Cyprus. That summer, motorcyclists trailing Greek flags tried to cross the buffer zone in the name of freedom, crying that they wanted to return to their homes. Most were stopped by United Nations soldiers, but one made it into Northern Cyprus, where he was beaten to death as cameras caught the gruesome mauling in vivid color. He was not only kicked and trampled by a mob of men, but he was also beaten with sticks studded with nails. A week later during the funeral procession that also took place along the buffer zone, his cousin darted past the U.N. guards and tried to climb a flagpole to bring down the Turkish flag that flew there. He was shot to death halfway up the pole, a cigarette dangling from his mouth.

In reporting the incidents, one of the right-wing, explicitly nationalist Greek Cypriot newspapers ran the headline, "Tourkos: Aionios Barvaros" (The Turk: Eternal Barbarian) and cited the many historical barbarities and slaughters committed by this "enemy of Christianity," especially those allegedly committed against Greek populations. The illustrations of the article made this even clearer: in the first illustration, one saw the beating of Tassos Isaac under the caption, "Turks hit with fury, satisfying their animal instincts on the lifeless body of Tassos Isaac." Another illustration then showed a 1958 photograph of the corpse of Kostas Mourris, who was beaten to death during that same year, during the intercommunal struggles that marked the end of British rule in the island. The caption read, "With the same animal instinct the Turks murdered Kostas Mourris."[1] Hence, in what the author called a "retrospective" on the Turk's "crimes and brutalities," she linked 200 years of regional history in an arc that sweeps across the present and into an implied future.

The main pro-government (center-right and nationalist) Turkish Cypriot newspaper said merely "Blood Flowed" and showed photos of the fighting, of a Turkish Cypriot who was injured, and of what one caption called "Greek bikers fanatic to shed blood." They also prominently displayed a photo of a Greek Cypriot youth—standing amongst others holding large wooden sticks—who had partially lowered his trousers and pulled out his private parts to display to the Turks a few hundred yards away. The caption of this photo declared, "They attacked with stones and sticks, and they made disgusting gestures."[2] The central government position was that this was a "provocation" (*tahrik*) intended to inflame sentiments and to have the effect that in fact it had, which was to bring Cyprus once again to the brink of war. The emphasis in much of the reporting was on the desire of these youths to violate Northern Cyprus' soil, their fanatical provocation, and disrespect.

This incident and its interpretations demonstrate much about conditions in Cyprus today and about the issues and ideologies that have divided the two communities in the past. On the one hand, some of the characterizations and accusations are near the extreme ends of the spectrum; on the other hand, the spectrum itself is always culturally constructed, as Peter Loizos has eloquently shown for Cyprus.[3] The ontologies described in the previous chapter manifest themselves in real actions and real decisions in the social and political world. When they do, they become ideological, not only providing a framework to interpret how things are, but also to predict how things will be and should be. In other words, when the real world is made to conform to a particular cultural logic, the result is an interpretation of that reality that is ideological.

I argue in this chapter that a particular vision of political reality that draws its ideals from liberal democracy appears to lead, through a brutal inevitability, to conflict. It does so through a promise of freedom, which in its realization is always freedom *for*. "Freedom," in historical reality, cannot be a metaphysical, metahistorical concept, but is instead a freedom realized *for* particular persons and communities *within* particular social, political, and historical contexts. Moreover, because democracy and its freedoms are *necessarily* exclusive, defined by the limits of the *polis* and limiting its freedoms to those within it, the battle to achieve freedom also becomes a battle to define what the *polis* should be.

Here, I contend that anonymous, democratic politics in Cyprus has always been conceived in ethnonational terms, even if the anonymity of ethnonationalisms existed in contradiction with the local-level responsibilities experienced by most Cypriots. It is a commonplace amongst both Greek and Turkish Cypriots to say that "we always got along together, we used to attend each others' weddings" and that it was the greed and rapaciousness of local politicians and international powers that divided the island.[4] Yet the emergence of an anonymous, democratic political space in the island also meant that the ideologies of freedom were primarily ethnonational, and hence exclusive, ones.[5]

By "ideologies of freedom" I mean those commonly held notions of what constitutes a proper relationship of state and people, and a proper ground upon which authority may be constituted. In other words, in Cyprus the politics of the village were replaced by the politics of the nation, so that ideologies of freedom in each community—framed here as "justice" versus "respect"—applied to entities that were no longer negotiable. And they were no longer negotiable because the very constitution of those entities as an outcome of "proper," popular politics meant that popular politics in Cyprus was inherently exclusive. As we will see, Greek Cypriots have demanded justice through those politics, while Turkish Cypriots have called for respect. Unfortunately, it has always been the other community that stood in the way of realizing those ideals of freedom and proper governance.

A central premise at work here will be that, historically speaking, a combination of capitalist intervention, colonial administration, and progressive aspirations has meant that the call for freedom and self-rule in many countries has been inextricably linked to self-realization within the ethnos. Another premise is that the ideologies and practices that define ethnic and national identities in modernity are indistinguishable, that one is no more primordial than another, and that both simply take the facts of cultural differentiation and translate them into political terms. The latter calls its members citizens; the former often aspires to. But both are based on a presumed link between land and people that often results in claims to political sovereignty.

One of the complications for making such a statement is the important literature that argues for the antiquity of ethnic identities, or for the endurance of ethnic differentiation as a part of social structure.[6] Now, certainly it is true that differentiation is part of our human condition. But even if we are to give credence to the idea that there have "always" been ethnicities, surely these entities cannot be construed as having the same meaning through time. The concept of "the public," for instance, has a similarly ancient history, but no one seems prepared to argue that the Roman *res publica* is the same as, let's say, Kierkegaard's conception of

"the public" as "a monstrous nothing."[7] While the roots of Kierkegaard's public are no doubt found in the Roman concept, Kierkegaard's
conception is self-reflective and immanently modern. Similarly for ethnicity: the very scope of ethnicities, their imagined nature, and their
historicized territoriality are some of the significant ways in which they
could be said to differ from ethnicities that pre-date the nation-state.[8]

In much of the literature on nationalism and ethnicity, scholars seem
at pains to differentiate the two and yet to understand their entanglement.[9] The nation, they say, teaches its citizens how to be national; the
members of ethnic groups already understand their belonging. But this
tends to privilege certain constructions of nation (especially the French)
that relied on revolt against internal tyranny and to ignore the potency of
historical enemies. It is well known in the anthropological literature on
segmentation that smaller groups may put aside differences to unite
against a common enemy. Exclusion may become "belonging" where
the differences are territorial and define one's right to existence.

A further premise, then, is that modern political systems are territori-
alizing and homogenizing in nature. Ethnicity is always invented, and it
seems beside the point whether it happens before the establishment of
the nation-state through the construction of a common enemy, or after
the construction of the nation-state through education and new ways of
life.[10] What seems to me to be the salient point is that nationalism and
modern forms of ethnicity make claims to territory (thereby legitimating
the state) and also claim that everyone within an ethnic group is equally
and always a member of that group. Furthermore, while the state may
not necessarily define the nation, the nation defines "the people" and
hence delimits the community of interests that provides legitimacy for
the state. Walker Connor traces this in part to writings of men such as
Locke: "In identifying *the people* as the font of all political power, this
revolutionary doctrine made the people and the state almost synony-
mous. *L'état c'est moi* became *l'état c'est le peuple*."[11] So, there tends to
be a confusion of freedom with democracy, and of equality with
homogeneity.

In tracing the emergence of ethnonationalist politics in Cyprus, then, I
also wish to demonstrate that we can see from the case of Cyprus the
fundamentally exclusionary principles of liberal democracy, which has
historically depended upon giving rights to some at the expense of others. Democracy's fundamental principle is one of exclusion
masquerading as inclusion: because democracy is a functioning political
system as well as an ideology, its limits are defined by the *polis*, or the

polity. And because democracy is a principle of equality and sameness, it defines not only what *is* but also what *should* be. In other words, the equality of democracy is not, for most people, easily distinguishable from the sameness of the ethnos.[12]

The reason for this, I will argue here, is that most people in the world do not think of themselves or those around them in terms of the pre-social, monadic individual required by Western democracy. Democracy, as we usually know and describe it, is predicated on an understanding of humans as individuals in possession of innate, pre-social rights. But for very many people in the world, it is an immanently social individual who is or should be the possessor of the rights, responsibilities, and free-doms of the polity. Therefore, for very many people, this principle of "universal" equality is always already delimited by the nation conceived as *ethnos*.[13] Unfortunately, such an Aristotelian view of the person exists in contradiction with the facile understanding of democratic rights char-acterized by Charles Taylor as "atomism," which arises from social contract theories and is predicated upon notions of individualism.

This thesis is already apparent in the vast literature—beginning with Marx—on liberalism's exclusionary principles. Democratic freedoms notoriously rose and flourished in countries known for their oppression of others, either through colonialism[14] or slavery[15] or through exploita-tion of the laboring classes. In Marx's famous phrase, exploitative capitalist enterprise constitutes "a very Eden of the innate rights of man." Hence, political freedoms have historically been purchased by denying those rights to others. More recently, scholars of the subaltern have begun to focus not only on these historical facts, but have also begun to ask how liberalism could also be racist and exclusionary at its theoretical core, or why democracy seems to result in the annihilation rather than the accommodation of difference.[16]

In tracing the entanglement of ethnonationalisms and democracy in Cyprus, then, I wish also to draw attention to certain contradictions inherent in our common understanding of democracy. The nationalisms in Cyprus were fundamentally democratic movements, founded on prin-ciples of popular representation. Yet they came into conflict with each other by necessity, since each defined a community of interests that wanted political guarantees. At the time of Cyprus' independence, Turk-ish Cypriots wanted certain guarantees that they would not, as the minority, be tyrannized by the majority; Greek Cypriots, on the other hand, believed that increased power for the minority was anti-democratic. This rift between the claims of liberal democracy to secure both representation and rights has been resolved in the literature on democratization by a call for cultivating democratic practices and assumptions within a strong civil society. The assumption at work here appears to be that democracy will emerge fully-formed when one has what Iliya Harik characterizes as "a certain degree of individualism, public-spiritedness, respect for and tolerance of others, and acceptance of winning and losing according to 'the rules of the game.'"[17]

This, however, is an illusory assumption. I should open a parenthesis here to note that the democratic model appears to be inclusive on the ethnic level only when inequality is cast in terms of class. For instance, in the case of the United States—whose model of political sovereignty was both civic and racist—blacks were universally excluded from the polity, while European ethnic groups lost their ethnic status in the name of a white identity. As Roger Sanjek notes, "The outcome of Anglo-conformity for non-British European immigrants has been an opportunity to share 'race' with whites with whom we do not share 'class.'"[18] Hence "equality" for whites was bought at the price of ethnic difference.

And so I pose some questions: in what sense, and under what circumstances, can democracy take account of difference within the state? And is "democracy" really a worthy political goal for everyone? What about other models—such as the Ancient Greek *isonomy* or the early American republic—which were explicitly opposed to democracy because of its dangers? To pose these questions is not to say that certain peoples are incapable of having "real" democracy; it is simply to say that we do not fully understand what "real" democracy is or the cultural price that it entails. But neither is the question intended as a statement of absolute cultural relativism; I certainly do not intend to say that peoples should abandon their struggle to increase the freedoms that democracy should guarantee. Rather, I believe that we should forefront democracy's insidious entanglement with the nation-state, which in all but certain very specific contexts has been based on or articulated through ethnonationalism.

"Democratization" has become an ideology that too often ignores the plural forms of democracy in practice. The practices of democracy can take and have taken many shapes, even in the capital of the most ardent proponents of democratization, namely the United States. Moreover, democracy is not the last word in freedom, and it has not always been the case that democracy was accepted as an unquestionable good. It seems to me that the problem for Cypriots—and the problem for many others caught in the pull of ethnicity—is not democracy *per se* but is, in Hannah Arendt's words, "the foundation of freedom, that is, the foundation of a body politic which guarantees the space where freedom can appear."[19] Freedom—as Cypriots and most other postcolonial peoples have discovered—means both much more and much less than democracy. As Thomas Holt notes, "Freedom's realization, for any people, is always specific and therefore historical, always contingent and therefore open to contestation."[20] Freedom, in other words, is political, material, and ideological, and democracy is only one part of this matrix.

This chapter, then, will trace the evolution of freedom in Cyprus, and along with it, the meaning of democracy. For Cypriots freedom was defined ethnically—as freedom *for* a particular group. As a result, democracy was imagined in those terms. This understanding of democratic representation was not incidental to but fundamental to Cypriot conceptions of a legitimate and just state. Moreover, various historical contingencies brought those imaginings of a true and just democratic ethnos into conflict. The themes of "justice" and "respect" that I employ here represent those aspirations and their seemingly inevitable conflict.

The forces of conflict

In the summer of 1996, when Tassos Isaac was murdered in the buffer zone, the assessment of blame and cries of victimization were widespread, vociferous and vehement, and many Cypriots saw the momentary attention that Cyprus received in the world press as a chance to prove the "truth" about the other. Greek Cypriots first blamed the radical pan-Turkish nationalist group, the Grey Wolves, whom they said Turkish Cypriot president Rauf Denktaş had brought from Turkey. But they then had to amend their accusations when the killers in the photos were identified as Turkish Cypriots, after which Denktaş was accused of being the "instigator" (*o ithikos autourghos*).[21] In an interview at the time, Denktaş himself told me first that these men had had loved ones killed by Greek Cypriots, whose names they shouted as they beat the young man to death. Then Denktaş told me that they had not yet identified the men, that the investigation was being held up by the refusal of his Greek neighbors to give him adequate evidence. Unofficially, I received information that the son of a former member of the radical nationalist guerrilla organization, EOKA B',[22] was collecting money for weapons to use against the 200 or so Turkish Cypriots still living in the

South. In another interview with Greek Cypriot president Glafkos Clerides, he acknowledged as much, and so I asked him why, in the face of that information, Greek Cypriot newspapers instead printed the "news" that the Turkish secret service had planned actions against Turkish Cypriots living in the south. He chose not to answer that question.

What is quite noticeable in these interpretations of a single event is that the official Greek Cypriot line portrays Turks as the eternal enemy, generally drawing no clear-cut distinction between Turkey and Turkish Cypriots. Occasionally that distinction is drawn heuristically, as when the Turkish Cypriots in Northern Cyprus are portrayed as unwilling captives of Denktaş and the Turkish military. For instance, many of my neighbors in Southern Cyprus, when they knew of my trips to the North, would ask, "How are they? Do they have enough to eat? Do they behave well towards you? Do they miss their homes?" This sort of concern might be expressed in the same sentence—even in the same breath—as an expression such as "*oi Tourchoi en shilloi*"—"the Turks are dogs." If asked, these neighbors would reply that their curses fell on the invading Turks. But that distinction has only domestic salience; it is not clear to outsiders and is even less clear to Turkish Cypriots. Saying that all Turks are bad except "our" Turks is an ambiguous qualification.

In turn, Turkish Cypriot officialdom consistently describes their neighbors as "fanatic" nationalists who still aim at uniting the island with Greece. When they do not so aim, they at least aim at destroying the hard-won freedoms of their Turkish Cypriot neighbors. In these portraits, Greek Cypriots ignore the "realities" of the situation—the long-standing division of the island and the presence of the Turkish military—in their fanatical pursuit of an ethnic ideal. Hence, any political maneuver, however benign, is interpreted as a move towards enosis, or union with Greece.

These are the nationalist discourses, the expression and realization of which spans the spectrum from devotion to disbelief. Before examining them further, I would like to remark that these are very powerful discourses that have personal resonances for many. Indeed, there is considerable overlap between many personal narratives and official histories. For instance, one blazing September day I arrived on the doorstep of an old teacher and anti-colonial resistance leader whom I will call here Kyriakos. This old teacher greeted me in a neat, dark suit and tie and led me through a hallway filled with books while his wife disappeared to bring lemonade. Kyriakos—like so many teachers of his age—was active in the revolt against colonial rule that was to have led to union with Greece, and he was imprisoned by the British for his role in that prolonged rebellion. He is a well-respected educationalist and an ardent nationalist who spent much of his childhood during the most repressive years of British colonial rule. Hence he knows from bitter experience about what he calls the "politics of waiting:" that patience that he believes constituted the political life of Cypriots from the twelfth to the twentieth centuries. In fact, Kyriakos says that for all of his primary school years he was not taught Greek history or geography but was brought up as a proper English boy. It was not until he went in 1937 to the Greek Gymnasium in Paphos that he encountered the combination of history and sanctity that would guide the future struggle. There, the teachers led prayers for union with Greece and taught the boys the Greek national anthem.

Kyriakos, like other fighters that I interviewed, felt it necessary to begin at the beginning, by explaining to me the history that made the struggle inevitable. He and other fighters accounted for the enthusiasm of small children for the struggle by reference to that glorious and ineluctable history. Another teacher who fought in the struggle summarized it well: "As small as they were in body, that's how large they were in spirit. It was a result—the vitality of EOKA—of our history." Kyriakos, like the other fighters, summarizes in several minutes the history that makes Cyprus a Greek island. Freedom meant enosis, he says. Freedom could be nothing less than enosis.

A year later and a world away, in the Turkish side of Cyprus, I found myself under a grape-covered trellis on a veranda that enjoys a panoramic view of the sea. Here, in the northwest corner of the island, the hills sweep down to a long, as-yet-uncluttered coastline, and from this distance one can barely see the waves folding against the shore. There, I had gone to see another old teacher, Ahmet Hulusi Menteş, who has a gentle, informal manner and a smiling face that belies his nearly eighty years. Menteş moved to this part of the island in the post-1974 period after having spent much of his life in Paphos. Born in 1918, he is about eight years older than Kyriakos.

Like many of the other Turkish teachers with whom I spoke, Menteş recounts history in terms of the very recent past, in terms of remembered wrongs and lived conflicts. Menteş does not tell me about Ottoman history; instead, he tells me about the history of the enosis movement and the fact that even in his own mixed village, there was "enmity" (*düşmanlık*). And in a brief autobiographical piece he describes how for his three years at the *rüştiye* school in Poli tis Chrysochou, he had to walk from his village along with Greek boys who constantly tried to fight the Turks. So many years later, he remembers the chants that they would use to tease the outnumbered Turkish boys, such as "Tourkoutia, Tourkoutia, ta matia sas loukoutia," (Little Turks, little Turks, your eyes are little sewers).[23] Such daily humiliations meant nothing to their antagonists and are not remembered today, but they are branded forever in the memories of those who suffered from them.

One notices at all levels that Greek Cypriot history partakes of the primordial, drawing upon "eternal" characteristics of the other, as well as an ancient history that supposedly describes one's self. One finds this expressed in claims to an everlasting, unchanging Greek "spirit" that unites the *ethnos* and imbues the land.[24] Hence, the claim that Cyprus is "3,000 years Greek" is "proven" by history. In contrast, the Turkish Cypriot version of history is pragmatic, contingent, constructivist, based on claims of conquest and validation of the status quo. So, Turkish Cypriots have a claim to the island not through some ethnic spirit but through the blood of "their martyrs" that soaks the land. For this reason, many of my Turkish Cypriot informants agreed with one old teacher who characterized their Greek neighbors as "obsessed by some notion of a 'pure' history. We could have gotten along together if not for this idea of purity." Or, as another informant put it, "If history is what the Greeks make of it, there's no room in the world for Turks." While Turkish Cypriots often try to counter Greek Cypriot histories with the claim that Cyprus historically belongs to the Turkish world because of the Ottoman conquest, my informants universally recognized that this was a much different claim from one which posited an ineluctable link of land and people through an ethnic spirit.

One sees this difference in, for example, the oft-expressed fears of Turkish expansionism and enosis. For very many Greek Cypriots, the eternal desire of Turkey to take Cyprus—what is generally referred to as "Turkish expansionism"—is a "fact" that is indubitably proven by the presence of Turkish troops in the island. Their presence "proves" that Turkey "always" wanted Cyprus and may take the entire island at some point in the future. For Turkish Cypriots, on the other hand, the primary fear is of enosis—a movement that divided the two communities and led, in its extreme forms, to persecution of Turks. Because of this, many Turkish Cypriots interpret everything done by their Greek neighbors as a move toward enosis, despite the fact that enosis died after 1974.[25]

What is important to note is that, as I remarked in the previous chapter, the accusations lodged take place at considerably different levels of abstraction. Greek Cypriots "demonstrate" the eternal imperialistic aspirations and plans of an entity of which they have no direct knowledge except as a military machine. In such discussions, "Ankara" becomes the seat of an evil empire (imagine the Kremlin, but darker) whose primary goal is and always has been to expand and crush all those surrounding it. Turkish Cypriots, however, "demonstrate" the continuing aspirations of those whose names and faces they know quite well. They discuss the alleged plans of people with whom they grew up and went to school. When newspapers discuss supposed plans for enosis, they dig up old photos of President Clerides standing with a Greek flag, hence blurring time and place enough to make the accusation seem plausible.

These divergent constructions of history have played and continue to play important roles in the legitimation of political power within each community. It is for this reason, I will argue, that Cypriot political life on both sides of the ceasefire line seems to be frozen in time: the political players get older, but they do not fade away. Rauf Denktaş has been the primary leader of the Turkish Cypriot community since the 1960s and has been president—first of the Turkish Federated State of Cyprus and then of the TRNC—since 1976. And Glafkos Clerides returned to power in 1994 in part on the grounds that, as Denktaş's old counterpart, he was the only one who could negotiate with him. "The Cyprus Problem," and each community's interpretation of it, continues to be what puts or keeps leaders in office. It is to this problem that I would like to turn now, discussing each community in turn. In particular, I want to show that while 1974 certainly altered politics within each community, certain fundamental themes have continued from the pre-1974 period. I believe that these are best encapsulated in the themes of "justice" and "respect" that have dominated and continue to dominate intracommunal politics and that evidence two divergent visions of the ideals of freedom.

To represent

In the spring of 1995, I strolled through Nicosia with a young Turkish Cypriot professional, chatting as we went about why she had returned to Cyprus after her many years abroad. Like so many Turkish Cypriots, her family had left for England during the troubled period between 1963 and 1974, when Turkish Cypriots had retreated to isolated enclaves to protect themselves from Greek Cypriot attack.[26] She had returned to Cyprus when she decided to marry and had since acquired an important public position. As we approached the barrier that divides the city,[27] she described to me what she said was her most vivid memory from her few years of childhood in Cyprus: walking through the streets of Paphos with her family, forbidden by her mother to speak Turkish. Always, she said, they were told to speak English. "We couldn't even speak our own language," she said with anger. "That was what it was like. And even today it's the same. There can never be a solution to the problem if the Greeks don't give us respect." She repeated several times—as others had told me many times—that Turkish Cypriots had to demand respect, and that with respect would come safety.[28]

As has been abundantly clear to Turkish Cypriots for much of this century, the dialogic sport of challenge and riposte inherent in negotiation cannot be carried out between parties of unequal status. For much of that time, the ubiquitous complaint and self-criticism of Turkish Cypriots was that they had no leader who could gain for them the respect needed in order for them to claim their rights.[29] Since 1974, Rauf Denktaş has monopolized public office because of his prior role as leader of the verbal and military battle against Greek Cypriots. He has been re-elected as president time and time again because of a widespread belief that no other politician could represent the nation in a way that would force Greek Cypriots to respect it. Despite challengers who have waved the banner of economic and political reform, until recently there have been few serious challenges to Denktaş's authority, because within him reside any national claims to have an authoritative voice.

Central to those claims is the demand for "respect" (saygı) that has dominated Turkish Cypriot politics for much of this century. Certainly, that demand arose at least in part from the experiences of a minority community faced for decades with the majority's demand to unite the island with a country that Turkish Cypriots had no reason to believe would welcome them. Greek Cypriots' demand for enosis, or union with Greece, was intended as the fulfillment of an historical destiny and was therefore framed in terms of "justice," as we will see somewhat later. Unfortunately, as we will also see, the demand for "respect"—when framed in opposition to a demand for "justice"—was a demand that by its very nature caused disrespect.

It was under such conditions that British administrators and Greek Cypriot antagonists alike asserted that the average Turkish Cypriot had no understanding of community or nation, and that any supposedly nationalistic action taken was "stirred up" by troublemakers in their leadership. In such a way, it was not necessary for the Greek majority to take seriously the claims of the Cyprus is Turkish Party, which seemed only a poor imitation of that faction of Greek Cypriots organizing for enosis. Similarly, the emergence of the TMT, the first Turkish Cypriot guerilla organization, came as a surprise to Greek Cypriots who had ignored the objections of Turkish Cypriots to enosis since the end of the nineteenth century. Indeed, they attributed the emergence of TMT to Britain's divide-and-rule tactics, claiming (in ways that interestingly echo British colonizers' comments about Greek Cypriots[30]) that the average Turkish Cypriot had no interest in politics and was just stirred up by troublemakers.[31]

Clearly, the Greek Cypriot demand for "justice"—perceived as a universal and timeless moral attitude towards their claims—ignored the Turkish Cypriot demand for "respect," which was rooted in the contingencies of daily life and the humiliations that Turkish Cypriots recall with vividness and feeling today. Within this context, it is worthwhile tracing the history of nationalism's entanglement with the desire to find a voice, to speak as "one man," that Turkish Cypriots hoped would enable them to wrest from their Greek neighbors the respect that they had, until then, refused to grant.

This sense of being disrespected began as early as the latter part of the nineteenth century, when—as I explained in Chapter 3—politics were being translated by Greek Orthodox in Cyprus into ethno-religious terms. One Turkish newspaper lamented,

> Our Christian compatriots, who for centuries have been living under the blessed protection of the great Sovereign [i.e., the sultan] ... have during several years that is to say since the change of the administration, gradually and without any reason changed their tongues and manners, and commenced to show strange and surprising manners .... As long as the indifference and apathy of the Government, and the patience and mildness of the Muslims are continuing, our Christian compatriots taking advantage of every opportunity do not abstain from showing demonstrations which are considered to be an insult to the Muslims, they carry it on in such degree that in their places of worship, in their meetings, and in the streets they are openly making such speeches, and showing such demonstration, which no conscience can bear, and which causes great excitement and anger.[32]

During the same period, the mufti officially complained to the secretary of state for the colonies that

> The change of the administration has converted the population into a different mould by the promulgation, all at once, of an excessive liberty, and has driven and incited the Christian population to a lot of unsound and nonsensical

7. "Kıbrıs Savaşçıları' (Cyprus Fighters) by Güner Pir, courtesy of the Turkish Republic of Northern Cyprus National Struggle Museum.

thoughts, as if that change was designed to bring about a revolution in morals and usages.[33]

There are two facets of these complaints and observations that are worthy of comment. The first is that the attitude of their Christian neighbors was clearly a novel experience, and one that would continue to inspire commentary for some time to come. Secondly, the commentators do not deny the communal rights of their neighbors, but simply deny their rights to behave in particular ways. This is evidenced, as well, fifteen years later, when the activities of Greek agitators such as the infamous Nikolaos Katalanos became the subject of complaint not because of their agitation *per se* but because of their offensive methods. The August 1910 editorial in *Sünuhat* cited in Chapter 2 is a good demonstration of this.[34]

Significantly for Muslims in this period (and later when the same group of Cypriots called itself Turkish), intercommunal life was made possible through a type of self-control—through the forms of intercommunal existence that reproduced the Ottoman ethos. Vamık Volkan is probably correct as regards much of the British period in Cyprus when he notes that, despite their minority status, the Muslims of the island, as heirs of an Ottoman legacy, "clung to their self-concept of lordliness and mastery pending the slow test of time and the impingement of reality."[35] Yet Volkan appears to be right in a limited sense: that Muslim Cypriots endured the insults of their neighbors because they clung to an idealized version of the Ottoman model of toleration, in which religious and juridical—as well as a certain amount of political—freedom was supposed to be granted to members of different *millets*, or religious communities, within the empire.

It is undoubtedly the case, as Volkan and others suggest, that many members of the Muslim minority in Cyprus had difficulty adjusting to a situation in which they were no longer the privileged community. However, evidence also suggests that the situation was considerably more complicated than that. Firstly, Muslim villagers without political or bureaucratic power had long been disenfranchised, while the Orthodox clergy had long wielded considerable power. Secondly, and equally importantly, however, evidence suggests that Muslim Cypriots were concerned—like other Ottomans—with comportment, public behavior, and public signs, such as dress. One sees this, for instance, in the fact that in the period of Ottomanism the fez was adopted as the "proper" hat of a "proper" Ottoman, only to be replaced in the period of Atatürk by the European hat. Similarly, in contemporary Turkey the controversy over women's wearing of the headscarf centers around the headscarf as a public, political symbol and a challenge to the supposedly secular, democratic principles of the state.

So, when I claim that Turkish Cypriots clung to an *idealized* version of the Ottoman model of toleration, I do not mean to imply that that model was ever fully realized[36] but only that it was in the breakdown of these ideals of public life that Turkish Cypriots most clearly perceived their disempowerment. In this case, clearly the breakdown of these forms continued to be the main source of intercommunal friction from the Turkish Cypriot perspective. As late as 1952—just three years before the outbreak of the Greek Cypriot anti-colonial rebellion—a poignant cry of frustration and injured pride came in the form of a letter from the village of Pyla.[37] The letter was addressed to *Halkın Sesi*, the newspaper of the Turkish party that would come to power after 1960. The author of the letter says that he writes "because there is no one else who will convey to the public things that our Greek compatriots have done against us and their lack of respect."

The author goes on to describe a play that had been performed in his village, apparently set in Macedonia during the period preceding Greek independence, and describing the supposed corruption and cruelty of Ottoman rule there. In the play, a schoolmaster is arrested by the Ottoman authorities but manages to escape by bribing his captors, and then is sentenced to death *in absentia*. When his pupils hear of this, they begin to cry. "At that moment," says the letter's author,

> a gentleman coming onto the stage says to the children these words: "The Turks are always like this. Know from the time that you are small to the time that you are old that they did these things to us, and always carry hatred against them in your heart!" But don't you agree that the real lack of respect was that in this speech Turks were called dogs?

The author of the letter goes on to lament the "terrible words" used by these "stupid fellows," and concludes by saying "in response to such inconsiderate people, 'Allah will give you your reward!'"[38] The writer of this painful account calls the insults contained in the play "disrespect" (*saygısızlık*), which seems a mild description of the lack of consideration that could have led to the presentation of such a play, especially in a mixed village where Turks would attend.

In this context, as I noted earlier, a peculiar adaptation of Turkish nationalism arose in Cyprus. The Turkish nationalism articulated by

Mustafa Kemal Atatürk began as a civic nationalism that could not hold up under the perceived need to reclaim a purely Turkish, pre-Islamic and pre-Ottoman past. It remained, however, a nationalism aimed at modernization, and the primary enemy was not some external power but the Ottoman past. Hence, the projects of secularization, linguistic purification, and educational renovation were carried out with great anti-traditional zeal. One could search the past for examples and exemplars, but primarily when those worked in the interests of modernization.[39]

Muslims in Cyprus immediately and voluntarily adopted these new statements about their identity, even while their presumed "brothers" in Anatolia were in the throes of cultural upheaval.[40] But they adopted them with a twist, for they had at hand an enemy—their Greek Cypriot neighbors—who was constantly agitating for a future that would not include Muslims. In other words, Turkish Cypriots adopted the modernizing framework, constructivist history, and future-oriented rhetoric of the new Turkish republic, but they combined this with a belief in a powerful enemy that has been the hallmark of ethnic nationalism.[41] This did not mean that they constructed Greek Cypriots as a *primordial* enemy; they did not. But they have constructed and continue to construct Greek Cypriots as an enemy who works against them, *always in the present*. The difference is that the primordial remembrance projects a reconstructed, imagined past onto the individual present, providing a timeless and therefore inescapable explanation of experienced events and possible future occurrences. The state of present recollection in which Turkish Cypriots find themselves is one that projects individual experience onto the collective present, simultaneously reducing the past to experienced event, and the present to an "always."

This combination of modernist historiography and threatened present is best seen in the constitution and legitimation of authority in the Turkish Cypriot state. In Turkish Cypriot nationalist mythology, 1963 is the defining moment—a moment that was experienced by the great majority of adult Turkish Cypriots still in Cyprus. This was the year of the first breakdown of the Cyprus Republic, when at Christmastime of that year, a group of extreme nationalists began a series of attacks on Turkish Cypriots in which women and children were shot and Turkish Cypriot homes were set ablaze. In response to a prolonged assault on the village of Erenköy (Greek: Kokkina) in northwestern Cyprus, almost 600 young Turkish men secretly returned from their studies abroad to defend the area surrounding the village. Even after the dramatic arrival of Turkish jets in August 1964 in the first Turkish military intervention, the siege continued for months as its young defenders went without food and clothing.

Unbeknownst to Greek Cypriots, this period of Greek Cypriot aggression served to define a new Turkish Cypriot history whose heroes would, after 1974, become leaders and protectors of the Turkish Cypriot state. Today, the men who were these young fighters make up a large part of the dwindling number of educated Turkish Cypriots remaining in the island. For instance, almost all holders of top political offices and all five of the 1995 contenders in the presidential election are veterans of Erenköy. Indeed, the history of the Turkish Cypriot state could be seen as a history of this battle, for it symbolizes both the irrevocable rupture caused by premeditated Greek brutality and the beginnings of the defensive battle that would culminate in the 1974 intervention of Turkish troops.[42]

In a 1995 interview with Denktaş, I questioned him at length about Erenköy and its fighters who have since become leaders. "But in this island," he said, "we're all fighters." And he cited numerous Greek Cypriot leaders, including the current president, who had fought for union with Greece. He then explained—apparently without realizing the implications of what he said—that in Northern Cyprus those fighters had since become members of all the parties, not only of the right, as in the South. And I was reminded of the gruesome photographs of war atrocities seen throughout Northern Cyprus—the stunned faces of the wounded, the staring eyes of the dead. In a place as small as Cyprus, these photos are not the anonymous faces of war but are intended as reminders of the fate of one's relatives, co-villagers, teachers, and friends. I was reminded, as well, of the wealthy businessman who had described to me how he had conquered the mountain village of Bellapaix in 1974. When one of his audience suggested that perhaps he had "rescued" it, he had leaned forward with a wide smile and said, "No, my dear, we conquered it. We conquered it and many other villages, as well."

As Hannah Arendt has most succinctly described in her analysis of the American revolution, any truly new political body has difficulties with "the beginning," for the act of foundation itself must provide a source that will define and grant authority.[43] It should not be surprising, then, that Turkish Cypriots make little attempt to disguise the aggressive, violent nature of their claims to authority. Rather, such claims are more successful the more unapologetic they are. While even the fighters I interviewed among Greek Cypriots spoke with some embarrassment and even sorrow of these violent periods in their history, my Turkish Cypriot friends and acquaintances spoke with great pride of their military maneuverings, and I was often taken to battle sites and war memorials as symbols of an embattled, but ultimately victorious, Turkish nationalism.

It is a truism to state that any revolution entails violence, whether physical, historical, or intellectual. But the nature of violence as a source of authority in Turkish Cyprus is revealed by the vested interest its leaders have in portraying the battle as an ongoing one. Although Denktaş and his fellows know quite well that enosis is an issue that died with the Turkish intervention, they portray it as a living struggle, and every Greek Cypriot move is one towards union with Greece. Children are taught this defensive posture from an early age, and their leaders are heroes of this defense. In a speech given some years ago in celebration of Children's Day, Denktaş told the crowd of students, "Learn well how we acquired our freedom, its value, and knowing what will happen if we lose it, you will live as fighters yourselves."[44] Or, in recent years, the Greek Cypriot attempts to enter the European Union have been called a move towards *de facto* union with Greece. Certainly, in the case of Cyprus, war has been—to paraphrase Clausewitz—the continuation of politics by other means.

More than simple actors in Cyprus' history, Denktaş and those who fought with him have created it. Moreover, with the 1974 Turkish intervention, a piece of island was seized, populations were exchanged, and Turkish Cypriots entered an entirely other, entirely Turkish world that has very few attachments to the world in which they once lived. And linked by a kinship of oppression, Turkish Cypriots have defined their current political arena as one of defense. They have recreated themselves in the process of creating a state: simply put, for Greek Cypriots historical time stopped at 1974, while for Turkish Cypriots it began there. And it was in this founding act that authority was constituted.

To summarize, then, we could say that Turkish Cypriots began very early in the British colonial period to lament their neighbors' disrespectful behavior. While they did not deny them their right to political action, they denied their right to allow that action to take an intolerant form. They found that form intolerant—and found that it became more so—in large part because it ignored them in both material and ideological terms. In Greek Cypriot nationalist history, Cyprus is 3,000 years Greek, and Turks are mere transient, and illegitimate, invaders. Moreover, as the numerical majority, Greek Cypriots were able, towards the end of the British period, economically to marginalize their Turkish neighbors. Hence, while adopting an ideology of modernization, Turkish Cypriots also developed an ethnic nationalism that viewed their Greek Cypriot neighbors as a continual threat to their safety and freedom. Rather than being primordial and essential, that threat is present and existent. Moreover, the enemy is not one of the mythic nationalist imagination but of lived experience. For such reasons, in negotiations since 1974 the Turkish Cypriot side has wanted an equal status as a group even at the expense of guaranteeing individual rights and liberties, such as rights to property and movement.

There are several conclusions to be drawn from this. First, freedom means respect for the autonomous status and identity of the community, and leaders have acquired their authority as guarantors of that respect. Second, violent rupture with the past has secured the foundation of a new state, but this presentist account of the nation and its enemies has meant the necessity for a constant reaffirmation of Greek Cypriots' continuing desire to unite with Greece. And third, for Turkish Cypriots, shared, lived experiences constitute the nation, and so personal memory becomes the legitimator of politics; for this reason, persons are pressured to conform their own memories to those of the state.

Finally, I should elaborate something about what I called the "idealized forms of tolerance." I noted that for Turkish Cypriots intercommunal life was made possible through a certain self-control— through the forms of intercommunal existence that made living together possible. I also remarked that this apparently attempts to reproduce an idealized version of the Ottoman ethos, in which religious communities acquired an independent political and legal existence. What I did not note is that in the Turkish Cypriot conception communal identity was clearly a public matter—i.e., it regulated the individual's interactions with the state and with its political and legal apparatuses. However, it was not a matter that should have governed individuals' interactions with each other. Hence, the public, political person was defined in communal terms, but the private individual was defined in a more complex set of ways. It was the intrusion of this public, political persona into the private realm that perplexed and disturbed many Turkish Cypriots and which they called "disrespect." It was the presumed triumph of the historicizing claims of communal life that Greek Cypriots would come to call "justice."

The problem

One year before the outbreak of the anti-colonial rebellion, an organization of university graduates gathered in Nicosia to receive a delegation from Greece that had brought encouragement from the "Free Motherland" to those engaged in the anti-colonial struggle, which at that moment was being carried out only in words. They issued a proclamation which announced:

> They declare their insistence on the one and only claim of the Greek people of Cyprus for union with motherland Greece, which is the only rightful solution of the Cyprus Question and through which alone the National Restoration of Cyprus can be effected, and that they, in their capacity as intellectual leaders of the Greek people of Cyprus, will not only continue supporting its struggle for Union with Greece, but being conscious of their obligations to it, they will intensify their activities together with its natural leadership, the Ethnarchic Church, in order that this claim of the Greek people in Cyprus may soon become a reality.[45]

The word used several times here is *dhikaioma*—claim or right—which is put forward as part of a timeless morality. *Dhikaioma* is related to *dhikaiosini*, or justice, and elsewhere the appeal was to "Liberty, Justice and Humanity, ideals which are so openly defied by the British government in Cyprus."[46] They assert that this is the only just or rightful solution to the "Cyprus Question," which was the question of Cyprus' fate when Britain finally decided to abandon the island—an eventuality that was assumed by most Cypriots. The great fear until World War I had been that Britain might return the island to the Ottomans, from whom Britain had rented and eventually taken it. Though that fear died away after Cyprus' annexation, during this period freedom—as many of my informants iterated to me again and again—simply could not be imagined except as union of the island with Greece.

There are three points to note here, which one might say constitute axioms of Greek Cypriot nationalist logic. The first is that Greek Cypriots' right to the island was absolute, framed in terms of universal justice. The second is that it was possible for it to be absolute because of primordialist claims on the island—that it is "the island of Aphrodite," that it is "3,000 years Greek." These claims were also very often framed in natural, or racial, terms. And third, the adoption of an ethnic identity that had actually been articulated in Greece led to certain contradictions with regard to the "eternal enemy," namely the Turks. It in fact led to the unsuccessful attempt of many Greek Cypriots cognitively to separate the Turks as conquerors from the Turks as neighbors.

As I noted in Chapter 3, by the beginning of the twentieth century a rhetoric of race and regeneration had overtaken Greek Cypriot political life, while almost all facets of public life were gradually being turned towards the movement for union with Greece. In fact, despite British attempts to quell it, "the movement"—*to kinima*—had, by the start of the anti-colonial rebellion, gradually succeeded in drawing almost all Greek Cypriots into its circle and demanding their sacrifices.[47] The movement's leaders were cocky with the self-confidence of absolute justification, and they quoted Gladstone and Churchill from those leaders' more philhellenic moments, when they had indicated some sympathy for the cause of enosis, or for the cause of those peoples struggling for self-rule. Until driven to rebellion by Britain's repeated refusals to grant their freedom, Greek Cypriot leaders seemed fully to believe that British justice and world opinion would eventually grant them union with their Mother Greece. Not only in Cyprus, but also in London, Athens, Cairo, and many other foreign capitals, Cypriots were organizing in a campaign that for many would be their life's work.

Following the 1931 riots, there were demonstrations in London, and Cypriots were mobilized to do their duty from the imperial capital. In Cairo, the Greek newspaper *La Semaine Egyptienne* published a banner headline, "Honneur aux Chypriotes tombés pour la Liberté," and devoted several editions to publishing the Cypriot cause. Even more importantly, however, newspapers in Greek sprang up abroad with the specified goal of promoting the cause of Cyprus' union with Greece. In the United States, *Kipriakos Agon* (Cypriot Struggle) was formed to enlighten the American public, to inform their "American Greek brothers" about the Cypriot question, and to unite Greek Cypriots in the U.S. in service to their "enslaved fatherland." "The Cypriot," they extolled,

> proud (*filotimos*), intelligent, hard-working, honorable, and above all a lover of his country (*filopatris*), in the imperative command of the salvation of the fatherland, puts aside every personal ambition and party quarrel and places himself with all his spirit under the flag of the National Ideology (*tis Ethnikis Idheologhias*).[48]

And the Athenian newspaper *Enosis tis Kiprou* similarly declared its single aim:

The *Enosis tis Kiprou* is published for one and only one sacred goal, with one and only one exalted ambition: to become the cry, the standard, and the enthusiastic [voice] of the great and implacable union struggle of the most Greek island (*tis ellinikotatis meghalonisu*).[49]

And the Athenian magazine, *Foni tis Kiprou*, called itself "The Panhellenic Publishing Organ for the Struggle for Freedom of the Greek Island." The struggle was kept alive as much by groups such as the Patriotic Committee of Cypriots in Egypt and the Cypriot Committee in Athens as it was in the island itself. They took it as their sacred duty to "enlighten public opinion" and so kept the question open despite Britain's attempts to cover it with the bandages of good intention.

In all of this ideological flurry, "the Turks" were always the eternal barbarians, the ones who had destroyed the Byzantine Empire and who stood in the way of its restoration. A very important part of the project of Greek "national restoration" was retaking Istanbul, the old Constantinople and former capital of the Byzantine realm. As I noted in earlier chapters, especially Chapter 3, there were often violent manifestations of those claims, such as Katalanos' announcement around the turn of the twentieth century that "the time to turn these irreligious doggish Turks on spits like kebabs has come."[50]

Clearly, there was always an ambiguity regarding the "real" enemy. In Greek historiography, the "eternal" enemy was always the Turks; while Greek Cypriots learned these histories, they also lived with Turks in their midst. For extreme nationalists, there could clearly be no difference, and there was no such thing as a "good Turk," as indicated by the fury aroused in many of the former EOKA leaders I interviewed when Turkish Cypriots were mentioned; this is best summed up in my informant's assessment of them as "*atakta paidhia*," or unruly children (see Introduction to Part Four). Similarly, one of the publications of EOKA during the anti-colonial rebellion was called "Cyprus in the Hands of the Turks," and it begins by describing the slaughter that accompanied the Ottoman conquest of the island in 1570–71. The authors then go on to state, "Now the Turks are crying that they have rights (*dhikaiomata*) in Cyprus because they conquered it with slaughter. By the same logic, Europe belongs to Hitler and the Nazis because they conquered it!"[51] This was the extreme, but there continues to be a confusion in Greek Cypriot discourse and the impossibility of reconciling a primordial history with lived experience. Hence, it is a common assumption even among leftist Greek Cypriots that the Ottoman centuries were the "black centuries" (*oi mavroi aiones*), the period of enslavement (*dhoulia* or *sklavia*). A rather unsuccessful attempt is made cognitively to separate the Turks in Cyprus from the "eternal barbarians" who still threaten the gates.

For such reasons, politics in the Republic of Cyprus has ceased at 1974. Each day, reading a newspaper is like experiencing déjà vu: there's nothing new in the world except the latest inroad or comment about "The Cyprus Problem" (*To Kipriako*).[52] Political life revolves around *To Kipriako*, which is always and invariably described as the problem of invasion and occupation.[53] The basic idea is that one has to remain united in the face of the "national issue." One Greek Cypriot political scientist calls the result "corporatism," which he blames for what he calls the "failure of politics in Cyprus"—i.e., "the failure to provide a functional framework for the peaceful coexistence of the two communities."[54] He goes on to cite the various ways in which this corporatism manifests itself in daily life, from the National Council (*Ethniko Symvoulio*), "an institutionalized forum of parliamentary leaders which usually stresses the need for national unity of 'voice' and even of 'soul' (*omofonia kai omopsychia*)"[55] to the manner in which nepotism and patronage have invaded the political parties, who divide and exchange favors and benefits. Moreover, there is no possibility of disagreement over the substance of "The Cyprus Problem," which is seen unquestionably to be invasion and occupation.

There are two conclusions that I would like to draw from this that relate to the current situation in Cyprus. The first is that, in Greek Cypriot politics, nationalism has consistently taken over personal experience, behavior, and memories. Before the anticolonial rebellion, as I discussed in Chapter 6, nationalism had invaded what we would think of as personal or family life, and nationalism also determined behavior. Many of my Turkish Cypriot informants commented that they could not go into the streets on Sundays, because it was the Greek "national day," and their neighbors would emerge from the churches inflamed by the rhetoric of the priests. Others told me of the students, teachers, neighbors, and colleagues, who would greet them on the street with "Enosis!" or lecture them about the Greek history of the island. For Greek Cypriots, the experiences of the "nation," the *ethnos*, constitute shared, lived experiences. During the colonial period, Greek Cypriots were mobilized to fight for an ideal: not simply an ideal of justice, or of freedom, or of a better life, but an ideal of enosis, which encompassed all of these. During the period since 1974, all of Greek Cypriot life has revolved around "The Cyprus Problem." Rather than the atomized individual creating the polity, the dream of ethnic unity has given shape to individuation.

Secondly, and as a consequence of this, politics becomes the legitimator of personal memory. Put simply, the dream of "progress" of a "better future" was, for Greek Cypriots, the fulfillment of an ethnic fantasy. "Progress," then, was not an objective universal and a political ideology[56] but the fulfillment of an immanent potentiality. Progress becomes predestination, and the state is but a realization and representation of that history. Hence, "justice," or the realization of these timeless claims, is today framed in terms of the eviction of the occupying Turkish forces and the return to one's lands.

An illustration: The missing persons

One can see that the two communities have diverged for reasons that are both ideological and historically contingent. Certainly, the divergent demands for justice and respect play themselves out in attempts at diplomatic solutions to the Cyprus problem. While Greek Cypriots claim that the problem is one of illegal invasion and occupation, Turkish Cypriots claim that it is one of securing recognition and safety for themselves as a group. But these divergent themes also play themselves out in daily life, as in the very different ways that the two groups have dealt with the question of missing persons. The question of missing persons has been both a thorny human rights problem and an important trope used in daily life to represent the personal violations of the past three decades.

In short, Greek Cypriots have charged that 1,619 of their own went missing during the invasion of 1974; they have had virtually no information about their fates since that time. Turkish Cypriots have numbered their own missing at between 600 and 900, some from 1963–64 and others from 1974.[57] The closest that the leaderships of the two communities have come to resolving the problem was in September 1997, when Denktaş and Clerides signed an agreement to exchange all information in their possession about the missing of the other community, dating as far back as 1964. It was agreed that where possible, they would exchange all remains so that families could bury their loved ones. Amongst Greek Cypriots, relatives of the missing made it clear that they would need convincing identification of the bodies, and so it was proposed that the families of all the Greek Cypriot missing contribute to a DNA blood bank to help in the identification of the remains. At the same moment,

Greek Cypriot members of parliament criticized as "unacceptable and provocative" the claims by Denktaş that all those missing since 1974 were dead. The chairman of the Missing Persons Committee declared that the committee would never accept this claim about the fate of the missing but would push to discover the fate of those believed still to be alive.[58]

Little progress has been made on the issue since that time, and of course there has been virtually no move to implement these tentative agreements. But even here one encounters the themes of justice and respect so important elsewhere. Greek Cypriots insist on having justice—i.e., full knowledge about the fate of those who went missing during 1974. This presupposes, of course, that the fates of all the missing are known, but that there is a deliberate attempt at obfuscation. Turkish Cypriots, on the other hand, say that this is an intentional attempt to slander them internationally, and that their Greek counterparts should simply accept that their loved ones are dead. Of course, as with so many similar themes, this results in a deadlock that is not only produced politically but also reproduced culturally.

And so at every national anniversary—indeed, at every opportunity—Greek Cypriot women in black are bussed to the checkpoint from which foreigners can cross to the Turkish north. Here they cry while holding photos of their missing husbands, fathers, brothers. No such thing ever happens in Northern Cyprus; indeed, no mention is made of their own missing except when Greek Cypriots cry loudest about theirs and begin to be heard on the international scene. There is no such furor among Turkish Cypriots, whose missing disappeared over the course of the decade prior to the Turkish military intervention. The certainty of their loved ones' deaths is as indubitable and inexpungable as are the memories of violence, death, and hunger that represent for them the decade before 1974.

It is clear that, because of the division of the island, talk about the missing mirrors talk about that other group of "missing:" namely, one's former neighbors who now live on the other side of a ceasefire line. For Greek Cypriots especially, that unseen and unknown world across the barrier is also the world into which one's husband, father, or brother may have disappeared. And so those lost in the war have come to represent the violence of those responsible for their disappearance. Here, the violence that turns inward, homogenizing the political domain, is reflected outward, onto the other.

And so, firstly, for both Greek and Turkish Cypriots, "the missing" symbolize rupture, though that rupture is necessarily located at different moments. For Turkish Cypriots, that rupture was both creative and definitive: their own missing were martyrs in the birth of a state, and the lack of interest in their fate appears to represent a homogenization of the violent past and an orientation towards the future, free of random Greek Cypriot violence. The fact of mass graves is enough of an explanation, and why dwell on a past that's so obviously gone? For Greek Cypriots, that rupture was both destructive and uncertain: this historical rupture was also the rupture of the island, and the suspension of the island's history, which was supposedly 3,000 years Greek. Paradoxically, Greek Cypriots cling to uncertainty, claiming that the fate of their missing is unknown, and hence suggesting that that fate is, in fact, knowable but that one's access to the truth is suspended or broken. Greek Cypriots cling to uncertainty as a way of salvaging history, of rescuing it from the completeness of its rupture. The insistence on "knowing" about the missing becomes a way of retrieving what they believe to be their rightful history.

We can see, secondly, that in these polarized cosmologies, the barbarians are those who disrupt history, whose history is the unimaginable opposite of one's own. For Turkish Cypriots, the refusal on the part of Greek Cypriots to accept that their missing are dead is only another denial of the historical "truth:" namely, the *de facto* partition of the island and the *right* of Turkish Cypriots to decide their own future and to make claims on the island. On the other hand, for Greek Cypriots the illegitimacy and deceptiveness of what they believe to be deliberate Turkish obfuscation with regard to the fate of the missing only reflects the illegitimacy and deceptiveness of Turkish claims on the island. And so the violence done to the missing represents a violence done to history, while the uncertainty of the "real" fate of the missing represents a suspension of the island's "real" history.

Conclusion: democracy and anti-democracy

Belief rests on imaginations of the future, and hence on visions of the past. As should be clear by now, it is utterly consistent with the foundations of nationalism in the Greek Cypriot community that they can express horror at a perceived erasure of the past in Turkish Cyprus while displaying bumper stickers that declare that Cyprus is Greek, distributing tourist brochures that call Cyprus the "island of Aphrodite" and emphasize its Greek heritage, and flying Greek flags on any special occasion. It is a triumph of a propaganda more amenable to Western European conceptions of the state that indeed much of the world believes that Cyprus is a Greek island. For British colonizers and democracy-touting diplomats, there is still something understandable in the goal of those who fought for enosis because they wanted Cyprus to join its Mother Greece as had so many other island children. For Greek Cypriots—and hence for much of the world—the invasion of the Turkish army was incomprehensible because Turkish claims on the island were so obviously illegitimate and childish. That invasion was not only a violent act that overturned their world; it was a rupture that suspended history, that violated the supposed 3,000 years of Hellenic culture of the island.

Similarly, there is no real contradiction in Turkish Cypriot references to the murder, arson, and mayhem that put them to flight in the pre-1974 period, and the fact that those same victims became victimizers during the war and after. Their own violence was defensive and creative; the violence of their opponents was obsessive, psychotic, and delusional. In a pragmatic history that accepts contingencies, the creation of an unbroken line of historical continuity is a laughable impossibility that ceases to be humorous when it becomes the basis for action. And so history becomes more than the motive force and justification for killing one's neighbors. History makes that violence not only explicable, but unavoidable.

Clearly, freedom for one group in Cyprus has been purchased at the expense of the other's freedom. Greek Cypriots initially wanted enosis against the vehement objections of the Turkish minority; they were then dissatisfied with the guarantees of the 1960 constitution and so did everything possible to impede its proper functioning. Turkish Cypriots, on the other hand, have purchased a certain limited freedom at the expense of their Greek neighbors. And, as Isaiah Berlin so tersely notes, "If the liberty of myself or my class or nation depends on the misery of a number of other human beings, the system which promotes this is unjust and immoral."[59] Yet, ironically, these violations have always occurred in the name of human rights and of the right of a people to determine its own form of representative government. Even more than that, the inability of Cypriots to conceive of their future freedom and of "proper" politics in any form besides that of representative, liberal democracy meant that that freedom was always already divided along communal lines.

The Cypriot anti-colonial battle was fought in the period after World War II when American power was ascendant, American capitalistic democracy and Soviet totalitarian communism were the unquestioned goods and evils of the day, and words and phrases such as "development" and "human rights" were beginning to echo in the halls of places such as the United Nations. Moreover, both communities of Cyprus had for a long time been oriented towards Europe and Westernization. Greek Cypriots—along with their Greek counterparts—had long declared themselves the living ancestors of the West.[60] And Turkish Cypriots—along with their Turkish counterparts—had recreated themselves in the interests of joining a future of progress and prosperity. Greek Cypriots claimed a European past and a primordial attachment to the ideals of European civilization; Turkish Cypriots claimed a European future and cast off the past with all the triumphalism of a truly modernizing spirit.

The supposedly European ideals of democracy and human rights were on the lips of all, but they were understood in only their crudest forms and not in all of their historical and cultural contingency. Hence, Greek Cypriots held a referendum in 1950 in which 95.7 per cent of eligible Greek Cypriot voters cast their ballots in favor of union with Greece.[61] Then and after the anti-colonial struggle it was considered a great injustice that they were not given what was the clear desire of the vast majority of the inhabitants of the island. Turkish Cypriots, on the other hand, demanded recognition of their rights as a community, even at the past and current expense of their Greek Cypriot neighbors.

In other words, the triumph in Cyprus of a popularized Western universalism and theories of right has unfortunately proved tragic. Obviously, the differences that I have described in these chapters will not be overcome easily. A simple demand for tolerance or insistence on rights brings one back to the same political mire. Ironically, hope may lie in what Mavratsas called the "corporatism" of Cypriot political behavior, in which at the political level the extreme individualism of Western politics cannot be seen to be fully operative. As I stated in the introduction, the supposedly pre-social individual of Western liberal democratic theory is applied with difficulty in parts of the world where social actors appear as immanently social beings. Indeed, I agree with Alasdair MacIntyre and Charles Taylor that "the individual" itself is not a pre-social, but an inherently social role played by those for whom individualism has become a worthy goal.[62] One can see this, for instance, in concepts such as those of respect and justice, which are applied both to individuals and to the community as a whole. *Saygı*, for example, has the further meaning of honor, but honor of a sort that recognizes another's worth. Peter Berger has noted that the concept of honor "implies that identity is essentially, or at least importantly, linked to institutional roles." He contrasts this with the modern concept of dignity at the heart of human rights discussions, which he says, "by contrast, implies that identity is essentially independent of institutional roles."[63] In other words, concepts such as justice or respect, while utilized in Cyprus for discussions of human rights, imply that the rights of humans are inextricably linked to the rights of communities.

This commitment to knowing and being known as members of communities and institutions could, in the case of Cyprus, be a good thing. If scrutinized with serious and sincere intent, it might be possible to use the corporatism and lack of anonymity or Western-style political individualism in order to develop new institutional forms or to revive older political ideals. In the Ancient Greek institution of *isonomy*, for example, it was agreed that humans are unequal by nature and need an institution, the *polis*, to make them equal. Arendt comments that in this system, "Equality existed only in this specifically political realm, where men met one another as citizens and not as private persons .... The equality of the Greek *polis*, its isonomy, was an attribute of the *polis* and not of men, who received their equality by virtue of citizenship, not by virtue of birth."[64] Similarly, even the authors of the United States' constitution were not originally concerned with the guarantees of private liberty, which they felt were the natural consequence of a just state and would be compromised only by a tyrannical ruler. Problems such as freedom of speech and movement were not to be resolved by a flat, universalized conception of human rights but by a working out within the polity of what would be accepted as good and just governance. They were more concerned with the space of political freedom—the space in which they could come together as equals engaged in a political project.

In his plea for balanced consideration of political possibilities rather than a single political solution to fit all, Isaiah Berlin remarks:

> The extent of a man's, or a people's liberty to choose to live as they desire must be weighed against the claims of many other values, of which equality, or justice, or happiness, or security, or public order are perhaps the most obvious examples .... That we cannot have everything is a necessary, not a contingent, truth.[65]

Clearly, in a case like that of Cyprus, the ideals of liberal democracy can be subverted to realize their opposite. Cypriots are largely dependent on the opinions and aid of international powers, and the platitudes of democracy and human rights can be invoked in the international arena to many different and contradictory ends. But the fate of the island ultimately lies in the Cypriots' own struggle to create a space of freedom, justice, and respect for all.

Conclusion:
Toward a Postnational Cyprus?

Since the beginning of 2003, Cyprus has experienced tremendous change, much of it following upon the opening of the buffer zone and the new opportunities for interchange that followed. Recent contacts between Turkish and Greek Cypriots show that there are many bonds of friendship and neighborliness that have survived the violence provoked by national-ist politics and the separation of decades. But the April 2004 failure at referendum of the Annan Plan to reunite the island indicates that contact does not automatically or necessarily produce reconciliation. At the polit-ical level, while Turkish Cypriots have engaged in a revolution that has marginalized their long-time leaders, Greek Cypriots have followed their own leaders into rejection of a plan that would have helped them to build a future together with their Turkish Cypriot neighbors. While Greek and Turkish Cypriots meet in their old villages and eat and drink together, there has been little serious discussion about how to mobilize those bonds of neighborliness as a form of critique and political action.

I believe that the history traced in this book points to at least one use-ful direction that such a critique might take. In recent work, Uday Mehta has used a Gandhian notion of political "friendship" as a point from which to critique liberal democracy's founding in "kinship."[2] The notion of fraternity at the heart of liberal democracy's promises of equality also inevitably leads to division and discrimination, as recognized by Gandhi earlier in the century. In opposition to this, Gandhi proposed a notion of political friendship, in which what he calls the "prejudices" of the other—those beliefs, such as religion, that the other finds constitutive of self—are tolerated in the name of a greater project. In other words, one forms an alliance.

The immediately obvious difficulty with the Gandhian notion is that it appears to provide no means for continuity: it is based on choice in the present. A political legitimacy founded in kinship or fraternity, on the other hand, guarantees the future. Hence, I would like to propose a third term: that of *neighborliness*. Nowadays, in much Euro-American experience, neighbors are those only contingently connected to one by proximity. In Cyprus and many other parts of the world, however, neighbors are those persons with whom one has always and presumably will always continue to live. In Cyprus, for instance, it is repeated again and again that neighbors always helped and never hurt each other. Even during periods of intercommunal conflict, it is unanimously agreed that neighbors never attacked one another, in fact protected and helped each other. The attackers always came from another village, never from one's own.

Neighbors, then, are those persons to whom one is historically connected through place and with whom one must live. This is what my Turkish Cypriot informant meant when he said that intercourse with his Greek Cypriot neighbors was "more an act of necessity, and not an act of affection." Affection, indeed, is not the point. Even the best neighbors may be nosy, may cause trouble, may know too much about one's comings and goings. Neighbors form a moral community and a tribunal. Neighborliness, then, is at least partially a pragmatic act.

But neighbors are also those persons in whose eyes one's identity is formed and judged. One "performs" one's identity partly in the home but primarily in the semi-public space of neighborhood or village, where one's performance—as father or mother, male or female, wise or foolish, rich or poor—is scrutinized and evaluated. It is in that often heterogeneous and uncertain space where identities are constituted. Certainly, the first, pragmatic understanding of neighborliness underpins and legitimates the project of the European Union of states. But even the second understanding of neighborliness is also in operation there, insofar as Europeans appear to be intensely aware of the European "neighborhood" as a performative space. As in the concept of fraternity, new legitimations of the state are extrapolated from an understanding of the "natural" relations of its units.

A political conception of neighborliness, however, presupposes not a contractual but a connective theory of human relations. As is well known, social contract theory—the precursor of modern liberalism—assumes a free, autonomous, whole individual, unfettered by the constraints of culture and at least theoretically in a constant war of all against all. Sociality, then, is a contract into which individuals enter for their own protection; according to Hobbes, the state's role is to guarantee that contract and to protect it from breach. While other "fathers" of contract theory, such as Rousseau and Locke, put various spins on the notion of the contract (in Rousseau's case by acknowledging the impossibility of a pre-social human), the problem is nevertheless articulated as one of binding the individual to society and its laws.

This explanation of sociality and hence of politics, while blatantly counterfactual and hence anti-anthropological, nevertheless serves as a starting point for liberal theory insofar as that theory begins from the rights of the individual. One possible alternative to contract theory is what the anthropologist Suad Joseph calls "connectivity," or the sense that one's personhood is inextricable from those persons to whom one is connected by kinship, history, or love. In the Lebanese case that she studies, Joseph observes that the self is not seen as bounded and whole, but as porous and open.[3] Such strong understandings of connectivity, especially to kin, when conjoined with Western theories of democracy as something based in a fraternal bond of equals, often lead to tragic results, as I observed in Chapter 8.

A political theory of neighborliness would begin from the assumption of connectivity as both the constitution of personhood and the ground of politics. Gandhi had similarly assumed that certain "prejudices"—i.e., aspects of culture—were constitutive of rather than incidental to definitions of self. Political friendship, then, would be a recognition of the ways in which one's own prejudices intersect with others'. Political neighborliness, however, would see such "prejudices" as interconstitutive and interdependent, never wholly bound within culture but as part of the ways in which differing humans interact, individually and collectively, in the world.

Such a possibility of political action would come into conversation with three fascinating strands of recent critique. The first is the postmodernist critique emanating from recent Islamist thought. Much of the Western postmodernist critique has focused on problems inherent in a modernist individualism and has called for a recognition of the rights of cultures. This position, in turn, has been criticized as reifying cultures by bounding them, "fixing" them, and immobilizing them beyond change. One important strand of the Islamist critique, however, has focused on the manner in which liberal democracy values rights over responsibilities, allowing the free rein of liberal capitalism in anti-democratic, authoritarian states. For many Islamists, the state's main role is to promote social justice, and Islamists have accused their own states of failing to fulfill its responsibilities to the people and to promote responsibility from within. This is why Islamist organizations in many countries are known for their successful organization at the grassroots level: because they take seriously the idea of humans as interconnected and responsible to each other. In Cyprus, this critique has been most powerfully embodied in the communist party, AKEL, which historically has gained widespread support in opposition to nationalist movements. The movement has not only been intercommunal, but its localized brand of communism primarily articulates the need for social justice and responsibility.

A second strand of critique that intersects with a notion of neighborliness is one that weaves its way through several areas of contemporary feminist thought. This is an idea articulated by Nel Noddings as an ethics of care and by Chris Cuomo, in her writings on animal rights, as "flourishing." While Cuomo intends the latter as a way for humans to judge when they have fulfilled their responsibilities to other living beings, it also clearly intersects with the ethics of care, which Noddings sees as based not on a human's supposed "basic" needs (food, water), but on a human's real needs (e.g., to have a home). An ethics of care would see humans in a community together as responsible for meeting needs that would lead to their flourishing. This is an idea that already has some foundation in Cyprus, where several women's groups have opposed the masculine oppression of war and division and have argued that women's voices—and the alternative ethics that they articulate—need to be heard. If joined to selfconscious critique of the ways in which "the feminine" has been utilized for nationalist purposes, this movement could represent an important direction in the rethinking of community in the island.

A final strand of recent thought with which a notion of neighborliness enters into conversation is that on the strange rise of the local within the global. Economic and technological globalization have simultaneously freed many persons and groups from dependence on the nation-state, and cast those same persons and groups into new hierarchies of oppression within the global order. Recent events in Cyprus are probably the most hopeful sort of consequence of globalization, as groups informed and empowered by possibilities within the new global order find ways to imagine beyond and therefore to resist a state of affairs that had for so long seemed the only real possibility.

In a globalized world and a renewed Cyprus, it seems time to take the local seriously. In Cyprus, taking the local seriously means taking seriously the neighborliness that has survived three decades of separation, a neighborliness that can now be put into political action. If ethnic fantasies have led to nightmares and the promises of liberal democracy have brought division, another path is certainly needed. My hope is that in a postnational Cyprus, the local will not be taken for granted or devalued but will instead become a starting-point for a critique from which Cypriots can carve out a new, juster world for themselves and their children.

Bibliography

Archives

Archive of the Archbishop of the Orthodox Church of Cyprus (AAOCC).
State Archive of the Republic of Cyprus (SA1).
State Archive of the Turkish Republic of Northern Cyprus (SATRNC).
Public Records Office, London (PRO).
Ministry of Foreign Affairs, Athens (MFA).
Archive of the Dragoumis Family, Gennaideion Library, Athens (Dragoumis).

Primary sources

Cyprus Annual Reports.
Cyprus Blue Book Reports.
Dhimitriadhis, Friksos (1994) (ed.), *Agogi ton Neon: To Paranomo Periodhiko tis EOKA ghia tous Mathites ton Dhimotikon Scholeion* (Limassol).
Papadhopoulos, Yiannis K. (1987), *Keimena Enos Agona: Paranoma Engrafa tou 1955–59* (Nicosia).
Report by Her Majesty's High Commissioner for 1887–88.
Standing Orders and Regulations of the Cyprus Police (Nicosia, 1896).

Secondary sources

Abu-Lughod, Lila (1986), *Veiled Sentiments: Honor and Poetry in a Bedouin Society* (Berkeley: University of California Press).
—— (1998) (ed.), *Remaking Women: Feminism and Modernity in the Middle East* (Princeton: Princeton University Press).
Al-Qattan, Najwa (1999), "*Dhimmis* in the Muslim Court: Legal Autonomy and Religious Discrimination," *International Journal of Middle East Studies*, 31: 3, pp. 429–44.
Alastos, Doros (1976), *Cyprus in History: A Survey of 5000 Years* (London: Zeno Publishers).
Amin, S., and Chakrabarty, D. (1997), *Subaltern Studies IX: Writings on South Asian History and Society* (Delhi: Oxford University Press).

Anderson, Benedict (1993), *Imagined Communities: Reflections on the Origin and Spread of Nationalism* (London: Verso).

Anderson, J. N. D. (1959), "The Family Law of Turkish Cypriots," *Die Welt des Islams*, V, pp. 161–87.

Anthias, Floya and Yuval-Davis, Nira (1992), *Racialized Boundaries: Race, Nation, Gender, Colour and Class and the Anti-Racist Struggle* (London: Routledge).

Apple, Michael (1979), *Ideology and Curriculum* (London: Routledge and Kegan Paul).

Arat, Zehra F. (1998a), "Educating the Daughters of the Republic," in Arat (1998b: 157–80).

—— (1998b) (ed.), *Deconstructing Images of 'The Turkish Woman'*, (New York: St. Martin's Press).

Arendt, Hannah (1963), *On Revolution* (New York: Penguin Books).

Argyrou, Vassos (1996), *Tradition and Modernity in the Mediterranean: The Wedding as Symbolic Struggle* (Cambridge: Cambridge University Press).

Armstrong, John A. (1982), *Nations before Nationalism* (Chapel Hill, NC: University of North Carolina Press).

Asad, Talal (1973) (ed.), *Anthropology and the Colonial Encounter* (Ithaca, NY: Cornell University Press, 1973).

—— (1993), *Genealogies of Religion: Discipline and Reasons of Power in Christianity and Islam* (Baltimore: Johns Hopkins University Press).

Attalides, Michael A. (1979), *Cyprus: Nationalism and International Politics* (New York: St. Martin's Press).

Barth, Fredrik (1969), "Introduction," in F. Barth (ed.), *Ethnic Groups and Boundaries: The Social Organization of Culture Difference* (Boston: Little, Brown and Co.), pp. 9–38.

Beckingham, Charles Fraser (1958), "Islam and Turkish Nationalism in Cyprus," *Die Welt des Islams*, V, pp. 65–83.

Berger, Peter (1984), "On the Obsolescence of the Concept of Honour," in Sandel (1984: 149–58).

Berkes, Niyazi (1964), *The Development of Secularism in Turkey* (Montreal: McGill University Press).

Bernal, Martin (1997), "Race, Class, and Gender in the Formation of the Aryan Model of Greek Origins," in V. Y. Mudimbe (ed.), *Nations, Identities, Cultures* (Durham, NC: Duke University Press), pp. 7–28.

Berlin, Isaiah (1984), "Two Concepts of Liberty," in Sandel (1984: 15–36).

Black-Michaud, Jacob (1975), *Cohesive Force: Feud in the Mediterranean and the Middle East*, with a foreword by E. L. Peters (New York: St. Martin's Press).

Blok, Anton (1972), "The Peasant and the Brigand: Social Banditry Reconsidered," *Comparative Studies in Society and History*, 14: 4, pp. 494–505.

Boissevain, J. (1979), "Towards a Social Anthropology of the Mediterranean," *Current Anthropology*, 20: 1, pp. 81–93.

du Boulay, Juliet (1986), "Women—Images of their Nature and Destiny in Rural Greece," in J. Dubisch (ed.), *Gender and Power in Rural Greece* (Princeton: Princeton University Press), pp. 139–69.

—— (1991), "Cosmos and Gender in Village Greece," in P. Loizos and E. Papatarxiarchis (eds.), *Contested Identities: Gender and Kinship in Modern Greece* (Princeton: Princeton University Press), pp. 47–78.

Bourdieu, Pierre (1977), *Outline of a Theory of Practice* (Cambridge: Cambridge University Press).

—— (1984), *Distinction: A Social Critique of the Judgement of Taste*, trans. Richard Nice (Cambridge, MA: Harvard University Press).

—— (1988), *Homo Academicus*, trans. Peter Collier (Cambridge: Polity Press).

—— (1990), *The Logic of Practice* (Stanford, CA: Stanford University Press).

—— and Passeron, Jean-Claude (1990), *Reproduction in Education, Society, and Culture* (London: Sage Publications).

Brandes, Stanley (1987), "Reflections on Honor and Shame in the Mediterranean," in Gilmore (1987: 121–34).

Braude, Benjamin (1982), "Foundation Myths of the Millet System," in B. Braude and B. Lewis (eds.), *Christians and Jews of the Ottoman Empire: The Functioning of a Plural Society* (London and New York: Homes and Meier Publishers), vol. 1, pp. 69–88.

Bringa, Tone (1995), *Being Muslim the Bosnian Way: Identity and Community in a Central Bosnian Village* (Princeton: Princeton University Press).

Browning, Christopher R. (1993), *Ordinary Men: Reserve Police Battalion 101 and the Final Solution in Poland* (New York: Harper Perennial).

Bryant, Rebecca (1998*a*), "Educating Ethnicity: On the Cultures of Nationalism in Cyprus," (unpublished Ph.D. thesis, University of Chicago Department of Anthropology).

—— (1998*b*), "An Education in Honor: Patriotism and the Schools of Cyprus," in Calotychos (1998: 53–68).

—— (2001), "An Aesthetics of Self: Moral Remaking and Cypriot Education," *Comparative Studies in Society and History*, 43: 3, pp. 583–614.

Burchell, Graham (1991*a*), "Peculiar Interests: Civil Society and Governing 'The System of Natural Liberty,'" in Burchell, Gordon, and Miller (1991*b*: 119–50).

——, Gordon, C., and Miller, D. (1991*b*) (eds.), *The Foucault Effect: Studies in Governmentality* (Chicago: University of Chicago Press).

Calotychos, Vangelis (1998*a*), "Interdisciplinary Perspectives: Difference at the Heart of Cypriot Identity and Its Study, " in Calotychos (1998*b*: 1–34).

—— (1998*b*) (ed.), *Cyprus and Its People: Nation, Identity, and Experience in an Unimaginable Community, 1955–1997* (Boulder, CO: Westview Press).

Camus, Albert (1956), *The Rebel* (New York: Random House).

Campbell, John (1964), *Honour, Family, and Patronage* (Oxford: Oxford University Press).

Chatterjee, Partha (1993), *The Nation and Its Fragments: Colonial and Postcolonial Histories* (Princeton: Princeton University Press).

Chatziioannou, Kyriakos (1976), *I Kataghoyi ton Tourkokiprion ke to Kipriako* (Nicosia: Kyriakos Chatziioannou).

Christodoulou, Demetrios (1992), *Inside the Cyprus Miracle: The Labours of an Embattled Mini-Economy* (Minnesota: University of Minnesota Press).

Chytry, Josef (1989), *The Aesthetic State: A Quest in Modern German Thought* (Berkeley: University of California Press).

Clark, D. L. (1957), *Rhetoric in Greco-Roman Education* (New York: Columbia University Press).

Clifford, James and Marcus, George E. (1986) (eds.), *Writing Culture: The Poetics and Politics of Ethnography* (Berkeley: University of California Press).

Cohn, Bernard D. (1985), "The Command of Language and the Language of Command," in R. Guha (ed.), *Subaltern Studies IV: Writing on South Asian History and Society* (Oxford: Oxford University Press), pp. 276–329.

—— (1989), "Law and the Colonial State in India," in J. Starr and J. F. Collier (eds.), *History and Power in the Study of Law: New Directions in Legal Anthropology* (Ithaca, NY: Cornell University Press, 1989), pp. 131–52.

Cole, Juan (1983), *Colonialism and Revolution in the Middle East: Social and Cultural Origins of Egypt's 'Urabi Movement* (Princeton: Princeton University Press).

Coleman, Joyce (1996), *Public Reading and the Reading Public in Late Medieval England and France* (Cambridge: Cambridge University Press).

Comaroff, Jean, and Comaroff, John (1991), *Of Revelation and Revolution: Christianity, Colonialism, and Consciousness in South Africa, Volume 1* (Chicago: University of Chicago Press),.

—— and Comaroff, John (forthcomng), *Of Revelation and Revolution, Volume 3: Reading, Writing, and Rioting* (Chicago: University of Chicago Press).

Comaroff, John (1987), "Of Totemism and Ethnicity: Consciousness, Practice and the Signs of Inequality," *Ethos*, 52: 3–4, pp. 301–23.

—— (1996), "Ethnicity, Nationalism, and the Politics of Difference in an Age of Revolution," in E. N. Wilmsen and P. McAllister (eds.), *The Politics of Difference: Ethnic Premises in a World of Power* (Chicago: University of Chicago Press), pp. 162–83.

Connor, Walker (1994), "A Nation is a Nation, is a State, is an Ethnic Group, is a …," in J. Hutchinson and A. D. Smith (eds.), *Nationalism* (Oxford: Oxford University Press), pp. 36–46.

Crawshaw, Nancy (1978), *The Cyprus Revolt: An Account of the Struggle for Union with Greece* (London: George Allen and Unwin).

Davis, John (1977), *Peoples of the Mediterranean: An Essay in Comparative Social Anthropology* (London: Routledge Kegan and Paul).

Davison, Roderic H. (1962), *Reform in the Ottoman Empire, 1856–1876* (Princeton: Princeton University Press).

Delaney, Carol (1986), "The Meaning of Paternity and the Virgin Birth Debate," *Man*, 21, pp. 494–513.

—— (1991), *The Seed and the Soil: Gender and Cosmology in Turkish Village Society* (Berkeley: University of California Press).

—— (1995), "Father State, Motherland, and the Birth of Modern Turkey," in S. Yanagisako and C. Delaney (eds.), *Naturalizing Power: Essays in Feminist Cultural Analysis* (New York: Routledge), pp. 177–99.

Denktaş, Rauf (1978), *Erenköy Dedikleri* (Nicosia).

—— (n.d.), *Kader Çizgisi* (Nicosia).

Deroche, François (1996), "Maîtres et disciples: la transmission de la culture calligraphique dans le monde ottoman," in Nicolas Vatin (ed.), *Oral et écrit dans le monde turco-ottoman* (Paris: Edisud), pp. 81–90.

Dhareshwar, Vivek and Srivatsan, R. (1997), "'Rowdy-Sheeters': An Essay on Subalternity and Politics," in Amin and Chakrabarty (1997: 201–31).

Dubisch, Jill (1995), *In a Different Place: Pilgrimage, Gender, and Politics at a Greek Island Shrine* (Princeton: Princeton University Press).

Dumont, Louis (1980), *Homo Hierarchicus* (Chicago: University of Chicago Press).

—— (1994), *German Ideology: From France to Germany and Back* (Chicago: University of Chicago Press).

Durakbaşa, Ayşe (1998), "Kemalism as Identity Politics in Turkey," in Arat (1998b: 139–55).

Durkheim, Emile (1956), *Education and Sociology* (Glencoe, IL: Free Press).

—— (1973) *Moral Education: A Study in the Theory and Application of the Sociology of Education* (New York: Free Press).

Eickelman, Dale F. (1978), "The Art of Memory: Islamic Education and its Social Reproduction," *Comparative Studies in Society and History*, 20: 4, pp. 485–516.

Ekdhosi Sindhesmou Tomearchon EOKA (1987), *Limeria tis EOKA 1955–59* (Nicosia: Ekdhosi Sindhesmou Tomearchon EOKA).

Englezakis, Benedict (1995), *Studies on the History of the Church of Cyprus, 4th–20th Centuries* (London: Variorum).

Evans-Pritchard, E. E. (1940), *The Nuer: A Description of the Modes of Livelihood and Political Institutions of a Nilotic People* (Oxford: Clarendon Press).

Ewing, Katherine P. (1986), "The Illusion of Wholeness: Culture, Self, and the Experience of Inconsistency," *Ethos*, 18: 3, pp. 251–78.

Fallers, Lloyd (1974), "Turkey: Nation-State out of Polyglot Empire," in *The Social Anthropology of the Nation-State* (Chicago: Aldine Publishing).

Ferry, Luc (1993), *Homo Aestheticus: The Invention of Taste in the Democratic Age*, trans. Robert De Loaiza (Chicago: University of Chicago Press).

Fleischer, Cornell (1983), "Royal Authority, Dynastic Cyclism, and 'Ibn Khaldunism' in Sixteenth-Century Ottoman Letters," *Journal of Asian and African Studies*, 18: 2, pp. 46–68.

—— (1994), "Between the Lines: Realities of Scribal Life in the Sixteenth Century," in *Studies in Ottoman History in Honour of Professor V. L. Menage* (Istanbul: Isis Press), pp. 45–61.

Fleming, K. E. (1998), "Women as Preservers of the Past: Ziya Gökalp and Women's Reform," in Arat (1998*b*: 127–38).

Foley, Douglas (1990), *Learning Capitalist Culture: Deep in the Heart of Tejas* (Philadelphia: University of Pennsylvania Press).

Foucault, Michel (1979), *Discipline and Punish: The Birth of the Prison* (New York: Vintage).

—— (1986), *The Use of Pleasure: The History of Sexuality Volume 2* (NewYork: Vintage Books).

—— (1991), "Politics and the Study of Discourse," in Burchell, Gordon, and Miller (1991*b*: 53–72).

—— (1997), "On the Genealogy of Ethics: An Overview of Work in Progress," in Paul Rabinow (ed.), *Ethics: Subjectivity and Truth: Essential Works of Foucault 1954–1984, Vol. 1* (New York: The New Press), pp. 253–80.

Gazioğlu, Ahmet C. (1996), *Enosis Çemberinde Türkler: Bugünlere Gelmek Kolay Olmadı* (Nicosia: Cyprus Research and Publishing Center).

Geertz, Clifford (1963) (ed.), *Old Societies and New States* (New York: Free Press).

—— (1973*a*) "After the Revolution: the Fate of Nationalism in the New States', in Clifford Geertz, *The Interpretation of Cultures* (New York: Basic Books), pp. 234–54.

—— (1973*b*), "Person, Time, and Conduct in Bali," in Clifford Geertz, *The Interpretation of Cultures* (New York: Basic Books), pp. 360–411.

Gellner, Ernest (1983), *Nations and Nationalism* (Ithaca, NY: Cornell University Press).

—— (1987), *Culture, Identity, and Politics* (Cambridge: Cambridge University Press).

Ghiangoullis, K. G. (2001), *Corpus Kipriakon Dhialektikon Poiitikon Kimenon* (Nicosia: Dhimosievmata tou Kentrou Epistimonikon Erevnon).

Giddens, Anthony (1990), *The Consequences of Modernity* (Stanford, CA: Stanford University Press).

Gillis, John (1996), *A World of Their Own Making: Myth, Ritual, and the Quest for Family Values* (New York: Basic Books).

Gilmore, David (1987) (ed.), *Honor and Shame and the Unity of the Mediterranean* (Washington, DC: American Anthropological Association).

Gingrich, Andre, and Fox, Richard G. (2002) (eds.), *Anthropology, By Comparison* (London: Routledge).

Giovannini, M. J. (1987), "Female Chastity Codes in the Circum-Mediterranean," in Gilmore (1987: 61–74).

Glass, James M. (1997), *Life Unworthy of Life: Racial Phobia and Mass Murder in Hitler's Germany* (New York: Basic Books).

Goddard, V. A. (1994), "From the Mediterranean to Europe: Honour, Kinship, and Gender," in V. A. Goddard, J. R. Llobera, and C. Shore (eds.), *The Anthropology of Europe: Identity and Boundaries in Conflict* (Oxford: Berg), pp. 57–92.

Goffman, Daniel (1994), "Ottoman Millets in the Early Seventeenth Century," *New Perspectives on Turkey*, 11, pp. 135–58.

Gökalp, Ziya (1959), *Turkish Nationalism and Western Civilization*, trans. Niyazi Berkes (New York: Columbia University Press).

—— (1978), *Türkçülüğün Esasları* (Istanbul: İnkılâp ve Aka Kitabevleri).

—— (1989), *Türk Medeniyeti Tarihi* (Istanbul: Toker Yayınları).

Goody, Jack (1977), *The Domestication of the Savage Mind* (Cambridge: Cambridge University Press).

—— (1987), *The Interface between the Written and the Oral* (Cambridge: Cambridge University Press).

—— and Watt, Ian (1963), "The Consequences of Literacy," in J. Goody (ed.), *Literacy in Traditional Societies* (Cambridge: Cambridge University Press), pp. 27–68.

Gordon, Colin (1991), "Governmental Rationality: An Introduction," in Burchell, Gordon, and Miller (1991*b*: 1–51).

Gramsci, Antonio (1971), *Selections from the Prison Notebooks* (New York: International Publishers).

Grant, Bruce (1995), *In the Soviet House of Culture: A Century of Perestroikas* (Princeton: Princeton University Press).

Güntekin, Reşat Nuri (1993), *Çalıkuşu* (Istanbul: İnkılâp Kitabevi).

Habermas, Jürgen (1992), *The Structural Transformation of the Public Sphere: An Inquiry into a Category of Bourgeois Society* (Cambridge, MA: Massachusetts Institute of Technology Press).

Hackett, J. (1901), *A History of the Orthodox Church of Cyprus* (London: Methuen).

Hadjipavlou-Trigeorgis, Maria (1998), "Different Relationships to the Land: Personal Narratives, Political Implications and Future Possibilities," in Calotychos (1998*b*: 251–76).

—— (2000), "The Role of Joint Narrative in Conflict Resolution: The Case of Cyprus," in Yashin (2000*b*: 159–79).

Hanioğlu, M. Şükrü (1985), *Osmanlı İttihad ve Terakki Cemiyeti ve Jön Türklük* (Istanbul: İletişim Yayınları).

Harik, Iliya (1994), "Pluralism in the Arab World," *Journal of Democracy*, 5: 3, pp. 43–56.

Heidegger, Martin (1959), *An Introduction to Metaphysics* (New Haven, CT: Yale University Press).

Heper, Metin (1976), "Political Modernization as Reflected in Bureaucratic Change: The Turkish Bureaucracy and a 'Historical Bureaucratic Empire' Tradition," *International Journal of Middle East Studies*, 7, pp. 507–21.

Herzfeld, Michael (1980), "Honour and Shame: Problems in the Comparative Analysis of Moral Systems," *Man*, 15, pp. 339–51.

—— (1982), *Ours Once More: Folklore, Ideology, and the Making of Modern Greece* (Austin: University of Texas Press).

—— (1984*a*), "The Horns of a Mediterraneanist Dilemma," *American Ethnologist*, 11: 3, pp. 439–54.

—— (1984*b*), *The Poetics of Manhood: Contest and Identity in a Cretan Mountain Village* (Princeton: Princeton University Press).

—— (1986), "Within and Without: The Category of 'Female' in the Ethnography of Modern Greece," in J. Dubisch (ed.), *Gender and Power in Rural Greece* (Princeton: Princeton University Press), pp. 215–34.

—— (1987), *Anthropology Through the Looking-Glass: Critical Ethnography in the Margins of Europe* (Cambridge: Cambridge University Press).

—— (1997), *Cultural Intimacy: Social Poetics in the Nation-State* (New York: Routledge).

Hess, Jonathan M. (1999), *Reconstituting the Body Politic: Enlightenment, Public Culture and the Invention of Aesthetic Autonomy* (Detroit: Wayne State University Press).

Heyd, Uriel (1950), *Foundations of Turkish Nationalism: The Life and Teachings of Ziya Gökalp* (Westport: Hyperion).

Hill, Sir George (1952), *A History of Cyprus, Volume IV: The Ottoman Province, The British Colony, 1571–1948* (Cambridge: Cambridge University Press).

Hirsch, Marianne (1983), "Spiritual *Bildung*: The Beautiful Soul as Paradigm," in E. Abel, M. Hirsch, and E. Langland (eds.), *The Voyage In: Fictions of Female Development* (Hanover, NH: University Press of New England), pp. 23–48.

Hitchens, Christopher (1989) *Hostage to History: Cyprus from the Ottomans to Kissinger* (New York: Farrar, Straus and Giroux).

Hobbes, Thomas (1962), *Leviathan* (New York: Collier Books).

Hobsbawm, Eric (1959), *Primitive Rebels: Studies in Archaic Forms of Social Movements in the Nineteenth and Twentieth Centuries* (New York: Norton).

—— (1969), *Bandits* (London: George Weidenfeld & Nicolson).

—— (1990), *Nations and Nationalism since 1780: Programme, Myth, Reality* (Cambridge: Cambridge University Press).

Hodge, B. and Lewis, G. L. (1966), *Cyprus School History Textbooks* (London: Parliamentary Group for World Government).

Holt, Thomas C. (1992), *The Problem of Freedom: Race, Labor, and Politics in Jamaica and Britain, 1832–1938* (Baltimore: Johns Hopkins University Press).

Hunt, Lynn (1992), *The Family Romance of the French Revolution* (Berkeley: University of California Press).

Hymes, Dale (1969) (ed.), *Reinventing Anthropology* (New York: Pantheon).

Iacorella, Angelo (1998), *Gönye ve Hilal: İttihad – Terakki ve Masonluk* (Istanbul: Tarih Vakfı Yurt Yayınları).

Iossifides, A. M. (1991), "Sisters in Christ: Metaphors of Kinship among Greek Nuns," in P. Loizos and E. Papataxiarchis (eds.), *Contested Identities: Gender and Kinship in Modern Greece* (Princeton: Princeton University Press), pp. 135–55.

İslâmoğlu, Mahmut (1994), *Kıbrıs Türk Kültür ve Sanatı: Araştırma-İnceleme Yazıları Tebliğler* (Nicosia: Yakın Doğu Üniversitesi Matbaası).

İsmail, Sabahattin (1988), *Kıbrıs Türk Basınında İz Bırakanlar* (Nicosia: KKTC Eğitim ve Kültür Bakanlığı).

—— (1989), *20 July Peace Operation: Reasons, Development and Consequences* (Istanbul: Kastas Publications).

—— and Birinci, Ergin (1989), *Atatürk Döneminde Türkiye-Kıbrıs İlişkileri* (Nicosia: Milli Eğitim ve Kültür Bakanlığı Yayınları).

Itzkowitz, Norman (1980), *Ottoman Empire and Islamic Tradition* (Chicago: University of Chicago Press).

Jayawardena, Kumari (1986), *Feminism and Nationalism in the Third World* (London: Zed Books).

Jennings, Ronald C. (1993), *Christians and Muslims in Ottoman Cyprus and the Mediterranean World, 1571–1640* (New York: New York University Press).

Joseph, Joseph S. (1985), *Cyprus: Ethnic Conflict and International Concern* (New York: Peter Lang).

Kandiyoti, Deniz (1991*a*), "End of Empire: Islam, Nationalism, and Women in Turkey," in D. Kandiyoti (ed.), *Women, Islam, and the State* (Philadelphia: Temple University Press), pp. 22–47.

—— (1991*b*), "Identity and Its Discontents: Women and the Nation," *Millennium: Journal of International Studies*, 20: 3, pp. 429–43.

—— (1997), "Gendering the Modern: On Missing Dimensions in the Study of Turkish Modernity," in Sibel Bozdoğan and Reşat Kasaba (eds.), *Rethinking Modernity and National Identity in Turkey* (Seattle: University of Washington Press), pp. 113–32.

—— (1998), "Some Awkward Questions on Women and Modernity in Turkey," in Lila Abu-Lughod (ed.), *Remaking Women: Feminism and Modernity in the Middle East* (Cairo: American University in Cairo Press), pp. 270–87.

Kant, Immanuel (1960), *Education* (Ann Arbor: University of Michigan Press).

Kapferer, Bruce (1988), *Legends of People, Myths of State: Violence, Intolerance, and Political Culture in Sri Lanka and Australia* (Washington, DC: Smithsonian Press).

Kaplan, Samuel (1996), "Education and the Politics of National Culture in a Turkish Community, circa 1990" (unpublished dissertation, Department of Anthropology, University of Chicago).

Kasaba, Reşat (1999), "Economic Foundations of a Civil Society: Greeks in the Trade of Western Anatolia, 1840–1876," in Dimitris Gondicas and Charles Issawi (eds.), *Ottoman Greeks in the Age of Nationalism: Politics, Economy, and Society in the Nineteenth Century* (New Jersey: Darwin Press), pp. 77–87.

—— (2002), "Izmir 1922: A Port City Unravels," in L. Fawaz and C. A. Bayly (eds.), with the collaboration of R. Ilbert, *European Modernity and Culture: From the Mediterranean Sea to the Indian Ocean* (New York: Columbia University Press), pp. 204–29.

Katsiaounis, Rolandos (1996), "Labour, Society, and Politics in Cyprus during the Second Half of the Nineteenth Century" (unpublished Ph.D. dissertation, University of London).

Kazamias, Andreas M. (1966), *Education and the Quest for Modernity in Turkey* (Chicago: University of Chicago Press).

Kazazis, Kostas (1992), "Sunday Greek Revisited," *Journal of Modern Greek Studies*, 10: 1, pp. 57–69.

—— (1993), "Dismantling Greek Diglossia," in Eran Fraenkel and Christina Kramer (eds.), *Language Contact – Language Conflict* (Balkan Studies, volume 1) (New York: Peter Lang). pp. 7–26.

Khaldun, Ibn (1981), *The Muqadimmah: An Introduction to History*, trans. Franz Rosenthal (Princeton: Princeton University Press).

Khalid, Adeeb (1998), *The Politics of Muslim Cultural Reform: Jadidism in Central Asia* (Berkeley: University of California Press).

Kierkegaard, Soren (1938), *A Kierkegaard Anthology* (New York: Modern Library).

—— (1962), *The Present Age and Of the Difference Between a Genius and an Apostle* (New York: Harper and Row).

Killoran, Moira (1998), "Nationalism and Embodied Memory in Northern Cyprus," in Calotychos (1998*b*: 159–70).

—— (2000), "Time, Space, and National Identities in Cyprus," in Yashin (2000*b*: 129–46).

Kinross, Lord (1965), *Atatürk: A Biography of Mustafa Kemal, Father of Modern Turkey.* (New York: Morrow).

Kitromilides, Paschalis (1979), "The Dialectic of Intolerance: Ideological Dimensions of the Ethnic Conflict," in Peter Worseley and Paschalis Kitromilides (eds.), *Small States in the Modern World: The Conditions of Survival* (Nicosia: The New Cyprus Association), pp. 143–84.

—— (1990), "Greek Irredentism in Asia Minor and Cyprus," *Middle Eastern Studies*, 26: 1 (January), pp. 3–17.

Kızılyürek, Niyazi (1993), *Ulus Ötesi Kıbrıs/I Kipros peran tou Ethnous* (Nicosia: Kasonlithis and Sons).

Knight, Kelvin (1998) (ed.), *The MacIntyre Reader* (Notre Dame, IN: University of Notre Dame Press).

Kodaman, Bayram (1991), *Abdülhamid Devri Eğitim Sistemi* (Ankara: Türk Tarih Kurumu Basımevi).

——and Saydam, Abdullah (1992), "Tanzimat Devri Eğitim Sistemi," in H. D. Yıldız (ed.), *150. Yılında Tanzimat* (Ankara: Türk Tarih Kurumu Yayınları), pp. 475–96.

Kogon, Eugen (1998) [first published 1950], *The Theory and Practice of Hell: The German Concentration Camps and the System Behind Them* (New York: Berkley Publishing Group).

Koliopoulos, Ioannis S. (1996), *Peri lichnon afas: I listia stin Elladha (19os. ai)* (Thessaloniki: Paratiritis).

Koloğlu Orhan (1991), *İttihatçılar ve Masonlar* (Istanbul: Gür Yayınları).

Kondo, Dorinne K. (1987), "Creating an Ideal Self: Theories of Selfhood and Pedagogy at a Japanese Ethics Retreat," *Ethos*, 15: 3, pp. 241–72.

—— (1990), *Crafting Selves: Power, Gender, and Discourses of Identity in a Japanese Workplace* (Chicago: University of Chicago Press).

Koselleck, Reinhard (1985), *Futures Past: On the Semantics of Historical Time* (Cambridge, MA: Massachusetts Institute of Technology).

Lambek, Michael (1990), "Certain Knowledge, Contestable Authority: Power and Practice on the Islamic Periphery," *American Ethnologist*, 17: 1, pp. 23–40.

Levinson, Bradley A., Foley, Douglas E., and Holland, Dorothy C. (1996) (eds.), *The Cultural Production of the Educated Person* (Albany: State University of New York Press).

Lewis, Bernard (1962), *The Emergence of Modern Turkey* (London: Oxford University Press).

Lincoln, Bruce (1994), *Authority: Construction and Corrosion* (Chicago: University of Chicago Press).

Loizos, Peter (1972), "Aspects of Pluralism in Cyprus," *New Community*; reprinted in Peter Loizos (2001), *Unofficial Views: Cyprus: Society and Politics* (Nicosia: Intercollege Press), pp. 13–23.

—— (1974), "The Progress of Greek Nationalism in Cyprus, 1878–1976," in J. Davis (ed.), *Choice and Change: Essays in Honour of Lucy Mair* (London: Athlone Press), pp 114–33.

—— (1975), *The Greek Gift: Politics in a Cypriot Village* (Oxford: Blackwell).

—— (1988), "Intercommunal Killing in Cyprus," *Man*, 23: 4, pp. 639–53.

—— (1998), "How Might Turkish and Greek Cypriots See Each Other More Clearly?," in Calotychos (1998*b*: 35–52).

Loukas, Ghiorgos (1974) [first published 1874], *Filologhikai episkepseis: Ton en to bio ton neoteron Kiprion mnimion ton Archaion* (Nicosia: Kiprioloyiki Vivliothiki).

MacIntyre, Alasdair (1984), *After Virtue: A Study in Moral Theory*, 2nd edn (Notre Dame, IN: University of Notre Dame Press).

—— (1998) [first published 1979], "Social Science Methodology as the Ideology of Bureaucratic Authority," in Knight (1998: 53–68).

—— (1998*b*) [first published 1987], "Practical Rationalities as Forms of Social Structure," in Knight (1998: 120–35).

Macpherson, C. B. (1962), *The Political Theory of Possessive Individualism: Hobbes to Locke* (Oxford: Oxford University Press).

Mahdi, Muhsin (1964), *Ibn Khaldun's Philosophy of History* (Chicago: University of Chicago Press).

Maratheftis, Michalakis I. (1992), *To Kipriako Ekpaidheftiko Sistima: Stathmi ke themata* (Nicosia: Michalakis Maratheftis).

Marcus, George, and Fisher, Michael M. J. (1986), *Anthropology as Cultural Critique* (Chicago: University of Chicago Press).

Mardin, Şerif (1969), "Power, Civil Society and Culture in the Ottoman Empire," *Comparative Studies in Society and History*, 11: 3, pp. 258–81.

—— (1991), *Türkiye'de din ve siyaset* (Istanbul: İletişim Yayınları).

—— (1992), *Din ve ideoloji* (Istanbul: İletişim Yayınları).

Marrou, Henri-Irenée (1956), *A History of Education in Antiquity* (London: Sheed and Ward).

Marshall, Byron K. (1994), *Learning to Be Modern: Japanese Political Discourse on Education* (Boulder, CO: Westview Press).

Mavratsas, Caesar (1998), "Greek Cypriot Economic and Political Culture: The Effects of 1974," in Calotychos (1998*b*: 285–300).

Mehta, Uday (1997), "Liberal Strategies of Exclusion," in Frederick Cooper and Ann L. Stoler (eds.), *Tensions of Empire: Colonial Cultures in a Bourgeois World* (Berkeley: University of California Press), pp. 59–86.

—— (1999), *Liberalism and Empire* (Chicago: University of Chicago Press).

—— (2003), "Kinship and Friendship: Two Conceptions of Political Action" (lecture given in the Society for the Humanities, Cornell University).

Melhuus, Marit (2002), "Issues of Relevance: Anthropology and the Challenges of Cross-Cultural Comparison," in Gingrich and Fox (2002: 70–91).

Messick, Brinkley (1993), *The Calligraphic State: Textual Domination and History in a Muslim Society* (Berkeley: University of California Press).

Mill, John Stuart (1961), "On Liberty," in Max Lerner (ed.), *The Essential Works of John Stuart Mill* (New York: Bantam Books), pp. 249–360.

Ministry of Education, Republic of Cyprus (1993), *I katechomeni ghi mas* (Nicosia: Dhiefthinsi Mesis Ekpaidhefsis).

Mitchell, Timothy (1991), *Colonising Egypt* (Berkeley: University of California Press).

Mosse, G. L. (1985), *Nationalism and Sexuality: Middle-Class Morality and Sexual Norms in Modern Europe* (Madison: University of Wisconsin Press).

Murray, D. W. (1993), "What is the Western Concept of the Self? On Forgetting David Hume," *Ethos*, 21: 1, pp. 3–23.

Myrianthopoulos, Kleovoulos I. (1946), *I paidhia en Kipro epi Anglokratias* (Limassol).

Nesim, Ali (1987), *Batmayan Eğitim Güneşlerimiz: Kıbrıs Türk Eğitimi Hakkında Bir Araştırma* (Nicosia: Milli Eğitim ve Kültür Bakanlığı Yayınları).

Norton, Robert E. (1995), *The Beautiful Soul: Aesthetic Morality in the Eighteenth Century* (Ithaca, NY: Cornell University Press).

Ohnefalsch-Richter, Magda (1994) [first published 1913], *Ellinika ithi ke ethima stin Kipro*, trans. from German by Anna K. Marangou (Nicosia: Cultural Center of the Popular Bank).

Ong, Walter J. (1967), *The Presence of the Word: Some Prolegomena for Cultural and Religious History* (New Haven: Yale University Press).

—— (1982), *Orality and Literacy: The Technologizing of the Word* (London: Methuen).

Orr, C. W. J. (1918), *Cyprus under British Rule* (London: R. Scott).

Ortner, Sherry (1974), "Is Female to Male as Nature is to Culture?," in M. Rosaldo and L. Lamphere (eds.), *Woman, Culture, and Society* (Stanford, CA: Stanford University Press), pp. 67–88.

—— (1978), "The Virgin and the State," *Feminist Studies*, 4, pp. 19–35.

Öztürkmen, Arzu (1998), *Türkiye'de Folklor ve Milliyetçilik* (Istanbul: İletişim Yayınları).

Pantelis, Stravros (1990), *The Making of Modern Cyprus: From Obscurity to Statehood* (London: Interworld Publications).

Papadakis, Yiannis (1993), "Perceptions of History and Collective Identity: A Comparison of Greek Cypriot and Turkish Cypriot Perspectives" (unpublished Ph.D. thesis, Cambridge University).

—— (1994), "The National Struggle Museums of a Divided City," *Ethnic and Racial Studies*, 17: 3, pp. 400–19.

—— (1998), "*Enosis* and Turkish Expansionism: Real Myths or Mythic Realities?," in Calotychos (1998b: 69–86).

Papadhopoulos, Theodoros (1964a), "Prosfati eksislamismi aghrotikou plithismou en Kipro", in *Kipriakai Spoudhai* (Nicosia: Etairia Kipriakon Spoudhon).

—— (1964b), *To ethnoloyiko provlima tou Ellinismou eis tin Kipriakin aftou fasin* (Nicosia).

Papagheorghios, S. (1979), *Dhia cheiros iroon* (Nicosia: Ekdhosis Epitanion).

Pateman, Carol (1988), *The Sexual Contract* (Stanford, CA: Stanford University Press).

Patterson, Orlando (1982), *Slavery and Social Death: A Comparative Study* (Cambridge, MA: Harvard University Press).

Peristiany, J. G. (1966*a*), "Honour and Shame in a Cypriot Highland Village," in Peristiany (1966*b*: 171–90).

—— (1966*b*) (ed.), *Honour and Shame: The Values of Mediterranean Society* (Chicago: University of Chicago Press).

—— (1968), "Introduction to a Cyprus Highland Village," in J. G. Peristiany (ed.), *Contributions to Mediterranean Sociology* (The Hague: Mouton), pp. 75–92.

Persianis, Panayiotis K. (1978), *Church and State in Cyprus Education: The Contribution of the Greek Orthodox Church of Cyprus to Cyprus Education during the British Administration (1878–1960)* (Nicosia).

Pettman, J. J. (1996), *Worlding Women: A Feminist International Politics* (New York: Routledge).

Pina-Cabral, João (1989), "The Mediterranean as a Category of Critical Comparison: A Critical View," *Current Anthropology*, 30: 3, pp. 399–406.

Pollis, Adamantia (1973), "Intergroup Conflict and British Colonial Policy," *Comparative Politics*, 5, pp. 575–99.

—— (1991), "The Missing of Cyprus—A Distinctive Case," *Journal of Modern Greek Studies*, 9: 1, pp. 43–62.

Prodhomou, Yeorghios (1984), *I ekpaidhefsi stin Kipro to 18. ke to 19. aiona* (Nicosia).

Proust, Marcel (1992), *The Remembrance of Things Past, Volume III: The Fugitive*, trans. C. K. Scott Moncrief and Terence Kilmartin (New York: Vintage).

Reddaway, John (1986), *Burdened with Cyprus: The British Connection* (London: Weidenfeld & Nicolson).

Rude, George (1995), *Ideology and Popular Protest* (Chapel Hill, NC: University of North Carolina Press).

Runciman, Steven (1970), *The Last Byzantine Renaissance* (Cambridge: Cambridge University Press).

Rybczynski, Witold (1986), *Home: A Short History of an Idea* (New York: Viking).

Sahlins, Peter (1989), *Boundaries: The Making of France and Spain in the Pyrenees* (Berkeley: University of California Press).

Sakellarios, Athanasios A. (1890), *Ta Kipriaka: Iti gheografia, istoria, ke glossa tis nisou Kiprou apo ton archaiotaton chronon mechri simeron* (Athens: P. D. Sakellarios).

Salih, Halil Ibrahim (1978), *Cyprus: The Impact of Diverse Nationalism on a State* (Birmingham: University of Alabama Press).

Sandel, Michael (1984) (ed.), *Liberalism and Its Critics* (New York: New York University Press).

Sanjek, Roger (1994), "The Enduring Inequalities of Race," in Steven Gregory and Roger Sanjek (eds.), *Race* (New Brunswick, NJ: Rutgers University Press), pp. 1–17.

Sant Cassia, Paul (1983), "The Archbishop in the Beleaguered City: An Analysis of the Conflicting Roles and Political Oratory of Makarios," *Byzantine and Modern Greek Studies*, 8, pp. 191–212.

—— (1986), "Religion, Politics, and Ethnicity in Cyprus during the Turkokratia (1571–1878)," *Archives Européennes Sociologie*, 27, pp. 3–28.

—— with Bada, C. (1992), *The Making of the Modern Greek Family: Marriage and Exchange in Nineteenth-Century Athens* (Cambridge: Cambridge University Press).

—— (1993), "Banditry, Myth, and Terror in Cyprus and Other Mediterranean Societies," *Comparative Studies in Society and History*, 35, pp. 773–95.

—— (1998/9), "Missing Persons in Cyprus as *Ethnomartyres*," *Modern Greek Studies Yearbook*, 14/15, pp. 261–84.

—— (1999), "Piercing Transformations: Representations of Suffering in Cyprus," *Visual Anthropology*, 13, pp. 23–46.

—— (2000a), "Bandits," in Peter N. Stearns (ed.), *Encyclopedia of European Social History, from 1350–2000, Volume 3* (New York: Scribner), pp. 373–82.

—— (2000b), "'Better Occasional Murders than Frequent Adulteries': Banditry, Violence and Sacrifice in the Mediterranean," *History and Anthropology*, 12: 1, pp. 65–99.

Schama, Simon (1990), *Citizens: A Chronicle of the French Revolution* (New York: Random House).

Schneider, David M. (1977), "Kinship, Nationality and Religion: Toward a Definition of Kinship," in J. Dolgin, D. Kemnitzer, and D. Schneider (eds.), *Symbolic Anthropology* (New York: Columbia University Press), pp. 63–71 [originally published in V. Turner (1969) (ed.), *Forms of Symbolic Action*, proceedings of the 1969 annual spring meeting of the American Ethnological Society].

—— (1980) [first published 1968], *American Kinship: A Cultural Account* (Chicago: University of Chicago Press).

Schneider, Jane (1971), "Of Vigilance and Virgins: Honor, Shame and Access to Resources in Mediterranean Societies," *Ethnology*, 10, pp. 1–24.

Shaw, Stanford and Shaw, Ezel Kural (1977), *History of the Ottoman Empire and Modern Turkey, Volume II: Reform, Revolution and Republic: The Rise of Modern Turkey, 1808–1975* (Cambridge: Cambridge University Press).

Shils, Edward (1964), *Political Development in New States* (New York: Monton).

Shusterman, Richard (1990), "'Ethics and Aesthetics are One': Postmodernism's Ethics of Taste," in Gary Shapiro (ed.), *After the Future: Postmodern Times and Places* (Albany, NY: State University of New York Press).

Simmel, Georg (1964), *Conflict, and the Web of Group-affiliations* (London: Free Press).

—— (1971) [first published 1908], "The Stranger," in D. N. Levine (ed.), *On Individuality and Social Form* (Chicago: University of Chicago Press), pp. 143–9.

Sirman, Nükhet (1990), "State, Village and Gender in Western Turkey," in A. Finkel and N. Sirman (eds.), *Turkish State, Turkish Society* (London: Routledge), pp. 21–51.

Smith, Anthony D. (1983), *Theories of Nationalism*, 2nd edn (London: Duckworth).

—— (1998), *Nationalism and Modernism: A Critical Survey of Recent Theories of Nations and Nationalism* (London: Routledge).

Sofokleous, Andreas K. (1995), *Simvoli stin istoria tou Kipriakou tipou* (Nicosia: Intercollege Press).

Spencer, Robert F. (1958), "Culture Process and Intellectual Current: Durkheim and Ataturk," *American Anthropologist*, 60, pp. 640–57.

Spiro, Melfold E. (1993), "Is the Western Conception of the Self 'Peculiar' within the Context of the World Cultures?," *Ethos*, 21: 2, pp. 107–53.

Spivak, Gayatri Chakravorty (1995), "Bonding in Difference, interview with Alfred Arteaga (1993–94)," in *The Spivak Reader* (London: Routledge), pp. 15–28.

Starrett, Gregory (1998), *Putting Islam to Work: Education, Politics, and Religious Transformation in Egypt* (Berkeley: University of California Press).

Stephens, Robert (1966), *Cyprus: A Place of Arms: Power Politics and Ethnic Conflict in the Eastern Mediterranean* (New York: Praeger).

Stevenson, Esme (1880), *Our Home in Cyprus* (London).

Stewart, Frank Henderson (1994), *Honor* (Chicago: University of Chicago Press).

Stirling, Paul (1965), *Turkish Village* (London: Weidenfeld & Nicolson).

Strauss, Claudia (1984), "Beyond 'Formal' versus 'Informal' Education: Uses of Psychological Theory in Anthropological Research," *Ethos*, 12: 3, pp. 195–222.

Street, Brian V. (1984), *Literacy in Theory and Practice* (Cambridge: Cambridge University Press).

Suha, Ali (1971), "Kıbrıs'ta Türk maarifi/Turkish Education in Cyprus," in *Milletlerarası, Birinci Kıbrıs Tetkikleri Kongresi* (Ankara: Türk Kültürünü Araştırma Enstitüsü), pp. 221–52.

Sutton, David (2001), *Remembrance of Repasts* (London: Berg).

Swedenburg, Ted (1995), *Memories of Revolt: The 1936–1939 Rebellion and the Palestinian National Past* (Minneapolis: University of Minnesota Press).

Talbot, J. W. and Cape, C. F. (1913), *Report on Education in Cyprus* (London).

Taylor, Charles (1989), *Sources of the Self: The Making of the Modern Identity* (Cambridge, MA: Harvard University Press).

—— (1984), "Hegel: History and Politics', in Sandel (1984: 177–99).

—— (1985*a*), "Foucault on Freedom and Truth," in *Philosophy and the Human Sciences: Philosophical Papers 2* (Cambridge: Cambridge University Press), pp. 152–84.

—— (1985*b*), "Atomism", *Philosophy and the Human Sciences, Philosophical Papers 2* (Cambridge: Cambridge University Press), pp. 187–210.

Thompson, E. P. (1963), *The Making of the English Working Class* (New York: Vintage Books).

Thomson, John (1985), *Through Cyprus with the Camera in the Autumn of 1878* (London: Trigraph).

de Tocqueville, Alexis (1969), *Democracy in America* (New York: Harper Perennial).

Tzapoura, C. M. (1892), "The Song of Hassan Poullis," in Ghiangoullis (2001: 38).

Visweswaran, Kamala (1996), "Small Speeches, Subaltern Gender: Nationalist Ideology and its Historiography," in Amin and Chakrabarty (1997: 83–125).

Volkan, Vamik (1979), *Cyprus—War and Adaptation* (Charlottesville: University of Virginia Press).

Weber, Eugen (1976), *Peasants into Frenchmen: The Modernization of Rural France, 1870–1914* (Stanford, CA: Stanford University Press).

Williams, Brackette (1996), "Introduction: Mannish Women and Gender after the Act," in B. Williams (ed.), *Women Out of Place: The Gender of Agency and the Race of Nationality* (New York: Routledge), pp. 1–33.

Willis, Paul (1981), *Learning to Labor: How Working Class Kids Get Working Class Jobs* (New York: Columbia University Press).

Wolf, Eric (1968), *Peasant Wars of the Twentieth Century* (New York: Harper and Row).

Wolseley, Sir Garnet (1991), *Cyprus 1878: The Journal of Sir Garnet Wolseley* (Nicosia: Cultural Centre of the Cyprus Popular Bank).

Woodhouse, C. M. (1980), "The Problem of Cyprus," in J. T. A. Koumoulides (ed.), *Hellenic Perspectives* (Lanham, MD: University Press of America), pp. 205–21.

Yashin, Mehmet (2000*a*), "Introducing Step-Mothertongue," in Yashin (2000*b*: 1–21).

—— (2000*b*) (ed.), *Step-Mothertongue: From Nationalism to Multiculturalism: Literatures of Cyprus, Greece and Turkey* (London: Middlesex University Press).

Yates, Frances A. (1966), *The Art of Memory* (London: Pimlico).

Yuval-Davis, Nira (1997), *Gender and Nation* (London: Sage Publications).

—— and Anthias, Floya (1989) (eds.), *Woman-Nation-State* (London: Macmillan).

Notes

The following abbreviations have been used in the notes:
Archive of the Archbishop of the Orthodox Church of Cyprus = AAOCC
Colonial Office Archive London = CO
State Archive of the Republic of Cyprus = SA1
State Archive of the Turkish Republic of Northern Cyprus = SATRNC

Introduction

1 It is also often contended by Greek Cypriots and by some Turkish Cypriot leftists that the Turkish Cypriot leadership encouraged or even forced these moves, and may have prevented some villagers from returning to their homes during periods of quiet. While this was undoubtedly the case in some areas, the evidence is too contradictory to draw such broad conclusions. In some areas of the island, persons who considered themselves to be members of the Turkish Cypriot "leadership" helped to rebuild village houses in the period of quiet around 1970. Hence, I state here only what is certain and well-documented: namely, that large numbers of Turkish Cypriots became internal refugees and were effectively prisoners of the enclaves for lengthy periods of time between 1963 and 1974.

2 One reader has commented that this formulation ignores the the wish of Greek Cypriot refugees to return to their properties. What I argue in the final chapters of this book, however, is that this powerful longing is, unfortunately, tragically self-defeating in that it is incorporated into a worldview that explains the loss of one's homes always and only in terms of "Turkish expansionism."

3 Asad (1973), Hymes (1969), and Clifford and Marcus (1986).

4 Gingrich and Fox (2002).

5 Melhuus (2002: 87).

6 Spivak (1995: 28).

Part One
Introduction

1 Ohnefalsch-Richter (1994). The title, "Greek Morals and Traditions in Cyprus," derives from *laografia*, or Greek folklore studies, a practice defined as the study of "morals and traditions."

2 The actual status and nature of the *millet*s, or religious communities, has been much debated in recent literature. Until recent years, most Ottoman historians had suggested that the legal and limited political autonomy of the millets of the Ottoman domains led to a relatively strict separation of those religious communities and formed the basis for later nationalist uprisings. However, as recent research has shown, this "foundation myth" of the Ottoman state constitutes a much later projection into the past of an institution that appears actually to have taken full shape only in the middle of the nineteenth century. Especially good examples of this literature include Al-Qattan (1999), Braude (1982), Goffman (1994), and Kasaba (2000). Kasaba notes that "[b]efore that time Ottoman society had resembled a kaleidoscope of numerous, overlapping and cross-cutting relations and categories more than it did a neatly arranged pattern of distinct elements" (ibid.: 9).

3 And upon the death of Sofronios, the administration hoped to eliminate the privileges granted in the berat. The queen's advocate, however, advised that "the Berats granted by the Sultan to the Archbishops of Cyprus must I think be regarded as conformations [sic] of ancient privileges and immunities of the Eastern Church rather than as grants of special jurisdiction to individuals" (SA1/1500/1900, memorandum from Lascelles, Queen's Advocate, to Colonial Secretary, September 24, 1900).

4 One should not see this, however, as an inevitable separation of church and state brought on by modernity and the supposed requirements of a civil society. A recent challenge to the delimitation of religion as an historical category has argued that this categorization itself in separation from a political sphere is a product of modernity, with its understandings of consciousness and agency (Asad 1993). This account has challenged, furthermore, the linear, Western European history of religions that sees the gradual secularization of the political sphere as the advance of a modernizing reason.

5 See in particular Thomson (1995).

6 Geertz (1973*b*).

7 Proust (1992: 657).

8 Charles Taylor has used the Heideggerian notion of "horizon" in his own analyses of modernity, where he argues that the Enlightenment and Romanticism molded the modern subject, "that our cultural life, our self-conceptions, our moral outlooks still operate in the wake of these great events." More importantly, however, these ideas now define the horizons of

the imaginable; pre-modern thought is no longer possible. Notes Taylor: "It is not just that we no longer believe these doctrines: we are not all unanimous about the defining doctrines of the Enlightenment or about expressivism. Rather it is that these earlier views have become strange to us; it is hard to recapture in imagination what they could ever have had going for them. Some watershed has been passed" (Taylor 1989: 393).

Chapter 1

1 SA1/E17/89, Paphos, letter from Delegates of Evkaf to High Commissioner, February 12, 1889. I should note that all such correspondence utilized in this book is found in the British colonial archives in Cyprus and so has already been translated. I utilize the available translations, though I have always checked the translations against the Ottoman original, where that was available.
2 Sutton (2001: 77–82) provides a description of the use of food to evoke the embodied memory associated with *ksenitia.*
3 Because the names of these offices have passed into use in English, they will henceforth be unitalicized.
4 It should also be noted that these military men, with their smattering of classical knowledge, had come to Cyprus with no preparation except their vague recollections of Herodotus. The first high commissioner commented, for instance, "Where are the forests we thought Cyprus was covered with? This is in everyone's mouth, yet no one can give a very satisfactory answer. Like everything else that made this country a splendid one in ancient times, the forests have disappeared under the influence, the blighting influence, of the Turk" (Wolseley 1991: 22). In fact, the forests had begun to disappear during the height of Cypriot copper mining in the fifth century; the British would abandon their own reforestation efforts in the 1920s.
5 ibid., p. 20.
6 "To Yiesil Gazino," from the brief memoirs of E. Paraskeva, published in a series of articles in *Neos Kipriakos Filaks*, May 29, 1936.
7 Interestingly, Cypriot nationalists of both Greek and Turkish persuasions cite this alleged incident as evidence of the long-standing desire of the Greek Cypriot population for enosis. For this reason, they also agree in seeing the 1821 execution of Archbishop Kyprianos and several hundred members of the Greek Cypriot elite as a result of that clergyman's covert involvement in the Greek War of Independence, which had just begun in the Peloponnese. See, for instance, Alastos (1976: 308); Gazioğlu (1996: 42–5); and İsmail (1989:16ff).
8 Katsiaounis (1996: 40–6).

9 Interesting examples among them are Bab'ullah, known as the Bab and founder of an offshoot of Bahai'ism, and Namık Kemal, the great nationalist poet of the Turkish language.
10 Norman Itzkowitz gives the standard recitation of the meaning of the "circle of equity":

1. There can be no royal authority without the military.
2. There can be no military without wealth.
3. The *reaya* produce the wealth.
4. The sultan keeps the *reaya* by making justice reign.
5. Justice requires harmony in the world.
6. The world is a garden, its walls are the state.
7. The state's prop is the religious law.
8. There is no support for the religious law without royal authority.

See Itzkowitz (1980: 88).
11 CO67/7, 339–340.
12 Alastos (1976: 307–18), and Pantelis (1990: 87); also Katsiaounis (1996). As early as January 1879, a reader of *Neon Kition* wrote to complain that he and other villagers of Anglisidhon, starving and unable to find work, had gone during the cold winter to cut wood. But since, in the English determination to reforest the island the cutting of wood was in most cases illegal, they were stopped by the police (*Neon Kition*, January 17, 1879).
13 As, for instance, when Russian peasants of the eighteenth century revolted against their landlords in the name of the tsar; see Rude (1995: 48ff). See also Wolf (1968) for similar observations on early twentieth-century peasant movements.
14 In the meantime, Sultan Abdülhamit II managed to embroil the British in a complicated battle over his own rights to various parcels of land in Cyprus. The voluminous correspondence and documentation on "The Sultan's Land Claims" served later as reference for those attempting to understand Islamic land laws and their application in Cyprus.
15 As in many Mediterranean island communities, use rights and possession of land and resources can be indefinitely parceled through the divisions of inheritance. Hence, a *dönüm* of land (about a quarter of an acre) could be divided among numerous relatives and villagers, while the water and trees on the land could belong to an entirely different set of owners. Even one tree could be legitimately claimed by numerous individuals or families, though this is normally true only of olive trees. In recent years, many of the olive trees in Northern Cyprus have been left to ruin, and in an informal interview Turkish Cypriot leader Rauf Denktaş remarked that the main difficulty in cultivating the trees is in judging who has rights to them (November 30, 1995).
16 These letters from town elites encapsulate their own interesting interpretation of British justice: "The official manner of this vandalous action is

protested, and we request official satisfaction. The English nation is a civilized nation, governed by a justice-loving government, and we hold the firm belief that it will not accept to hear of this illegal action," in "I Katadhiki ton ieron" (The Sentence of the Priests), *Neon Kition*, June 25, 1879.

17 It was, no doubt, also known to many that the British were generally horrified by the state of the bodies and clothing of the village priests. The prison guard who shaved the priests in question claimed that they had lice, while other officials speculated that villagers chose the most disreputable and filthiest among them for the holiest position.

18 SA1/1474/1899, letter from Commissioner of Kyrenia to Colonial Secretary, June 2, 1899, and SA1/302/1900, letter to the Limassol Commissioner of Police, January 21, 1900.

19 In its initial form, this body was composed of the high commissioner plus not less than four and not more than eight other members, half being official and half unofficial. After complaints from the Cypriot population and an extensive report to the Colonial Office, the constitution was granted and the Legislative Council reorganized.

20 CO67/35, 15475, confidential letter to Earl of Derby from High Commissioner Biddulph, August 29, 1884.

21 SA1/2136/90.

22 SA1/2790/90, translated letter to the High Commissioner.

23 ibid.

24 SA1/3534/90, letter from High Commissioner Bulwer to Sir William White, Consul General, Istanbul; my notes in italics.

25 SA1/2052/91, from High Commissioner Bulwer to Lord Passfield, June 2, 1891.

26 Unfortunately, I have been unable to find records about this issue outside those of the British administration. There were no Turkish-language newspapers at that time, and no reference is made to the problem after the turn of the century. Contemporary historians of the Turkish community in Cyprus make no mention of the controversy.

27 Biographical information available in Sofokleous (1995: 25–31), as well as in SA1/811/1883, letter from Konstantinidhis to the Colonial Secretary, January 23, 1883.

28 With nearly 1,500 more distributed to Cypriots abroad (Cyprus Blue Book returns for 1889–90).

29 Cyprus Blue Book returns for 1889–90.

30 Herzfeld (1982).

31 This quotidian diglossia continued until novelists, poets, and journalists began a rebellion in the 1960s against the use of *katharevousa* in print. In 1976 *katharevousa* was dismantled as the official language of Greece and has subsequently disappeared from public use, but there are still many words and phrases that have entered *dhimotiki* from *katharevousa* and

would be considered diglossic. On the latter point, see Kazazis (1992 and 1993).

32 It is possible, in fact, that Cypriot Greek would have been considered different enough from *dhimotikí* in the nineteenth century for it to have been classified as a separate language, perhaps comparable to the differences between Spanish and Portuguese. With the spread of education and electronic media, Cypriot Greek has been modified so that it is now (relatively unambiguously) classified as a dialect.

33 Especially Goody (1987) and Goody and Watt (1963).

34 Coleman (1996).

35 Although reports on the question are sketchy and anecdotal, it is clear that readers were aware of the kinship and political affiliations of publishers, and of how those affiliations may have affected their reporting of events.

36 SA1/388/1909.

37 SA1/442/1900.

38 The tone of the periodical arises from the conceit that the *choriatis* of the title is a villager who has left his sheep to come into the town and publish a newspaper that will tell the townspeople what's what. Hence, the dialect is sprinkled with the sorts of *katharevousa* elements that might be found in the speech of an "uppity" villager.

39 But it would be collected in a massive volume less than a decade later by Sakellarios (1890).

40 It should be noted that Michaelidhis was following in the footsteps of the uncle who had raised him—a great *poiitaris* in his own time. Sofokleous (1995: 139–40).

41 In the Orthodox community, the central problem was a ten-year dispute over the election of a new archbishop. The seat was eventually won by a young cleric who was a self-proclaimed nationalist. In the Muslim community, the dispute was between a kadi wishing to resuscitate Ottomanism and a modernizing mufti. For more on these issues, see Chapters 3 and 4.

42 Interestingly, Turkish-speaking Cypriots appear usually to have been well-versed in the Turkish tradition of *âşık* poetry, but competed with Greek Cypriot *poiitaridhes* in the Cypriot Greek dialect. For examples of well-known Muslim *poiitaridhes*, see İslâmoğlu (1994: 105–24).

43 "Ratio" here refers to the actual ratio of Christians to Muslims in the population. The poem complains that the legislative council was not representative, because it gave a disproportionate number of seats to Muslim members in order to allow the combined forces of Muslim and British members to outvote Orthodox members.

44 "Osmanli" here is no doubt intended to refer not to average Muslim Cypriots—who were typically called "Mousoulmanoi" or less commonly "Tourkoi" by their Orthodox neighbors—but to their educated leaders and

clergy who participated in the larger Ottoman realm and thought of themselves as "Osmanlı."

45 *Keravnos*, April 15, 1882, in Sofokleous (1995: 78).
46 Anderson (1992).
47 In Cyprus at this time, the idea of a public opinion was used in both senses
mentioned by Habermas: both as an uncertain judgment and as "what one
represents in the opinion of others" (Habermas 1992: 89).
48 Koselleck (1985).
49 SA1/63/1889, Q1/6, Chief Medical Office, Dr. Heidenstam, Chief Medical
Officer, to the Chief Secretary, October 3, 1889.
50 ibid.
51 ibid.
52 SA1/2696/1889, memorandum to Chief Secretary from R. E. Swittenham,
August 21, 1889,
53 Extract from *Alitihia*, 445, August 31, 1889, reprint of article, "The Cypriot
Affairs," from the *Metarithmisis* of Alexandria.
54 Extract from *Salpinks*, 239, August 19,1889.
55 Extracts from *Alithia*, 444, August 24, 1889.
56 SA1/130/91, to the Chief Secretary from the Commissioner of Nicosia,
August 25, 1891.
57 SA1/ 2298/1900, report from Collet, acting British Delegate of Evkaf, to the
Chief Secretary, August 15, 1900.
58 SA1/3063/1889.
59 Habermas (1992: 104).
60 On this point, see especially Asad (1993: 210).
61 From the newspaper *Salpinks*, April 1884, quoted in Sofokleous (1995).
62 Giddens (1990: 38).

Chapter 2

1 *Standing Orders and Regulations of the Cyprus Police* (1896).
2 SA1/1474/99, memorandum from Police Chief Chamberlayne to Chief Secretary, June 2, 1899.
3 SA1/302/1900, memorandum of trooper Artemis Christodoulou to Limassol
Commissioner of Police, January 21, 1900.
4 SA1/286/1909.
5 Dhareshwar and Srivatsan (1997: 201–31).
6 What Dhareshwar and Srivatsan call "the *excessive* body of the rowdy" in
opposition to "the disincoporated body of the citizen" (ibid., p. 223; emphasis in original).
7 Foucault (1977).
8 ibid., p. 139.

9 The literature on British colonial legal and administrative practice is vast. Among those dealing with the questions addressed here, some of the most noteworthy are Chatterjee (1993), Cohn (1985 and 1989), Comaroff and Comaroff (1991), and Mitchell (1991).

10 Mehta (1997: 61, emphasis in original).

11 SA1/1122/1913, letter from Chief Justice to Governor, October 16, 1946.

12 Mill (1961).

13 SA1/1217/1891, Sir Henry Bulwer, High Commissioner, to Lord Holland, Secretary of State for the Colonies, August 17, 1891.

14 *Report by Her Majesty's High Commissioner for 1887–8*, "Report by the Chief Justice", June 27, 1888, p. 17.

15 Despite the rising fear of crime, however, no stigma was necessarily attached to elites jailed for a crime. Indeed, many of the elite class were jailed for crimes such as repeated libel or disturbance of the peace, and this appears to have been an accepted and ordinary part of dealings with the government. (See, for example, SA1/2136/1890, for the case of a jailed publisher applying to have the editorship of his newspaper changed during his imprisonment.) In fact, Legislative Council members proposed at one point to eliminate the penalty of hard labor for those jailed for certain types of non-violent crimes.

16 CO67/105, 5846.

17 As, for example, when a shepherd might invite another to go to "eat roast meat," meaning that he invited him to go on a sheep-stealing expedition. See especially Herzfeld (1984*b*). Also see, for example, CO67/10162, 1886, for Cyprus.

18 The fact that the first local newspaper was produced in 1878 was a matter of coincidence and not directly associated with the arrival of the British. The first publisher, Theodhoulos Konstantinidhis, had already secured the permission of the Ottoman *kaymakam* of Larnaca and had brought printing equipment from Egypt by the time the British arrived. On this see Sofokleous (1995: 11).

19 *Foni tis Kiprou*, February 17, 1894.

20 *Parliamentary Papers, 1887–1905*, enclosure 20, Sir Henry Bulwer to Lord Knutsford, received April 13, 1891.

21 ibid.

22 Quoted in Katsiaounis (1996: 244).

23 ibid.

24 SA1/1962/1897.

25 Whipping was apparently a widespread form of extortion and humiliation, as Juan Cole remarks that it was commonly practiced in Egypt in order to extract taxes from the peasants. See Cole (1983: 85–9).

26 *Parliamentary Papers, 1887–1895*, p. 51.

27 ibid., p. 50.

28 See Hill (1952: 207–9); and *Cyprus Annual Reports for 1879*, p. 195.

29 In Cyprus, as elsewhere, an independent Christian court did not develop, and religious minorities often sent cases of personal status to the shari'a court, where they were judged by the local kadi. For early Ottoman rule in the island, see Jennings (1993). For later periods there is scattered evidence in Hill (1952), as well as in documents relating to the British occupation. Politically, however, the archbishop enjoyed special privileges, such as the right to use the local police force to collect tithes from his congregation. Other church privileges, such as its autocthony, were preserved from the early Byzantine period.

30 The Ottoman legal reforms of the nineteenth century were part of a general restructuring and "modernization" of the imperial administration. For standard accounts, see Davison (1963), and Shaw and Shaw (1977).

31 *Cyprus Annual Report for 1883*; also Orr (1918: 114–20).

32 CO67/13/18868, Biddulph 332, August 10, 1880.

33 Messick (1993: 161).

34 *Cyprus Annual Report for 1882*, report by Chief Commandant of Military Police, A. Gordon.

35 *Parliamentary Papers for 1887–95*, p. 21, Sir Henry Bulwer to Sir H. T. Holland, enclosure 1, minute by the High Commissioner on the subject of the prevalence of crime in the Paphos district.

36 Orr (1918: 76).

37 *Cyprus Annual Report for 1881*, report by Arthur Young, Commissioner of Paphos.

38 CO67/13260, enclosure in despatch 136, June 9, 1897.

39 CO67/21628, enclosure 2 in Cyprus despatch 110, June 22, 1911; report on a law "To Amend the Knives Law of 1888," John A. Bucknill, King's Advocate, June 12, 1911.

40 SA1/1468/1909.

41 SA1/725/1912.

42 There is an enormous literature on honor, shame, and violence in Mediterranean societies. Among the earliest and best known of these are Campbell (1964) and Peristiany (1966b). For the "classic" perspective on these problems see also Black-Michaud (1975), Boissevain (1979), Davis (1977), Gilmore (1987), Giovannini (1987), Schneider (1971), and Stirling (1965). For more critical perspectives on the importance of the "honor and shame complex" and on the presumed unity of the Mediterranean, see Abu-Lughod (1986), Brandes (1987), Goddard (1994), Herzfeld (1980 and 1984a), Pina-Cabral (1989), and Stewart (1994). For the most succinct analysis of honor and shame in Cyprus, see Peristiany (1966a and 1968).

43 SA1/1122/1913, letter from Chief Justice to Governor, October 16, 1946.

44 Berger (1984: 154).

45 *Parliamentary Papers, 1887–95*.

46 Foucault (1979); for an overview of Foucault's analysis of the role of policing and security in the liberal state, see Gordon (1991).
47 Sant Cassia (1993: 784).
48 SA1/CO337/1887.
49 Stevenson (1880: 122).
50 SA1/388–389/1887.
51 It is worth noting here that for many years after this "purification" the issue
   of the *linovamvakoi* and of converts generally dropped from sight, until the
   Greek Cypriot revolts of the 1950s against the British colonial government.
   Then, Turkish Cypriot opposition to enosis became more strident the closer
   the Greek Cypriot dream seemed to realization; Turkish Cypriots eventually
   won their cause with the establishment of the independent Republic of
   Cyprus, guaranteed by Great Britain, Greece, and Turkey. In response,
   Theodhoros Papadhopoulos, one of the founders of the Cyprus Research
   Center, set himself the task of using population data and tax records to prove
   a bit of Greek Cypriot folklore: namely, that almost all the Turks in the
   island were really converted Greeks (Papadhopoulos 1964*a* and 1964*b*).
   This might have seemed a strange move at first, except that his conclusions
   were entirely predictable: namely, that since the so-called Turkish Cypriots
   were in fact Greek by blood, there was no Turkish minority in the island,
   and hence no impediment to the realization of the dream of enosis. For more
   on this point, see Chapter 7.
52 Herzfeld (1997: 3).
53 Especially the two major works by E. J. Hobsbawm on the subject (1959
   and 1969). For other, anthropological views that draw on the literature on
   the Mediterranean, see especially Blok (1972) and Sant Cassia (1993,
   2000*a*, and 2000*b*).
54 Blok draws similar conclusions when he remarks that "[t]he myth of the
   bandit (Hobsbawm's social bandit) represents a craving for a different society, a more human world in which people are justly dealt with and in which
   there is no suffering." He further notes that bandits are essentially conservative and that "actual brigandage expresses man's pursuit of honour and
   power" (Blok 1972).
55 Koliopoulos (1996: 250).
56 ibid., p. 251.
57 ibid., p. 259.
58 In the period before nationalisms in the island began to demand linguistic
   homogenization, it was quite common for Muslims to speak Cypriot as their
   first language, and many well-known Muslim folk poets composed in Cypriot. For examples of the latter, see İslâmoğlu (1994).
59 Quoted in Katsiaounis (1996).
60 CO67/105, 5846, Annual Report of Paphos District, 1895–96.
61 ibid., report from police headquarters, July 17, 1896.

62 ibid.

63 I should note here that in the most thorough discussion of this particular gang of Cypriot bandits, Rolandos Katsiaounis (1996) marshals considerable evidence to make the claim that widespread poverty in this period must have been responsible for a considerable part of the crime. In this regard, he sees the Hassanpoulia as akin to Hobsbawm's "primitive rebels." However, this does not seem to be a sufficient explanation for crimes in the villages, given the considerable evidence that villagers saw the "bad characters" who committed crimes as an intrinsic part of village life. Moreover, "bad characters" were often supported by or related to powerful persons in the villages. Bulwer comments, for instance, that at the village of Potamion, "[s]ome of the thieves are connected with the best families in the village, and are protected by them. Some are poor and steal on that account, but others are well-to-do and steal because it has become a habit with them," *Parliamentary Papers, 1887–95.*

64 Tzapoura (1892).

65 Regarding this, one interesting publication by a union of former EOKA fighters, EOKA (1987), provides maps of the caves in which guerilla fighters hid.

66 See especially Christodoulou (1992) and Mavratsas (1998).

67 Mavratsas (1998: 285).

68 ibid., p. 293.

Part Two
Introduction

1 AAOCC, Box IE, letter from Dellios, Headmaster of the Pancyprian Gymnasium,to the Archbishop, December 20, 1895.

2 Author's collection.

3 AAOCC, Box ΛΔ, letter from Ghiorgos N. Kalvati to Archbishop Sofronios, January 6/18, 1895.

4 CO67/105, confidential despatch 8189, from High Commissioner Walter Sendall to Lord Chamberlain, April 7, 1897; and SA1/1259/1896, letter from Commissioner of Nicosia to Chief Secretary, July 4, 1896.

5 SA1/1515/1905.

6 An idea formulated most trenchantly and extremely by Ernest Gellner:

The basic deception and self-deception practiced by nationalism is this: nationalism is, essentially, the general imposition of a high culture on society, where previously low cultures had taken up the lives of the majority, and in some cases of the totality, of the population. It means that generalized diffusion of a school-mediated, academy-supervised idiom, codified for the requirements of reasonably precise bureaucratic and technological communication. It is the establishment of an anonymous, impersonal society, with mutually substitutable atomized individuals, held together above all by a shared culture of this kind, in place of a previous complex structure of local groups, sustained by folk cultures reproduced locally and idiosyncratically by the micro-groups themselves. That is what *really* happens (Gellner 1983: 57).

7 Sir George Hill mentions the charge in a note (Hill 1952: 506).
8 "The dialectic of antiquity tended towards *leadership* (the great individual and the masses—the free man and the slaves); so far the dialectic of Christendom tends toward *representation* (the majority sees itself in its representative and is set free by the consciousness that it is the majority which is represented, in a sort of self-consciousness); the dialectic of the present age tends toward *equality*, and its most logical—though mistaken—fulfillment is leveling, as the negative relationship of the particular units to one another." Kierkegaard, "The Individual and 'The Public'" (Kierkegaard 1938: 260).
9 Kierkegaard, "The Present Age" (Kierkegaard 1938: 264–5).
10 Fleischer (1983).
11 It is worth quoting the passage in full: "Until Rousseau's time, God created kings, who, in their turn, created peoples. After *The Social Contract*, peoples create themselves before creating kings. As for God, there is nothing more to be said, for the time being. Here we have, in the political field, the equivalent of Newton's revolution. Power, therefore, is no longer arbitrary, but derives its existence from general consent. In other words, power is no longer what is, but what should be" (Camus 1956: 115).
12 Hobbes (1962: 271–5).
13 Khaldun (1981: 74–8, 155–60) and Mahdi (1964: 86–99).
14 Lincoln (1994).

Chapter 3

1 Privileges granted by the Emperor Zenon in the late fifth century, in acknowledgment of the claims of the Church of Cyprus to apostolic preeminence. According to legend, the Apostle Barnabus appeared to the Archbishop Anthemios in a dream and told him the location of his grave, in which was also found a copy of the Gospel of St. Matthew written in Barnabus' hand and laid there by Mark. This discovery guaranteed the independence of the Church and gained for it the above-mentioned privileges.
2 *Salpinks*, 716, November 12, 1897, and 727, November 15, 1897.
3 See on this point in particular Gramsci (1971: 7–8), who comments regarding the Western European intellectual classes that

since these various categories of traditional intellectuals experience through an "*ésprit de corps*" their uninterrupted historical continuity and their special qualification, they thus put themselves forward as autonomous and independent of the dominant social group. This self-assessment is not without consequences in the ideological and political field, consequences of wide-ranging import. The whole of idealist philosophy can easily be connected with this position assumed by the social complex of intellectuals and can be defined as the expression of that social utopia by which the intellectuals think of themselves as "independent", autonomous, endowed with a character of their own, etc.

4 SA1/3198/1900, report to the High Commissioner.
5 Ohnefalsch-Richter (1994: 281–2).
6 SA1/2666/90, Mehmet ibn Fellah Ali of Avlona, September 13, 1890.
7 Englezakis (1995: 446).
8 *Salpinks*, 508, December 24, 1894, quoted in Hackett (1901: 294–5).
9 ibid., p. 295.
10 SA1/1607/1889, Commissioner of Kyrenia to Chief Secretary, July 29, 1889.
11 "O patriotismos," *Foni tis Kiprou*, July 6, 1900.
12 ibid.
13 See, for instance, Koloğlu (1991); Hanioğlu (1985: 75–92); and Iacorella (1998). The latter two works also provide extensive bibliographies on the subject.
14 Dan Gilgoff, "Devil in a Red Fez: The Lie About the Freemasons Lives On," *U.S. News and World Report*, August 26, 2002.
15 The police reports of the time are filled with reports of the influence of his teachings in the villages:

Yesterday (Monday) afternoon the church bell of the village of Peristeropiyi began to ring violently. The unceasing sound of the bell having made the said village's Muslims, retired to their beds, to suppose that a fire has broken out, they hastened in the direction of the church, where they met with a great gathering of Christians, and understood that the ringing of the bell was for Katalanos, the cursed, who had arrived there and was making an address to the people. The Muslims, on finding out that in honor of Katalanos the bell was ringing, wanted to go back, but the expression of the following words, viz., "In whatever way those barbarous Turks have ____ our wives and daughters before, now we should in like manner ____ their wives and daughters on their knees," made by Katalanos in the course of his speech infuriated them, the Muslims, to such an extent that a terrible quarrel occurred. During the quarrel one could hear the following and other similar words, 'Hit those doggish and infidel Turks.' At this quarrel they have, through the instigation of Katalanos and the Greek mukhtar, thrown stones and fired revolvers at the Muslims."

(Suleiman Shevket, schoolmaster of Peristeropiyi, in letter to *Sünuhat*, 191, September 1, 1910).

16 SA1/539/1901, *Evaghoras*, 577.
17 See, for example, "Ekviasmos mathiton," *Evaghoras*, February 23, 1901.

18 SA1/C622/1902, extract from *Evaghoras*, 619, December 12/25, 1901.
19 SA1/C622/1902, extracts from the halfsheet of *Evaghoras*, December 14/27, 1901.
20 SA1/C560A/1901, letter from Holy Synod, April 6, 1901.
21 SA1/1056/1908, letter from Chief Commissioner of Police to Chief Secretary, April 14, 1908.
22 SA1/1753/1910, from speech given by Katalanos in Marathovouno and reported in *Sünuhat*, 189, August 18, 1910.
23 Heidegger (1959: 103).
24 SA1/1753/1910, letter from Numan, kadi, and Mehmet Ziyaeddin, mufti, to High Commissioner, August 26, 1910.
25 ibid.
26 SA1/C226/1895, memorandum from the Colonial Secretary to the High Commissioner, reporting a meeting with the mufti and other representatives of the Muslim community of Nicosia.
27 SA1/C226/1895, letter from the magistrate of Nicosia to the Chief Secretary.
28 ibid.
29 SA1/C226/1895, extract from *Kıbrıs*, 136, April 15, 1895.
30 SA1/178/1896, letter from Ali Rıfkı, mufti, to the Secretary of State for the Colonies, May 5, 1895.
31 SA1/897/1910, letter from kadi complaining of article in *Salpinks*, 1486, May 18, 1912.
32 SA1/876/1912, police office, Limassol, August 21, 1912.
33 SA1/1491/1906, letter from Commissioner of Paphos to Chief Secretary, May 5, 1906.
34 Heidegger (1959: 101).

Chapter 4

1 SA1/2064/1901, judgment of Ottoman Ministry of Interior, forwarded to kadi, June 19, 1901.
2 SA1/C515/1900 and SA1 1881/1900.
3 SA1/2273/1897.
4 SA1/1881/1900, statement of Armenian translator, Mr. Hajj, July 21, 1900.
5 SA1/2108/1899.
6 SA1/1962/1900, translation of telegram made by state translator; July 9, 1900 (original unavailable).
7 SA1/1881/1900, report of Chamberlayne, Commissioner of Larnaca, July 21, 1900. The report is part of a long correspondence regarding the onset of the kadi's insanity.
8 SA1/2300/1899.

9 A 1917 application to publish a newspaper to be called *Minja-i-Islam* led the colonial secretary to comment that no Turkish paper was at that time published in the island and that the publication of a paper with obviously political intent "might tend to revise animosities within the Moslem community at present more or less dormant outwardly" (SA1/620/1917).

10 Mitchell (1988).

11 SA1/2566/1900, letter from Ali Rıfkı, mufti, to the High Commissioner, September 7, 1900.

12 SA1/1896/1898, letter from Ali Rıfkı, mufti, to the High Commissioner.

13 Asad (1993: 210).

14 SA1/C491/1900, Ali Rıfkı, mufti, to High Commissioner, January 14, 1900.

15 SA1/1881/1900, telegrams dated July 8, 1900.

16 SA1/465/1912, extract from *Seyf*, 26, August 25, 1912.

17 Messick (1993: 161).

18 For information about Hafız Ziyai Efendi, see Nesim (1987: 61–3).

19 ibid., p. 61.

20 Blue Books for 1890–91 and 1894–95.

21 Berkes (1964: 160).

22 Kodaman and Saydam (1992: 485).

23 SA1/2896/1898, letter from Ali Rıza, headmaster of the *i'dadî* school, to the Inspector of Schools, August 18, 1898.

24 SA1/830/1899, letter from mufti Ali Rıfkı to High Commissioner, March 23, 1899.

25 There is a vast literature on the Ottoman bureaucracy and those who passed through its service. For information particularly relevant to the question of literacy and Ottoman bureaucracy, see Davison (1963), Fleischer (1994), and Kazamias (1966).

26 SA1/2987/1899, letter from Ali Rıza Efendi, headmaster of *i'dadî* school, to Chief Secretary, and response of Inspector of Schools, November 3, 1899.

27 *Report by Her Majesty's High Commissioner for the Year 1879*, report from Colonel Gordon on the Nicosia district, p. 245.

28 SA1/1093/1904.

29 Şerif Mardin (1991: 286).

30 SA1/753/1910, editorial in *Sünuhat*, 189, August 18, 1910.

31 SA1/2766/1904.

32 SA1/4057/1902. See also Kodaman (1991: 126–7).

33 SA1/C685/1902, letter from Halil Bey, headmaster of *i'dadî* school, December 17, 1902.

34 SA1/2866/1904.

35 SA1/2866/1904, official regulations for the control of *i'dadî* schools, 1902.

36 ibid.

37 Peristiany (1966a).

Part Three
Introduction

1 Bourdieu and Passeron (1977: 4).
2 SA1/1314/1881, report of Director of Education to Chief Secretary, July 25, 1881.
3 Goody (1977, 1987), Goody and Watt (1963), and Ong (1967).
4 For very interesting observations on the practices involved in this veneration and sacrality, see Nesim (1987) and Prodhomou (1984).
5 Maratheftis (1992), Myrianthopoulos (1946), Persianis (1978).

Chapter 5

1 CO67/240/11, file 41397, document 243/1, letter from Governor Storrs to Cunliffe-Lister, February 22, 1932.
2 ibid.
3 Bryant (2001).
4 For two interesting studies of the development of our own notions of intimate home and family life, see Gillis (1996), and Rybczynski (1986). Gillis very persuasively locates the Anglo-American ideal of the "traditional" family at the end of the nineteenth century.
5 SA1/1494/1927, extract from *The Cyprus News*, March 7, 1931.
6 This phrase is one reported for Turkey and Central Asia, as well. See Kaplan (1996) and Khalid (1998).
7 Prodhomou (1984).
8 *Report by Her Majesty's High Commissioner for the Year 1884.*
9 "Dhia tin paidhian," *Foni tis Kiprou*, July 13, 1900.
10 SA1/1314/1881, draft memorandum from Spencer to Chief Secretary, July 25, 1881.
11 *Report by Her Majesty's High Commissioner for 1881*, enclosure 9, report by the Director of Education, Josiah Spencer.
12 *Report by Her Majesty's High Commissioner from 1st January 1883 to 31st March 1884*, report by J. Spencer to the Chief Secretary, June 10, 1884.
13 *Report by High Commissioner W. J. Sendall for the Year 1895–6*, report by the Chief Commissioner of Larnaca, C. Delaval Cobham.
14 SA1/1491/1906, letter dated May 5, 1906, emphasis in original.
15 Persianis (1978: 24).
16 SA1/1314/1881, report from Spencer to Chief Secretary, July 25, 1881.
17 Talbot and Cape (1913: 30).
18 ibid., p. 32.
19 Persianis (1978: 157).
20 Foucault (1979).
21 See, for instance, Anderson (1993), and Herzfeld (1982).

22 See Bryant (2001).
23 Eickelman (1978: 511).
24 Especially Messick (1993).
25 Khalid (1998).
26 "Mia lisis tou anatolikou zitimatos," *Kipriakos Filaks*, 318, April 28, 1912.
27 See, for instance, Alastos (1976: 208) and Pantelis (1990: 7).
28 For instance, Gazioğlu (1996), İsmail (1988 and 1989).
29 Comaroff and Comaroff (1991: 25).
30 SA1/1074/1911, confidential letter from Newham to Chief Secretary, July 18, 1912.
31 ibid.
32 "Evghe Neotis," *Foni tis Kiprou*, March 2, 1901.
33 *Foni tis Kiprou* , December 21, 1901.
34 Foucault (1979: 36).
35 The author continues by noting that "the ethnic school for these reasons forms the national crucible in which are smelt and opened wide and forged the great and high characters in those advanced persons who accomplish great things," *Kipriakos Filaks*, 340, September 29,1912.
36 Benedict (1993: 77).
37 Marrou (1956: 196).
38 AAOCC, 500, letter from Leontios, Bishop of Paphos, to Governor Palmer, November 18, 1935.
39 SA1/646/1916/1, extract from *Neon Ethnos*.
40 For a succinct explanation of the development of these concepts, see Shaw and Shaw (1977: 340 ff).
41 Nesim (1987: 65).
42 ibid.
43 SA1/1314/1881, letter from Spencer to Chief Secretary, July 25, 1881.
44 Talbot and Cape (1913: 14).
45 There is, indeed, a vast literature on this subject alone. See especially Kandiyoti (1991*a* and 1991*b*); Arat (1998*a*); and Fleming (1998).
46 Deniz Kandiyoti, while not framing the problem in the same terms, makes similar observations about the culturally specific nature of Turkish appropriations of Western ideas when she suggests that "the specificities of the societies in question may have played as determining a role as the history of their encounters with the West. Indeed, it could be argued that, far from being random, the selection of Western sources by local reformers reflected processes of internal negotiation and struggle between factions of political elites with different visions of the 'good society,'" (Kandiyoti 1998: 272). For paradigmatic observations of the period in question, see Gökalp (1978) and what is often seen as the prototypical Turkish nationalist novel, Güntekin (1993).

47 Partha Chatterjee, for instance, remarks that in India "[t]he world was where the European power has challenged the non-European peoples and, by virtue of its superior material culture, had subjugated them. But, the nationalists asserted, it had failed to colonize the inner, essential identity of the East, which lay in its distinctive, and superior, spiritual culture" (Chatterjee, 1993: 121).

48 SA1/426/1919, letter from Necmi Potamyalızâde to the High Commissioner of Cyprus for transmission to the Prime Minister, December 26, 1919.

49 SA1/465/1912, extract from *Seyf*, 26, August 25, 1912.

50 SA1/465/1912, *Doğru Yol*, 3.

51 For a very interesting comparison, see Khalid (1998: 135–6).

Chapter 6

1 Ghiorgos Grivas was from the village of Trikomo in northeast Cyprus, near Famagusta. He participated in the Greek invasion of Asia Minor and distinguished himself during World War II. He became the military leader of the EOKA campaign and took the *nom de guerre* "Dhighenis" after Dhighenis Akritas, the eponymous warrior-hero of a famous Byzantine epic.

2 Such, at least, was the opinion of Turkish Cypriot journalists, who were careful observers of Greek Cypriot politics. See, in particular, articles in *Bozkurt* and *İstiklal* on purported extortion involved in the 1950 plebiscite. See also a 1952 series of articles by Mim Varoğlu in *Bozkurt*, "Rumlar Arasında Ayrılık."

3 This observation is based on interviews with former teachers who had worked in the villages in the 1940s and 1950s, who insisted that the labor-intensive agricultural economy of Cyprus could not support large numbers of secondary school graduates until the post-war period and that it was only at that time that children in poorer villages were allowed to complete their primary education.

4 Durkheim (1973: 37).

5 Bourdieu (1977: 31).

6 Foucault (1979). Durkheim had also seen discipline in its positive sense as the foundation for moral action. He asks rhetorically, "Must one view discipline simply as an external, palpable police force, whose single *raison d'être* is to prevent certain behaviors and which, beyond such preventive action, has no other function? Or, on the contrary, may it not be, as our analysis leads us to suppose, a means *sui generis* of moral education, having an intrinsic value which places its own special imprint upon moral character?" (1973: 77).

7 Dhimitriadhis (1994: 52).

8 The British were accused of attempting to spread the "gospel of mishellenism" as early as 1903, when an uproar was created over use of Edmond

About's popular novel *Le roi des montagnes*, in the English School (SA1/ 3237/1903). However, it was not until the early 1950s that the term "dehellenization" (*afellinismos*) came into use as a fully formed explanation for British action with regard to the schools. See in particular documents from AAOCC, Box ΞH.

9 AAOCC, Box ΞH, 1.

10 The law had been passed while the legislative council was still a functioning body, and three Greek elected members had been persuaded to vote in its favor. They were unable to run for re-election to their seats. CO67/247/10, secret dispatch to Cunliffe-Lister, report on the political situation, 1926–32, from Sir Robert Storrs, June 9, 1932.

11 CO67/246/13, dispatch to Sir Philip Cunliffe-Lister from H. Henniker-Heaton, acting Governor.

12 CO67/228/13, secret dispatch to Amery, Secretary of State, from Sir Robert Storrs, Governor of Cyprus, January 18, 1928.

13 CO67/248/3, confidential letter to Cunliffe-Lister from H. Henniker-Heaton, acting Governor, September 7, 1932.

14 The most frequently cited evidence for this consistent British desire is an incident that took place when High Commissioner Biddulph suggested in 1880 that Greek might be replaced by English in the schools. Lord Kimberley in his reply deemed this suggestion not only unnecessary but foolhardy, since the Greek schools of Cyprus were provided with adequate books and educational materials from Greece. Turkish Cypriot schools were not included in this scheme, since they were, by treaty, still part of the educational system of the Ottoman Empire. Biddulph's ill-fated proposal has since become part of Greek Cypriot lore, and it is seen as proof of the consistency of British schemes. See also above, p. 138.

15 Persianis (1978: 135).

16 AAOCC, Box ΞH, 1/4.

17 ibid.

18 Maratheftis (1992: 154).

19 ibid., p. 143.

20 AAOCC, Box ΞH, 1/4.

21 ibid., 330, April 1, 1956.

22 Myrianthopoulos (1946: 119).

23 See, for instance, Persianis (1978: 167).

24 AAOCC, Box ΞH, 1/4, 265, May 31, 1954.

25 ibid., 266, June 16, 1954.

26 ibid., 334, June 15, 1956.

27 Dhimitriadhis (1994: 50).

28 AAOCC, Box ΞH, 1/4, 266.

29 AAOCC, Box ΞH, 1/3.

30 AAOCC, Box ΞH, 1/5.

31 ibid.
32 SATRNC, CO247/58, June 12, 1958.
33 CO67/238/14, enclosure 1, in governor's dispatch 115, letter from Mehmet Zekia Bey to Governor Storrs, March 27, 1931,.
34 "Maarif işleri çocuk oyuncağı oldu," *Söz*, July 16, 1931.
35 CO67/238/14, Cyprus 115, Governor Storrs to Lord Passfield, Secretary of State for the Colonies, March 27, 1931.
36 SA1/931/1926, Programme: Moslem Elementary Education, May 10, 1926.
37 "Maarifimizin vechesi ne olmalıdır?," *Söz*, March 19, 1931.
38 *Gençlik Dergisi*, May 19, 1955.
39 Ahmet C. Gazioğlu, "Kültür İhtiyacı," *Halkın Sesi*, August 26, 1951.
40 Nazıf Süleyman Eboğlu, "Kültür ve Medeniyet," *İstiklal*, December 27, 1949.
41 Ziya Gökalp, whose writings served as the foundation for much of Atatürk's nationalism, discussed culture as the realm of emotion, saying that civilization is "economics, religion, law, morals, etc., and all such ideas" while culture is "religion, morals, and all the emotions of beauty." He would go on to say that "because the emotions produced by culture come from inside and are intimate, it is very difficult for them to be seen or examined" Gökalp (1989: 9–10).
42 For the specific question of the Durkheimian roots of Turkish nationalism, see Spencer (1958).
43 For interesting parallels to this use of culture, see Bringa (1995) and Grant (1995). Such a vision is also implicit in Khalid (1998).
44 SA1/931/1926, Programme: Moslem Elementary Education, May 10, 1926.
45 *Halkın Sesi*, June 29, 1962.
46 Nazıf Süleyman Eboğlu, "Kültür ve Medeniyet," *İstiklal*, December 27, 1949.
47 On this question, see in particular Mardin (1992).
48 This took place under the direction of the Türk Dil Kurumu, or Turkish Language Society, beginning in 1926 (see Shaw and Shaw 1977: 376). For an excellent analysis of Turkish folklore studies, see Öztürkmen (1998).
49 As when Turkish Cypriot writers encouraged the community to "purify" its culture and for the "intellectuals" to teach the villagers that it was unnationalistic, for instance, to worship Christian saints. "I wonder what the difference is," one asks, "between a Turk who's just a copy of a Turk, who visits the monastery of Apostolos Andreas, kneels before the cross, lights candles, and does I don't know what other unutterable nonsense, and a pork-eating Christian?' ("Domuz eti yiyen bir Hristiyan gibi!," *Halkın Sesi*, September 22, 1954).
50 *Halkın Sesi*, June 23, 1955.
51 The first articulation of this stance appears to have been that of Ziya Gökalp, who was also strongly influenced by the Comtean strain of sociology that

had by his time entered Turkish nationalist circles. Gökalp argued in an influential early work that "a civilization is the common property of diverse nations. Because every civilization was created in order to enble the common life of those nations to which it belongs. For this reason all civilizations are 'international.' But in every civilization, each nation produces its own particular manners or ways, and these are called culture (*hars*)" (Gökalp 1989: 3). See also Gökalp (1959), and Heyd (1950).

52 Foucault (1979). For reflections on implications of Foucault's argument, see Burchell, Gordon and Miller (1991).

53 Anderson (1993: 144).

Part Four
Introduction

1 Peter Loizos' important and troubling article (Lozios 1988) contextualizes interviews with such men from his own family's village. Loizos notes that while the men themselves may have had psychopathic tendencies, those tendencies were culturally directed.

2 Simmel (1964).

3 Especially Hitchens (1989).

4 Especially Pollis (1973).

5 Kitromilides (1979 and 1990).

6 Especially Kızılyürek (1993), who opens his essay with the claim that "Cypriot elites treated Cyprus within the framework of the Greek and Turkish nations and applied all sorts of 'national' measures to prevent the development of a local identity" (p. 13). This "leader-victimization" view has become familiarly accepted in leftist discourse in the island, whose articulators seem not at all disturbed by this romanticized (and often condescending) view of the presumably illiterate villager. Aside from the disturbing lack of agency ascribed to the villager, there also tends to be another problematic consequence: that this view glorifies a Cypriot identity, denies other forms of communal identity, and appears to replicate the British colonial view of nationalisms and their possible futures in Cyprus.

7 Browning (1993), Glass (1997), and Kogon (1998).

8 Loizos (1988).

9 Argyrou (1996: 59).

10 *Molohiya* is a long-stemmed plant with medium-sized, green leaves that grows in fields in Cyprus and is a distinctive part of Turkish Cypriot cuisine, as it is part of the cuisine of some other parts of the eastern Mediterranean, such as in Egypt (though not, interestingly, in Turkey). Turkish Cypriots highly prize *molohiya*, in either fresh or dried form, as a leaf with which to make flavorful stews. Picking the leaves is labor intensive, and women often pick them in groups. Many families also keep a supply of dried *molohiya*

leaves for use in winter. Greek Cypriots do not, to my knowledge, use *molohiya* at all, and I have not yet found a Greek Cypriot who knows of its existence. This points to a probable factual problem in my informant's story, though his mention of *molohiya* suggests everyday intimacy.

11 Loizos (1998: 37).

Chapter 7

1 In recent years, writers especially concerned with the implications for nationalism of the uses of gendered models have begun to suggest that kinship is more than "just" a metaphor but may actually be essential to the workings of nationalism, especially in the West. See, for instance, Delaney (1995), Schneider (1977), Williams (1996), and Yuval-Davis (1997). On a related point, see also Hunt (1992). Michael Herzfeld (1987 and 1997), for instance, argues that nationalism enlarges the sphere of "natural" relations, taking as its models the local relations of families and patrilines.

2 The tendency to focus on similarities derives from the understandable desire to uncover the ways in which the nation-state, while claiming to liberate, has created new forms of inequalities, often defined along the "natural" lines of gender. The best-known analysis of the relationship between the rise of the modern state and the rise of modern patriarchal relations is Pateman (1988). For discussions of the relationship between nationalist ideologies and gender relations, see especially Chatterjee (1993), Jayawardena (1986), Kandiyoti (1991b), and Yuval-Davis and Anthias (1989). On the discursive strategies that allow this process to work, especially in the postcolonial world, see Abu-Lughod (1998), Mosse (1985), and Visweswaran (1996).

3 Pettman (1996: 49).

4 With regard to Turkey, for instance, Delaney (1995) emphasizes the symbolic association of the *Anavatan*, or motherland, with the passive female and her "soil" which may be in danger of being implanted with foreign "seed." Kaplan, while not denying this usage, also finds others, such as the association of land with the forefathers. See Kaplan (1996).

5 Schneider (1980: 25).

6 While not stating the argument precisely in these terms, Paul Sant Cassia notes that "the public virtues of Greek life, the virtues that were publicly commended as peculiarly Greek, the virtues which children were especially taught to appreciate were the virtues of Hellenism, striving for union with Greece, which became almost an expression of holiness and of an extreme religious fervour" Sant Cassia (1983: 194). He goes on to argue that Greek nationalism in Cyprus, represented in the person of Archbishop Makarios, was inextricable from religious belief. For Turkish Cypriots, Moira Killoran comes close to the argument that I make here when she remarks that blood is a common metaphor and that "the land or soil which has been 'inseminated'"

by the blood of the fighters (martyrs) creates a national family that is not merely linked to a land, but *is* the land." (Killoran 1998: 164)

7 Papagheorghios (1979: 15).
8 AAOCC, Box ΞH, 500, letter from Leontios, Bishop of Paphos, to Governor Palmer, November 18, 1935.
9 Ministry of Education (1993: 9).
10 *Halkın Sesi*, October 26, 1952.
11 Quoted in Killoran (1998: 163).
12 Maratheftis (1992: 148).
13 Dhimitriadhis (1994: 281).
14 ibid., p. 191.
15 AAOCC, Box MZ, 93, letter to Colonial Secretary Drummond Shields from the Administrative Council of the Pancyprian Greek League of Volunteers, October 15, 1930.
16 SA1/160/1909.
17 Dubisch (1995), du Boulay (1986 and 1991), and Herzfeld (1996).
18 Dubisch (1995: 244). See also Iossifides (1991) and Sant Cassia (1992).
19 Herzfeld (1987).
20 Peristiany (1966*b*: 182).
21 Furthermore, the relationship between virginity and differentiation is at least implied in several of the most important works on the meaning of virginity and virginity rites. See Delaney (1991), Ortner (1978), and Schneider (1971). All of these works suggest that virginity is important in symbolizing the relationship between the family unit and the larger social order.
22 See especially Herzfeld (1997).
23 Iossifides (1991: 150).
24 It is common in many versions of Christianity to discuss the Church as the "bride" and Christ as the "bridegroom."
25 On this point, see also Yuval-Davis and Anthias (1989).
26 Ministry of Education (1993: 23).
27 Sant Cassia (1999). This is also clear in the aforementioned middle school textbook devoted to the "occupied lands" that concludes with a reprint of a 1960 retelling of Christ's martyrdom. One presumes that in the context of the textbook the story is used allegorically.
28 SA1/876/1912, Police Office, Limassol, August 21, 1912.
29 Nesim (1987: 325).
30 Kaplan (1996: 346).
31 ibid., p. 344.
32 Delaney (1995 and 1991).
33 Delaney (1995: 182).
34 ibid., p. 179 ff. She is never clear, however, about precisely what she takes the relationship between *Devlet Baba* and *Anavatan* to be. For other views

on the meaning of *Devlet Baba*, see Sirman (1990) and Stirling (1965). See also Mardin (1969).

35 This designation is so common, in fact, that in Turkish airports, flights of the northern Cyprus airways, Kıbrıs Türk Havayolları, are abbreviated as KYV, or Küçük Yavru Vatan, i.e., "little babyland."

36 Turkish Cypriots did eventually begin to speak of blood in an ethnic sense, but this usage became pervasive only when certain Greek Cypriot writers attempted to show that Turkish Cypriots were actually converted Greeks, and hence Greek by blood. Not wanting to be denied their ethnic claims, Turkish Cypriots responded in kind. See İslâmoğlu (1994).

37 For Turkey, Kaplan describes how a doctor in a state hospital had explained to him why many village men do not want blood from a donor: because they fear that the donor may be impotent and would damage the man's virility (Kaplan 1996: 346–7).

38 Nesim (1987: 334).

39 On this point, see, for instance, Anderson (1959).

40 *Halkın Sesi*, June 8, 1950.

41 *Halkın Sesi*, April 4, 1950.

42 *İstiklal*, August 13, 1950.

43 Simmel (1971: 143–9).

44 SA1/972/1924.

45 The Turkish Grand National Assembly awarded the title while the country was still divided between the forces of the Ottoman administration still in Istanbul and those of the Assembly and Kemal's associates, located in Ankara. See Shaw and Shaw (1977: 361).

46 Sant Cassia (1983)

47 The adulation that both of these figures inspired deserves a separate study. Many Greek Cypriots spoke of their love for Makarios, giving examples such as the way that men burst into tears upon hearing Makarios' sonorous voice on the radio in 1974, when he assured the Cypriot public that he was still alive after the assassination attempt against him. Turkish Cypriots who experienced the early Atatürk years often spoke to me of participating in a communal spirit of what they called *Atatürk sevgisi*, or "Atatürk love."

48 Ortner (1974).

49 Schneider (1980: 116).

50 Kitromilides (1979). For examples of this dynamic from Papadakis' work, see especially Papadakis (1993 and 1994).

51 Papadakis (1998). The very different constructions of history on each side of the island have been noted in some form by many observers. See, for instance, Hadjipavlou-Trigeorgis (1998 and 2000), Killoran (2000), and Loizos (1998).

52 Papadakis (1998: 79).

53 Comaroff (1996).

54 Papadhopoulos (1964*a*: 47).
55 ibid.
56 Papadhopoulos (1964*b*).
57 Chatziioannou (1976: 32).
58 ibid., pp. 33–4.
59 Address by the minister of education at the Leventis Foundation International Archaeological Symposium, September 1993.
60 *Near East*, August 4, 1927, cited in Nesim (1987: 117).
61 İslamoğlu (1994: 34).
62 Anderson (1993: 9.
63 *Halkın Sesi*, January 18, 1943, quoted in Nesim (1987: 119).
64 Akay Cemal, "Hükümetin bizi getirdiği nokta," *Halkın Sesi*, October 20, 2000.
65 Papadakis (1998: 74).
66 ibid.
67 Comaroff (1996: 176).
68 Comaroff (1987).
69 Delaney (1991 and 1995).
70 See especially Delaney (1995).
71 Bringa (1995: 30).
72 ibid.
73 Swedenburg (1995).
74 Comaroff (1996: 176).
75 ibid., p. 177.
76 Kapferer (1988: 179).

Chapter 8

1 *Simerini*, September 4, 1996.
2 *Kıbrıs*, August 12, 1996.
3 Loizos (1988).
4 It should be remarked, however, that this is much more commonly heard amongst Greek Cypriots, for reasons that will be discussed in this chapter. On this point see Argyrou (1996), as well as Vangelis Calotychos' critical comments on Argyrou in Calotychos (1998*b*).
5 The important exception to this rule was the emergence at the beginning of the century of a radical, internationalist labor movement that drew large numbers of Greek and Turkish Cypriots and became the major source of intercommunal political action. Because of their communist allegiances, labor movement members were ostracized by the Church and nationalists in the Greek community and by Turkish Cypriot nationalists who owed their anti-communism to that of Turkey.

6 From the perspective of anthropology and sociology, some of the most important proponents of the essential nature of ethnicity have been Shils (1964) and Geertz (1963 and 1973). From outside those disciplines, others, such as Martin Bernal, have read back into literary evidence to argue that we find conceptions of ethnic identity even in the most ancient periods of our history (Bernal, 1997). Another strand of social anthropology—beginning with Evans-Pritchard's famous outline of Nuer segmentary lineage organization—emphasizes not the internal sense of community but the forms of ethnic differentiation, which are necessary but mutable (Evans-Pritchard 1940). Another early explanation may be found in Simmel (1964), and later seminal definitions in Barth (1969), and Comaroff (1987). Attempts to link these two views (primarily from a political-science perspective) may be found, for example, in Armstrong (1982), and Connor (1994). Useful overviews of these various proposals (again, primarily from a political-science perspective) may be found in the preface to Smith (1983), and in Smith (1998).

7 Kierkegaard himself draws the distinction; see above, p. 77.

8 Similar views have been expressed most notably and clearly by Anthony Smith, who argues "that ethnicity forms an element of culture and social structure which persists over time and reappears in every generation, with varying force, in most areas of the world." He insists, however, that more recent "revivals" of ethnicity differ from previous manifestations, "[f]or what was lacking in those earlier revivals, was an ideology of national self-determination and a belief in popular sovereignty; these are the new ideas which have given the present-day revival its revolutionary, change-seeking and mass-mobilising impetus" (Smith, 1983: xxxi–xxxii).

9 For a useful assessment of this literature and the confusions that it entails, see Connor (1994) and Smith (1998).

10 The latter view is expressed quite cogently by both Ernest Gellner and Eric Hobsbawm, each of whom argues in his own way that nations are products (or inventions) of nationalism. See Gellner (1983) and Hobsbawn (1990).

11 Connor (1994: 38).

12 Those familiar with the literature on Cyprus may note that the following argument bears certain resemblances to Paschalis Kitromilides' (1979) analysis of what he calls the "dialectic of intolerance." There, Kitromilides outlines ways in which the ideological extremes of the two communities fed off of each other and "deprived nationalist ideas of their original democratic impulse" (p. 172). From this statement it should be clear that my starting-point is different and that I see the "democratic impulse" itself as one of the main causes, rather than a supposed mitigating factor, of nationalist intolerance in Cyprus.

13 To quote Charles Taylor again: "... [T]he doctrine of the primacy of rights is not as independent as its proponents want to claim from considerations

about human nature and the human social condition. For the doctrine could be undermined by arguments which succeeded in showing that men were not self-sufficient ... —that is, that they could not develop their characteristically human potentialities outside of society or outside of certain kinds of society" (Taylor, 1985: 193).

14 Mehta (1997 and 1999).

15 See especially Patterson (1982).

16 The best of these is without doubt Mehta (1999). Many of the conclusions drawn there are also summarized in Mehta (1997). See also Macpherson (1962), Taylor (1984), Pateman (1988), and Burchell (1991a).

17 Harik (1994: 43).

18 Sanjek (1994: 9).

19 Arendt (1963: 125).

20 Holt (1992: 402).

21 The Republic of Cyprus opened a suit in the International Court of Human Rights to press for prosecution of the murderers, who could not be arrested by their government. They also requested the arraignment of Rauf Denktaş as "instigator" of the murderers (*Fileleftheros*, September 2, 1996).

22 EOKA must be credited with having achieved Cyprus' independence. However, EOKA had a radical nationalist agenda, and some of its original members ultimately had little patience with Cyprus' independent status after having fought for union with Greece. Some of these men later formed a second guerrilla organization, EOKA B', whose members were also violently anti-Turkish in a way that EOKA members had not consistently been. With the aid of the Greek *junta* government in 1974, EOKA B' staged a *coup d'état* against the elected president of the republic, Archbishop Makarios, and began a campaign of terror against both Greek and Turkish opponents. The Turkish military intervened ostensibly to restore order, but the Turkish army has remained in the island since 1974.

23 Nesim (1987: 370).

24 For a fascinating historical analysis of the emergence of "the ideology of ancestral worship" that sustained the Modern Greek claims to glory, see Kitromilides (1979).

25 For more on these particular mythical constructions of the other, see Papadakis (1998).

26 By 1970, relations between the two communities had significantly improved, but many Turkish Cypriots continued to be wary, and many continued to emigrate.

27 The "Green Line" that divides Nicosia was established on December 30, 1963 as a result of the first serious intercommunal troubles in the city. See, for instance, Pantelis (1990: 199ff).

28 I should note here that others have complained of the opposite problem: namely, that they were forced by the "Turkish leadership" to speak Turkish.

In the 1950s and 1960s, for instance, one author claims that "they [the Turkish authorities of Cyprus] were punishing Turkish-Cypriots by making them pay money for each Greek word they used" (Mustafa Gökçeoglu, *Tezler ve Sözler*, vol. 3, Nicosia, 1994, quoted in Yashin 2000*b*: 7). While I certainly do not wish to ignore the experiences of those who lost their first language—Cypriot—in favor of Turkish or a more standardized Greek, my aim here is to understand the processes by which certain ideas became hegemonic and made that loss seemingly inevitable.

29 This complaint was reiterated throughout the British period. For elaboration on this point, see Chapters 3 and 5.

30 For details on this point, see Bryant (1998*a*).

31 What Governor Ronald Storrs called "the taunt of Greek political agitators that the Turkish population of Cyprus is supine" (CO67/238/14, Cyprus, 115, March 27, 1931).

32 SA1/C226/1895, extract from the Turkish newspaper *Kıbrıs*, 136, April 15, 1895.

33 SA1/C226/1895, letter from Ali Rıfkı, mufti, to the Secretary of State for the Colonies, May 5, 1895.

34 See above, p. 117.

35 Volkan (1979: 38).

36 Or even that it is as ancient as is often claimed. On the novelty of this model, see Kasaba (1999). There, Kasaba also discusses the nineteenth-century emergence of new forms of Ottoman civic life and argues that "the turning point in the transformations of the Ottoman Empire should be sought not in the institutional changes that affected Ottoman bureaucracy, but in the development of a qualitatively new relationship between the Ottoman state and the non-state arena that can be characterized as a nascent civil society" (p. 85).

37 Currently the only remaining fully mixed village in Cyprus, situated on the ceasefire line that divides the island.

38 "Pile Rumlarının maskaralıkları!," *Halkın Sesi*, April 25, 1952.

39 As in reference to a pre-Arabized and -Persianized "pure Turkish" presumably spoken by tribal Turks, or by reference to the equality of male-female relations and to female warriors in the pre-Islamic Turkish past. The latter, of course, was part of the effort to create a "new Turkish woman." On both these points, see Durakbaşa (1998); Kandiyoti (1997 and 1998).

40 Beckingham (1958); İsmail and Birinci (1989).

41 Kitromilides (1979) makes a similar point, though describing this reaction as part of a larger conspiracy of the reactionary Turkish Cypriot leadership.

42 Denktaş (1978).

43 Arendt (1963).

44 Denktaş (n.d.: 58).

45 AAOCC, Box ΞH, 1/9, Association of Greek Cypriot Intellectuals, Resolution of Greek Cypriot Scientists, June 6, 1954.
46 AAOCC, Box ΞH, 1/3, "The Policy of the British Government on Greek Education in Cyprus" (circular of the Archbishopric of the Orthodox Church of Cyprus).
47 At the same time, the communist or labor party AKEL drew large numbers of supporters for an internationalist, rather than nationalist, cause that included both Greek and Turkish Cypriots. Many members of AKEL became targets of EOKA oppression during the anti-colonial rebellion as well as after independence. While AKEL is often cited as an instance of relatively large-scale resistance to the hegemonic Greek nationalist ideology, its stance was also ambiguous: quite a number of older AKEL members have expressed to me pride in their Greek heritage and have noted that AKEL members finally did not want to appear as 'traitors' during the anti-colonial rebellion. Furthermore, most Greek Cypriot AKEL members remained believers in the Orthodox faith and so many continued to submit themselves in spiritual matters, at least, to Archbishop Makarios, who was also the leader of the nationalist, anti-colonial resistance.
48 "Kipriakos Aghon," n.d., archive of the Dragoumis family, Gennaideon Library, Athens.
49 "I Enosis tis Kiprou," May 22, 1932, archive of the Dragoumis family, Gennaideon Library, Athens.
50 SA1/1753/1910, letter from Numan, kadi, and Mehmet Ziyaeddin, mufti, to High Commissioner, August 26, 1910.
51 Yiannis Papadhopoulos (1987: 140).
52 *To Kipriako* literally means "The Cypriot"; it is used as shorthand for *To Kipriako Provlima*, "The Cyprus Problem." It is standard in Greek to use an adjective to stand for a noun when there is a known antecedent; the adjective is in gender agreement with the antecedent, and so it is clear to what it refers. In this case, *To Kipriako* refers to *the* problem, the one and only problem.
53 Mavratsas (1998); Papadakis (1998).
54 Mavratsas (1998: 291).
55 ibid., p. 293.
56 See, for instance, Gramsci (1971: 357–8).
57 For a detailed analysis of the numbers of those missing, see Pollis (1991: 43–62).
58 "Missing claim 'unacceptable,'" *Cyprus Weekly*, August 29–September 4, 1997.
59 Berlin (1984: 19).
60 On Greece, see Herzfeld (1987).
61 Pantelis (1990: 151).
62 MacIntyre (1984) and Taylor (1985).

63 Berger (1984: 154).
64 Arendt (1963: 31).
65 Berlin (1984).

Conclusion

1 http://www.radikal.com.tr/veriler/2003/04/28/haber_73499.php.
2 Mehta (2003).
3 I might note that during three years of teaching the history of social theory at the American University in Cairo, the concept with which students had the most difficulty was always the idea of a pre-social individual and of persons bound by a social contract.

Index